Richard Nixon

Published by

Western Islands
Belmont, Massachusetts 02178

Manufactured in the United States of America

Table Of Contents

I   Liberals Get The Action,
       Conservatives Get The Rhetoric 1

II   The UN-Free Agent 31

III   The Establishing Of Establishments 55

IV   The Elephant That Brays 87

V   Little Man In A Big Hurry 125

VI   Purging The Party Of Patriots 165

VII   "We Are Not Going To Be Outbid" 199

VIII   Goldwater Over The Dam 227

IX   Be Sincere Whether You Mean It Or Not 243

X   Sincere Advice From The Unsilent Minority 269

XI   The Pachyderms Return 275

XII   President Of The Universe 289

XIII   The More It Changes 315

XIV   The Great Socialist Revival 345

XV   The End Is Power 393

XVI   Turn The *Insiders* Out 403

       Epilogue 421

       Index 425

CHAPTER I

Liberals Get The Action,
Conservatives Get The Rhetoric

While in a particularly expansive mood one day, Richard Nixon's Senate floor leader, the very Liberal Hugh Scott of Pennsylvania, boasted to a reporter: "We [Liberals] get the action and the Conservatives get the rhetoric."[1] This yeasty admission of the Nixon Administration's Liberalism in action doubtless would have come as a distinct shock to most of the 32 million citizens who voted for Richard Milhous Nixon for President of the United States in 1968. They expected Conservative actions to follow the laudable Conservative rhetoric of the campaign. The Nixon campaign landed many a strong verbal clout on the snout of squishy-soft Liberalism, whose permissive policies at home and abroad had brought the country to the brink of a nervous breakdown from frustration, if not financial, moral, and military collapse. While stumping the hustings, candidate Nixon promised again and again "new leadership" that would restore law and order, stop aid and trade with our Communist enemies, terminate the ceaseless war in Vietnam, scuttle unworkable socialist spending programs, dash virulent inflation, restore fiscal sanity, stuff the genie of big government back into the bottle, and, in general, "throw the rascals out."

Liberal columnists, widely believed to be Mr. Nixon's implacable enemies, have seemed both surprised and highly pleased at the "New Nixon," who gives the Conservatives the rhetoric and the Liberals the action. One of the tip-offs came even before the election in an amazing column by the late

Ralph McGill, formerly a staunch enemy of Richard Nixon. McGill, editor of the *Atlanta Constitution* and a nationally syndicated columnist, was a member of the semi-secret Council on Foreign Relations, called "the CFR," otherwise known as "the invisible government" or the "Eastern Liberal Establishment." (The CFR will be dealt with in greater detail in Chapter Three.) McGill, one of America's most vocal anti-anti-Communists, wrote in a column titled "All Civilized Persons Are Indebted To Nixon":

> An important change has come to Richard Nixon. The nation, and, for that matter, civilized persons everywhere, are in his debt.
> Nixon has changed his once rigid views about the necessity to maintain relations and a dialogue with the Communist world, including Red China, when that now chaotic country has a government that can be responsive. He did so because the facts have changed.
> Nixon built his political career on opposition to Communism. He had made himself the darling of the Birch-type mentalities, and of all the various extreme right-wing nut organizations that carry on witch hunts and character assassination in the name of anti-Communism.
> The New Nixon policy was made public before his nomination at Miami. He said in a press conference that he had "revised" some of his earlier views, largely because the Communist world itself has shifted in new directions.
> Nixon suggested further that the era of "confrontation" with the Communist world has ended. It has been replaced, he believes, with an era of negotiations.
> Whoever is President, he said, in the next four and eight years, "must proceed on the assumption that negotiations with the Soviet world, negotiations eventually with the leaders of the next superpower, Communist China, must take place. This is a change that has come about, and therefore, your policy must change."
> Nixon said, with admirable candor, that his 1960 acceptance speech, with its inflexible position against any talks with the Communist world, "would be irrelevant to the problems of today."

"As the facts change," he said, "any intelligent man does change his approaches to the problems. It does not mean that he is an opportunist. It means only that he is a pragmatist."[2]

The "New Communists" proceeded to embarrass the "New Nixon" by shortly thereafter breaking their non-aggression treaty with Czecho-Slovakia and invading that country to brutally crush an apparent move toward independence.

Shortly after the election, Liberal columnists were gloating that Nixon could do more for Liberalism simply because he was a Republican who was widely believed to be a Conservative. Robert J. Donovan of the *Los Angeles Times* observed in an article titled "Nixon Will Protect the Center From the Left and Right":

> He knows he cannot make strides at home until he gets rid of the burden of the war. He has promised to end the war. His associates say he is aware that in order to do so he may have to make unpopular concessions that only a new President and only one who, like himself, feels safe against charges of being "soft on communism" would risk making.
>
> As one of his closest friends explained recently, "The American people know Dick Nixon wouldn't sell the country out to the Communists." Or as Sen. Jacob K. Javits (R.-N.Y.) was quoted as having said the other day, "I'm confident that Nixon will end the war . . . if Humphrey would do what Nixon is going to do on Vietnam, Humphrey would be shot or impeached. Nixon will end the war."[3]

Widely syndicated Liberal columnist Sydney Harris was not exactly downcast at the thought of a Nixon Administration:

> It is probably better for the nation that Nixon was elected than Humphrey, for social realities will force Nixon to do pretty much the same things Humphrey would have done, but Nixon will encounter less bitterness and opposition than Humphrey would have.[4]

Look magazine's Washington correspondent Richard Wilson wrote in his newspaper column:

> A rather impressive list has accumulated of things that are not going to be done in the Nixon administration:
> The Office of Economic Opportunity (poverty program) is not to be abolished.
> The 10 per cent income surtax is not to be dropped.
> The Johnson budget is not to be cut substantially.
> Southern public schools are not to be permitted to squirm out of ending segregation through freedom of choice plans.
> A significant rise in the rate of unemployment is not to be encouraged as a concomitant of arresting inflation.
> Consumer-protection activities are not to be abandoned.
> The "security gap" in national defense is not found to be as wide as it appeared last October.
> If such policy decisions seem at variance with Nixon's stance in the presidential campaign, it is because so many people had formed a different idea of what the Nixon administration would be like.
> If there is to be no significant change in budgetary policy, no significant change in tax policy, no significant change in economic policy, then much of what was said during the campaign can be classified as the usual political bombast.[5]

Columnist Wilson noted that "the agony in Nixon's early days is among Republicans who think their legitimate interests aren't being protected, while the ecstasy is among Liberals and Democrats who have discovered that Richard Nixon isn't half as bad as they expected."[6]

Stewart Alsop, old warhorse of the Fabian Socialist Americans for Democratic Action (ADA), told his *Newsweek* readers in a column titled "The Demonsterization of Nixon":

> Something very important has happened during Richard M. Nixon's first month as President: a great many people who supposed or at least suspected that Mr. Nixon was a sort of human monster have discovered that he isn't.[7]

All these assorted Nixonophobes now find themselves puzzled and discomfited. For where is the Richard Nixon they so happily hated?

They may find him again, of course — honeymoons always end. Yet the sudden, sharp fading of Nixonophobia seems to be more than a function of the usual Presidential honeymoon. It could be a basic and perhaps even a permanent change in public attitudes toward the new President . . . .

It is interesting to speculate on the reasons for the change. For one thing, President Nixon, as a suspected monster, gets a lot of credit for not being a monster. He gets credit for not doing all sorts of things that a President Humphrey, for example, would have got no credit at all for not doing — not abandoning the cause of school integration; not instituting a witch-hunting "clean-out" of the State Department; not demanding "clear-cut superiority" in nuclear weapons as a condition of negotiating with the Russians. President Nixon, in short, gets credit for not doing things candidate Nixon hinted he might do.

Later, Alsop was to joyously crown Mr. Nixon "The Great Pre-Emptor":

The President's basic political technique is now entirely obvious. He appeases the right with reassuring rhetoric, conservative appointments and such gestures as the unleashing of Vice President Spiro T. Agnew and the veto of the HEW bill. At the same time, he busily pre-empts, purloins, or filches all the major issues of his natural enemies, the liberal Democrats.

There are plenty of examples of the President in action in his role as The Great Pre-Emptor. A national minimum income was just burgeoning forth as a major liberal Democratic issue when the President snatched it away. The draft lottery bore the Kennedy brand before the President captured it, and so did tax reform. The "New Federalism" was the brainchild of Robert F. Kennedy, but it has now been legally adopted by the President. And so on.[8]

Since Mr. Alsop is a Liberal, he naturally found all this highly praiseworthy as he continued:

...In short, Mr. Nixon has turned out to be a far better politician than most political journalists (again, including this one) thought him to be a year ago. He may turn out to be a better President, too. To be a good President it is first necessary to be a good politician. Moreover, the issues that Mr. Nixon has pre-empted from the liberals are good issues — they involve doing things that badly need to be done. Perhaps, to be fair, that is also a reason why The Great Pre-Emptor has pre-empted them.

Alsop was also pleased that Conservatives are neutralized through this policy of giving the rhetoric to them while the Left gets the action: "The rhetoric has had a marvelously soothing effect on the Republican right; there has been hardly a peep from Senators Goldwater, Tower, Thurmond and company." After all, what can these men say? They went far out on a limb to support Mr. Nixon in 1968 and they are now in a highly embarrassing position.

Few have gushed over the New Nixon as has the nationally syndicated columnist Roscoe Drummond, a member of the Council on Foreign Relations Establishment. Drummond began even before President-elect Nixon took office, by declaring RMN to be a "secret liberal":

The most significant political fact of the hour is now so evident it can't be seriously disputed:

President Richard M. Nixon is a "secret liberal."

He may not welcome the description. He resists labels and sees himself as a pragmatist, a problem-solver — neither liberal nor conservative — who wants to do what needs to be done.

But Nixon is already proving himself a liberal-in-action if not a liberal-in-theory — and this is what counts.

The evidence:

Lyndon Johnson initiated and Congress approved the largest volume of social legislation of any president in history. And Nixon prepares to carry forward every major Johnson measure.

During the eight Eisenhower years 45 new welfare programs were passed. During the five Johnson years some 435 welfare programs were passed and Nixon is not proposing to dismantle them. He is proposing to build on them and his goal is to make sure they achieve their purposes more effectively.

Finally, Nixon has committed his administration to a big open-ended increase in Social Security benefits by advocating that they be boosted regularly to match higher living costs.

But the fact remains that Nixon is not going to disrupt, decrease or dismantle the vast, help-people, help-the-states programs he inherited from the Great Society any more than Dwight Eisenhower did those he inherited from the New Deal.

Ike accepted the reform of the New Deal as part of the fabric of modern society and cites as his proudest presidential achievement the extension of Social Security to cover more than 12 million more people.[9]

Six months later, after Mr. Nixon announced his Family Assistance Plan, a thinly disguised Guaranteed Annual Income, which he had opposed during the campaign, the dumbfounded Drummond was predicting that Richard Nixon, of all people, might go down in history as the FDR of the 1970s:

> Whatever happened to conservative Richard Nixon?
>
> Here he is in the lead for the most far-ranging, groundbreaking, daring social-welfare reform since the early years of the New Deal.
>
> The President has seized the initiative on the most crucially needed domestic reform and has stolen the best clothes of the Democratic liberals.
>
> Strange to contemplate but the time may come when people will think of Richard M. Nixon as the Republican Franklin D. Roosevelt of the 1970s!
>
>   * * *
>
> But none of this alters the fact that conservative Richard Nixon is acting to carry out an immensely liberal concept and liberal program.
>
> How liberal? If you define modern liberalism as a willingness to use the federal government to achieve major social ends, the President's new Program is very liberal .... [10]

Drummond also told his sophisticated Liberal readers in such papers as the notoriously Leftist *Washington Post* to ignore the fact that Democrats have to denounce Nixon as a Conservative for political purposes:

> Despite epithets from liberals, the record of the Nixon administration thus far is on the progressive side in both policy and action.
>
> It is much more midroad than conservative and perhaps even a little left of center.
>
> The labels don't matter. What does is whether the President is acting wisely and effectively.
>
> It is doubtful if Nixon's Democratic critics are doing themselves much good politically. It doesn't do the administration any harm to be called conservative by its opponents, particularly when it isn't very conservative. And the conservatives have no place to go except to Nixon. [11]

Drummond also bulldoggedly noted that Mr. Nixon on Vietnam, contrary to all past promises, has seized the Eugene McCarthy plank out of the 1968 Democratic National Convention:

> The areas of agreement between the responsible doves and President Nixon are far greater than many realize.
>
> This is revealed by two facts.
>
> All the leading Democratic doves voted for the minority Vietnam plank at the 1968 Democratic National Convention.
>
> Today Nixon is carrying out every provision of that plank and — at points — more.
>
> The dove-supported Democratic plank advocated "phased withdrawal" of all foreign troops from Vietnam. Richard Nixon has gone further . . . . [12]

Mary McGrory, Liberal *femme fatale* of the *Washington Star,* noted early in the game (in the February 11, 1969 issue) that loyal Republican Congressmen were in for short shrift:

Innocently, [Republicans] assumed that they would have their pick of choice jobs for their friends and instant access to the White House. They are getting fewer plums and fewer calls . . . . The Republican members [of Congress] have not yet addressed themselves to the first policy moves of the President which seem likely to please the Americans for Democratic Action more than Strom Thurmond.

Miss McGrory was also all atwitter at the fact that a Republican had done the unthinkable and appointed an officer of the ultra-Leftist Americans for Democratic Action, Daniel Patrick Moynihan, as a Presidential advisor. She wrote: "Moynihan . . . knows that his basic idea about the poor, money, work and family is now on its way, respectable Republican doctrine at last." [13]

It was the Family Assistance Plan, drafted largely by Moynihan, that evoked the greatest surprise and the loudest cheers from the portside pontificators. The *Washington Star's* Carl T. Rowan, a former JFK appointee, wrote:

Imagine someone telling you 20 years ago that a Republican president would ask the federal government to guarantee a minimum annual income to every family.

You would have laughed your informant out of town.

Especially if he told you that this Republican would advocate a welfare program that covered 25 million Americans instead of 10 million and cost $10 billion instead of $5 billion.

Yet, after months of debate within his administration, President Nixon went on nationwide television to make just such a revolutionary proposal to the American people. [14]

Earlier Rowan had pointed out: "Richard M. Nixon is clearly not what he said he was, not what Democrats feared he was, nor even what Republicans hoped he was during the presidential campaign. [15]

Even the *New Republic*, for fifty years the voice of intellectual socialism, was gleeful to welcome Nixon and his

Family Assistance Plan to the ranks of the creeping socialists:

> ...President Nixon informed the Neanderthal men that he
> had accepted and would assert creeping socialism, the principle of
> the Federal Government guaranteeing a minimum income to all
> disadvantaged Americans. [16]

Even Joseph Kraft, probably the most far-out Leftist
among syndicated columnists, has had words of praise for
RMN's Liberalism. Kraft, a member of the Establishment's
Council on Foreign Relations and a man who recently praised
Lenin as having "transmitted to the Communist world the
ideals of equality and progress and peace,"[17] was particularly
impressed by the President's hypocrisy in repudiating campaign promises:

> ... the Administration's slow start has made it possible to fob
> gently off into oblivion some of the least enlightened things said
> and done during the campaign. Attaining nuclear superiority over
> the Russians has been replaced by going for "nuclear suffi-
> ciency." Crude notions of trading a little more unemployment for
> a little less inflation are only an echo. So is non-enforcement of
> the laws against segregation. And "law and order" sounds like a
> quaint slogan of the same vintage as "54-40 or Fight" and
> "Tippecanoe and Tyler, Too." [18]

Rank and file Republicans would be most shocked at the
consistent praise heaped upon Mr. Nixon by the *New York
Times'* house savant, James Reston. Reston, also a member of
the CFR, is regarded as the official "unofficial spokesman"
for the Eastern Liberal Establishment, now that Walter
Lippmann has retired after fifty years of laundering the
minds of the American public. Reston praised the President
for "wiping out the old political stereotypes of Richard
Nixon the partisan politician, the darling of the professional
anti-communists." [19]

Reston later wrote a column congratulating the President,

after his first five months in office, on "a good beginning." Among the things that particularly pleased the Liberal sage of the Potomac were Nixon's appointments, which he termed neither "political nor ideological." Reston described these men as "competent modern pragmatists, who may not be very imaginative, but who are more interested in the facts and the national interests, than in the conservative theories or political interests of the Republican party." [20]

This naturally ignored the fact that most people in voting for Mr. Nixon did so believing that they were voting for Conservative theories to cure the disastrous effects of the Liberal theories that had held sway for nearly forty years. Of course, many Republicans fail to understand why Democratic Administrations have the privilege of being partisan and of building the Democratic Party at every turn, while the Republicans must be constantly non-partisan and always make concessions in the direction of the Liberals.

In the same column Reston told his more sophisticated readers that the name of the game is "The Conservatives get the rhetoric, the Liberals get the action":

> Nixon has, of course, said a lot of things that please the hawks, the Republican conservatives, and the authoritarians who want to be militant in Vietnam and on the campuses and in the cities, but he has acted prudently, and stuck to his priorities on ending the war, controlling the inflation and moving toward an accommo- dation with Moscow on the control of military arms and the reduction of military budgets.
>
> Even his support of the antiballistic missile system, which looked so hawkish, was probably a move toward an arms control accommodation with the Soviet Union . . . .

Reston also provided us with an analysis — in this case an accurate one — of why the country constantly moves to the Left, regardless of whether Republicans or Democrats are in office:

President Eisenhower acquiesced in all the New Deal reforms the Republicans opposed in the 30s and 40s, and [so did] Nixon as his deputy. He came to office as a minority president, accused of being a war-monger who was indifferent to the internal social and economic problems of the cities and the races, but he is now arguing for peace, and social justice — talking like a conservative but acting like a progressive.

Arthur Schlesinger Sr. makes the same point in his study of "The Tides of National Politics." The chief liberal gains of the past, he says, "generally remain on the statute books when the conservatives recover power . . . liberalism grows constantly more liberal, and by the same token, conservatism grows constantly less conservative . . . ."

This may not be true of the conservatives like George Wallace who are out of power, but it seems to be true of Nixon. He is zig-zagging to the left. [21]

If Liberals like Reston can convince Conservatives that it is somehow ungentlemanly ("you can't turn the clock back") to undo the damage done by previous Leftist administrations, then the Republicans are doomed to meekly promising to administer socialism more efficiently. This, of course, is exactly what is happening and the Liberals love it. Observed Reston:

All the President's ambiguous and even contradictory state-ments of foreign and domestic policy have been analyzed here with the greatest care. One day he is saying the Vietnam war may be one of our "finest hours," and the next he is withdrawing American troops from the battlefield. One day he is submitting to the conservative instincts of the American Medical Association or placating the southern senators on the school integration guide-lines, and the next he is supporting welfare state policies he had opposed over the last 20 years. [22]

Like other Liberals, Reston was ecstatic over Nixon's guaranteed annual income plan:

The main thing about President Nixon's proposals for dealing

with poverty in America is that he recognizes the government's
responsibility for removing it. He has been denouncing the
"welfare state" for 20 years, but he is now saying that poverty in
America in the midst of spectacular prosperity is intolerable and
must be wiped out . . . .

A Republican president has condemned the word "welfare,"
emphasized "work" and "training" as conditions of public
assistance, suggested that the states and the cities be given more
federal money to deal with their social and economic problems,
but still comes out in the end with a policy of spending more
money for relief of more poor people than the welfare state
Democrats ever dared to propose in the past.

This is beginning to be the story of American politics . . . .

. . . And now on the most controversial question of domestic
policy, he changes the rhetoric, the philosophy and the administration, but proposes more welfare, more people on public
assistance, which will take more federal funds than any other
president in the history of the Republic . . . .

Nevertheless, Nixon has taken a great step forward. He has
cloaked a remarkably progressive welfare policy in conservative
language . . . . [23]

Reston concluded this column by claiming that Nixon
believes that Americans favor the Marxian concept of
redistributing the wealth:

He has repudiated his own party's record on social policy at
home and even his own hawkish attitudes abroad, and this tells us
something both about the President and the country.

For he has obviously concluded that the American people are
for peace abroad and for a more decent distribution of wealth at
home, and the chances are that this will prove to be both good
policy and good politics.

Actually most Americans realize that by "peace abroad,"
Mr. Reston means further appeasement of the Communists'
global power grab, and that the poor can only be helped
through gainful employment, which the plan promises, but
which nobody seriously thinks it will deliver. The other side

of the "welfare state" coin at home is the acceptance of a
softer attitude toward Communism abroad, on the basis that
it is somehow changing and has mellowed. Reston wrote in
the August 6, 1969 *Long Beach Press-Telegram*:

> The tide is going out. The President is turning around, waving
> to the right one day and to the left the next — but the
> overwhelming impression in the capitol is that he is consciously
> zig-zagging toward peace in Vietnam and an accommodation with
> Moscow . . . .
>
> Washington is more sensitive than New York or other places to
> the general direction of Presidents and politics. It is more
> interested in the over-all tendencies of Presidents than in the day
> to day White House statements, and it seems to feel that Nixon is
> now engaged in a delicate retreat from his hawkish and
> anti-Communist record of the past.

By September 30, 1970, Mr. Reston, in what may have
been an effort to get Liberals to look at what Nixon does and
not what he says, was telling readers of the *Press-Telegram*
that Mr. Nixon was desperately attempting to "liberate
himself from his conservative and anti-Communist past":

> . . . It is true that Nixon rose to power as an anti-Communist,
> a hawk on Vietnam, and an opponent of the New Deal, but once
> he assumed the resonsibilities of the presidency, he began moving
> toward peace in Vietnam, coexistence with the Communist world
> of Moscow and Peking, and despite all his political
> reservations, even toward advocacy of the welfare state at
> home.
>
> Nixon's policies toward Social Security, welfare payments,
> arms control and coexistence with the Communist world are
> quite different from the policies he supported when he was a
> congressman, a senator and vice president under Eisenhower. He
> has been struggling between his political prejudices of the past
> and his responsibilities as President, and he has moved in the last
> two years toward an accommodation with his old adversaries both
> at home and abroad.
>
> This has not been easy. He is still torn between his old

anti-Communist cold war instincts and his new presidential duties. He has been arguing for arms control, he has been supporting the nonproliferation of nuclear weapons, he has been supporting the reconciliation of the West Germans and the Soviets, he has been approving more trade between the Western and the Communist worlds — most of the time against the prejudices of most of the conservative Republicans who supported his bid for the presidency in the first place.

The likelihood is that Nixon is going to be President for the next six years. He is at a critical point in his career. He has been trying to liberate himself from his conservative and anti-Communist past, and work toward a progressive policy at home and a policy of reconciliation with the Communists abroad . . . .

Although there were hints during the 1968 campaign that this was what Mr. Nixon was up to, only the most sophisticated conservatives, who were familiar with Mr. Nixon's background as a sometime member of the Eastern Liberal Establishment's CFR, could interpret the message. Most of the campaign rhetoric dealt with strengthening America in its dealings with the Communists and a castigation of the policies of past inadequate leadership, which had led us from one disaster to another. But in 1970 Reston was telling us: " . . . it would probably be wise to follow the administration's slogan: 'Watch what we do rather than what we say.' " [24]

Even David Broder of the *Washington Post*, just about the most Leftwing daily this side of the Iron Curtain, has had praise for Nixon. Broder, who describes himself as a "radical liberal," chastises Mr. Nixon for not having brought order to the federal government's chaotic bureaucracy:

. . . if we are fated to be governed by conservatives, this isn't the worst set we could have, by a long shot.

They are rather stuffy and occasionally sour, but on the substantive questions they're not nearly as bad as they might be. We could have conservatives who are hell-bent on fattening the military; these men have put the Pentagon on its leanest rations in years. We might have conservatives determined to remove communism from every village in Vietnam; Mr. Nixon wants mainly to get out, though he sometimes scares you out of your wits with a Cambodian operation in the process.

The harshest sustainable indictment of these Republicans is that they lack the one virtue conservatives are supposed to be born with: competence as managers. Despite three major reorganizations and a massive increase in the White House staff, this Administration is still a "pitiful, helpless giant," stumbling over its own feet. Its record in handling Congress, the economy, the campuses and the other trouble spots is consistently one of arriving breathless, shortly after the crisis has occurred. [25]

Those whom we have quoted (with the exception of Mary McGrory) represent the elite, the *crème de la crème* of the Eastern Liberal Establishment's coterie of intellectual commentators. They obviously approve of Mr. Nixon and are trying to tell their readers to forget what Mr. Nixon says in order to pacify those who voted for him, and pay attention to what he does. This is also good advice for Conservatives. While the Washington press corps of hack correspondents have traditionally neither liked nor trusted Richard Nixon, they are blinded by passé stereotypes and their own knee-jerk Liberalism. The Drummonds, Alsops, Krafts, Broders and Restons are in an entirely different class. They serve as a transmission belt for the Liberal elite in and out of the government, the foundations, the communications industry and the academy. The fact that foaming-at-the-mouth college radicals, psychotic black militants, neurotic professors, and politically motivated Liberal Democrats continue to damn Mr. Nixon as what they consider a "right-wing-capitalist-pig-exploiting-imperialist" serves only to enhance and protect Mr. Nixon's reputation with the so-called silent majority. It doesn't hurt him, it is a necessity to keep those who voted for the President from realizing that candidate Nixon and President Nixon are as different as Dr. Jekyll and Mr. Hyde.

It is not only the philosopher-king intellectuals of the Establishment who have noted that "Shifty Dick" has shifted Left. Even the publications in the "middle of the road" (a position which has been shifting Leftward for going on four decades) have taken notice. An eye-opening article in the Dow Jones Corporation's *National Observer* of July 21, 1969, titled "Two Positions: Liberal and Less Liberal — The Conservatives Find Themselves Boxed In," stated that all the Conservatives could expect from the Nixon Administration was "meaningless baubles." *National Observer* correspondent Jude Wanniski continued:

The most important thing to understand about the ideological churning in the Capitol is that it is taking place within an extremely narrow range of debate. And that range has been circumscribed by congressional liberals of both parties.

Unlike earlier conflicts of ideology in Washington, there is now no fundamental dispute over commitments, only a narrow haggling over technique. There are artificial "liberal" positions and "less liberal" positions, with the pulling and hauling largely between Senate Democrats and the White House, but the conservatives have been foreclosed from debate. Because the liberals have been surprisingly efficient in organizing the loyal opposition, Congressional conservatives have no choice but to join in support of the somewhat "less liberal" White House. . . . Here we have Sen. Strom Thurmond, who would like an abrupt halt to all federal desegregation moves, lightly applauding the new approach to school-desegregation guidelines because they would give a few school districts a little extra time. Here are other conservatives, Sen. John Tower of Texas among them, approving the Nixon voting-rights plan because it applies to the nation a civil-rights formula that now applies only to the South. If Mr. Nixon lately has been seen in the company of conservatives it is only because they have moved onto liberal terrain in order to support him.

Conservatives who looked forward to abolishing the Office of Economic Opportunity have found themselves in the odd position of promoting renaissance of the agency along new lines, the liberals defending the status quo. Old guard Republicans who last year thought razing was too good for the Job Corps camps this year passionately defend the Administration's decision to keep half the camps open . . . . The conservatives want to merely double the federal commitment to feeding the poor. The liberals want to triple the commitment. On the entire range of domestic issues there is scarcely one on which conservatives are not occupying ideological ground that was held by liberals only a year or two ago . . . . The "conservative" campus-unrest bill that was blocked in the House Education and Labor Committee last month was so mild as to be meaningless, but as mild as it was the legislation was opposed by the President . . . . On foreign-policy issues, too, the debate falls within a narrow range, the old guard conservatives moving to traditional liberal terrain to support Mr. Nixon. The President will visit Communist Rumania in the kind of east-west bridge-building that President Kennedy and President Johnson talked about. But here are the liberals criticizing the trip because it might upset Moscow. And here comes the Old Guard – the Mundts, Towers, Hruskas, Dirksens – galloping to Mr. Nixon's defense.

The conservatives seem comfortable enough arguing for Mr. Nixon's Safeguard anti-ballistic missile system, but even here the ground has shifted. A year ago the Richard Russells and Strom Thurmonds wanted nothing less than an ABM net to protect American cities against attack while many liberals would have considered the Safeguard defense of the U.S. nuclear deterrents a triumph of reason and peace . . . . Nowhere, it seems, has the spectrum shifted more than in the Vietnam debate. Senators who two years ago were still talking about bombing Hanoi and Haiphong are pushing disengagement. Sen. John Stennis of Mississippi, chairman of the Armed Services Committee, only eight months ago was still not ruling out the possibility of employing nuclear weapons in Vietnam. Now he is endorsing the enclave theory of Gen. James Gavin, a theory which seemed a panacea to doves in 1967 . . . .

Perhaps the liberals should be happier with this condition than they are. But in fact they seem more frustrated than they ever were in the Johnson era. As much ground as they cover in seeking an issue, Mr. Nixon follows, yanking the Old Guard with him.

But at least the liberals should feel pride of authorship, serving the nation well in leading the loyal opposition as vigorously as they have. If they had been in disarray, unable to bring forceful pressures on the White House for necessary policy changes at

home and abroad, Mr. Nixon would have been forced to move
even more cautiously than he has.

The *Wall Street Journal*, which tries to stay in the middle
of the road, has consistently called attention, usually
approvingly, to Mr. Nixon's "Liberalism in action." *Journal*
correspondent Alan Otten wrote early in the game on March
4, 1969: " . . . There will clearly be no big cutbacks in
Government spending; in fact, all signs are that spending will
rise pretty much on Lyndon Johnson's schedule . . . . "

Otten quotes an unnamed White House staffer that "the
Nixon Administration talks quite conservatively much of the
time, yet ends up acting with comparative liberalism." Otten
also notes that a Republican who has a Conservative image
can get away with things no Liberal could. " . . . The same
proposal would sound like another alarming step down the
road to state socialism" coming from the Democrats, writes
Otten.[26] This is, of course, the very road Mr. Nixon is
travelling, and the fact that a Republican is now leading the
way serves to neutralize much of the opposition to it.
Conservative correspondent Walter Trohan of the *Chicago
Tribune* sadly wrote on October 15, 1969:

> Conservatives should be realistic enough to recognize that this
> country is going deeper into socialism and will see expansion of
> federal power, whether Republicans or Democrats are in power.
> The only comfort they may have is that the pace will be slower
> under Richard M. Nixon than it might have been under Hubert H.
> Humphrey.
>
> * * *
>
> Conservatives are going to have to recognize that the Nixon
> administration will embrace most of the socialism of the
> Democratic administrations, while professing to improve it . . . .

Conservative acquiescence in the basic theory of Marxism
that "socialism is inevitable" seals the doom of liberty in
America.

Even such a staunch and long-time Nixon advocate as Trohan, who is the *Chicago Tribune's* senior political writer, has confessed in print that, "more in sorrow than in anger, this commentator is beginning to find himself puzzled by Richard M. Nixon's start in the Presidency." He added: "There would seem to be some cause for uneasiness." One thing that made Trohan uneasy was " . . . the praise Nixon heaped on the State Department staff when he called on his round of federal establishments. No less enthusiastic praise has been heaped on others of the entrenched Democratic party. This also contrasted sharply with his call for change during the campaign." [27]

Columnist Ralph de Toledano, an erstwhile Nixon supporter who once wrote a laudatory biography of the President, complained:

> While President Nixon has basked in the approving smiles of the liberal establishment, a cloud once no bigger than a man's left hand has begun to grow darker on Washington's political horizon. That cloud has a storm potential which could badly rock Mr. Nixon's ship as he moves toward the 1970 and 1972 elections.
>
> It is no longer possible to ignore this, or not to comment on its significance. It adds up to one important fact: The conservatives won the election for Richard Nixon — and they are losing the election to him. It can no longer be denied that those to the right of center who carried November 6 for Mr. Nixon have gotten less than the back of his hand for their effort.
>
> Obviously the spoils are going to those who did their worst, or best, to see Nixon's opponents triumph. In fact, a kind of political alliance between the present administration and the anti-Nixon coalition seems to be in the making.[28]

A nervous James Jackson Kilpatrick, a former editor of the *Richmond News Leader*, gave as his tentative judgment that "Mr. Nixon, thus far, disappoints." What concerned the columnist most was that:

Mr. Nixon has not cleaned house. To be sure, a new cabinet is in office, but what of that? Bureaucracy is a kind of root vegetable; what counts is underground. It is at the third and fourth levels that memorandums are drafted, regulations enforced, speeches prepared, and policies shaped. If Mr. Nixon fails to dig down to these levels, and to put in new men with new ideas, he will harvest the same old thing. [29]

William Loeb of the *Manchester* (N.H.) *Union Leader* didn't take what he thought was Nixon's double-cross quite so gracefully. Loeb accused Nixon of "throwing it away" and noted, quoting an informant, a long-time Washington observer:

"Had Mr. Nixon and his cabinet officers exposed the wrongdoing of the Kennedy and Johnson Administrations in the various departments and in the branches of the government in Washington — and throughout the world — President Nixon could have consolidated himself in office and built the Republican party up so it would be strong for years to come.

"Instead," our friend concluded, "Mr. Nixon is attempting a course of action which never in the history of politics or government has been successful. He is favoring his enemies and offending his friends." [30]

By January 24, 1970, *Human Events*, the staunch Conservative weekly newsletter from Washington, which vociferously supported Mr Nixon in 1968, had itself become largely disillusioned with the President's actions. Surveying the scene after one year, the paper stated:

. . . it seems to us that the President ignored most of his own rhetoric during the first year. Instead of ruthlessly examining existing domestic legislation and eliminating the unnecessary, he kept all the Kennedy-Johnson programs, called for increased funding of them in some instances and even dreamed up a new welfare scheme which he acknowledges will cost more than the existing welfare set-up.

* * *

The President can be seen embracing the views of liberal leprechaun Daniel Moynihan one morning and then that afternoon siding with the conservative Arthur Burns. Nixon condemns the anti-poverty program as a waste, but then pushes for its extension for at least two years. He permits Atty. Gen. Mitchell to lobby for the Whitten anti-school-busing amendment in the House, but when it passes, lo and behold, he benches Mitchell and suits up Finch, who sinks it in the Senate . . . .

It has become a truism under Liberalism that old subsidies never die, and, as *Human Events* pointed out, Nixon has made "no effort — no effort at all — to roll back the bureaucracy. Indeed some observers might conclude there was an effort to *entrench* established programs [emphasis in original]." Administrations come and go, while millions of government workers go right on folding, spindling, and mutilating. As the *Chicago Tribune* observed, quoting the French proverb, "The more it changes, the more it remains the same."

Among the most articulate Conservative critics of Mr. Nixon has been the Republican *Battle Line,* the publication of the American Conservative Union. In its February-March 1969 issue, *Battle Line* bluntly told its readers with regard to Nixon's appointments: "Slowly but surely it has finally dawned on Republican party regulars across the nation that they have been taken." The non-partisan approach to filling appointments was a convenient excuse for retaining Democratic holdovers and moving Liberal Democrats into important slots. This is not exactly what Republicans had been led to expect. According to *Battle Line*:

. . . candidate Nixon admitted publicly, as when he spoke to Republican delegates in caucus at Miami Beach last August, that one of the greatest failures of the Eisenhower administration was the complete lack of White House action in building up the Republican Party organization. It appears that GOP history not only repeats itself, it stutters badly.

Later, in June 1970, *Battle Line* was to note of Mr. Nixon's own personal staff:

> ... Perusing an organizational chart of the White House staff, the traditional Republican is struck by the presence of so few avowed conservatives in any capacity, and those few are assigned non-policymaking jobs . . . .

Battle Line in February had warned that the Administration was straying away from its traditional role as the Conservative party:

> Since its founding the Republican Party has generally held itself out to be the responsible party concerning national economic policy. The Republicans have fought the "budget busting" Democrats who in their profligacy "tax, spend and elect." Limited government, balanced budgets, lower taxes have always been GOP watch words. That all may be changing now.

Concerning Nixon's domestic policies, the American Conservative Union concluded in the June issue of *Battle Line*:

> One should start with the obvious historical premise that almost every major domestic policy theme the President has adopted during his term of office has favored not just the liberal side, but at times, the ultra-liberal. Nixon has heartily embraced welfare programs that would have made Dwight Eisenhower blush. He has championed big spending to the tune of billions and budget cuts in name only. One of the largest increases ever in the national debt has just passed the House and the Nixon budget, designed as a model of fiscal rectitude, has drowned in a swirl of red ink and inflation.

In February of that same year (1970) the ACU newsletter had commented:

> Not only does Nixon seek new ways to spend Federal tax money, he has greatly increased spending for programs started by Kennedy and Johnson. Secretary of HEW Finch's department will

get $6 billion more than the $52 billion it spent last year, although all but $1 billion of this results from increases already written into law — Social Security boosts, welfare, Medicare, etc. Nevertheless, another billion dollars goes to HEW. "Considering the tight budget," said an HEW official, "we did very well."

It should be remembered that the vast majority of Republican Senators and Congressmen wholeheartedly opposed these Kennedy-Johnson Socialist programs when they were originally before Congress. As *Battle Line* remarked:

If it were not so tragic it would seem humorous — a Republican Administration tossing away billions of tax dollars for socialistic schemes that make the New Deal look like a penny ante game . . . .

The Conservative Republican group also pointed out that the Party was abandoning, particularly with reference to Vietnam, its traditional anti-Communist position, a position once championed by Richard Nixon himself. *Battle Line* observed in December 1969:

What worries many is that the President may have abandoned even a remote intention of winning this costly struggle against Communism; that our goal of victory has been replaced with withdrawal and acceptance of defeat. If that is so, all that remains is to play out the traditional Asian game of saving face.

In the Nixon Administration "appearances are everything," concluded *Battle Line* in August 1969. The Conservatives get the rhetoric . . . . In June 1970 *Battle Line* pointed out:

All this is not to say that the words have not been there. Between his [Nixon's] own milder utterings and the conservative-sounding rhetoric of Vice President Agnew, most Republicans have been able to assuage their consciences with the vacant thought that "they sure do sound good." As we've said many times before, conservatives get the words, liberals get the action.

Nixon's "New Leadership" has virtually removed the Conservative viewpoint from the congressional spectrum. The August 1969 *Battle Line* mournfully noted:

> The truth is that President Nixon's advocacy of all sorts of liberal domestic and foreign policies seems to have foreclosed conservatives from debate. Many conservative Republicans in Congress, especially in the House, have adopted what has now become the President's own standard operating procedure; they talk conservative but go along with the liberalism the President has been espousing more and more each week. The vote on the surtax proposal found many Republicans reversing themselves as they supported the President's back-turning on a campaign issue. Demands for "unity" do wonders as more and more legislators follow their President down the liberal road in spite of prior conservative records and campaign promises in the past elections.

Political commentators from Left, Right, and that non-existent ideological position known as the "Center" all agree that the Nixon Administration is far more Liberal than it pretended it would be during the 1968 campaign, that Conservatives receive only "meaningless baubles," and that the administration talks Conservative and acts Liberal. The Nixon Administration, moving Leftward, has pulled the Republican Party with it.

The head of the American Conservative Union, Congressman John Ashbrook of Ohio, has pointed out that the Nixon Administration is using the excuse of "party unity" to high-pressure Congressmen into supporting increased government spending and power. Ashbrook stated:

> A few months after a hard-fought and close national election, it appears that some Republican leaders would make you believe that it is a question of "not supporting" the President or the

party when you vote against him when he fails to carry out his campaign promises. I will support him steadfastly in his efforts to bring about the changes he promised the American people. I will just as vigorously oppose him if he endeavors to go in the opposite direction. I am not one of those Republicans — and they are apparently in the majority — who could view with alarm under Johnson last year and point with pride to the same thing under President Nixon this year. There are always changing factors to consider but some things are clearly central and basic to our Republican philosophy. If as a part of our basic philosophy we opposed something last year, it should still be wrong this year. If it was right last year, it should be right this year. [31]

But apparently many Republicans have decided Sam Rayburn was right when he said, "To get along, go along." Most Republican Congressmen have gone along in what Republican *Battle Line* refers to as "legislative amnesia." *Battle Line* in October 1969 said that:

> ... the Republican Party in Congress, long a bastion for conservatism, seems to be suffering from legislative amnesia. GOP leaders don't lead and their members, for the most part, seem paralyzed by the presence of a Republican in the White House. Congressmen with long voting records based on sound GOP conservative principles now forgotten have followed like sheep as the Nixon Administration has proposed new legislative confirmation for many liberal Democrat programs first enacted under Kennedy and Johnson.

The political proof is in the voting. The effects of the go-along-to-get-along, party-unity-above-principle policy has shown up in the voting records of Republican Congressmen. The *Washington Star* of February 12, 1970, reported:

> Americans for Constitutional Action, whose ratings of congressional voting records are frequently relied upon as a measure of conservative influence in the House and Senate, says there has been "a distinct drop" in conservatism in both houses, particularly among Republicans . . . .

In a statement accompanying the ratings, ACA President Charles A. McManus said:

"There is no question that we are disappointed at the ratings received by a number of members of Congress, mostly Republicans, and particularly as the new ratings fall far below the high-water mark achieved in the ACA ratings by the conservative members of Congress covering the final session (1968) of the liberal Johnson administration."

ACA President McManus further stated:

The new figures revealed that many conservative Republicans have taken positions on rollcall votes contrary to their former position on similar legislation, some for the first time in their legislative career. Their voting records in 1969 reveal support of some liberal Kennedy-Johnson Administration programs continued by the Nixon Administration. [32]

The extent to which many Republican Congressmen who would have fought Hubert Humphrey tooth and nail have been neutralized by the Nixon Administration is revealed by the ACA tabulations. The Conservative voting indices of numerous GOP lawmakers dropped precipitously. For example, the late Congressman James Utt, a long-time champion of Conservatism through thick and thin, through vice and sin, had a cumulative Conservative voting record with the ACA of ninety-five per cent. His record in the 91st Congress, believe it or not, was sixty-seven per cent. This is an increase from voting Liberal five per cent of the time to voting Liberal nearly thirty-five per cent of the time — an increase of almost seven hundred per cent. The voting records of other California Republican Congressmen were typical of the increasing Liberalism and decreasing Conservatism of GOP legislators across the country. Don Clausen fell from seventy-nine to fifty-nine per cent; Charles S. Gubser, from seventy-two to forty per cent; William S. Maillard, from fifty-three to twenty-nine per cent; Robert

Mathias, from seventy-one to forty-seven percent; Burt Talcott, from eighty to forty-seven per cent; Charles Teague, from eighty to fifty per cent; Charles Wilson, from eighty-two to fifty-four per cent; and Craig Hosmer, from seventy-five to fifty per cent.

Concerning the disastrous effects of the Nixon Administration on GOP voting records, *Battle Line* stated:

> Nowhere has the President's liberalism had a more depressing result than among Republicans in Congress. *Congressional Quarterly* in its 1969 year-end study of the voting habits of congressional Republicans found a decided move to the left. Most of the Nixon congressional victories did not result from the traditional conservative coalition of a majority of the GOP plus the bloc of southern Democrats. Rather Nixon most often won with a liberal-dominated coalition including Eastern GOP members, many Democrats outside the South plus just enough "normally" conservative Republicans who are willing to go along with liberal bills because the President wants them.[33]

David Broder, writing in the *Washington Post* said:

> This fact shows most clearly in the figures on individual members' support of the President. Within each party the strongest support for the Nixon program was the East ... [although] high on the list of his Democratic backers were such liberals as Democratic National Committee Chairman Fred Harris of Oklahoma and Rep. Morris K. Udall of Arizona. Rep. Peter Frelinghuysen, Republican of New Jersey, another liberal, led all House Republicans in support of the President ... and the Republican foes of the President were the ultra-conservatives in the House led by none other than Rep. H.R. Gross of Iowa, who voted against the Republican President 64% of the time.[34]

Battle Line commented further:

> Interestingly by comparison, the 1969 annual conservative ratings by Americans for Constitutional Action (ACA) gave Rep. Frelinghuysen, Nixon's most frequent GOP supporter, a rating of

only 20% conservative. Rep. Gross, Nixon's most frequent GOP
opponent, rates 100% conservative with ACA.[35]

In other words, the Nixon Administration has proven to be
an absolute disaster in the fight against socialism at home and
Communism abroad. The Nixon Administration, for all its
campaign promises and patriotic Conservative rhetoric, is not
part of the solution, it is part of the problem. Grass-roots
Republicans and GOP Congressmen must now swallow their
pride and realize that they have been conned by a smooth-
talking automobile salesman from Whittier, and must heed
St. Paul's recommendation to the Ephesians: "Follow not a
multitude to do evil."

References
1. *Battle Line*, February 1970.
2. *Indianapolis Sunday Star*, August 18, 1968.
3. *Los Angeles Times*, November 7, 1968.
4. *Deseret News*, December 2, 1968.
5. *Long Beach* (Calif.) *Press-Telegram*, February 10, 1970.
6. *Battle Line*, February-March 1969.
7. *Newsweek*, February 24, 1969
8. *Ibid.*, February 2, 1970.
9. *Indianapolis News*, January 22, 1969.
10. *Washington Post*, August 16, 1969.
11. *Ibid.*, July 12, 1969.
12. *Indianapolis News*, October 21, 1969.
13. *Battle Line*, August 1969.
14. *Washington Star,* January 21, 1970
15. *Washington Star*, February 16, 1969.
16. *National Review,* October 7, 1969, page 1013.
17. *Indianapolis Star*, April 24, 1970.
18. *Los Angeles Times,* April 15, 1969..
19. *Long Beach* (Calif.) *Press-Telegram*, February 7, 1969.
20. *Ibid.*, June 23, 1969.
21. *Ibid.*, August 13, 1969.
22. *Ibid.*, August 6, 1969.
23. *Ibid.*, August 11, 1969.
24. *Indianapolis News*, February 27, 1970.
25. *Los Angeles Times*, September 17, 1970.
26. *Wall Street Journal*, August 20, 1969.
27. *Chicago Tribune*, February 7, 1969.
28. *Indianapolis News*, February 26, 1969.
29. *Los Angeles Times,* February 15, 1969.
30. *Manchester Union-Leader,* reprinted in *Independent American,* April-May, 1969.
31. *Battle Line,* July 1969.
32. *Human Events*, February 21, 1970.
33. *Battle Line*, February 1970.
34. *Washington Post*, quoted in *Battle Line*, February 1970.
35. *Battle Line*, February 1970.

CHAPTER II

The UN-Free Agent

It must seem a great irony to many that as the Nixon Administration moves Left, the country as a whole is moving Right. That this is true is attested by the fact that the President often resorts to Conservative rhetoric and uses Vice President Spiro Agnew as a tool to placate Conservative sentiment in the nation.

On November 5, 1968, over 73 million Americans tramped to the polls and elected Richard Nixon President with 43 per cent of the vote. On this basis America's powerful Liberal pundits and social savants announced in a shrill chorus that Mr. Nixon was a minority President, and that in order to govern properly he should form a sort of coalition government to include "the alienated urban poor and the dissident youth." When John Kennedy won a squeaker over Nixon in 1960, thanks to civic-minded voters from the Great Beyond in Chicago and Texas, these same soothsayers trumpeted that the returns were a "mandate" for the march to a New Frontier of the Left. Not one southpaw scribe suggested that Richard Nixon undertake a "dialogue," much less seek a coalition government, with the alienated, disaffected, and dissident ten million who had put their X on the ballot beside the name of George Corley Wallace. Unlike the Black Nationalists and New Lefties, the ten million Wallace supporters were deemed to be beyond the political and ideological pale — awful creatures to be isolated and treated as lepers.

31

The Liberal pundits ignored the fact that Nixon and Wallace polled a combined 57 per cent of the vote, which constituted the greatest four-year shift of voter sentiment against an incumbent party in the nation's history. Led by Lyndon Johnson in 1964, the Democrats got 61 per cent of the vote against Barry Goldwater. Four years later they were swamped when more than 18 per cent of the electorate changed their minds. The Nixon-Wallace 57 per cent represented a clear Conservative majority. This, of course, makes it all the more strange that the President should prove to be a Liberal in action.

It is certainly not that the President is unaware of the meaning of the 1968 contest, for one of his campaign assistants has delivered to him an exhaustive breakdown of national voting moods and patterns. Kevin Phillips, Mr. Nixon's principal "vote patterns" and "trends" analyst and Special Assistant to Nixon campaign manager John Mitchell during the campaign, assembled the results of his study in a book, *The Emerging Republican Majority*. The conclusion of Mr. Phillips that Conservativism is the real wave of the political future is particularly significant, since this graduate of the Harvard Law School is far from being a Conservative on many issues. As one who walks carefully along the center stripe, Phillips cannot be accused of letting his personal prejudices color his conclusions – a charge which reviewers applied to similar conclusions of the brilliant M. Stanton Evans at the time he published *The Future of Conservatism* in 1968. Actually the Phillips book, written after the election and based on a careful scrutiny of the returns, proves that Mr. Evans was less a partisan than an accurate analyst and shrewd forecaster of the temper of the American trend.

Republican *Battle Line*, in September 1969, called the Phillips book "no less than a blueprint for Republican Party control of the White House for the remainder of the century. And it is based on a mass of maps, charts, election trend statistics and historical facts that in combination reflect the author's deep sense of scholarship and keen analytic mind."

The "Phillips Strategy" in a nutshell is to build a Republican presidential majority based upon combining the Heartland (Midwest), the Sun Belt (from Charleston, S.C., across the Southwest to Southern California), and the West. The twenty-five states that comprise the Heartland, for example, cast 223 of the 270 electoral votes needed to elect a President of the United States. Whereas Nixon carried only 17 of these in 1960, in 1968 he carried 21. The "Phillips Strategy" abandons the Northeast, saying in effect, "There's no way, baby."

Phillips has sent Liberals into absolute conniptions, and they have damned his plan as "the Southern Strategy." Actually, it is not a "Southern Strategy," but a national strategy that includes the South. Unfortunately, Liberals have not psychologically re-admitted the South into the Union. They love the sidewalks of New York, not the suburbs of Atlanta. What they hate most about it, of course, is that the "Phillips Strategy" is a Conservative strategy to build a coalition of Republicans, Catholics, and Southern Democrats. Following the 1970 mid-term elections, Liberals, including Democratic chieftain Lawrence O'Brien, fell all over themselves announcing that the "Southern strategy" had flopped, since many GOP candidates had gone down the drain in Dixie. But the misnamed "Southern Strategy" is a Presidential strategy, not a gubernatorial or congressional strategy. Certainly the GOP would like to elect governors, senators, and congressmen in the South, and someday they may, but the facts of the matter are that many Southerners vote for Conservative Democrats in these races. However, this does not mean they will swallow a Hubert Humphrey, Edmund Muskie, or Teddy Kennedy in a presidential race. They will either vote Republican, if the candidate is a Conservative, or they will vote for a third party candidate like Governor George Wallace in an attempt, at the very least, to throw the election into the House of Representatives, where they could bargain.

"Ah," say the Liberals, "but you don't build a party by reading people out of it. You build a party by bringing people into it. We must attract the young, the poor, and the black." Of course, no party should exclude people because of race, age, or economic status, but the Republican Party should exclude socialists — be they millionaires or welfare recipients. It is truly tragic that many of the young, the poor, and the black have been convinced that their economic salvation lies in socialism — the primary cause of the problems they have. The Republican Party must not cater to their mistaken ideas. The cliché that socialism is the cancer of liberty and has never worked is true. Following the path of the welfare state with its increasing numbers of people on the dole, high taxes, and perpetual inflation is not only immoral and the road to national disaster; but it is not even politically expedient. Phillips, relying on stark statistics, shows that no amount of Republican concern for Negro welfare can gain their mass support. He points to returns which show that neither Michigan ex-Governor George Romney nor Illinois Senator Charles Percy got more than 19 or 20 per cent of the black vote, despite their all-out effort to win it. Phillips adds: "Indeed, the Negro-Democratic mutual identification was a major source of Democratic loss . . . in many parts of the country . . . " and conversely, the lack of GOP-Negro identification helped the Republicans nationwide.

With an impressive array of vote statistics culled from Northeastern and urban precincts, Phillips demolished the Liberal Republican argument that the GOP must cater to big city Liberals to gain votes. He calls this "one of the greatest political myths of this decade — a product of liberal self-interest . . . the actual demographic and political facts convey a very different message." The "Big City strategy" aimed at the Northeast, as advocated by GOP Liberals, assures only a Republican debacle. The big cities are losing their power. The real growth of America is in the suburbs and particularly in the suburbs of the fast-growing areas of the South-Southwest and West — targeted by Phillips as the base of his emerging Republican majority. The electoral votes of the Sun Belt almost tripled in the half century between 1920 and 1970, outstripping the declining urban Northeast in the process. Equally important, the Republican share of the suburban vote is on the increase.[1] Richard C. Wade of the University of Chicago wrote: "The great growth area of the country is the suburbs — and they are going to be for a long time . . . the suburbs are likely to stay strongly Republican."[2] However, the decisive turning point has come just recently. A report by the Republican National Committee on the 1966 elections stated: "The balance of political power in the nation's major metropolitan areas has swung sharply in the direction of the suburbs in the past four years." In his book, *Conservatism and the GOP*, Frank W. Mezek Jr. went on to say:

> In 1962 the metropolitan area vote was about evenly divided between the cities and their suburbs, but in four years the suburban vote grew by more than 12 percent while the urban vote declined 11.5 percent.
> *Thus, in the 1966 elections, the suburban share of the total metropolitan vote rose to 56 percent!* . . . . [Emphasis in the original]

U.S. News & World Report told us in its June 2, 1969 issue: "Four-fifths of the national growth will be found to have taken place in the suburbs, where nearly 20 million people have been added in a decade."

Phillips asserted that a large segment of the Democratic electorate is in the process of breaking away. The old urban-labor coalition which has served the Democratic party so faithfully and well in the past is breaking down. "The Democratic coalition is now a basket case. Its body is emaciated, and its arms or legs are broken, or paralyzed, or sliced right off," wrote Stewart Alsop.[3] Theodore Sorenson, the late President Kennedy's chief adviser, said: "The old urban coalition has split to smithereens. The unions can no longer deliver their members, their preachers can no longer deliver the Negroes and the ward captains can no longer deliver the precincts."[4]

The children of the masses of first- and second-generation Americans, who were often ignorant or illiterate and crowded into large cities, where they were dependent on the Democratic precinct captain for vital services or jobs, have now moved to the suburbs. Frank Mezek notes:

> ... the laboring man is becoming affluent, suburbanized, conservative and Republican — usually in that order. The American worker is no longer Roosevelt's "forgotten man" of the Depression, and he would probably be insulted if this were insinuated today . . . .[5]

Addressing the Western States Democratic Conference in Los Angeles on August 26, 1967, Postmaster General Lawrence F. O'Brien, referring to "American workers who live in the suburbs, pay taxes, support church and community activities and hope to send their children to college," went on to say, "We are making a serious error if we look at union memberships as if they were living back in the 1930's. Today the party that forgets that about 50 percent of union families are in the $7,500 to $15,000 range does so at its peril."[6]

Pat Brown, the former Democratic Governor of California, said after his 1966 loss to Ronald Reagan: "Workers used to ask about workmen's compensation and disability insurance. Not this time. The workers have become aristocrats, they became Republicans."[7]

As laboring families move to the suburbs, and one-half of all laboring families and 75 percent of union members under age 40 now live in suburbia, they do not automatically desert the Democratic Party for the Republican. It is more a process of attrition. As they pay property taxes, become more closely oriented to their local government, and are influenced by the proximity of Conservative and Republican thought, they tend to become Conservative and Republican themselves. The rise of the suburbs reflects a growing middle-class and growing affluence in the United States. Studies by the AFL-CIO have shown that as people move to the suburbs they gradually become more Conservative, looking to the federal government not as a benefactor, but as a menace. They become aware not of what government can "give" them, but of what it can take away.[8]

While Phillips, Evans, and Mezek all agree that labor is becoming increasingly sympathetic to courting by Conservatives, the 1970 Congressional elections showed that labor tends to return to the womb when the economy sours and the specter of unemployment rises. Nixon's refusal to control inflation by cutting government spending and taxes doubtless cost the Republicans dear in the off-year elections, despite the fact that he was basically following Phillips' campaign recommendations and making a Conservative appeal.

Another factor in favor of forging the "New Consensus" is that the number of blue-collar workers is decreasing as a percentage of the total population. Increased educational opportunities and the force of an increasingly scientific and technological society are changing the makeup of the work force. There are now six and a half million more white-collar than blue-collar workers in our country.[9]

A major segment of the "New Consensus" is the South, where century-long attachments to the Democratic party are breaking down. Phillips peers at his election statistics and determines that the whole future of the Republican party lies in moving far enough to the Right to persuade Southern Wallace voters, who are mostly Democrats, to get off their donkey and mount the elephant. He writes:

> The common denominator of Wallace's support, Catholic or Protestant, is alienation from the Democratic party and a strong trend — shown in other years and other contests — towards the GOP. Although most of Wallace's votes came from Democrats, he principally won those in motion beween a Democratic past and a Republican future . . . . Three quarters or more of the Wallace electorate represented lost Nixon votes. [10]

In an interview with *Human Events* on August 16, 1969, Phillips further elaborated on the Wallace vote:

> . . . of the states Wallace carried, four of them had been among the six to vote for Goldwater in 1964. Obviously much of the Wallace electorate there, and beyond those states as well, was a Goldwater electorate. And to that extent it came from voters who had been in a Republican voting pattern.
>
> But you can go beyond this and you can look at areas that were showing a trend to the Republicans in 1960 that was quite sharp and then rolling up a heavy Wallace vote in 1968. The indication is that an awful lot of these voters, although Democrats by party identification, were exactly the segment of the Democratic electorate that is in the process of breaking away.
>
> . . . Third parties have almost always served as way stations between the parties, and these Wallace voters seem definitely to be in a transitional phase.

Loyalties to the Democratic Party that were built in the South after the Civil War are being displaced as the Democratic Party becomes more and more the creature of the Eastern Liberal Establishment. Phillips observed:

> What you have in the works politically is a deterioriation of Democratic tradition among people, often very conservative people, whose loyalty to the Democratic party is based on old Democratic party cultural, regional and ethnic loyalties. And as

those deteriorate and fall apart, their cohesion starts transferring itself to the GOP. Mainly because there are many aspects of the Republican party, whether in foreign policy or social policy or economic policy, that are more appealing to these people once their old traditional loyalties become to them obsolescent and no longer purposeful . . . .[11]

However, it is doubtful if many of these potential pachyderms have been converted by the actions of the Nixon Administration, despite the occasional "meaningless bauble" thrown their way.

Liberal Stewart Alsop sees Mr. Nixon moving Left (for his "New Consensus") because that is where he believes most of the voters lie:

This two-way nibbling explains why the President who unleashed Agnew and nominated Clement F. Haynsworth Jr. and G. Harrold Carswell is the same President who first proposed a floor under incomes and a multibillion-dollar attack on pollution. Judging by the polls and other evidence, the nibbling is going so well that the President is much closer to creating his majority than would have seemed likely a year ago.

If the majority is to be solid and lasting, most of the votes will have to come from the Democratic center rather than the Wallace right, because that is where most of the votes are. This is why the Nixon technique of pre-emption of the liberal Democratic issues is his chief political instrument. He has used it so far with consummate skill.

. . . His object is to create a solid majority for the Republican Party and Richard Nixon, which will be the mirror image of the Democratic majority created by Franklin Roosevelt.

Roosevelt's majority stretched from the outer edges of the pro-Communist left to the outer edges of the hard-core Republican right. Mr. Nixon's majority is designed to stretch from the edges of the Wallace right to the edges of the hard-core liberal Democratic left. And he is nibbling away at both edges just as hard as he can.[12]

Mr. Nixon obviously would like to be all things to all people.

Liberals in general, and Liberal Republicans in particular, have tried to convince Republican politicians that the country is overwhelmingly Liberal and that the word "Conservative" has a poisonous image. For them it does. But not to the American public. The truth is that "Conservative" has far more acceptance — by as much as a two-to-one margin — than does the term "Republican." Current surveys reveal that barely one-quarter of the American people now consider themselves Republicans, but a far higher percentage, up to one-half of the electorate, think of themselves as Conservatives. In a 1963 Gallup Poll, voters were asked, "Suppose there were two major parties in the United States, one for liberals and one for conservatives, which one would you be most likely to prefer?" Fifty-one percent answered Liberal, forty-nine percent answered Conservative.[13] In other words, the Conservatives would only have to proselytize one percent of the Liberals to achieve parity.

In a September 1966 interview Gallup admitted that Conservative strength in America seemed to be on the increase, and added: "The country is split almost evenly between 'conservatives' and 'liberals.' Strangely enough, the word 'conservative' doesn't carry the onus that the word 'Republican' does."

A Harris survey in 1964 found Conservatism on a key number of issues to be not merely strong but overwhelming. Harris concluded that voters agreed with Goldwater on prayer in the schools (88 per cent), government security regulations (94 per cent), the demoralizing effect of government welfare programs (60 per cent), and the general increase of government power (60 percent). The fact that these same voters were preparing to cast their ballots against the candidate who represented their own views on these questions, and in favor of the candidate who opposed them, illustrates the difficulty of putting a strictly ideological interpretation on any given set of election results. If the 1964 election had been run on issues instead of TV ads showing Social Security cards being torn up and little girls vaporized in mushroom clouds, Goldwater would have won. But former Census Bureau chief Richard Scammon observed that many voters thought Johnson was the Conservative candidate and Goldwater the "radical" one. Harris found that almost half the voters polled by his organization chose the designation "radical" rather than "conservative" to describe Goldwater's position.[14]

If there are more Conservatives than is generally believed, then why have they lost so many presidential elections to Liberals? The chief answer, according to Evans, is that American elections are not ideological plebiscites but highly complicated affairs in which popular sentiment is divided by many other factors. Also, it is difficult to determine cause and effect, because politicians most often do not conduct their campaigns in terms relevant to ideology. Equally important is the fact that Conservatives over the years have been outclassed by the Liberals in presenting their case to the public. But Richard Nixon proved in 1968 that a candidate could run as a Conservative and win.

Mr. Nixon, a firm realist when it comes to politics, obviously realizes that despite the howls of Republican Liberals, Messrs. Phillips, Evans, and Mezek know what they are talking about. Republican campaign strategy in 1968 and 1970 reflected an awareness that those who have come to be known as "the silent majority" are a large and politically forceful group. This does not mean that they are well-informed Conservatives who have studied political philosophy, economics, or history from other than the Liberal point of view. These people, for the most part, attended the same institutions of higher *leaning* and rely for their information on the same Establishment-controlled slick magazines and television commentators as the Liberals. But they are intuitive Conservatives who look around and see the real world as it is. Innately they are appalled at crime, rioting, inflation, high taxes, and an America-last foreign policy. What Richard Nixon realizes is that most of these people have short memories and basically want to forget about politics and go back to minding their own business after the election. Most of them are lulled to sleep by the continuing Conservative rhetoric and don't notice that the Liberals are getting the lion's share of the action.

Doubtless Mr. Nixon would like to carry on this charade through the '72 election. After that it will be "Katy bar the door." Until then, the realities of the Phillips strategy must be observed — though officially denied. Since writing his book, *The Emerging Republican Majority,* Mr. Phillips has become officially an un-person. Now that he is no longer with the Nixon Administration, when his name is mentioned, top party leaders say, "Kevin who?" Columnists Evans and Novak detailed in the *Los Angeles Times* of September 30, 1969, how the White House has decided to handle this hot potato:

> President Nixon's highly critical answer at Friday's press conference when asked about Kevin Phillips' "The Emerging Republican Majority" was no snap response but had been carefully prepared in advance as part of a concerted White House effort to disavow the book and muzzle the author.
>
>   A few days before the President's public rejection of the lily-white strategy implicit in the book, the muzzle was applied. It was made clear from on high in the Administration that Phillips, a 29-year-old special assistant to Atty. Gen. John N. Mitchell, ought to curtail his public appearances. As a result, he quietly bowed out of a scheduled debate on NBC's Today show last Wednesday morning . . . .
>
>   Early in September, a senior White House aide (not Dent) prepared a highly critical memorandum on the book for Mr. Nixon. It recommended that, when asked, the President should say he had not read the book but still indicate clearly that he does not agree with it (advice he followed at Friday's press conference).[15]

Evans and Novak reported that Phillips had been thoroughly muzzled by the Administration until he left his job as Mitchell's aide. But you can be certain that Mr. Nixon and Attorney General John Mitchell, who will reportedly manage Mr. Nixon's campaign once again in 1972, have virtually memorized every chart, table, and graph in *The Emerging Republican Majority*. *Battle Line* pointed out in December 1969:

> . . . if conservatives are pleased with the words of Agnew and Mitchell, they should not lose sight of the many liberal actions the Nixon Administration has been taking. It is fairly obvious that the President and his political advisors have understood and accepted the thesis advanced in Kevin Phillips' book *The Emerging Republican Majority*. Being pragmatic, they naturally tend to do whatever they feel necessary to win the support of this new national conservative majority . . . .

You can also be certain that the Democrats will cooperate by nominating a "super-Liberal" who will frighten many Americans into reluctantly supporting Mr. Nixon and his seemingly more moderate socialism. It will be the old "lesser of two evils" flim-flam once again. And why not? It works! And it will continue to work until Americans realize that the choice they are given — between taking the freeway to socialism and going by way of the back alleys — is a false alternative. Both lead to the same destination; one route merely gets there slightly later than the other.

Numerous rationalizations are offered for the conflict between what Mr. Nixon does and what he says. One major excuse is that he does not control Congress. This is true from a numerical standpoint, but it would be quite possible to forge an ideological majority with a Republican-Southern Democrat coalition.

If he wanted to, the President could take giant steps toward reducing socialistic controls over the citizens of this country without the assistance of a single senator or congressman. Many of the most dictatorial laws that have partially enslaved Americans were not passed by Congress at all. These are "Executive Orders," which are entered into the *Federal Register* by the Executive Department and at the end of thirty days have the force of law. Nowhere in the Constitution will you find a grant of power to make "Executive Orders." Historically, presidents issued these "Executive Orders" to cover things like holidays and working schedules for government employees. But Franklin Delano Roosevelt perverted this harmless mechanism into a weapon for establishing one-man tyrannical rule by bypassing Congress. For example, the reason you cannot own gold is not that Congress passed a law against it, but that FDR issued an "Executive Order." Mr. Nixon has said much (and done nothing) about returning the power of government to the people. By "the people," he does not mean individuals, but state and local governments. Mr. Nixon could take a gigantic step towards increasing individual liberty simply by systematically repealing literally thousands of un-Constitutional "Executive Orders" that are on the books. Instead, Mr. Nixon has increased their number and strengthened some of the most dangerous ones.

The concept that the federal government is a Frankenstein monster run amuck, which cannot be controlled, is another oft-used excuse for the contradiction between Nixon's promises and his performance, as in this example by the *Wall Street Journal's* Alan Otten:

> . . . there's the possibility, sure to be rejected by conservative philosophers, that the Presidency simply forces a man to be more liberal — that once in office, facing the magnitude and intensity of unsolved problems and the tremendous backlog of unmet needs, a man concerned about his place in history almost inevitably becomes an activist, ready or even eager to order new and bigger Federal programs. Greater action by the private sector

and state and local governments may be fine campaign themes, and Mr. Nixon will surely push for such action in the months ahead. But the levers and money the President actually controls are Federal power and Federal funds, and more and more he uses these to meet the problems he feels must be met.[16]

Certainly it takes courage to reduce government, because every bureau, every subsidy, every program represents strong vested interests. But public sentiment is, in general, strongly in favor of cutting back the expensive giveaways — many of which could be abolished by cancelling the "Executive Orders" that created them. Instead, Mr. Nixon is moving in just the opposite direction, adding onto New Deal, Fair Deal, New Frontier, and Great Society programs as well as creating "New Nixon" giveaways of his own.

Another rationalization offered for Mr. Nixon's seemingly inconsistent Liberal actions is that he is prevented by public opinion from doing otherwise. But this is just the reverse of the truth. As the February 1970 *Battle Line* observed:

> Nor can it be plausibly argued that Nixon is simply being as conservative as public opinion will allow. Quite the opposite. He is obviously suggesting to the public that he is more conservative than is actually the case — implying that public opinion would not only countenance more rightward action but is earnestly in want of it. If the administration's objective is to move things as much toward traditionalism as possible, it should be willing to be at least as conservative as its advertising says it is.

The obvious question is: Why is Nixon leading into socialism? He campaigned as a Conservative, virtually lifting George Wallace's campaign theme lock, stock, and barrel. There was hardly a dime's worth of difference between a Nixon campaign speech and a Wallace campaign speech, except for Wallace's more colorful colloquialisms. The long-standing argument over whether a man can win the Presidency by campaigning as a Conservative has finally been settled. Now millions are wondering why Nixon's actions as President should be so different from his campaign promises. What motive could he have?

Every amateur psychiatrist and "pop" psychologist from Burbank to Boston has been trying for two and a half decades to discover the "real" Nixon. It is a pastime almost as popular as playing Monopoly, or mini-skirt watching. Theories abound like ants at a midsummer's picnic. We shall not spend time on any of these theories for we believe most of them are inconsequential, except that friend and foe unanimously agree that Mr. Nixon is fired by an all-consuming ambition. We think Mr. Nixon is summed up in an unguarded remark he made to an acquaintance of ours when he was first running for Congress in 1946, before he had acquired the cool reticence of today: "Look, you drove up to this meeting in a beautiful new Cadillac. I came here in a battered secondhand Chevrolet. But all of that is going to change. I'm going to get mine, no matter what it takes." This inordinate ambition has been both Mr. Nixon's greatest asset and, from the country's point of view, his Achilles' heel. This fervid desire to scratch his way to the top of the political heap has driven him to spend countless hours preparing himself for the presidency. It drove him to tour the country tirelessly, not only in his own behalf but for other Republican candidates. It allowed him to rise from the ashes like a phoenix after his defeat in the 1962 California gubernatorial election, in which virtually every observer in the nation had read Nixon's political epitaph. Richard Nixon is far from being the first man to have borne the scars of childhood poverty and had them turn into a mania of ambition for wealth or power. Mr. Nixon became a politician quite by accident (as we shall see later), much as a man might fall into a career in advertising or as a stockbroker. Had he not become a politician he might have become a real live Cash McCall, or another Joe Kennedy. But such was not his fate.

One can readily understand how a man of inordinate ambition may become an opportunist or, as Mr. Nixon is most often called, a pragmatist, i.e., one who does what appears to be practical without regard to any set of principles.

While Nixon's most vociferous backers have for the most part been Conservative, he does not himself profess to be a Conservative. When asked where he stood on the ideological spectrum, Mr. Nixon replied, "I'm perhaps at dead center."[17] Being "at dead center," however, is a convenient, a pragmatic position. One can move in either direction from there, very quickly and without attracting great attention. But, as we have said before, the "middle of the road" is a totally unstable position. It is theoretically a position between competitive free enterprise on the right and revolutionary Communism on the left. The "center" is not the place of moderation its adherents claim it to be. As the world's greatest economist, Ludwig von Mises, has shown, "The middle of the road leads to socialism." In every election campaign the "middle of the roaders" have to promise more and more "free" government goodies to those beguiled individuals who believe that there is such a thing as something for nothing. And in each election we enfranchise more and more people who do not work for a living and therefore don't pay the taxes that finance the "free" government handouts. This is why the "middle of the road" has been steadily shifting Leftward since the election of FDR. Many centrist goals today (such as a guaranteed annual income) would have been considered ultra-Leftwing less than a decade ago. Many, if not most, Americans consider themselves "middle of the roaders" because they feel it is a sensible position between extremes. A politician can run as a "centrist" and attract support from most people on the political spectrum, foregoing the allegiance only of those who are termed "extremists." This false conception of what the political spectrum is has been the secret weapon of the Fabian Socialists, who would bring the theories of Marx to fruition one painful step at a time. By the middle '50s the late old-time socialist Norman Thomas could look around and proclaim that practically all of the planks of the Socialist Party platform of 1932 had been adopted by the Democrats and Republicans. In April 1957, Thomas, six-time candidate for President of the U.S. on the Socialist ticket, stated that "the United States is making greater strides towards socialism under Eisenhower than under Roosevelt."[18] And Norman Thomas, who liked Ike, would be absolutely delirious over Richard Nixon.

The concept that Mr. Nixon is a "centrist," a "middle of the roader," a "pragmatist" — empty terms that sound meaningful — is widely promoted by the press. Alan Otten, in the *Wall Street Journal*, expressed what is generally accepted as the lack of any guiding philosophy within the administration when he wrote: " . . . the Nixon Administration appears to have no convictions at all — to be merely holding its finger to the political winds and swaying back and forth," and he further observes that the President "is above all a pragmatist, addressing himself matter-of-factly and non-philosophically to the domestic and foreign problems facing the country and the political problems facing himself and his party; that he will seek aggressively to command as much of the middle of the road as possible; and that this means he will probably zigzag back and forth . . . "[19] Columnist Robert Semple of the *New York Times* would have us believe the same thing:

> Yet in the end one suspects that the underlying cause of much of the confusion is the absence of any firm ideological thrust in Mr. Nixon's mind or in the minds of his principal associates. "A political man," he is fond of calling himself, and that is what he is: a creature of that extraordinarily shapeless heritage known as "moderate Republicanism," a centrist whose principal political ambition is to occupy neither the right nor the left, but to enlarge the middle.

Hence he zigs and he zags, and if he is zigging rightward today
— and no one should be surprised by this, in view of his campaign
promises — then he may zag in the other direction tomorrow.
Intellectually supple and politically sensitive, he is trying to build
a complicated platform from which he can preside — and win
again.[20]

Max Frankel put forth the same Establishment line on the
President: " . . . the President abhors controversy and keeps
trying to embrace all points of view . . . "[21]

The *Wall Street Journal's* Edward Behr predicted on July
17, 1969, that apparent ideological confusion will continue
to reign throughout Nixon's first administration:

It may well be . . . that no one action will mean much, that the
oft-confusing crosscurrents marking the President's first six
months will persist indefinitely and that even by January 1973
the Nixon regime will show no clear-cut pattern or philosophy.

You can bet a clear-cut pattern will emerge *after* January
1, 1973.

On January 24, 1970, *Human Events* interpreted Mr.
Nixon's actions in much the same way:

We don't accuse the Nixon Administration of being truly
liberal, or even blindly middle-of-the-road. More often than not,
it appears confused and at cross purposes with itself. Too
frequently it seems as if the President has no real philosophy, that
his entire goal is to tranquilize the electorate rather than to lead it
in a certain direction. When the conservatives get uppity, Spiro
Agnew comes to the fore with all his hard-line rhetoric. But as the
liberals become incensed, Agnew fades offstage and the spotlight
suddenly focuses on Robert Finch, who has been patiently
waiting in the wings with his latest liberal spectacular.

While superficially it appears that Mr. Nixon wouldn't take
a stand on what time it is without consulting a hatful of
watches and is widely regarded as America's foremost

political weathervane, this merely serves to mask what is
really happening. The political winds are blowing to the
Right, and Mr. Nixon acknowledges this while at the same
time moving Leftward. Congressman Robert Nix (R.-Pa.)
commented: " ... the Nation [is] being asked to do the
'Nixon foxtrot' − one step forward, two steps backward,
then three steps sideways and take a 15-minute break." We
think two steps Left and one step Right is a more accurate if
less colorful description. In Marxist terminology this is
known as *dialectics.*

Establishmentarian Max Lerner of the *New York Times*
would have us believe Nixon may not know what he is doing:

> If some leaders govern by love and some by fear, Mr. Nixon
> generates neither but governs by puzzlement and indirection. He
> runs foreign policy and suffers domestic policy, but in both his
> chief quality is a shrewdness which keeps his opponents con-
> stantly off balance by timing, compromise and diversion and also
> the quality of detachment which enables him to use a Henry
> Kissinger and Daniel Moynihan as well as a Spiro Agnew and a
> Mitchell for purposes that none of the four may understand − if
> indeed the President himself understands them. [22]

But we think there is method in this madness. As Alan
Otten noted: " ... to a large extent his [Nixon's] policy has
been one of studied ambiguity."[23] We think the "studied
ambiguity" is a smokescreen behind which Nixon can
continue the same policies of taking the country Leftward
that were practiced by Roosevelt, Truman, Eisenhower,
Kennedy, and Johnson. The faces change, but the policies
never do. In its February 1970 issue *Battle Line* observed:

> What is the ideological significance of all this? It is suggested
> that Nixon's policy is a kind of fabianism in reverse − an inching
> back toward traditional GOP principles, in which Nixon moves as
> far to the right as conditions will permit . . . . this is obviously not
> the case. What has transpired is not a movement toward
> conservatism, but continued momentum along the path of

liberalism, albeit at a slower pace than might have been expected if Hubert Humphrey rather than Nixon were in the White House.

The Nixon Administration is not Fabianism in reverse, it is Fabianism in second gear forward. Nixon sees himself as a modern Disraeli, a man with a Conservative image who implements socialist programs. Alan Otten wrote concerning Mr. Nixon, in the *Wall Street Journal* of August 20, 1969:

> ...He had been reading a life of Disraeli, the conservative [*sic*] Prime Minister who pushed through some of Britain's earliest laws to improve slum conditions, protect factory workers and extend the franchise. Both appraising Disraeli and paraphrasing one of his quotations, Mr. Nixon said he realized it was "Tory men with liberal principles who enlarged democracy."
> ...But the Nixon comment does call attention to an oft-forgotten fact of political life: Conservatives pursuing a liberal course can on occasion succeed better than liberals could have, while liberals on occasion can advance a conservative cause better than conservatives could.

The cold, hard facts are that Mr. Nixon is neither a Liberal, nor a Conservative, nor a "pragmatist," nor a "centrist," although at times he can pretend to be any of these. He is simply a man with all-consuming ambition. And as a professional politician, naturally a man with his desire to get to the top of the heap would seek the ultimate in political power — the Presidency. But Mr. Nixon could not have become President unless he had been willing to work with or join the oligarchy that has the power to make or break those with presidential aspirations.

After losing to Pat Brown in the California gubernatorial race in 1962, Nixon had universally been consigned to the political trash heap. He left his practice as an attorney in California and went to New York, where he moved in as a neighbor of Nelson Rockefeller, the man who is supposedly his archenemy, in a $100,000-a-year apartment in a building owned by Rockefeller. Then Mr. Nixon went to work for the law firm of Mr. Rockefeller's personal attorney, and in the next six years spent most of his time touring the country and the world, first rebuilding his political reputation and then campaigning to get the 1968 Republican nomination. At the same time, according to his own financial statements, his net worth multiplied many times and he became quite wealthy. Nelson Rockefeller, the man who helped make Nixon acceptable to Conservatives by appearing to oppose him, and his colleagues of the Eastern Liberal Establishment, rescued him from political oblivion and made him President of the United States. Does it not make sense that Mr. Nixon, the man of passionate ambition whose career had sunk to the bottom, had to make some deals in order to reach his goal? And did he not acquire massive political debts in return for being made President by the Eastern Liberal Establishment?

The President is obviously an un-free agent. Mr. Nixon gets the glory, gets to live in the White House, flies across the nation and the world in a giant jet, and makes numerous decisions and appointments, but the real power lies with a clique based in New York. This clique is interested in building an all-powerful government that it will control. This is the real reason Mr. Nixon moves Left while talking like a Conservative. He has no choice. Despite highly convincing statements about cutting spending and decentralizing government, almost everything he does increases government spending and concentrates more and more power in the federal government. Certainly it is not exclusively a one-way street. That would be too obvious. The "Nixon Fox Trot" — two steps Left, one step Right — serves to disguise the real intent and direction of the Nixon Administration. As *Battle Line* pointed out in February 1970:

> For those who have watched the President's career in politics the past year should really be no surprise. Nixon has always

prided himself on being a pragmatic "centrist." What was surprising in 1968 was that so many staunch Republican conservatives should have granted Mr. Nixon the nomination, which they surely had the power to deny, without gaining some assurance that his presidential policies would at least reflect elemental conservative tendencies. Indeed the mass of conservative minded voters who elected Richard Nixon can be forgiven their lack of political sophistication. They heard what candidate Nixon said and to them it sounded conservative, matched their state of mind, and so they elected him.

Many key Conservatives were given private assurances during the campaign that the Nixon Administration would be very Conservative. But this was simply bait. Mr. Nixon was already firmly committed to carrying out the will of the clique to whose members we shall hereinafter refer to as the *Insiders*, who had resurrected him from political oblivion.

If this is true, and it is, the obvious questions are: What is this mysterious clique, and why are its members interested in building a socialist government?

References

1. M. Stanton Evans, *The Future of Conservatism: From Taft to Reagan and Beyond,* New York, Holt, Rinehart & Winston, 1968, pp. 44-46.
2. Frank W. Mezek Jr., *Conservatism and the G.O.P.*, Chicago, Charles Halberg & Co., 1968, p. 15.
3. *Saturday Evening Post*, 1967, p.29.
4. Frank W. Mezek Jr., *op. cit.*, p. 16.
5. *Ibid.*, pp. 17-18.
6. *Ibid.*, p. 18.
7. *Time*, November 18, 1967, p. 27.
8. M. Stanton Evans, *op. cit.*, pp. 47-48.
9. Frank W. Mezek Jr., *op. cit.*, p. 17.
10. Kevin Phillips, *The Emerging Republican Majority*, New York, Arlington House, 1969.
11. *Human Events*, August 16, 1969.
12. *Newsweek*, February 2, 1970.
13. M. Stanton Evans, *op. cit.*, p. 58.
14. *Ibid.*, p. 61.
15. *Los Angeles Times*, September 30, 1969.
16. *Wall Street Journal*, March 4, 1969.
17. Jules Witcover, *The Resurrection of Richard Nixon*, New York, C.P. Putnam's Sons, 1970, p. 106.
18. *Harvard Times-Republican*, April 18, 1957.
19. *Wall Street Journal*, March 4, 1969.
20. *New York Times,* July 13, 1969.
21. *Battle Line*, June 1969.
22. *Boston Herald-Traveler*, January 7, 1970.
23. *Wall Street Journal*, March 4, 1969.

CHAPTER III

The Establishing
Of Establishments

The word "Establishment" is badly overused and misused today, thanks to the young people who employ it to categorize parents, teachers, policemen, all government employees, all businessmen, and virtually anyone who has drifted across the magical age line of thirty. This is unfortunate, for there is in the country what truly amounts to an Establishment. As we use the word in this book, it means people and organizations connected with the immensely powerful and highly secret Council on Foreign Relations — the CFR.

One of the extremely infrequent articles concerning this Council that have appeared in the national press was published in the *Christian Science Monitor* of September 1, 1961. It began this way:

> On the west side of fashionable Park Avenue at 68th Street [in New York City] sit two handsome buildings across the way from each other. One is the Soviet Embassy to the United Nations .... Directly opposite on the southwest corner is the Council on Foreign Relations — probably one of the most influential semi-public organizations in the field of foreign policy.

Although the formal membership of the CFR is composed of fourteen hundred of the most elite names in the worlds of government, labor, business, finance, communications, the foundations, and education — and despite the fact that it has staffed almost every key position of every administration

since FDR's — it is doubtful that one American in a hundred
so much as recognizes the Council's name, or that one in a
thousand knows anything at all about its structure or purpose. Indicative of the CFR's power to maintain its
anonymity is the fact this writer discovered after poring over
decades of volumes of the *Readers' Guide to Periodical
Literature*: that, despite its having been operative at the
highest levels for fifty years, and having from the beginning
counted among its members the foremost lions of the
communications media, the CFR has been the subject of only
one article in a major national journal — and that one in
Harper's, hardly a mass-circulation periodical. Similarly, only
a handful of articles on the Council have appeared in the
nation's great newspapers. Such anonymity — at that level —
can hardly be a matter of mere chance.

Strangely, if you write to the CFR asking for information,
you will receive an expensively printed Annual Report which
lists officers, members, publications, and expenses for the
previous year. But this is just about all you can learn about
the CFR. We don't know who really sets its policy, and its
meetings are secret. In fact, the bylaws call for the expulsion
of any member who discusses in public what goes on at CFR
meetings.

The *Christian Science Monitor* did note in the article of
September 1, 1961, that:

> Its roster . . . contains names distinguished in the field of
> diplomacy, government, business, finance, science, labor, journal-
> ism, law and education. What united so wide-ranging and
> disparate a membership is a passionate concern for the direction
> of American foreign policy.

The CFR's passionate concern for the direction of American foreign policy has amounted to an attempt — highly
successful — to make certain that American foreign policy
continues marching Leftward toward World Government.

The CFR was criticized for precisely this by the Reece Committee, a Special Committee of the House of Representatives established in 1953 to investigate abuses by tax-free foundations. In the case of the Council on Foreign Relations, the Committee found that "its productions are not objective but are directed overwhelmingly at promoting the globalism concept."

Despite nearly incredible pressure to remain silent, the Reece Committee disclosed that the CFR had in fact come to be almost an employment agency for key areas of the U.S. Government — "no doubt carrying its internationalist bias with it." The investigation also showed that the CFR's influence was so great that it had almost completely usurped the prescribed activities of the U.S. State Department. The *Christian Science Monitor* article confirmed this conclusion as follows:

> *Because of the Council's single-minded dedication to studying and deliberating American foreign policy, there is a constant flow of its members from private to public service.* Almost half of the Council members have been invited to assume official government positions or to act as consultants at one time or another. [Emphasis added.]

The policies promoted by the CFR in the fields of defense and international relations become the official policies of the United States Government with a regularity that defies the laws of chance. As Liberal columnist Joseph Kraft, himself a member of the CFR, noted of the Council in *Harper's* of July 1958: "It has been the seat of . . . basic government decisions, has set the context for many more, and has repeatedly served as a recruiting ground for ranking officials." Kraft, incidentally, aptly titled his article on the CFR, "School for Statesmen" — an admission that the members of the Council are drilled with a "line" of strategy to be carried out in Washington.

As the *Christian Science Monitor* admits, almost half of
the members of the CFR have served in the government
under one administration or another. There are CFR members who serve in Democratic administrations and CFR
members who serve in Republican regimes. There is a great
game of musical chairs when a new administration takes
office, although no matter who is in power, many members
seem to stay on in key positions, particularly in the State
Department. Since the public knows nothing of the CFR, it
accepts the public relations image that many of these men are
political enemies, not realizing that they are in fact all parts
of the same power-seeking organization.

So completely has the CFR dominated the State Department over the past thirty-eight years that every Secretary of
State except Cordell Hull, James Byrnes, and William Rogers
has been a CFR member. And though Rogers himself is not
CFR, Professor Henry Kissinger, the President's chief foreign
policy advisor, came to the job from the staff of the Council
on Foreign Relations.

The CFR has one primary goal: the abolition of the United
States. This is not an exaggeration, although it is hardly the
way they express it. Our Founding Fathers set up a sovereign
United States. The CFR wants to abolish the sovereign
United States and set up a world government. That is why
the CFR was founded in 1919. The CFR makes no bones
about *world government* being its goal. "Study No. 7,"
published by the CFR on November 25, 1959, openly
advocates "building a new international order [which] must
be responsive to world aspirations for peace [and] for social
and economic change . . . an international order . . . including
states labeling themselves as 'Socialist' [Communist]." To
accomplish this, the CFR says, we must "gradually increase
the authority of the UN" until it becomes the official
government of the world.[1] Since you cannot have sovereignty at the national level and at the international, UN level

at the same time, the CFR is advocating the abolition of the United States as a sovereign government.

Richard Rovere, in his half-kidding and wholly-in-earnest treatise called *The American Establishment*, referred to the CFR as the American "Presidium." This is an accurate description, for like the Russian Presidium, the CFR only presides. It is the Establishment, but not the inner core, or "inner steering committee" as George Orwell called it, of the Establishment. Fortunately, someone who has been on the inside, or very close to it, has written a book about it. He is Dr. Carroll Quigley, professor of history at the Foreign Service School of Georgetown University. He formerly taught at Princeton and Harvard as well as at the Army and Navy War Colleges. Professor Quigley's monumental book, *Tragedy and Hope*,[2] contains amazing revelations concerning the clique of kingmakers who run international politics and international finance. W. Cleon Skousen, Ph.D., who served for sixteen years in the FBI (including several years as personal assistant to J. Edgar Hoover), and who now teaches at Brigham Young University, stated in his recently published, 130-page review of Quigley's book:

> Political conspiracies also have a way of reaching the public, because someone on the inside is willing to tell the story. I have waited for thirty years for somebody on the inside of the modern political power structure to talk. At last, somebody has.[3]

Dr. Skousen, who calls his review *The Naked Capitalist*, begins by commenting:

> When Dr. Quigley decided to write his 1,300 page book called *Tragedy and Hope*, he knew he was deliberately exposing one of the best kept secrets in the world. As one of the elite "insiders," he knew the scope of this power complex and he knew that its leaders hope to eventually attain total global control. Furthermore, Dr. Quigley makes it clear throughout his book that by and large he warmly supports the goals and purposes of the

"network." But if that is the case, why would he want to expose this world-wide conspiracy and disclose many of its most secret operations? Obviously, disclosing the existence of a mammoth power network which is trying to take over the world could not help but arouse the vigorous resistance of the millions of people who are its intended victims. So why did Dr. Quigley write this book?

His answer appears in a number of places but is especially forceful and clear on pages 979-980. He says, in effect, that it is now too late for the little people to turn back the tide. In a spirit of kindness he is therefore urging them not to fight the noose which is already around their necks. He feels certain that those who do will only choke themselves to death . . . .[4]

Quigley's qualifications for writing about the international conspiracy are as imposing as are those of ex-FBI man Skousen, author of the national best seller *The Naked Communist*, for exposing the real import of *Tragedy and Hope*. Quigley says of this *Insider* conspiracy:

I know of the operations of this network because I have studied it for twenty years and was permitted for two years, in the early 1960's, to examine its papers and secret records. *I have no aversion to it or to most of its aims and have, for much of my life, been close to it and to many of its instruments.* I have objected, both in the past and recently, to a few of its policies . . . but in general my chief difference of opinion is that *it wishes to remain unknown*, and I believe its role in history is significant enough to be known. [Emphasis added.][5]

Skousen observes:

Dr. Quigley admits he is telling more than his comrades-in-arms would care to have disclosed. They want their conspiratorial subversion to be kept a secret. Dr. Quigley thinks it is time people knew who was running things . . . .

The real value of *Tragedy and Hope* is not so much as a "history of the world in our time" (as its subtitle suggests), but rather as a bold and boastful admission by Dr. Quigley that there actually exists a relatively small but powerful group which has succeeded in acquiring a choke-hold on the affairs of practically the entire human race.

Of course, we should be quick to recognize that no small group could wield such gigantic power unless millions of people in all walks of life were "in on the take" and were willing to knuckle down to the iron-clad regimentation of the ruthless bosses behind the scenes . . . .[6]

Who is behind this conspiracy to control the world? Skousen writes:

He [Quigley] points out that during the past two centuries when the peoples of the world were gradually winning their political freedom from the dynastic monarchies, the major banking families of Europe and America were actually reversing the trend by setting up new dynasties of political control through the formation of international financial combines.

Dr. Quigley points out that these banking dynasties had learned that all governments must have sources of revenue from which to borrow in times of emergency. They had also learned that by providing such funds from their own private resources, they could make both kings and democratic leaders tremendously subservient to their will. It had proven to be a most effective means of controlling political appointments and deciding political issues.[7]

Quigley reveals that these international banking dynasties established a vast network to control government through the control of money. Quigley writes:

The greatest of these dynasties, of course, were the descendants of Meyer Amschel Rothschild (1743-1812) of Frankfort, whose male descendants, for at least two generations, generally married first cousins or even nieces. Rothschild's five sons, established at branches in Vienna, London, Naples, and Paris, as well as Frankfort, cooperated together in ways which other international banking dynasties copied but rarely excelled.

* * *

The names of some of these [other] banking families are

familiar to all of us and should be more so. They include Baring, Lazard, Erlanger, Warburg, Schröder, Seligman, the Speyers, Mirabaud, Mallet, Fould, and above all Rothschild and [J.P.] Morgan.[8]

We should here caution the reader that we are not talking about his personal banker down on the corner, who has nothing to do with the international intriguers we are discussing.

Secrecy has always been the byword of the international bankers. According to Quigley:

> The influence of financial capitalism and of the international bankers who created it was exercised both on business and on governments, but could have done neither if it had not been able to persuade both of these to accept two "axioms" of its own ideology. Both of these were based on the assumption that politicians were too weak and too subject to temporary popular pressures to be trusted with control of the money system . . . . To do this it was necessary to conceal, or even to mislead, both governments and people about the nature of money and its methods of operation.[9]

The aims of this stealthy crew are spelled out by Quigley:

> In addition to these pragmatic goals, the powers of financial capitalism had another far-reaching aim, nothing less than to create a world system of financial control in private hands able to dominate the political system of each country and the economy of the world as a whole. The system was to be controlled in a feudalist fashion by the central banks of the world acting in concert, by secret agreements arrived at in frequent private meetings and conferences.[10]

Through this system the international bankers hope to gain control over the world's natural resources, finance, transportation, and commerce. In order to do this they must first eliminate their competitors. The only way they can do it is by gaining control of government and establishing socialism. To accomplish this on a world-wide basis you need a world government — a socialist world government. Most people cannot understand why many of the super-rich like the Rockefellers, Kennedys, and Fords are socialists. "They have far more to lose under socialism than I," is a typical comment. People make that statement because they believe that socialism is really what the super-rich want them to believe socialism is, i.e., a movement to divide the wealth. But if these super-rich international bankers wanted to divide their wealth they could do it right now. There is no law against the Rockefellers giving away their billions. Instead, the super-rich almost totally avoid paying the taxes that finance the socialistic giveaway programs they force on the middle-class. They hide their wealth in foundations where it compounds tax-free. The concept that socialism is a divide-the-wealth program is held by revolutionaries, visionary utopians, and misguided idealists, who are promoting, in the name of fighting the super-rich, the socialism the *Insiders* want. Socialism in practice is not a share-the-wealth program but a consolidate-and-control-the-wealth program. When you understand this, the seeming paradox of the promotion of socialism by the power-hungry super-rich described by Quigley, becomes no paradox at all. Most people mistakenly believe that wealthy people are conservative, that they believe in free enterprise and are opposed to government controls. In many cases this is true, but it is not true of the super-rich cartel monopolists who want to control the world. These people are not on the Right, but on the Left. They don't want competition, they want monopoly. They work through the Left because the Left promotes government controls, and only by government controls can these monopolists eliminate their competition.

Robert Bartley of the *Wall Street Journal*, which does not consider itself Conservative, has observed: "Today the

Establishment has unquestionably adopted liberalism . . . ."[11]
The Establishment opposes Conservatives because Conservatives oppose government controls and a world super-state.
The Left advocates controls and a world government. This is
why these billionaires work and finance revolutionary movements whose objective is ostensibly to destroy the super-rich.

Quigley admits in effect that there is a conspiracy bigger
than the Communist conspiracy. He writes:

> There does exist, and has existed for a generation, an
> international Anglophile network which operates, to some extent,
> in the way the radical Right believes the Communists act. In fact,
> this network, which we may identify as the Round Table Groups,
> has no aversion to cooperating with the Communists, or any
> other groups, and frequently does so.[12]

Why has this Establishment conspiracy never been exposed? Many people have tried to expose it. The chief
weapon used to stop the exposure is ridicule. Nobody likes to
be ridiculed. If one calls attention to the strange alliance
between the international bankers and their cohorts, and the
Left, the retort is usually a sneering, "Obviously you believe
in the conspiracy theory of history." In most cases that stops
the person who is trying to expose the conspiracy. The
connotation is that a person who believes there is a
conspiracy seeking financial and political control of the
world is a paranoid who believes that every Liberal college
professor gets his orders for the day in a special morning
telegram from conspiracy headquarters. Since sneering at the
idea of a conspiracy is fashionable, millions of well-meaning
people who know absolutely nothing about it repeat the
sneering statements of ridicule. Nobody tries to refute the
facts. They cannot be refuted. And why try when ridicule
works so effectively?

But ridicule is only half of the Establishment's weapon
system to avoid exposure. The Establishment's media simply

never discuss the existence of the interlocking organizations and individuals within the CFR's orbit. CFR members control such mass media as the *New York Times, Los Angeles Times, Washington Post, Life, Time, Newsweek,* and the Columbia Broadcasting System and National Broadcasting Company. The Establishment has also spent enormous amounts of money to steer historians away from subjects it feels are dangerous. Professor Harry Elmer Barnes wrote in his *The Struggle Against the Historical Blackout*:

> It may be said, with great restraint, that never since the Dark and Middle Ages, have there been so many powerful forces organized and alerted against the assertion and acceptance of historical truth . . . . The Rockefeller Foundation and the Council on Foreign Relations . . . intend to prevent, if they can, a repetition of what they call in the vernacular the debunking journalistic campaign following World War I . . . .[13]

Whittaker Chambers, the man who exposed Alger Hiss (CFR) as a Soviet spy, made this observation:

> No one who has, even once, lived close to the making of history can ever again suppose that it is made the way the history books tell it. With rare exceptions such books are like photographs. They catch a surface image. Often as not, they distort it. The secret forces working behind and below the historical surface they seldom catch.[14]

But people do not reject all conspiracies. They can believe businesses conspire to fix prices. They can believe in the conspiracy of organized crime — Cosa Nostra. It is not that they reject conspiracy *per se*, they just reject the idea that there is an international conspiracy that uses the Communists and other Leftwing movements, and works to gain control over governments. Cosa Nostra is an example of how people will accept conspiracy in one area of human activity while they reject it in another. Until Joseph Valachi sang to a Congressional committee some years ago, people knew so little about Cosa Nostra that they didn't even know its name. They called it the Mafia, and many people vehemently denied that such an organization existed.

What is the difference between Cosa Nostra man Lucky Luciano and, say, Nelson Rockefeller? The only essential difference is that Rockefeller had wealth, background, and education. Totally cunning and absolutely ruthless, Luciano scratched his way to the top of the Cosa Nostra heap. Though altogether despicable, he was an able, ambitious, and talented man. If Luciano had been born to a patrician family, had attended swank private academies and then matriculated at Harvard, possessing the same brilliant mind and amoral personality, he would have come to an inescapable conclusion: Why spend your time pushing numbers, drugs, and dames, when you can get into government where the real money and power are? A socialist government controls people, and when one controls people one has absolute power over their economic activity too. The advance of Socialism in the world is no natural phenomenon, as the Internationalists pretend. Like depressions, it is a sinister promotion by the *Insiders* and their allies.

The Old Testament is full of conspiracies, most of them for power over government. Even a cursory study of Rome or Athens shows the role played by numerous conspiracies. As we climb the historical ladder to modern times, the number of political conspiracies increases; but we are not to believe that any are operative today – *that* is the "conspiracy theory of history." What is a conspiracy? Liberals would have us believe that Conservatives conjure up mysterious men in long black overcoats and slouch hats who meet in closets and mysteriously issue orders or exchange information. Here is the ridicule technique in action! All a conspiracy is, is men planning together for an unlawful purpose. "Conspiratorialists" — those who hold the "conspiracy theory of history" — agree with FDR, who said, "Nothing just happens in politics. If something happens you can be sure it was planned that way." The idea of "smoke-filled rooms" suggests secret plans being made, does it not? There are only two theories of history — (1) that things happen because they were planned that way, and (2) that everything happens by accident and nobody makes any plans. The latter is the idea that ought to be ridiculed, for it considers the observable reality — that America has been moving Left for thirty-five years, that we have persistent inflation, that we fight endless "no-win" wars, and that for twenty-five years we have been constantly losing to the Communists — to be a total accident. As former Secretary of Defense James Forrestal once remarked, "Consistency has never been a mark of stupidity. If they were merely stupid they would occasionally make a mistake in our favor."[15] Abraham Lincoln observed in his "House Divided" speech:

> We can not absolutely know that all these exact adaptations are the result of preconcert. But when we see a lot of framed timbers, different portions of which we know have been gotten out at different times and places and by different workmen — Stephen, Franklin, Roger and James, for instance — and when we see these timbers joined together, and see they exactly make the frame of a house or a mill, all the tenons and mortices exactly fitting, and all the lengths and proportions of the different pieces exactly adapted to their respective places, and not a piece too many or too few — not omitting even scaffolding — or, if a single piece be lacking, we can see the place in the frame exactly fitted and prepared to yet bring such piece in — in such a case, we find it impossible to not believe that Stephen and Franklin and Roger and James all understood one another from the beginning, and all worked upon a common plan or draft drawn up before the first lick was struck.[16]

The very essence of a conspiracy is that its perpetrators

must convince the public that it does not exist. This, of course, necessitates lying. In order to be a conspirator one must be a liar — and a convincing one, who conveys sincerity in whatever he says. The conspiracy also must mask its goals in order to get idealists to do its work for it, and it does so by using humanitarian terms like "seeking social justice," "ending poverty," and "bringing about world peace." Those who think they are helping the poor are only solidifying the power of the rich. The great historian Oswald Spengler realized this half a century ago, and wrote in his monumental *Decline and Fall of the West*:

> There is no proletarian, not even a Communist, movement, that has not operated in the interests of money, in the directions indicated by money, and for the time being permitted by money — and that without the idealists among its leaders having the slightest suspicion of the fact.

Quigley picks up the threads of the two-centuries-old movement to control the world by discussing the role of Cecil Rhodes in England during the latter part of the last century. Rhodes, working as a front man for Lord Rothschild, had conquered Southern Africa with its enormous mineral wealth. Rhodes' friendly biographer, Sara Millin, reveals his goal: "The government of the world was Rhodes' simple desire." With a world government under their control, Rhodes and his international banker partners would control the wealth of the world. Quigley notes:

> In the middle 1890's Rhodes had a personal income of at least a million pounds sterling a year (then about five million dollars) which was spent so freely for his mysterious purposes that he was usually overdrawn on his account. These purposes centered on his desire to federate the English-speaking peoples and to bring all the habitable portions of the world under their control.[17]

Frank Aydelotte, a founding member of the CFR, in his

book, *American Rhodes Scholarships*, tells of Rhodes will setting up a "secret society":

> The seven wills which Cecil Rhodes made between the ages of 24 and 46 [Rhodes died at age forty-eight] constitute a kind of spiritual autobiography . . . . Best known are the first (the Secret Society Will . . .), and the last, which established the Rhodes Scholarships . . . .
>
> In his first will Rhodes states his aim still more specifically: "The extension of British rule throughout the world . . . the foundation of so great a power as to hereafter render wars impossible and promote the interests of humanity."
>
> The "Confession of Faith" enlarges upon these ideas. The model for this proposed *secret society* was the Society of Jesus, though he mentions also the Masons. [Emphasis added.]

Aydelotte tells us, "In 1888 Rhodes made his third will . . . leaving everything to Lord Rothschild."

Apparently for strategic reasons, Lord Rothschild was subsequently removed from the forefront of the scheme. Professor Quigley reveals that Lord Rosebery "replaced his father-in-law, Lord Rothschild, in Rhodes' secret group and was made a Trustee under Rhodes' next (and last) will."

Professor Quigley writes of the formalization of Rhodes' "secret society":

> They were remarkably successful in these aims because England's most sensational journalist William T. Stead (1849-1912), an ardent social reformer and imperialist, brought them into association with Rhodes. This association was formally established on February 5, 1891, when Rhodes and Stead organized a secret society of which Rhodes had been dreaming for sixteen years. In this secret society Rhodes was to be leader; Stead, Brett (Lord Esher), and [Alfred] Milner were to form an executive committee; Arthur (Lord) Balfour, (Sir) Harry Johnston, Lord Rothschild, Albert (Lord) Grey, and others were listed as potential members of a "Circle of Initiates," while there was to be an outer circle known as the "Association of Helpers" (later organized by Milner as the Round Table organization).[18]

The "secret society," which fitted into the structure of the much older *Illuminati*, was organized on the pattern of "circles within circles," as was the Order of the Illuminati itself. The Round Table organization, which was not part of the innermost circle of the Great Conspiracy, was later to spawn the Council on Foreign Relations.

During World War I the Round Table group and its allies actually promoted and financed the Russian Revolution, despite the fact that Russia under the Czar and under Kerensky was an ally of Britain and the U.S. The Communists had made a deal with the Germans to make peace if they took over and thereby to free the German armies to fight the Americans and British on the Western front. Therefore any encouragement by Englishmen or Americans of the Communist takeover of Russia was clearly treason.

Possibly the best source of information on the financing of the Russian Revolution is *Czarism and the Revolution* by an important White Russian named Arsène de Goulevitch, founder in France of the Union of Oppressed Peoples. In this volume, written in French and since translated into English, de Goulevitch notes:

> The main purveyors of funds for the revolution, however, were neither the crackpot Russian millionaires nor the armed bandits of Lenin. The "real" money primarily came from certain British and American circles which for a long time past had lent their support to the Russian revolutionary cause . . . .

De Goulevitch reveals that Milner, the key man in the secret Round Table organization, was in Russia at the time of the Communist Revolution and was deeply involved. A footnote to the previous quotation contains this critical addition:

> On April 7, 1917, General Janin made the following entry in his diary ("Au G.C.C. Russe" – at Russian G.H.Q. – *Le Monde Slave*, Vol. 2, 1927, pp. 296-297): Long interview with R., who

confirmed what I had previously been told by M. After referring to the German hatred of himself and his family, he turned to the subject of the Revolution which, he claimed, was engineered by the English and, more precisely, by Sir George Buchanan and Lord [Alfred] Milner. Petrograd at the time was teeming with English . . . . He could, he asserted, name the streets and the numbers of the houses in which British agents were quartered. They were reported, during the rising, to have distributed money to the soldiers and incited them to mutiny.

The man who apparently was the major financial contributor to the overthrowing of Kerensky (remember, the Czar had already been overthrown) was Jacob Schiff of the Rothschild-connected banking firm of Kuhn, Loeb and Company in New York. The *New York Journal-American* noted on February 3, 1949: "Today it is estimated by Jacob's grandson, John Schiff, that the old man sank about 20,000,000 dollars for the final triumph of Bolshevism in Russia."

At the time of the Communist Revolution it was widely known and reported by American, British, French, and Dutch journalists and intelligence men in Russia that the international bankers were bankrolling the Bolsheviks. What was not understood was the reason. The international bankers hoped to get a full-blown world government out of World War I, but failing that, at least they could obtain a geographical base for their operation. Whether these international bankers today actually control Russia or whether they just cooperate with the Soviets is a moot point. But obviously they do not fear the Communists. Quigley admits, as noted earlier, that "this network, which we may identify as the Round Table Groups [including the CFR], has no aversion to cooperating with the Communists, or any other groups, and frequently does so."[19] We know that after the Bolshevik Revolution the *Insiders* controlled Russia. It is doubtful that they would allow themselves to lose control. If they have somehow done so, it has not altered their attitudes and policies towards helping Communism.

Evidence revealed in the three-volume work, *The United States and Soviet Economic Development*, by Antony Sutton of Stanford University's Hoover Institution for War, Revolution and Peace, shows that CFR members began in 1919 to transfer American technology and know-how to the Soviet Union; they continue to do so today, with the blessing of the Nixon Administration. Russian Communism is the hammer and Finance Capitalism is the anvil. With these two instruments the world is to be pounded into one unified mass run by an elite group of international civil servants serving their masters, the *Insiders*. Former FBI-man W. Cleon Skousen, commenting on the Quigley book, states:

> . . . In a nutshell, Dr. Quigley has undertaken to expose what every insider like himself has known all along — that the world hierarchy of the dynastic super-rich is out to take over the entire planet, doing it with Socialistic legislation where possible, but having no reluctance to use Communist revolution where necessary.[20]

The Communists are merely the "hatchet men" of an evil conspiracy that is far more sinister and diabolical than Communism itself. Communism did not create the Conspiracy, but the Conspiracy created Communism. And the men at the top of the Conspiracy are not Communists in the sense that the public understands the word. They are not loyal to Moscow or Peking or the United States. They are loyal to their own group of *Insiders*, who are seeking total world control. The late Dr. Bella Dodd, a former member of the National Committee of the Communist Party USA, who later became an active anti-Communist, told Dr. Skousen: "I think the Communist conspiracy is merely a branch of a much bigger conspiracy!"[21] Skousen adds:

Dr. Dodd said she first became aware of some mysterious super-leadership right after World War II when the U.S. Communist Party had difficulty getting instructions from Moscow on several vital matters requiring immediate attention. The American Communist hierarchy was told that any time they had an emergency of this kind they should contact any one of three designated persons at the Waldorf Towers. Dr. Dodd noted that whenever the Party obtained instructions from any of these three men, Moscow always ratified them.

What puzzled Dr. Dodd was the fact that not one of these three contacts was a Russian. Nor were any of them Communists. In fact, all three were extremely wealthy American capitalists!

Having the Communist world as an "enemy" provides an excuse for establishing ever higher taxes and ever more controls at home. We are kept fighting "the perpetual war for perpetual peace," just as in Orwell's *1984*. (Orwell, incidentally, was a Communist Party member who became aware that the Communist movement was merely a pawn in a conspiracy of gangsters.) "Busy giddy minds with foreign quarrels," one of Shakespeare's characters recommends. Eventually, in the not far distant future, Americans will be beguiled into accepting a world government to "save us from Communism" and end the endless Vietnam-type wars. It is the old throw-Br'er-Rabbit-into-the-briar-patch ploy.

The *Insider* conspirators had hoped to achieve this world government as a result of World War I, under the League of Nations. But while President Woodrow Wilson was doing his best to restructure the world at Versailles, the anesthesia induced back home by internationalist propaganda was rapidly wearing off. As the negotiations revealed that one side had been about as guilty as the other, and all the glitter of the "moral crusade" evaporated with Wilson's vaunted "Fourteen Points," the "rubes back on Main Street" began to stir and wake. Reaction and disillusionment set in.

Americans hardly wanted to get into a World Government

with double-dealing European crooks whose specialty was secret treaty hidden behind secret treaty. The guest of honor, so to speak, stalked out of the banquet before the poisoned meal could be served. And without American participation there could be no effective World Government.

Aroused public opinion made it obvious that the U.S. Senate dared not ratify a treaty saddling the country with such an internationalist commitment. The American public had somehow to be sold the idea of internationalism and World Government, and it was for precisely that purpose that the CFR was made to order.

When the members of the Round Table group saw the handwriting on the wall, they decided to form a network of front organizations in the major Western nations to "educate" the nationalistic boobs to accept world government. This led to the founding of the Council on Foreign Relations as a part of this network. According to Professor Quigley:

> At the end of the war of 1914, it became clear that the organization of this system [the Round Table Group] had to be greatly extended. Once again the task was entrusted to Lionel Curtis who established, in England and each dominion, a front organization to the existing Round Table Group. This front organization, called the Royal Institute of International Affairs, had as its nucleus in each area the existing submerged Round Table Group. In New York it was known as the Council on Foreign Relations, and was a front for J.P. Morgan and Company in association with the very small American Round Table Group. The American organizers were dominated by the large number of Morgan "experts," including Lamont and Beer, who had gone to the Paris Peace Conference and there became close friends with the similar group of English "experts" which had been recruited by the Milner group. In fact, the original plans for the Royal Institute of International Affairs and the Council on Foreign Relations were drawn up at Paris. The Council of RIIA (which by Curtis's energy came to be housed in Chatham House, across St. James's Square from the Astors, and was soon known by the name of this headquarters) and the board of the Council on

Foreign Relations have carried ever since the marks of their origin.[22]

As the decades have passed, the Morgan group has faded in strength and been replaced by the Rockefellers, whose number one business now is not oil, but banking. But all of the major international banking families are represented in the CFR and have been since its founding. These families include such familiar names as the Rockefellers, the Morgans, the Lamonts, the Lehmans, the Schiffs, the Warburgs, the Kahns, and their hirelings. Their scions were often closely linked together by business and family ties both here and in Europe. Quigley says:

> . . . the relationship between the financial circles of London and those of the eastern United States . . . reflects one of the most powerful influences in twentieth-century American and world history. The two ends of this English-speaking axis have sometimes been called, perhaps facetiously, the English and American Establishments. There is, however, a considerable degree of truth behind the joke, a truth which reflects a very real power structure. It is this power structure which the Radical Right in the United States has been attacking for years in the belief that they are attacking the Communists. This is particularly true when these attacks are directed, as they so frequently are, at "Harvard Socialism," or at "Left-wing newspapers" like *The New York Times* and the *Washington Post*, or at foundations . . . .[23]

There is a strong interlocking directorate between the CFR and the socialism-promoting Rockefeller, Ford, and Carnegie Foundations. These and many other foundations have been working for decades to bring socialism to America and to promote concepts of world government. In doing so they had no aversion to employing men with Communist backgrounds, until a Congressional investigation forced them to replace Communist-linked Leftists with Establishment Leftists. Quigley admits:

It was this group of people [the Eastern Establishment], whose wealth and influence so exceeded their experience and understanding [*sic*], who provided much of the framework of influence which the Communist sympathizers and fellow travelers took over in the United States in the 1930's. It must be recognized that the power that these energetic Left-wingers exercised *was never their own power or Communist power but was ultimately the power of the international financial coterie*, and, once the anger and suspicions of the American people were aroused, as they were by 1950, it was a fairly simple matter to get rid of the Red sympathizers. [Emphasis added.] [24]

This, of course, raises the question of just who is using whom? It is always assumed that it is the Communists who dupe others into doing their work. In most cases this is undoubtedly true; however, it strains credulity to believe that men who are the world's shrewdest businessmen and bankers can be perennial suckers in dealing with Communists. Clearly there are *Insiders* manipulating both ends of the show.

The Reece Committee attempted to investigate this matter. Norman Dodd, chief investigator for the Committee, was told by the then-President of the Ford Foundation that the purpose of his Foundation "was to so alter American society that it could be comfortably merged with that of the Soviet Union." Dodd was then told that this was being done on "orders from the White House." Quigley says of the Reece Committee's investigation of tax-exempt foundations:

It soon became clear that people of immense wealth would be unhappy if the investigation went too far and that the "most respected" newspapers in the country, closely allied with these men of wealth, would not get excited enough about any revelations to make the publicity worth while, in terms of votes or campaign contributions. An interesting report showing the Left-wing associations of the interlocking nexus of tax-exempt foundations was issued in 1954 rather quietly. [25]

Dodd maintains that when the investigation began probing

into "the so-called legitimate world" that is the real nerve center of the Communist movement, the investigation was quashed.

Dan Smoot, like Skousen a former FBI agent, reveals that Communists have operated within the CFR itself:

> Among the most influential of CFR members during the late 1930's and early 1940's, when the CFR cabal was taking control of policy-making functions inside the federal government, were such people as Alger Hiss and Lauchlin Currie, later identified as Soviet espionage agents; and Owen Lattimore, later identified as a "conscious, articulate instrument of the Soviet international conspiracy."
>
> I do not intend to imply that the Council on Foreign Relations ever was a communist organization. Boasting among its past members four Presidents of the United States (Hoover, Eisenhower, Kennedy, Nixon) and many other high officials, both civilian and military, the CFR can be termed, by those who agree with its objectives, a "patriotic" organization.
>
> The fact, however, that communists worked for many years as influential members of the CFR indicates something about the CFR's objectives. The ultimate aim of the Council on Foreign Relations (however well-intentioned many of its members may be) is the same as the ultimate aim of international communism: to create a one-world socialist system and make the United States a part of it.[26]

The CFR serves as a giant lobby within the government, the foundations, banking, big business, communications, and the academy to promote its one-world designs. It does this by promoting increased aid and trade with the Communist countries, disarmament, increased foreign aid, endless no-win wars, and the surrendering of sovereignty to world organizations. The primary vehicle is to be the United Nations, which will serve to run the *Insiders'* world monopoly. The UN is largely the creature of the CFR (sometimes called the Council For Revolution). Forty-seven CFR members attended the San Francisco Conference that founded the UN, and the Rockefeller family donated the New York City land upon which the UN building was constructed.

Dan Smoot, considered by many to be the most sound and penetrating researcher and reporter of our time, published a book called *The Invisible Government*. In his foreword Mr. Smoot wrote:

> . . . I am convinced that the Council on Foreign Relations, together with a great number of other associated tax-exempt organizations, constitutes the invisible government which sets the major policies of the federal government; exercises controlling influence on government officials who implement the policies; and through massive and skillful propaganda, influences Congress and the public to support the policies.
>
> I am convinced that the objective of this invisible government is to convert America into a socialist state and then make it a unit in a one-world socialist system. [27]

CFR members have virtually run the administrations of Franklin D. Roosevelt, Harry Truman, Dwight Eisenhower, John Kennedy, Lyndon Johnson, and Richard Nixon. This is the real reason why "there isn't a dime's worth of difference" — why despite campaign promises our policy of appeasing the Communists never changes. As the *Chicago Tribune* noted, in referring to the Nixon State Department: "The more it changes, the more it remains the same."

One of the primary goals of the Council on Foreign Relations has always been to make the Democrat and Republican parties as much alike in their actual policies as possible. The game is to make the two parties appear to the public to be different while they act the same — the real control being hidden in the inner sanctum of the CFR headquarters in New York. Is it not natural that conspirators would try to control both, or all, sides of the conflict, political or otherwise? This has always been the strategy of the Marxists, and it was also followed by the J.P. Morgan interests in America even before the founding of the CFR. According to Professor Quigley:

> . . . they [the Morgan partners] expected they would be able to control both political parties equally. Indeed, some of them intended to contribute to both and to allow an alternation of the two parties in public office in order to conceal their own influence . . . .[28]

Quigley adds:

> More than fifty years ago the Morgan firm decided to infiltrate the Left-wing political movements in the United States. This was relatively easy to do, since these groups were starved for funds and eager for a voice to reach the people. Wall Street supplied both. The purpose was not to destroy, dominate or take over . . . .[29]

The purpose was to guide the Left into doing what the *Insiders* wanted. Many of these movements were later absorbed into the Democratic Party, and when this happened their Wall Street-international banker connections went with them. "The associations between Wall Street and the Left . . . are really survivals of the associations between the Morgan Bank and the Left. To Morgan all political parties were simply organizations to be used, and the firm was careful to keep a foot in all camps."[30]

When the English Round Table Groups started the Council on Foreign Relations in conjunction with the Morgan-Rockefeller organizations, this policy became standard operating procedure for the CFR. The Morgan partners have divided themselves between the Democratic and Republican parties. The Rockefellers have traditionally been Republicans, while other international banking families active in the CFR, like the Schiffs, Warburgs, Kahns, Lehmans, and Harrimans, have been Democrats.

CFR members include such Democratic party powers as

Dean Acheson, George Ball, William Benton, Chester Bowles, McGeorge Bundy, Ellsworth Bunker, David Dubinsky, Henry Fowler, John Kenneth Galbraith, Arthur Goldberg, Hubert Humphrey, Nicholas Katzenbach, Eugene McCarthy, the late Walter Reuther, Walt W. Rostow, Dean Rusk, Arthur Schlesinger Jr., Stuart Symington, Cyrus Vance, Adam Yarmolinsky, and the late brothers Robert and John Kennedy. Among the CFR members who are major movers and shakers of the Republican party are Clifford Case, Thomas E. Dewey, Paul Hoffman, Jacob Javits, Ogden Reid, David, John, and Nelson Rockefeller, and Harold Stassen. CFR members in one party are supposed to be the mortal political enemies of those in the other party. It is like going to the theater to see a play. In the cast are heroes and villains and we become emotionally involved, cheering for the good guys and yearning for the bad guys to get their just deserts. But after the play is over the whole cast goes out to have pizza together. They aren't really enemies, they are friends. They work for the same script writer, the same director, and the same financial "angels" behind the scenes. And, of course, you buy a ticket to see the play. The CFR play has been showing in Washington for forty years, and the tickets have been very expensive in both money and blood. The *Chicago Tribune's* editorial of December 9, 1950, on the CFR still applies:

> The members of the Council [on Foreign Relations] are persons of more than average influence in the community. They have used the prestige that their wealth, their social position, and their education have given them to lead their country toward bankruptcy and military debacle. They should look at their hands. There is blood on them — the dried blood of the last war and the fresh blood of the present one [the Korean War].

The tickets to the CFR play in Vietnam have cost America nearly 350,000 dead and wounded in that "no-win" war.

As in many plays, the actors can, if need be, play interchangeable roles. An example of CFR bipartisanship was contained in an exclusive interview given to *U.S. News & World Report* shortly after the election by Democratic President Lyndon Johnson, who stated:

> I am very proud of the contributions made to the Administration by so many outstanding good Republicans ... such as Secretaries McNamara and Dillon (Secretary of Defense Robert S. McNamara and Secretary of the Treasury Douglas Dillon), CIA Director John McCone, Special Assistant for National Security Affairs McGeorge Bundy, and distinguished Republican business and community leaders such as John McCloy and Robert Anderson.

All the Republicans mentioned by LBJ were members of the Communist-appeasing Council on Foreign Relations. Naturally, none of these appeasement-minded Republicans could support the anti-Communist position of Senator Barry Goldwater during his campaign against LBJ.

The CFR, unknown to all but a comparative handful of Americans, has made a tragicomedy out of Republican vs. Democrat politics at the Presidential level. The CFR has concentrated on the executive branch, and competition between parties at the congressional level is much more real. When someone points out that there is not a dime's worth of difference between the Democrats and the Republicans, even in this inflationary age, they mean at the apex of the party, not the grass roots. At the grass-roots level the Republican Party is basically conservative and the Democrat Party (outside of the South) is basically liberal. If you go to a Young Republican meeting and then a Young Democrat meeting, you won't have the feeling that there isn't a dime's worth of difference! But as you go up the political ladder from the grass roots of both parties, they become more and more similar until they merge behind the scenes at the top.

Grass-roots Republicans and Democrats may hack and kick at each other all they want, but the policies at the top never change.

The typical American gets excited during an election by campaign promises like Nixon's to bring "new leadership," because "we can't be led into the '70's by the men who stumbled and bumbled and fumbled their way through the 60's." But after the election when the same disastrous policies are followed, Mr. Typical shrugs his shoulders and returns to his TV set with the fading hope that the next administration will somehow bring to government as much common sense as is found among taxi-drivers. He does not realize that the election promises were bait and that he is really being given the choice between ex-CFR member Tweedle-Dick and present CFR member Tweedle-Dumphrey. As far as the election goes, it made little difference to the nation as a whole, because the CFR hierarchy is going to continue to call the shots; but it made an enormous amount of difference to Mr. Nixon and Mr. Humphrey. While Mr. Nixon lived the life of a king (with the responsibilities of a king, to be sure) and accepted the perquisites of the office, Mr. Humphrey was freezing his toes off as a teacher at Macalester College in Minnesota. Serving as President for the CFR is much like being the student body president of a high school. Nobody seriously believes that the high school student body president really runs the high school, but he does have some power and lots of glory and prestige. Being President of the United States sure beats teaching Poli-Sci I to smart-aleck sophomores at Macalester College. (Mr. Humphrey, of course, has now escaped the great unwashed at Macalester and returned to the Senate, where he can once again be a fiery radical for the downtrodden international bankers behind the CFR.)

Mr. Nixon joined the Council on Foreign Relations in 1960. (They ask you to join, you don't ask them. Try writing to the CFR saying that you have heard they are a very democratic organization and you would like to join. Oh, do they discriminate!) According to former FBI man Dan Smoot, Mr. Nixon was a member of the CFR until 1964. Nixon's official attitude about the CFR and his former membership in it was expressed in a very defensive form letter which his staff sent in answer to inquiries during the 1968 political campaign. The following is a quotation from the letter:

> Mr. Nixon has never attended a meeting of the Council on Foreign Relations. He is not currently a member, although several years ago he shared membership with former President Eisenhower, former President Hoover, and a host of other distinguished Americans . . . .
>
> The Council on Foreign Relations . . . is purely and simply a group which supports independent research in world affairs. It takes no positions. It is not a policy-making body. It advocates nothing but research of foreign affairs as a contribution to public opinion. The individual member is in no way bound to any such findings.[31]

The standard defense of the CFR is that it is an organization whose membership has included some of our most wealthy, famous, and powerful men. This, of course, begs the question. It is also passed off as a mere advisory body, but this is misleading. As ultra-liberal columnist Joseph Kraft, himself a member, admitted in his "School for Statesmen" article in *Harpers* it is much more than that, and "has been the seat of . . . basic government decisions, has set the context for many more, and has repeatedly served as a recruiting ground for ranking officials."[32]

The idea that the CFR "advocates nothing but research" is absolutely untrue. Its "Study No. 7," published in *A Strategy for the Sixties*, makes very clear the fact that it advocates an extremely radical program of accommodation with the Communists. It is true that a member is not technically bound by any of the CFR's findings, and there are a handful of members who have rebelled against the brainwash; but the Establishment's control goes far beyond the mere bylaws of the CFR.

Nixon's CFR membership became an issue in 1962, during his Republican gubernatorial primary contest with Joe Shell in California. After that Mr. Nixon either dropped out of the CFR or went underground. The CFR admits that it is sometimes necessary for its members to go underground. On page 42 of its 1952 Report, the CFR stated: "Members of the Council are sometimes obliged, by their acceptance of government posts in Washington and elsewhere, to curtail or suspend for a time their participation in Council activities." Notice that Mr. Nixon's form letter mentioned no reason for his having dropped out of this organization that he so staunchly defends. Was the reason political expediency? He has never repudiated the CFR and supports all of its policies. He also wrote an article in October 1967 for the 45th Anniversary Issue of the CFR's publication, *Foreign Affairs Quarterly.* The article was entitled "Asia after Vietnam," and was an obvious attempt to court the Liberal intellectuals who read *Foreign Affairs,* for in it he said things that were clearly different from his standard campaign rhetoric. The article followed the CFR line 100 per cent, calling for "the evolution of a new world order" based on "regional approaches to development needs." These proposals later became known as "the Nixon doctrine."

Whether or not Mr. Nixon is a secret member of the CFR is a moot point. He is obviously much further up the Establishment ladder than mere CFR membership would indicate. The proof of the political pudding is in the appointing, and Mr. Nixon's appointments show that his administration is as much dominated by the Communist-accommodating, one-world-promoting CFR as those of his last five predecessors. As of January 1971, Mr. Nixon had appointed to high political position no less than 107 members of the CFR. In fact, Mr. Nixon seems to be going for the record. Imagine, Mr. Nixon appoints 107 members of an organization from which he apparently dropped out for reasons of political expediency — because his membership in it was a political hot potato.

To illustrate the extent of CFR power in Washington at the present time, consider some of these important CFR appointments made by President Nixon:

Henry A. Kissinger, Chief foreign policy advisor (directly from the paid staff of the CFR);

Henry Cabot Lodge, chief negotiator at the Paris Peace Talks;

Charles Yost, Ambassador to the United Nations (also a paid staff member of the CFR);

Arthur Burns, chairman of the Federal Reserve Board;

Harlan Cleveland, U.S. Ambassador to NATO;

George Ball, foreign policy consultant;

Robert Murphy, special consultant on international affairs;

Dr. Paul McCracken, chief economic aide;

Ellsworth Bunker, U.S. Ambassador to Saigon;

Gen. Andrew J. Goodpaster, chief military policy advisor;

Dr. Glenn T. Seaborg, chairman of the Atomic Energy commission;

Joseph J. Sisco, Assistant Secretary of State for the Middle East and South Asia;

Jacob Beam, Ambassador to the Soviet Union; and

Gerald Smith, director of the Arms Control and Disarmament Agency.

References

1. Jay Cerf and Walter Posen, *Strategy for the Sixties*, New York, Praeger, 1962, p. 95.
2. Carroll Quigley, *Tragedy and Hope — A History of the World in Our Time*, New York, The Macmillan Co., 1960.
3. W. Cleon Skousen, *The Naked Capitalist*, Salt Lake City, W. Cleon Skousen, 1970, p. 4.
4. *Ibid.*
5. Quigley, *op. cit.*, p. 950.
6. Skousen, *op. cit.*, pp. 5-6.
7. *Ibid.*, p. 7.
8. Quigley, *op. cit.*, pp. 51-52.
9. *Ibid.*, p. 53.
10. *Ibid.*, p. 324.
11. *Wall Street Journal*, August 14, 1969.
12. Quigley, *op. cit.*, p. 950.
13. Harry Elmer Barnes, "The Struggle Against the Historical Blackout," reprinted as Chapter One of *Perpetual War for Perpetual Peace*, Caldwell, Idaho, The Caxton Printers Ltd., 1953.
14. Whittaker Chambers, *Witness*, New York, Random House, p. 331.
15. *Review Of The News*, August 5, 1970, pp. 27-28.
16. Abraham Lincoln, speech, Republican State Convention, Springfield, Ill., June 16, 1856.
17. Quigley, *op. cit.*, p. 130.
18. *Ibid.*, p. 131.
19. *Ibid.*, p. 950.
20. Skousen, *op. cit.*, p. 25.
21. *Ibid.*, p. 1.
22. Quigley, *op. cit.*, pp. 951-952.
23. *Ibid.*, p. 956.
24. *Ibid.*, pp. 951-952.
25. *Ibid.*, p. 955.
26. *Dan Smoot Report*, May 19, 1969.
27. Dan Smoot, *The Invisible Government*, Dallas, The Dan Smoot Report, Inc., 1962, p. xi.
28. Quigley, *op. cit.*, p. 73.
29. *Ibid.*, p. 938.
30. *Ibid.*, p. 945.
31. *Dan Smoot Report*, June 4, 1969.
32. *Harper's*, July 1958.

CHAPTER IV

The Elephant That Brays

Control over the GOP by the Establishment *Insiders* is not something new or ephemeral; it dates back at least to 1936. The Establishment has controlled the Pachyderm Party by wheeling and dealing to control its Presidential nomination. Every Republican convention pits the Conservative Congressional wing against the Establishment-controlled Presidential wing. Naturally, the media try hard to make it appear that the Conservatives, always dubbed the "Old Guard," are a minority pitted against the "progressive" or "moderate" wing of the party, which represents the grass-roots "little people" of the international banking fraternity.

The story behind this wheeling and dealing to keep the nomination in the control of the Establishment is one of great importance. If real Republicans are ever to recover their party, they must understand the powers they are dealing with.

As the 1920's roared on, the stock market climbed to dizzy heights, fueled by ever-increasing amounts of paper money pumped into circulation by the Federal Reserve, which had been established following an enormous lobbying campaign by Colonel Edward M. House, a founder of the Council on Foreign Relations; Felix Warburg, a charter CFR member; and other Wall Street *Insiders*. The Federal Reserve was supposed to make America depression-proof, and to represent a giant step forward in "democracy." Just why numerous international bankers were so interested in "de-

mocracy" was not explained. In the summer of 1929, after
eight years of easy money promoted by an artifically low
interest rate set by the Federal Reserve, the "Fed" reversed
itself and, in order to stop runaway inflation, bounced the
interest rate sky high. This in effect stuck a pin into the stock
market balloon, which began its crash in October 1929,
proving that America indeed was not "depression-proof."
Popular mythology has it that the stock market crash was a
great blow to Wall Street. To the vast majority of patriotic
and honest bankers and brokers it was, since Wall Street
became a whipping boy during the '30's. But if you are an
Insider, more money is made faster during a depression than
at any other time. *Insiders* who got out of the market at its
height, in the middle of 1929, were able to buy stocks back
at an 80 per cent discount four years later. Others made
enormous wealth by being "short" in the market and riding
the Dow-Jones-average toboggan down to great profits.

In 1932, the Democrats elected Franklin D. Roosevelt to
office on one of the most Conservative platforms ever written
by any party in the history of the United States. Of course,
the platform was mere pretense — "dialectics," as the
Communists would call it. FDR had been a Wall Street
banker, and he was propelled into office by the *Insiders*, who
saw a chance to capitalize on the chaos they had caused.
When FDR in his fireside chats railed against the "malefac-
tors of great wealth," building the dialectical image that he
was "a traitor to his class," he was really throwing the
Insiders into the briar patch, right where they wanted to be,
like Br'er Rabbit in the Uncle Remus stories. FDR began
deficit spending, which over a period of years has resulted in
hundreds of billions of dollars of interest profits to bankers.
The bulk of these profits have gone to a handful of New
York banks.

In order to perpetuate deficit spending and launch an
"America last" foreign policy, the *Insiders* had to assert the

same control over the Republican Party that they already possessed over the Democrat Party. In 1936, in a confidential meeting in keeping with the political legend of the smoke-filled hotel room, a group of *Insiders* laid long-range plans to control the Republican Party. We know of the meeting from an account by Dr. Glenn Frank, president of the University of Wisconsin, whom the *Insiders* mistakenly believed they could trust.[1] The presiding *Insider* at this secret meeting in the royal suite on the 21st floor of the Waldorf-Astoria Hotel in New York was Thomas Lamont (CFR), senior partner in J.P. Morgan & Company. According to Professor Quigley, Lamont was the most important connection between the international bankers and the hard-core Left in America. Quigley states that the chief evidence against the Lamont family

> . . . can be found in the files of HUAC which show Tom Lamont, his wife Flora, and his son Corliss as sponsors and financial angels to almost a score of extreme Left organizations including the Communist Party itself . . . . During this whole period of over two decades, Corliss Lamont, with the full support of his parents, was one of the chief figures in "fellow traveler" circles and one of the chief spokesmen for the Soviet point of view . . . .[2]

Six other prominent financiers and industrialists were also present. The purpose of the meeting was to "decide" who the Republican nominee for President should be. At the meeting it was generally agreed that their support would be thrown to Governor Alfred M. Landon of Kansas, who, of course, never stood a chance to win, because there was no beating Roosevelt in 1936. Support of Landon by the Lamont clique was significant. Influential Liberal Republicans such as "Ogden Mills [CFR], Eugene Meyer [CFR, financier and owner of the *Washington Post*], Winthrop Aldrich [CFR; a Rockefeller relative], recognized that . . . Landon might be adapted to their own purposes."[3] Landon had boasted, "I have cooperated with the New Deal to the best of my ability," and had even issued public praise of New Deal designer Rexford Guy Tugwell, devoted radical socialist.[4] When Landon went down the electoral drain, the New Deal was safe for four more years. The *Insiders* had had nothing to lose either way.

Nineteen forty was a crucial year for the *Insiders*. Through appeasement of Hitler, who had been financed and protected by the Round Table clique, the world was being maneuvered into a war. The *Insiders* know that it is in a time of crisis during war or depression that dictatorial power can be concentrated in the federal government. It was essential to the *Insiders* that the "America last" international policies and welfare state deficit spending be continued. However, there was considerable doubt as to whether the American public would accept an unprecedented third term for FDR. Therefore, it was necessary to take control of the Republican party away from the real Republicans and make sure that the 1940 Presidential candidate was a man acceptable to the *Insiders*. The *Insiders* found their man in Wendell Willkie.

The man behind Wendell Willkie was the late Russell Davenport, a Democrat who belonged to such world-state-promoting outfits as the World Citizenship Council, Atlantic Union Committee, and Federal Union, and served on the council of advisors of Student Federalists, which later merged with United World Federalists. Davenport was associated with Americans for Democratic Action (ADA) and was later a founder of Republican Advance, the ADA of the Republican Party.[5] Davenport was one of the founders of *Fortune* magazine for the late Henry Luce (CFR). A Leftist from the beginning, he felt his ideas could be sold to businessmen through this slick magazine.[6] After the 1940 election Davenport set down his philosophy in *Fortune*. His article, "USA: The Permanent Revolution," was widely syndicated in the press as "the American credo." It was a clever attempt to sell the idea that American capitalism had lost its fight and that ours was now a "mixed economy" — half socialist and half free. To Davenport this represented a great "social achievement." Boiled down, his argument was that America can prevail over Russia only if it borrows many of Russia's ideas and applies them to America. Davenport applauded the fact that "every year more businessmen see the light and some few of them become missionaries [for the new concept of capitalism]. The result is that American business is erecting a social structure that many a state planner would envy. A true industrial democracy is emerging." ("Industrial democracy" is a code phrase for socialism among Marxists.)

Much of what we know of the *Insiders'* maneuvering of Willkie into the Republican nomination comes from the auto-biography of Davenport's wife, published in 1967. Marcia Davenport tells us that her husband was holding sessions of a discussion group known as the "Fortune Round Table" (was the choice of words a coincidence?), whose participants were chosen for their "eminence" in their chosen fields. The round table group included "leading industrialists, bankers, finan-ciers, scholars, labor union leaders, sociologists, economists and technical specialists." Mrs. Davenport writes: "Russell came home from his Roundtable meeting and walked into the house saying, 'I've met the man who ought to be the next President of the United States.' " His name was Wendell Willkie.[7] In describing Willkie, Marcia Davenport says:

> Some people called him [Willkie] the advocate of free enterprise; some, the spokesman of big business against the government. These were mostly mistaken summations of Wendell Willkie. He was an old-fashioned, hell-raising, hard-wrangling liberal . . . . He was a Democrat, a man of the people . . . .[8]

Willkie was in fact a registered Democrat who only five years earlier had been elected by Tammany Hall to the New

York County Democratic Committee.[9] As a student at Indiana
University he had been a member of the Socialist Club. [10] Willkie, the high-salaried head of a large utility company, had never
done anything in or for the Republican party and was completely unknown outside his own limited but highly influential
circles. What apparently sold the Establishment *Insiders* on
Willkie was, as Mrs. Davenport puts it, that he was "outspoken
in opposition to what was then a classic isolationist position in
the Republican party."[11] Mrs. Davenport claims that the Willkie for President idea occurred to a number of individuals simultaneously, including "Harry [Henry] Luce and other members of Time, Inc., who met him in our house." [12] According to
Mrs. Davenport, the leadership from the financial community
was "headed by Thomas W. Lamont." She adds:

> Willkie did not just happen to the Republican party . . . . Sever-
> al times each week we had people to dinner, sometimes by careful
> plan, when it best served the purpose to enclose the occasion in
> the form of an agreeable social meeting . . . .[13]

The Establishment worked hard to sell Willkie to the
American public through a gigantic publicity spree, which
columnist George Sokolsky called "the advertising agent's
holiday." Through their financial and other contacts throughout the communications media, the *Insiders* made it appear
that there was spontaneous public interest in Wendell Willkie.
Willkie was catapulted into the political arena by an article in
the *Saturday Evening Post*, which was followed by articles
suggesting Willkie for the Republican nomination that suddenly blossomed in leading newspapers and magazines. His
picture "spontaneously" appeared on the covers of *Time* and
other popular magazines, and the unknown lawyer mysteriously appeared as an author in Sunday magazines. He was
given prestige in business circles by a laudatory article in
Fortune, and in popular circles by a feature article in *Life*
(*Life, Fortune*, and *Time* were all Luce publications).

The Willkie boom was engineered by top advertising executives from Madison Avenue, who planted news articles in magazines and newspapers, stimulated petitions, chain letters, advertisements, telegrams, and fund raising, and started Willkie clubs and Willkie mailing committees. Seven weeks before the Republican convention, the Gallup Poll reported that Willkie was the favorite of only 3 per cent of Republican voters.

As the convention approached, one big stumbling block remained for Willkie — Senator Robert A. Taft, the choice of party Conservatives. Fearing that perhaps they might not be able to put Willkie over after all, the *Insiders* decided to make an attempt to buy Taft. The week before the convention opened, Senator and Mrs. Taft were invited to a New York dinner party given by Ogden Reid (CFR), publisher of the *New York Herald Tribune*, and Mrs. Reid. The details of the dinner party are set forth in *One Man: Wendell Willkie*, by C. Nelson Sparks. The major facts have been thoroughly corroborated by both Robert Taft and Wendell Willkie.

Present at this dinner party were Thomas Lamont (CFR), senior partner of J.P. Morgan & Company, and Mrs. Lamont; Lord Lothian of the Round Table, then Ambassador to the United States from Great Britain; Mr. and Mrs. John Pillsbury of the Minneapolis milling family; and Mr. and Mrs. Wendell Willkie. Following the dinner Lord Lothian, a member of the British Liberal Party who had accompanied socialist George Bernard Shaw in his loving pilgrimage to Moscow, was asked to make a few remarks.[14] The substance of his speech was that it was the duty of the United States to go all out at once to aid Britain in the war. This was in June 1940, a year and a half before Pearl Harbor. Lamont was then called on, and expressed himself as being wholly in accord with Lord Lothian. Willkie was called on next. He enthusiastically endorsed everything that Lord Lothian and Lamont had said,

maintaining that it was our duty to go to war at once to aid
England. By this time, the plot was pretty clear to Taft. He
realized that he had been invited to the Reid dinner for the
purpose of ascertaining whether he was willing to pay the
price to get the support of the *Insiders* for the Republican
nomination — namely, an all-out war declaration that would
satisfy the New York banking interests and the British
Ambassador. Taft knew that if he endorsed the remarks of
Lothian, Lamont, and Willkie, he would automatically
become acceptable to the financial interests and thereby
greatly improve his chances of winning the nomination. Taft,
however, was a man of rare principle, and he declined this
opportunity to win the support of the *Insiders*. When called
on, he simply observed that he could add nothing to his
remarks in the Senate, where he had declared that Americans
did not want to go to war to beat a totalitarian system in
Europe if they were to get socialism here when it was all
over. A few days later, the *New York Herald Tribune*
announced its unequivocal support for Willkie, with a
three-column appeal to the delegates on the front page calling
Willkie "Heaven's gift to the nation in its time of crisis."

When the Republican national convention convened in
Philadelphia, Willkie had only 105 delegates. Even the Gallup
(CFR) Poll reported that Willkie was the favorite of a mere
17 per cent of Republicans. Only the politically naive could
believe that hundreds of delegates suddenly went overboard
for Willkie out of sheer fascination with "the barefoot boy
from Wall Street." Some Republicans saw through the
publicity blitz, and forty Republican Congressmen called for
a "real Republican." Congressman Usher Burdick declared:

> I believe I am serving the best interests of the Republican party
> by protesting in advance and exposing the machinations and
> attempts of J.P. Morgan and other New York utility bankers in
> forcing Wendell Willkie on the Republican Party . . . . There is
> nothing to the Willkie boom for president except the artifical

public opinion being created by newspapers, magazines and the radio. The reason back of all this is money. Money is being spent by someone and lots of it. This is a good time to find out whether the American people are to be let alone in the selection of a Republican candidate for the Presidency, or whether the "special interests" of this country are powerful enough to dictate to the American people.[15]

At the convention the galleries were packed with noisy Willkie supporters who chanted "We Want Willkie" hour upon hour in an attempt to stampede the convention and give the erroneous impression that the Willkie bandwagon came from the grass roots. Lamont money could buy anything.

Professionals around the country hired girls to get on the telephone and stimulate a deluge of pro-Willkie telegrams to the delegates. Not all the telegrams were signed. Also, the *Insiders* sought to influence delegates by having the mortgage holders and bankers to whom they owed money call them on behalf of Willkie.[16] The chairman of one delegation stated that he was offered $19,000 for the expenses of his delegation if he would deliver his state's votes for Willkie. [17] And so one of the great show biz successes of the Twentieth Century was staged in Philadelphia, as the *Insiders* succeeded in heading off Taft and making sure that New Deal foreign and domestic policies with their deficit spending and resulting millions in interest to bankers were secure.

In her autobiography Marcia Davenport describes the Willkie campaign:

> The campaign began. It was one thing for a small group of inspired men to incite the American people to demand the nomination of Wendell Willkie and to ram him down the throats of the Republican party. It was quite another thing to mount a presidential campaign on the shoulders and through the resources of that party . . . .
> . . . I marvel today at the audacity of a handful of amateurs

[*sic*] who drove in the nomination of Willkie over the heads of
the whole Republican old guard.[18]

Willkie's campaign of glorifying the New Deal both at
home and abroad led, of course, to a staggering defeat. In
spite of all their efforts to nominate him, the Establishment
Insiders couldn't have cared less that Willkie lost. Their
objective had been to ensure that the voters were not given a
choice, to wrap their tentacles around the Republican party,
and to deal a death blow to the two-party system.

In assessing the Willkie movement Mrs. Davenport calls
Willkie's defeat:

> . . . the most constructive defeat a candidate ever met . . . . It
> changed the direction of the Republican policy during the war
> and in the harried years of non-peace afterwards . . . . No Repub-
> lican since has taken a leading place in American and world affairs
> who did not follow the path that [liberal Democrat] Willkie
> blazed. And when the old guard, after twenty-four years of
> battling his ghost and his echo, nominated one of their own for
> the presidency, Goldwater went down to the most crushing
> defeat in presidential campaign history.[19]

Mrs. Davenport provides us with this significant anecdote
about the end of the Willkie campaign:

> The night after the 1940 election Russell and I were alone at
> home . . . . The doorbell rang, about eleven o'clock. I went to the
> door — to Harry Hopkins [Roosevelt's aide]. I had never met him
> *though Russell had more times than he admitted*. Hopkins was like
> a walking corpse, bone-pale, emaciated, bent and stooped with
> weakness. He shuffled into the drawing room with me, saying to
> Russell, "Tell me about it. Tell me how you did it." [Emphasis add-
> ed.][20]

Following his election defeat Willkie continued to serve
the *Insiders*. During the war years few pro-Communist
propaganda moves were more successful than Willkie's

round-the-world trip. As columnist George N. Crocker describes it:

> The flighty Wendell Willkie, after losing in his try for the presidency in 1940, "suddenly got religion" and became an ebullient emissary for Roosevelt, traveling to London, Moscow and Chungking in an Army Transport plane, emotionally overcome by his precipitate arrival in the upper regions of international fame. His much publicized slogan "One World" served well to cover up the real state of affairs . . . . Whether other Republican leaders, such as Hoover and Taft, and dissident Democrats such as former Secretary of War Harry H. Woodring, looked upon these antics of Wendell Willkie as those of an opportunistic hypocrite or an impressionable dupe we know not. They themselves had no hallucinations about a "grand coalition of peoples, fighting a common war of liberation."[21]

A companion of Willkie on his trip and the ghostwriter of his book, *One World* (the title is very significant),[22] was Communist party member Joseph Fels Barnes (CFR), a relative of the Rothschild banking dynasty. Later Barnes was to ghostwrite Dwight D. Eisenhower's book, *Crusade In Europe.*

In 1944, with a war going on, the *Insiders* had little to fear from the Republicans. However, they took no chances. Polls taken by CFR member George Gallup showed that the GOP could not win unless it continued the New Deal foreign policy and named candidates who would appeal to left-leaning Democrats. The Gallup Poll also "announced" that 68 per cent of Republican voters were for Thomas E. Dewey (CFR), and that he was the only Republican with a chance to win. Dewey carried on a weak campaign and refused to mention, because of the personal request of George C. Marshall, the Republicans' best issue: how Roosevelt had invited and encouraged the Pearl Harbor attack. Dewey knew that FDR had refused to negotiate with the pro-American government of Prince Konoye of

Japan, and had given its successor an ultimatum that meant war. Dewey knew that we had broken the top Japanese code before Pearl Harbor, and also was aware that FDR, his Secretaries of War and Navy, and Chief of Staff George C. Marshall, had had advance warnings of the Japanese attack. He knew that Pearl Harbor was a "set-up" and a disaster for which the Commander-in-Chief should have been held personally responsible.[23] The American people had the right to know too, but they never found out. *Insiders* don't tattle — with the possible exception of Dr. Carroll Quigley, if he really is one.

In 1948, despite the Republican party tradition against nominating a loser, the *Insiders* successfully trotted the lackluster Dewey back on stage once again, complete with CFR Gallup Polls showing that he was a sure thing. To insure the nomination, the Deweyites spent money and made deals and promises that Taft would never have made. After the convention one delegate ran for the train and died of a heart attack on it. He had $1500 in fresh money on him, and the other delegates claimed it should be divided among them. [24]

One of the deals made by the Dewey managers was with Congressman Charles Halleck, who was promised the Vice Presidential nomination if he could deliver the Indiana delegation to Dewey; but the *Insiders* did not trust Halleck. Their house organ, the *New York Times*, declared:

> Surely not Mr. Halleck! Mr. Halleck would bring into the campaign the perfect record of a Republican isolationist. Mr. Halleck voted against Selective Service in the summer of 1940 . . . . Mr. Halleck voted against Lend-Lease . . . . He voted against the British loan, he voted against the Hall Reciprocal Trade program in 1940 . . . . He led the plan to cut appropriations under the Marshall plan . . . .

Here's a good summary of the kind of candidate the *Insiders* will not tolerate. They will not allow a candidate on the ticket – even in second place – unless he has a foreign policy acceptable to the New York financiers and banking interests who profit so greatly from the New Deal internationalist foreign policy.

Earl Warren of California was chosen as the Vice Presidential nominee. Warren had begun his political career as a hard-fighting enforcer of anti-Communist and anti-crime laws. However, following the mysterious and never-solved murder of his father, Earl Warren had suddenly changed, almost as if he had been blackmailed, and went on to establish his notorious pro-Communist record.[25]

Dewey and Warren did not campaign on the major issue of that year, which was Communist infiltration in government. The exposure of Alger Hiss, Harry Dexter White, and other Communists in high government positions had given Republicans their best issue – but Dewey and Warren did not discuss it.

Dewey went into the '48 election with everything in his favor. He was faced not by the invincible Roosevelt, but by a highly vincible Harry Truman. The Democrats had been in office for four long and troublesome terms. Truman was not a popular President, and the Democratic party was split three ways, with Henry Wallace siphoning off far-Left voters and with the Dixiecrats in the South. The country was ripe for a change. All the pre-election polls showed Dewey far out in front, but, accepting in almost every particular the liberal analysis of how to run a campaign, he proceeded to blow it. Dewey's campaign was a textbook study of liberal Republican strategy. Its ideological bias leaned heavily toward Liberalism – a fact Dewey underlined by virtually disowning the Republican Party in Congress and steering particularly clear of arch-rival Robert Taft.

Truman pitched his campaign against the Republican 80th Congress. Dewey made his fatal mistake when he did not defend it. The Republican 80th Congress, under the leadership of Taft, had made the greatest record of any Congress in the Twentieth Century. For the first time since the start of the New Deal, it reduced taxes, balanced the budget, and reduced the national debt. It had exposed numerous Communists who had infiltrated the New Deal. It had enacted the Taft-Hartley law over Truman's veto. It had authorized the Hoover Commission to reorganize the government, and had passed the 22nd Amendment to the Constitution, limiting the President to two terms.

Dewey assumed that the Midwestern heartland of the party was secure and that his job was to corral Liberal votes in the East. He also assumed that the key to Republican success was in the big cities — another theorem presently favored by the Liberal GOP.

What happened? Dewey accomplished the major strategic objectives he thought were necessary to his election. He carried supposedly decisive New York State and triumphed in Pennsylvania and New Jersey, running strongly in the major metropolitan centers. Yet he lost the election because he failed to carry the Republican base he thought he could take for granted. It was the crowning irony of the New York-big city strategy that the 1948 election was lost through defection of the Midwestern farm vote. Dewey lost the key Midwestern states of Ohio, Illinois, Iowa, and Wisconsin by an aggregate of less than 100,000 votes, and thereby lost the election. Dewey's campaign was so Liberal that Midwesterners found Truman more to their liking. Pollster Samuel Lubell observed:

> Truman rather than Dewey seemed the conservative candidate to many voters .... The harshest fact about the 1948 voting from the Republican viewpoint was how many ordinarily conservative persons feared a Republican victory ....
>
> The net significance of the Dewey debacle was that it demonstrated the political liabilities of being neither fish nor fowl.[26]

The accuracy of this comment is suggested by the fact that Dewey got fewer votes in 1948 than he did in 1944. Some 682,000 voters in the election did not bother to mark a ballot for either Presidential candidate, and in sixteen states the vote for Congressional candidates was larger than that for Presidential aspirants. Dewey himself observed, in the aftermath of the election, that it "looks as though two or three million Republicans stayed home."[27] It is also possible that voters felt there was no apparent difference between the candidates to make it desirable to vote for the Republican. Dewey was doubtless personally humiliated, but the *Insiders* had plenty of their men around the hapless Harry Truman, a small-time outsider who had been hoisted into national politics by the notorious Pendergast machine of Kansas City.

Following the '48 election Democrats bragged about the trick they had pulled. Jack Redding, former publicity director of the Democratic National Committee, in his book, *Inside the Democratic Party*, quoted Democratic National Chairman Robert Hannegan as saying in a Democratic strategy huddle:

> Actually, if the Republicans were smart, they'd run Taft. He'd make a better candidate and would probably be harder for us to beat because he would fight harder. Don't make the mistake of underrating Taft . . . . The fact is Taft is a fighter and will make a terrific fight for what he represents. Dewey will be "me-too" all over again . . . . Hit Taft hard and often; maybe we can stop him from getting the nomination and at the same time embarrass Dewey.[28]

Harold Ickes put it more bluntly. He said: "With the bases loaded, the Republicans sent to the plate their bat boy. They could have sent their Babe Ruth — Bob Taft."[29] Dewey had indeed snatched defeat from the jaws of victory for the Republicans, but either way it was a victory for the *Insiders*, who cared not a whit whether their man Dewey or the perfectly acceptable substitute, Harry Truman, sat in the White House.

The *Insiders* realized that 1952 would be a turning-point year in American history. It was almost a foregone conclusion that after thirty years of Democrat rule the nation was gasping for a change. The Truman scandals, the Korean War, Communist infiltration in government, plus the fact that for the first time in twenty years the GOP did not face an incumbent President, all combined to make the Republican Presidential nomination a valuable prize. Although the *Insiders* had been selecting Republican candidates since 1936, their hold on the Republican Party for 1952 looked tenuous. The Taft Conservative forces had been gaining in strength and were preparing to make an all-out assault on the Presidency. But the *Insiders* were determined to make the two parties as much alike as Tweedle-Dum and Tweedle-Dee.

Colonel Edward M. House had established the Council on Foreign Relations to carry out Karl Marx's dictum: "Infiltrate both or all of the political organizations — eliminate all opposition and confuse the people." Americans for Democratic Action (ADA), which included numerous CFR members in its membership, had served well as the Fabian Socialist movement within the Democratic party. Russell Davenport of Willkie campaign fame, himself a behind-the-scenes wheelhorse in the ADA, was determined that the GOP should have its own ADA, which would serve as a leftwing Trojan horse within the Republican party. The ADA-type organization for the GOP was called Republican Advance; it was bankrolled by Nelson Rockefeller (CFR) and Sidney Weinberg.[30] In hearings held before the Select Committee on Lobbying Activities on July 7, 1950, former FDR Attorney General Francis Biddle gave the following testimony:

"Mr. Brown: Have you [ADA] become more active in the Republican party recently, your organization?

Mr. Biddle: No — we have not, except — well, in this sense. *Our influence has been rather striking.* I do not know if you have noted the organization of a similar movement in the Republican party — I don't think they have a name for it — led by Russell Davenport.

Mr. Brown: You mean Republican Advance or something like that?

Mr. Biddle: Something like that. I thought it might be called Republicans for Democratic Action, but that did not seem quite appropriate .... [Emphasis added.][31]

Republican Advance had its beginnings in 1950. On the Fourth of July that year, twenty-one Republican Congressmen joined what they termed a "revolt" against the Taft wing of the party. They announced their support of the new Republican group calling itself "Advance," which had been launched in semisecrecy the week prior to the announcement in Philadelphia. Advance hoped to unseat Senator Taft and to dilute the influence of Conservatives within the party, and of other Conservatives. The Advance statement was issued in opposition to the GOP statement of policy adopted in February 1950 by House and Senate Republicans and concurred in by the Republican National Committee. The statement said that the case was merely "liberty versus socialism." The "Statement of Policy" issued by Republican Advance announced the intention to have the GOP "play down" its campaign against socialism and Communism within the government. It would commit the party instead to a strong civil rights platform and a welfare state along Roosevelt-Truman lines.

The *Los Angeles Times* of July 14, 1950, reported that twenty-one Republican Congressmen endorsed the principle that the Republican Party must "place strong emphasis on civil and social rights as a keystone for national unity." The principal ideological paragraph in Advance's manifesto asserted:

> *The real issue against the Democrats does not lie with the*
> *goals* .... The real issue ... lies with the means of achieving
> these goals .... The Republicans have failed to sell themselves by
> attacking the product of the Democrats. They have not presented
> satisfactory alternatives to the Democratic projects they have
> attacked. [Emphasis added.]

Prior to the formation of Republican Advance the main
thrust of the Republican Party was exposing Communism
and fighting socialism. These two aspects were dropped in
favor of fighting for civil rights, social legislation, and
internationalism.

Although at the time the Republican Advance statement
was brushed off by the Republican National Committee,
which promised to keep up a hot war against the Marxists,
for the first time the Left was organized within Republican
Congressional ranks. The turning-point had been passed: the
Republican Party had made a decisive turn to the Left.

Among the twenty-one Congressmen on the original list of
Congressional sponsors of Republican Advance were John
Davis Lodge (CFR; brother of Henry Cabot Lodge, CFR),
Clifford Case (CFR), Christian Herter (CFR), Jacob Javits
(CFR), Kenneth Keating, Thruston Morton, Hugh Scott, and
Richard M. Nixon (CFR).

Many of the twenty-one Congressmen were merely
"fronts" for the CFR leaders of Advance, such as Thomas E.
Dewey and John Foster Dulles. Among other political figures
involved were Herbert Brownell, who became Attorney
General in the Eisenhower cabinet, Senator Henry Cabot
Lodge (CFR), Senator Ralph Flanders, and Sherman
Adams.[32] Also supporting Advance was the nation's most
influential publisher, Henry Luce (CFR) of *Time, Life* and
Fortune.

Advance was soon to emerge from its cocoon and become
Citizens for Eisenhower. Much of the background of the
Citizens for Eisenhower movement is provided for us by an

article by Paul Hoffman (CFR) in *Colliers* magazine of
October 26, 1956, entitled "How Eisenhower Saved the
Republican Party." This article can be read in any major
library and is one of the most illuminating documents by
or about the *Insiders* ever made public. Hoffman and his
wife, Leftwing Democrat Anna Rosenberg, have been key
figures in the capture of the GOP by the Left. Hoffman
was described by *U.S. News & World Report* of December
30, 1955, as "an influential, though unofficial, Presidential
advisor," and was a key man in the nomination and
election of Eisenhower. Before he became involved in
politics, Hoffman's chief claim to fame was that he had
piloted the Studebaker-Packard Corporation over the rapids
of financial collapse. His qualifications for restructuring the
Republican party included his career as a "professional
spendthrift with other people's money" through foreign
aid, and his advocacy of the thesis that American foreign
aid should be not temporary but permanent; he had also
advocated giving cabinet rank to the agency that dispensed
the money.[33] In December 1948, months after General
Marshall himself had abandoned any such idea, Hoffman
was still calling for a coalition government with the Communists in China.[34] He has served as a trustee of the
Committee for Economic Development (CED), the major
propaganda arm of the Council on Foreign Relations, and
of the Ford Foundation, a horn of plenty for Leftwingers
and Leftwing projects on every continent; he was also a
trustee of the CFR-spawned Institute of Pacific Relations,
called by the Senate Internal Security Subcommittee an
"instrument of Communist policy, propaganda and military
intelligence." Hoffman has been a member of such one-
world outfits as the UN Association of the United States,
the American Committee on United Europe, and Americans
United for World Government. Now involved with the
United Nations Special Fund, Hoffman, a close friend of

the late publishing magnate Henry Luce, has been responsible for channeling money to Castro's Cuba and other
Communist nations. Former Ambassador Spruille Braden
once remarked:

> The kindest thing I can say about Hoffman is that he is a damn
> fool. I would be sorry to think he knew that this whole business
> of foreign aid has been a fulfillment of Soviet policy. But if he
> doesn't know it he is a damn fool. Lenin and Stalin both said it
> was the purpose of Soviet Communism to get the developed
> countries to send financial help to the underdeveloped coun-
> tries.[35]

Hoffman has been one of the financiers of the National
Committee for an Effective Congress, a group which is
somewhat to the left of the ADA.[36]

Hoffman, a top *Insider* himself, is married to Anna
Rosenberg. In the early 1950's Mrs. Rosenberg, who was later
to be the brains behind Nelson Rockefeller's political career,
was working in the Defense Department, picking key
personnel for the entire defense establishment. Despite the
fact that the Senate confirmed her appointment, Mrs.
Rosenberg is seriously suspect. Nobody wants to discuss or
expose her for fear of being called anti-Semitic, but criticism
of Mrs. Rosenberg's background has nothing to do with her
religion, only with her politics. All of her adult life she has
been on the Marxist side of the world revolution. Born in
Hungary, she worked closely for many years with the
revolutionary Marxist, Sidney Hillman. For years she wrote
for Red organs, lectured to Red groups, and promoted Red
activities. The December 8, 1942 issue of the official
Communist publication, *New Masses*, contains an article by
her. The magazine introduced her as "New York Regional
Director, War Manpower Commission," the title which the
future Assistant Secretary of Defense held under President
Roosevelt at that time. That issue of *New Masses* showed a

drawing of the author in connection with the article. Placing the drawing beside a photograph of Mrs. Anna Rosenberg shows that it was not a case of mistaken identity, as she claimed.

Ralph DeSola, a former Communist, testified under oath that he had attended meetings of the Communist John Reed Club with Mrs. Rosenberg in the mid-1930's, and that she was a member of the Communist Party. Although DeSola identified her by sight as the same Anna Rosenberg whom he knew to be a Communist, Mrs. Rosenberg steadfastly maintained that it was a case of mistaken identity. DeSola's testimony could not be refuted, but neither could it be corroborated. It was brought out that there were forty Anna Rosenbergs in New York City at that time, and that six had signed Communist petitions. Another Anna Rosenberg, who had since moved to California, claimed that she had been a member of the John Reed Club during the '30's, so that DeSola's testimony was clouded.

However, Mrs. Rosenberg did contradict her own testimony. She testified, "I re-read the Dies Committee report and the Anna Rosenberg [of the John Reed Club] was a writer. I am not a writer . . . . I have never written anything." But a little later, on November 29, 1950, Mrs. Rosenberg told the same Senate Committee, "I have a full list of the organizations to which I have belonged, and of *everything I have written* . . . . " (Emphasis added.) Mrs. Rosenberg then submitted a long list of articles she had written, thus showing that she had testified falsely under oath in stating that she had "never written anything." It is significant, too, that she failed to list the article she had written for the Communist *New Masses* of December 8, 1942. She admitted she "wrote for New School for Social Research" and "gave courses on collective bargaining at New School for Social Research, 1940." The New School for Social Research, as various official investigations show, is a hotbed of Marxists of all varieties. General Eisenhower was an old friend of Mrs. Rosenberg and knew her favorably long before her patron, George C. Marshall, took her into the Defense Department as a manpower expert.[37]

The opposition to her Defense Department appointment was violently and vehemently attacked by official Communist organs and by the multitude of Communist fronts and *Insider*-controlled publications throughout the country. By the vehemence of their defense of Mrs. Rosenberg, Hoffman's wife, the Communists and *Insiders* showed that she was of special importance in their plans.

In the *Colliers* article, "How Ike Saved the Republican Party," Hoffman described meeting Senator Arthur Vandenberg of Michigan to discuss blocking the nomination of Taft in 1952. Vandenberg, who wanted to nominate Eisenhower, explained the "quandary" faced by the Republican Party (as related by Hoffman):

> Half the Republican leadership, many of them utterly sincere men, could not, it seemed, grasp the overriding fact that we lived in a very dangerous world . . . . Half our party — the isolationist, fortress-America half — seemed equally unable to grasp the fact that America has changed at home too; that labor unions were here to stay; that *government had a partner's role to play in preserving free enterprise*; that ordinary people needed some insurance against the dangers that go with our free system of economic abundance.
>
> There was another half of our Republican party too, a modern-liberal half, whose work and philosophy was demonstrated in the achievements of *such great state governors as Sherman Adams, Tom Dewey and Earl Warren.* This half had come to grips with the problems of the 20th Century and had worked out a program, both at home and abroad, that seemed to be better than anything the Democrats could offer. [Emphasis added.][38]

Hoffman made several trips to Europe to induce Eisenhower to run. He said in *Colliers*:

> I returned to Paris again in November of 1951. That week we spoke several times — away from his offices at SHAPE where he could not let politics enter . . . . Many men, far more important, had been urging him to run . . . . When I returned to New York, I felt I could confidently spread the word: "We have a candidate."[39]

Hoffman took a "four months' leave of absence" from the Ford Foundation "to devote full time to the campaign."

The Citizens for Eisenhower movement, according to Hoffman, was:

> . . . vitally important both in the strategy of the campaign and in Eisenhower's political education. Strategically it was the brainchild of Cabot Lodge [CFR], who saw it as an instrument to bring pressure to bear on the Old Guard regulars who controlled the party's machinery, a lever to exercise the power of millions of unorganized and independent and Democrat votes where this power could count. [40]

The campaign then became one to convince Democrats and independents that the Republicans could out-Liberal the Democrats.

The first man who publicly attempted to induce Eisenhower to run for President was Leonard Finder, one of the founders of the Leftwing Anti-Defamation League (ADL), later headed by Dore Schary of the United World Federalists. Finder, who became a "Republican" only in 1952, had wanted Ike to run as a Democrat in 1948. In an article for *Colliers* of November 3, 1951, titled "Why Ike Will Run," Finder confirmed the fact that he initiated the "Ike for President" movement, and the General wrote him a letter dated January 22, 1948, when he decided not to risk a try for the Presidency that year. In the *Colliers* article Finder named as Eisenhower supporters such ultra-Leftists as Paul Douglas, Wayne Morse, David Dubinsky, Adolph Berle, James Roosevelt, Claude "Red" Pepper, Chester Bowles, Helen

Gahagan Douglas, Jake Arvey, and Adlai Stevenson. Finder
said that, in 1948, "most Democrats were elated with the
news that he had not acted with definite adverseness. But
something happened within those few weeks to alter his
attitude and make him hold adamant against the nomination."

Finder went on to state, "On every appropriate occasion,
General Eisenhower has reiterated that he has no party
affiliations." Because Ike "believes in the two-party system,"
Finder hinted that the General would decide to run as a
Republican in 1952. Although he did not rule Eisenhower
out as the Democratic candidate in 1952, Finder said that the
public was feeling the Democrats had been in office too long.
But, said Finder, "Do these considerations mean that the
Democratic nomination is ruled out absolutely? Not at all. At
least one situation exists, in my opinion, that would make
General Eisenhower accept the Democrat bid . . . . That
condition would be the Republican nomination of Senator
Taft . . . . " In 1948, Ike had told Finder, "If the Republicans
were to nominate a reactionary, you know what my answer
would have to be."

Finder said of Ike's liberal politics that, while they "might
not make as much speed as would satisfy impatient extreme
liberals or radicals, it would mean progress forward at an
appreciable rate." Even if the ADL for which Mr. Finder
spoke were not an extreme Left organization, one could
hardly fail to catch the full implication of that statement.
Eisenhower would follow the same course as the extreme
"liberals or radicals," though less rapidly. Finder stated:

> The election of General Eisenhower on the Republican ticket
> would strengthen democracy on all sides. At present, the
> Democratic party claims to be the only haven for Americans
> who believe more in growing with the future than in retaining
> the status quo. The Republican party is under the influence of
> its most conservative members. With General Eisenhower

leading the Republicans, that party too would become liberalized.[41]

A more blatant call for the takeover of the Republican party by non-Republicans of the Left would be difficult to imagine.

The fact that it was the extreme Left wing of the Democratic party that wanted Eisenhower to run for the Presidency as a Democrat in 1948 should have given Republicans a clue to Ike's true beliefs. Among those supporting an Eisenhower candidacy were Adlai Stevenson, Eleanor Roosevelt, and Walter Reuther of the ADA. In hearings held on January 7, 1950, before the Select Committee on Lobbying Activities, the following testimony was given:

> *Chairman*: Did the national organization [ADA] actually take a position for Eisenhower for President?
> *Mr. Loeb*: For Eisenhower or Justice [William O.] Douglas .... The position taken at the Board meeting in Pittsburgh in April 1948, was for Eisenhower or Douglas.[42]

In his book, *Crusade in Europe*, Ike revealed that Harry Truman had offered to support him for the presidency in 1948. Eisenhower's chief ghostwriter for *Crusade in Europe* was Joseph Fels Barnes, who had written *One World* for Willkie. Barnes, a CFR member, had shortly before this time traveled to Russia with the General's brother Milton. Barnes, a relative of the Rothschild banking clan, has been independently identified as a Communist agent in sworn testimony, on their personal knowledge, by Whittaker Chambers, Louis Budenz, General Alexander Barmine, Dr. Carl Wittfogel, and Hede Massing.[43] John Gunther, after visiting Eisenhower's headquarters in Paris, confirmed Barnes' role in the writing of *Crusade in Europe*.[44]

Another behind-the-scenes international banker-kingmaker

who worked both sides of the political street was the late
Bernard Baruch, who discussed his relationship with Eisenhower in his autobiography:

> The country was fortunate in the choice it was offered in
> 1952. Adlai Stevenson certainly is one of the outstanding men in
> public life today. During the campaign, both he and General
> Eisenhower were kind enough to ask my views. I told them both
> that in my opinion the control of inflation, the strengthening of
> our defenses, and the securing of peace were the major goals.
>
> General Eisenhower and I became close friends after the war. I
> saw him frequently at Columbia University, as I had when he was
> Chief of Staff, and developed a warm affection and regard for
> him. One question which interested us both, and which we often
> discussed, was the relationship between the individual and his
> government — how to strike a balance between laissez-faire and
> paternalism. The discussions between us on this subject, while
> Eisenhower was president of Columbia, led him to initiate a study
> of the problem at the University. Out of such conversations I
> gained an appreciation of his ability, and of his quick and open
> mind.
>
> I myself concluded that, apart from the advantages which
> might accrue from a change after so long a Democratic tenure,
> General Eisenhower could best provide the leadership which the
> attainment of these goals required. I also felt that he could bring
> unity to the country.[45]

Another backer of Eisenhower for the Democratic candidacy in 1948 was Sidney Hillman, with the CIO. Hillman had
been an active revolutionary in the Russian Revolution and
was a lifelong promoter of Communist causes in America. In
the *Atlanta Journal* of September 17, 1951, labor columnist
Victor Riesel gave details of Eisenhower's relations with
Hillman. Riesel was present at the CIO convention when the
leftwing union boosted Ike. He said:

> The first Eisenhower for President boom was sounded by
> union chiefs. Until now that story has never fully been told. It
> began back in 1945, when the man who drove into Germany as a

conquering hero cabled Sidney Hillman to fly into the bombed-out Reich . . . .

Soon Eisenhower was invited to speak at the Atlantic City CIO convention in '46 — a great coup for the CIO, for Eisenhower was on the paths of glory and a much sought after man.

In describing events at the convention Riesel says:

That night two men were called in by aides of Mr. Hillman. I know. I was one of those [newsmen who were told] . . . that the CIO thought it would be a great thing for the nation if Eisenhower were nominated in '48 . . . .

The reason Ike chose not to run as a Democrat in 1948 could have been the adverse publicity stemming from the fact that, while president of Columbia University, he had granted the Communist government of Poland a Chair of Polish studies at the school. Dr. Arthur P. Coleman, assistant professor of Polish at Columbia, who saw how Poles were being slaughtered by the Communist government, lost the fight to keep Eisenhower from accepting the Red Chair. The Chair was subsidized by a $25,000-a-year grant from the Polish Communist government. [46]

As 1952 approached, the *Insiders* who had been grooming Ike switched him from potential Democratic candidacy to Republican candidacy, even though he shared none of the traditional GOP philosophy.

Eisenhower was no champion of free enterprise, and showed that he had little if any knowledge of the workings of free economy when he gave his answer to the inflation problem to a group in 1947: "Inflation could easily be licked any time by the simple action on the part of the industrialists and other business leaders of the nation. They merely decide, by joint voluntary agreement, to forego all profits for a year — or two if necessary." [47] In his article on the CFR, "School for Statesmen," Joseph Kraft quoted a Republican member of the Council as saying: "Whatever General Eisenhower knows about economics he learned at the study group meetings." Another participant at the same group recalls that: "Eisenhower came with a vague predilection in favor of building up Europe. When he left, European aid was a ruling conviction."[48] It was the General's internationalism that endeared him to the *Insiders*. Thomas Dewey, writing in *Look* magazine of September 11, 1951, stated: "I am an internationalist. That's why I am for Eisenhower. Eisenhower is a Republican at heart — but more important than that, he is an internationalist."[49]

Not only did Eisenhower turn out to be a Republican in 1952, but his campaign manager, Henry Cabot Lodge (CFR), went along with the story and claimed that Ike had been a life-long Republican.[50] The *New York Times* of May 1, 1951, had written:

> One of the weaknesses of the Eisenhower drive is that the General has never declared whether he was a Republican or Democrat. Another is that no one can say, with certainty, that he would accept the nomination. He is being represented, however, as definitely opposed to the nomination by the Republicans of an "isolationist" candidate like Senator Robert A. Taft of Ohio . . . .

Robert Sherwood in his book, *Roosevelt and Hopkins*, said that Eisenhower told him personally in London, in March 1944, "that his family had always been Kansas Republicans, but he himself had never voted in his life."[51] Harry Truman, with whom Eisenhower had been in very close contact, thought right up to the fall of 1951 that Eisenhower would unquestionably accept the Democrat nomination.[52] It was Wendell Willkie all over again.

In a feature story in the *New York Times* on April 15, 1952, Warren Moscow, that paper's New York political reporter, wrote:

There is some degree of similarity between the Willkie drive and the movement to nominate General of the Army Dwight D. Eisenhower. The same financial and publishing interests or their counterparts are behind the Eisenhower movement . . . . If they nominate General Eisenhower, it will be because *the controlling minority* in the convention believes it needs him to win, and because the Eisenhower forces *will have whipped up, back home, sentiment approaching the hysteria of the Willkie drive.* [Emphasis added.]

The newsletter *Human Events* noted on July 9, 1952: "For months the big money from New York has been flowing into the Eisenhower movement's coffers . . . . Presidents of every big bank in New York save one are behind the General." The treasurer of the Citizens for Eisenhower movement was the ubiquitous Sidney Weinberg, an international banker with Goldman, Sachs, and an intimate of FDR, who had discovered during the Willkie campaign that he could support Republicans as well as Democrats.

Writing in the April 9, 1952 *Human Events*, scholar Frank Chodorov asked:

Why is Big Business backing General Eisenhower for the Presidency . . . ? Things being as they are in this country Big Business looks to Washington for its living; if the next head of the Washington establishment is a spender of proportions, Big Business may hope to live at the cocktail standard to which it has been accustomed by the New-Fair Deal. General Eisenhower is reported to have strong leanings toward the big spender role.

The other serious contender for the Republican nomination, Senator Taft, is of doubtful value to Big Business . . . he has shown a distaste for the policy called internationalism, which is a euphemism for profligacy, and he seems to be temperamentally unfit for the job of wasting other people's money. It is expected that Mr. Taft, if elected, would be inclined to pull the national purse strings tight . . . .

Putting the individualistic Mr. Taft aside, Big Business could place its bets on any of the present entries in the race and be sure to come up with a winner; that is, with a President who would assure them of a steady intake of the taxpayers' dollars, via contracts, interest payments, loans, etc.

The pre-convention campaign featured rough, tough in-fighting. *Human Events* of March 26, 1952, remarked:

> The Wall Street supporters of General Eisenhower were jubilant [about Taft's withdrawal from New Jersey]. Such moneymen as George Whitney [CFR], Clarence Dillon [CFR], Harold Talbott, John Hay Whitney [CFR], and Winthrop Aldrich [CFR] [all Big Bankers], who are supporting Eisenhower and masterminding his campaign, operate as business men do in ruthless competition, forgetting that the primary is a prelude to a General Election and that nothing should be done in the primaries which will have the effect of a cumulative spite vote in the General Election.

Human Events, which now no longer mentions the words "international bankers," commented strongly on January 23, 1952, on their involvement in denying Taft the nomination:

> Specifically, we can report that pressure is now being applied (by these banking interests) on businessmen who favor Taft but have the misfortune to owe money to these Eastern bankers. We have, on investigation, spotted several cases in which businessmen (leaders in their trans-Appalachian communities) have received communications from their New York creditors, urging them to join pro-Eisenhower committees and to raise or contribute funds thereto. These debtors happen to favor Taft and/or MacArthur and are not happy about the communication. For, they want no trouble with the gentlemen who hold the notes. At this moment, we cannot as yet ascertain just whether or not the debtors will surrender their political independence.
>
> First of all, it is being eloquently argued that, on the plane of principle, Taft can be urged to make an issue of this. Bankers and financial interests which play ball with and profit from the Fair Deal (in contrast to those who engage in "straight" banking) are just as much a menace to the weal of the country as Socialists, Communists and corruption practitioners. These elements of high finance played a role, and a big one, in getting us into both World

Wars. What they are up to now should be discussed in the public forum.

Naturally Eisenhower had all the *Insider* news media going for him, including some newspapers, such as the *New York Post*, owned by Dorothy Schiff, granddaughter of Jacob Schiff, the financier of the Russian Revolution, and the *Washington Post*, owned by the late financier Phillip Graham (CFR). The two *Posts* support a Republican every third blue moon. Even John Cowles' (CFR) *Minneapolis Star* supported Ike; and in its March 19, 1952, issue, it revealed that Minnesota's leftwing Democratic farmer-labor voters were supporting Eisenhower too. Historian George Morgenstern commented in the October 8, 1952, *Human Events*:

> Yet, sight unseen, and even in advance of any personal profession of party attachment, the General's candidacy was espoused by an unlikely set of New Deal newspapers and syndicated columnists, all declaring the sudden conviction that the nation's well-being demanded that the two-party system be preserved through a change of administrations.

Although Eisenhower had the support of the *Insiders'* mass media, he did not have the support of anti-Communist General Douglas MacArthur. Columnist George Sokolsky wrote: "He [MacArthur] supports Taft; he opposes Eisenhower; . . . the international bankers can exercise no influence on General Mac Arthur." [53]

Standing in the way of the *Insiders'* attempts to steal away with the Republican party was Robert A. Taft. Historian George Morgenstern describes this man of impeccable principle as follows:

> Three times Mr. Taft picked his party off the floor following defeat and put it together again. Morally and intellectually he was its unchallenged leader, and in himself personified the values

which the party was supposed to represent. Miss Dorothy
Thompson was never more cogent than when, in expressing the
outlook of Taft's followers, she quoted a carpenter who urged her
to support Taft, and described in his terms what those values
were:

"We are the people who pay our taxes even when we hate what
the government does with them; who regard it as a disgrace to
expect our fellow citizens to support us; who believe we should
get what we earn but earn what we get; whose sons are the first to
volunteer in America's wars and who expect if we get in them to
win them; and who know darn well nobody is ever going to
protect America but Americans. We are the Vanishing Americans,
pushed around by big business, big labor, big government and big
military. And if we lose this election we are finished. Eisenhower
won't win it for us even if he wins. He'll win it for another branch
of the same people who are running the country now."[54]

In Taft's book, *A Foreign Policy for America*, he expressed
this simple premise, which made him anathema to the
Insiders: "The ultimate purpose of our foreign policy must
be to protect the liberty of the people of the United States."
This attitude had led people like Arthur Hays Sulzberger,
publisher of the *New York Times*, to say he was supporting
Eisenhower and opposing Taft for the Presidential nomination "because it is so frightening at [*sic*] the thought of
Mr. Taft."

As the time for the Republican convention approached,
Taft apparently had enough delegates to win the nomination
on the first ballot, while Eisenhower was at least 150
delegates short. The *Insiders* were desperate and needed a
gimmick to capture a few crucial delegates from Taft. The
opportunity presented itself in Texas. They devised a scheme
whereby they would ignore the legally elected Taft delegates.
The ploy was to hold rump meetings to which they would
invite Democrats who had no intention of voting for any
Republican in the November election, and have this illegal
body "elect" Eisenhower delegates, who would then try to
unseat the Taft delegates at the convention.

The Eisenhower managers ran advertisements in Texas newspapers, and mailed out vast quantities of postcards addressed to "Occupant," which invited Democrats to come to Republican party meetings and "vote" for Eisenhower. These ads stated, "You are not pledged to support the nominee of the Republican party nor does it prohibit you from voting in the July Democratic primary nor does it prohibit you from voting for whomever you please in the November election."[55] Such a procedure was clearly contrary to Texas law. When Taft and his supporters protested this illegal action, one of the *Insiders*' hatchet men came up with a brainstorm — accuse Taft of stealing delegates! Of course the *Insiders* were trying to steal the Republican Party, but that fact was lost in a deluge of propaganda from anti-Taft newspapers who accused Taft of the "big steal." Masked bandits with guns paraded the streets of Chicago carrying placards reading "Taft Steals Votes." Henry Cabot Lodge (CFR), Sherman Adams (CFR), and the other Eisenhower managers were screaming "Dishonesty" and "Fraud!" to the media, which treated the charges as if they were true. Like 1940, it was great show biz.

When the illegally elected Eisenhower delegates arrived at the Republican national convention in Chicago, the job was to get them officially seated in place of the Taft delegates, in order to take away Taft's narrow margin of victory. By high-pressure propaganda and hypocritical bleating about the moral issue, the *Insiders* brought about a change in the rules for seating delegates under which every previous convention had functioned. Although this rules change was contrary to common sense as well as to every principle of parliamentary procedure, it was called the "Fair Play Amendment."[56]

Once the rules were changed, the second battle at the '52 convention was over the seating of the contested delegates. By promising Earl Warren the first appointment to the Supreme Court and Richard Nixon the Vice Presidency, the *Insiders* persuaded the California delegation — without hearing any of the evidence — to vote to expel the regular Georgia, Louisiana, and Texas delegations and seat the Eisenhower delegates.

When the convention opened, the Taft headquarters had signed pledges from 604 delegates, the narrow majority he needed out of 1203. Eisenhower had only 400 plus. But behind the scenes, wheeling and dealing by *Insiders* whittled away at Taft's majority and cost him the margin of victory. The Taft headquarters received reports of delegates who were bodily put on the train for home, leaving their alternates to vote for Ike. Delegates were threatened with loss of their jobs *and calling of their bank loans* unless their vote was for Eisenhower. Money flowed in great quantities everywhere. The *Chicago Tribune* on July 11 summed up the convention like this:

> While yelling, "Steal!", they stole. While piously condemning evil, they entered the bagnio with it. With holy airs, they prejudged the issues, and with piety — and a lot of patronage — they cried corruption while corrupting their own small souls. It was a sickening spectacle.
>
> On Monday the cry was "Fair play." On Wednesday all pretense of fairness was forsaken. On Monday the old rules of 1948 were bad. On Wednesday the bad old rules and precedents of 1948 were cited by the same people, and now they were good. The rule of seating Delegates in 1948, was lamentable on Monday. On Wednesday the precedent of 1948 was invoked to seat Delegates, so long as they were for Eisenhower.

Without hearing any of the evidence the convention overruled the credentials committee, overruled the Republican National Committee, threw out the Taft delegations from Georgia, Texas, and Louisiana, and seated Eisenhower delegates. Ike won on the first ballot.

The big question in Chicago was not a Southern delegation

"steal." It was the question of whether or not the GOP would become *de facto* an arm of a permanent Democratic Administration. Eisenhower forces had made great capital out of the image slogan, "Taft Can't Win." In retrospect it is quite clear Taft indeed could have won in 1952, as he probably would have done in 1948. The issues and the time were not merely ripe for a Republican victory, but overripe. Even Liberal commentators like Lubell acknowledged that Taft could have harvested a victory over Stevenson as Eisenhower did, although no doubt by a smaller margin. There was, nevertheless, a grain of truth in the argument: Taft was simply a less merchandisable item than the returning war hero, Ike. The "Can't Win" slogan was, in part, a reflection of the new age of image politics, which the *Insiders* use so masterfully. The slogan itself was an example of image politics and was an exercise in self-fulfilling prophecy, a variation on the theme that has been developed by Liberal Republicans for use against Conservatives in every intra-party combat since 1940.

In a memorandum written by Taft in late 1952, circulated privately among his close friends, and published in the December 2, 1959 *Human Events*, giving reasons why he lost the nomination, Taft said:

> First, it was the power of the New York financial interests and a large number of businessmen subject to New York influence, who selected General Eisenhower as their candidate at least a year ago. There was a strong and substantial minority of Taft supporters among business leaders, but they were a minority, particularly in the East. Second, four-fifths of the influential newspapers in the country were opposed to me continuously and vociferously and many turned themselves into propaganda sheets for my opponent.

Thus did the *Insiders* deal a possibly mortal blow to the two-party system in the United States, while denying the

Presidency to one of the great men of American history and guaranteeing to themselves hundreds of billions of future taxpayers' dollars.

References

1. C. Nelson Sparks, *One Man: Wendell Willkie*, pp. 5-7.
2. Carroll Quigley, *Tragedy and Hope – A History of the World in Our Time*, New York, The Macmillan Co., 1960, pp. 945-946.
3. Arthur M. Schlesinger Jr., *The Politics of Upheaval*, Boston, Houghton-Mifflin Co., 1960, p. 539.
4. *Ibid.*, p. 533.
5. Rose L. Martin, *Fabian Freeway*, Belmont, Mass., Western Islands, 1966, p. 402.
6. Marcia Davenport, *Too Strong for Fantasy*, New York, Charles Scribner & Sons, 1967, p. 141.
7. *Ibid.*, p. 268.
8. *Ibid.*, p. 269.
9. Joseph Barnes, *Willkie*, New York, Simon & Schuster, 1952, p. 152.
10. Donald B. Jackson, *The Republican Party and Wendell Willkie*, Urbana, Ill., University of Illinois Press, 1960, p. 50.
11. Davenport, *op. cit.*, p. 272.
12. *Ibid.*, p. 273.
13. *Ibid.*, p. 274.
14. Martin, *op. cit.*, p. 33.
15. *Congressional Record*, June 19, 1940. p. 12960.
16. Sparks, *op. cit.*, p. 18.
17. *Ibid.*, p. 20.
18. Davenport, *op. cit.*, pp. 283-284.
19. *Ibid.*, p. 293.
20. *Ibid.*
21. George Crocker, *Roosevelt's Road to Russia*, Chicago, Henry Regnery Co., pp. 50-51.
22. Wendell Willkie, *One World*, New York, Simon & Schuster, 1943, p.x.
23. Ralph de Toledano, *The Winning Side*, New York, G.P. Putnam's Sons, 1963, p. 84.
24. Jules Abeles, *Out of the Jaws of Victory*, New York, Henry Holt & Co., 1959, p. 63.
25. *San Francisco Chronicle*, May 16, 17, 18, 1938; *Los Angeles Times*, May 17, 1938.
26. M. Stanton Evans, *The Future of Conservatism*, p. 248.
27. *Ibid.*
28. Jack Redding, *Inside the Democratic Party*, New York, The Bobbs-Merrill Co., Inc., 1958, pp. 44-45.

29. *Human Events*, February 23, 1963.
30. Martin, *op. cit.*, p. 402.
31. *Lobbying, Direct and Indirect*, Hearings Before the Select Committee on Lobbying Activities, House of Representatives, 2nd Session, 81st Congress, Washington, D.C., U.S. Government Printing Office, 1950, p. 16.
32. Martin, *loc. cit.*
33. *San Francisco Chronicle*, June 16, 1952.
34. *National Review*, August 1, 1956, p. 5.
35. *San Francisco Call-Bulletin*, June 15, 1956.
36. *Our Sunday Visitor*, November 16, 1958.
37. *New York Times*, December 9 and 23, 1950.
38. *Colliers*, October 26, 1956.
39. *Ibid.*
40. *Ibid.*
41. *Colliers,* November 3, 1951.
42. *Lobbying, Direct and Indirect*, p. 16.
43. Senate Internal Security SubCommittee Hearings: *Institute of Pacific Relations* (Parts 1 and 2); Chambers' testimony of August 16, 1951; Budenz's testimony of August 22, 1951; Barmine's testimony of July 30, 1951; Wittfogel's testimony of August 7, 1951; and Massing's testimony of August 2, 1951.
44. *The Freeman*, March 10, 1952.
45. Bernard M. Baruch, *Baruch: The Public Years*, New York, Holt, Rinehart & Winston, Inc., 1960 (Giant Cardinal Edition, Pocket Books, Inc.,) New York, 1952, pp. 384-385.
46. *Los Angeles Examiner*, July 13, 1948; *Saturday Evening Post* editorial, November 6, 1948, p. 184.
47. John Gunther, *Eisenhower: The Man and the Symbol*, New York, Harper & Brothers, 1951, pp. 130-131.
48. Joseph Kraft, "School for Statesmen," *Harpers*, July 1958, p. 66.
49. *Look*, September 11, 1951, p. 97.
50. *New York Times*, January 7, 1952.
51. Robert E. Sherwood, *Roosevelt and Hopkins*, New York, Harper & Brothers, 1948, p. 915.
52. *U.S. News & World Report*, January 18, 1952, p. 1.
53. *Human Events*, March 26, 1952.
54. *Ibid.*, October 8, 1952.
55. Phyllis Schlafly, *A Choice Not an Echo*, Alton, Ill., Pere Marquette Press, 1964, p. 57.
56. *Ibid.*, p. 59.

CHAPTER V

Little Man
In A Big Hurry

The Nixon story begins almost as if it had been written by Horatio Alger. Reared in a hard-working Quaker family, Richard Milhous Nixon was early inspired by his father's commitment to overcoming economic hardship through diligent effort. As the former Vice President has said, "My dad was an individual – he'd go to his grave before he took government help. This attitude of his gave us pride." And no doubt it did. The schoolboy Nixon worked in the family's small grocery store in Whittier until nine or ten o'clock at night, and after it closed for the night would study until two or three in the morning.

In Nixon's junior year at Whittier High School, in keeping with his Quaker philosophy of individual responsibility and personal dignity, young Nixon's father gave him complete charge of the vegetable counter in the family grocery store. Dick did the buying, driving to the Los Angeles public market before sunrise to haggle with the local produce growers and hurrying back to arrange his displays before he left for school. All the profit he could make was his, and all that he could save went into a college bank account. It was superb training for a boy.

In describing Richard Nixon as boy and young man, his schoolmates employ two adjectives repeatedly: "determined" and "persistent." After that come "brilliant," "serious," "clever," "calculating," "reserved," "cold," "industrious," and "game."

An excellent student who was willing to pay the price of long hours of study to achieve academic excellence, young Nixon also became entranced with debating. His high school debating coach, Mrs. Clifford Vincent, remembers that she used to feel "disturbed" at his superiority over his teammates. "He had this ability," she recalls, "to kind of slide round an argument instead of meeting it head on, and he could take any side of a debate."[1]

Nixon has always prided himself on his skill with an audience and on the practiced urbanity and self-control that he patiently developed in those early years. His teenage skill at debating may have been honed by six weeks as a barker for a wheel of chance at the Slipper Gulch Rodeo in Prescott, Arizona. There "he learned the knack of drumming up customers and then letting them have it," Phillip Andrews wrote in *This Man Nixon*. "His booth, it is said, became the most popular one in the show."

While working his way through Whittier College, Richard Nixon majored in history and again covered himself with distinction as a debater; he also distinguished himself as an actor in school dramas. Dr. Albert Upton, who directed Nixon in one of the Whittier College plays, is still awed when he recalls how adept the young collegian was at producing tears. "It was beautifully done, those tears," he remembers, confessing to having "twinged" when he saw photos of Nixon weeping on Senator William Knowland's shoulder after the famous "Checkers" speech. Dr. Upton says he never dreamed that his former student would go into politics, but adds: "I wouldn't have been surprised if, after college, he had gone on to New York or Hollywood looking for a job as an actor."[2] Some cynics believe he did!

According to Earl Mazo, his most friendly biographer, "Nixon classified himself a 'Liberal' in college, 'but not a flaming liberal.' Like many law students of that period, his public heroes were Justices Brandeis, Cardozo and Hughes, then the Supreme Court's progressive minority."[3] At Duke Law School on a scholarship, he graduated third in his class. Stewart Alsop quotes a former classmate: "My impression was that Richard Nixon was not an exceptionally brilliant student. However, he was outstanding because of his ability and willingness to do prodigious amounts of work. He pursued his ambition to stand at the head of his class with an intensity that few people are capable of."

The biggest excitement of his law school days came when he and two classmates became overeager to learn of their class standing at the end of the second year and, in the words of one of them, Bill Perdue, "broke into the dean's office during the summer to find out where they stood."[4]

Upon graduation, Nixon had his heart set on the "big apple" — New York. Although he graduated third in a class of twenty-six, none of the New York firms to which he applied showed any interest. Then he made application to the FBI, and accounts vary as to whether there was any response from that agency. In any case, Nixon returned to Whittier and entered law practice in his home town. After Pearl Harbor, Nixon hied himself to Washington looking for a job. According to Harvard's John Kenneth Galbraith (CFR):

> . . . the Office of Price Administration, where I was in charge of price control, rescued him — and hired Mrs. Nixon too. The primary credit goes, I believe, to Thomas I. Emerson, later Professor of Law at Yale, a valiant supporter of Henry A. Wallace and by all odds the most radical member of this very liberal agency. But Leon Henderson, who was in general command, gets bureaucratic credit and so do I. It hurts me that I never met Mr. Nixon in those days. I'm glad he's still under my influence.[5]

Nixon found life as an OPA bureaucrat suffocating, and in the spring of 1942 he applied for a Navy commission, disregarding the fact that as a Quaker he could easily have claimed exemption from active service. In the famous

"Checkers" speech of 1952, Mr. Nixon described his war record in these words:

> My service record was not a particularly unusual one. I went to the South Pacific. I guess I'm entitled to a couple of battle stars. I got a couple of letters of commendation, but I was just there when the bombs were falling, and then I returned.

That isn't just how it was. In fact, Stewart Alsop noted in *Nixon and Rockefeller* that " . . . Nixon had a non-combat job far from the battle lines . . . " For a few weeks, though, his naval unit was on the *fringe* of a combat area. But though he received a citation for efficiency in providing supplies — something he had been doing effectively with cabbages and parsley since the age of seventeen — he was certainly entitled to no battle stars.

During the long lonely nights in the backwaters of the Pacific war, Nixon did develop a talent that has doubtless stood him in good stead ever since. The young lieutenant became an expert — and very cagey — poker player. "He was the finest poker player I ever played against," fellow officer James Udall said. "I once saw him bluff a lieutenant commander out of $1,500 with a pair of deuces."

Another officer, Lester Wroble, said he never saw Nixon lose at the game — five-card stud or draw, nothing wild. "He was consistent. He might win $40 or $50 a night," Wroble said.

When Nixon entered politics by running for Congress from Whittier, his few thousand dollars of savings included money won at the poker table.[6]

Richard Nixon's entrance into politics was one of those quirks of fate. In a feature story the *Los Angeles Mirror* once observed: "It's still a matter of some amusement to Dick Nixon how he was transported from a small-town lawyer into a legislator. He answered a newspaper ad."[7] In reality it wasn't quite that simple. Republicans in Nixon's home district had for ten years been endeavoring unsuccessfully to unseat Democratic Congressman Jerry Voorhis. A candidate-finding "Committee of One Hundred" was formed to select an opponent to Vorrhis who had enough pizazz to defeat the veteran Congressman. The committee took its first step by sending to twenty-six newspapers in the district a publicity announcement describing its aims. What they wanted, it said, was a newcomer in politics with qualifications that might make him a match for the incumbent. The committee promised that its endorsement and financial support would not obligate the candidate in any way. An old friend of the Nixon family, Herman Perry, head of the Bank of America's Whittier Branch, fired a telegram to Nixon, who was awaiting his discharge from the Navy in Washington. Nixon tele-phoned Perry and told the banker he was definitely interested. Nixon was flown home for a November 1, 1945 appearance before a screening committee at the William Penn Hotel in Whittier. He told the assembled men that there were two schools of thought about the nature of the American system:

> One advocated by the New Deal is government control in regulating our lives. The other calls for individual freedoms and all that initiative can produce. I hold with the latter viewpoint. I believe the returning veterans — and I have talked to many of them in the foxholes — will not be satisfied with a dole or a government handout. They want a respectable job in private industry where they will be recognized for what they produce, or they want an opportunity to start their own business. If the choice of this committee comes to me, I will be prepared to put on an aggressive and vigorous campaign on a platform of progressive liberalism designed to return our district to the Republican Party.

Despite the fact that his closing sentence seemed to contradict what he had said before, Richard Nixon was tapped by the committee to carry the Republican banner into political battle against the seemingly unbeatable Mr. Voorhis. The "Committee of One Hundred" had hired an appealing symbol — one that could be well merchandised. He was young, industrious, well-educated, and very ambitious. His background exemplified the wholesome Protestant ethic of hard work and diligent self-improvement. Here was a young man who was going places.

Up to then, Richard Nixon says, he had had little interest in politics, but he accepted the offer with alacrity: "Why did I take it? I'm a pessimist, but if I figure I've got a chance, I'll fight for it." As the friendly Stewart Alsop observes: "Nixon became a politician, in short, more because it seemed a good idea at the time than because of any profound political convictions. Having thus entered politics more or less by accident, one suspects that he thought of a political career much as another young veteran back from the wars might think of advertising, or meat packing, or bond selling — as a way to make a living and get ahead."

Nixon's opponent, Jerry Voorhis, was a true maverick. Voorhis at one time had been a registered Socialist and was a staunch supporter of the New Deal's welfare and business control measures. But Voorhis broke with FDR on the question of the Federal Reserve System and deficit spending. Most Leftist politicians would rather slide down a bannister that turns into a razor blade than criticize the international banking fraternity, which probably contributes more money to the Democratic Party than do the labor unions. But Voorhis committed the unpardonable sin of introducing a bill into Congress calling for the end of the international banker-controlled Federal Reserve System. Voorhis then compounded the crime by writing a book called *Out of Debt, Out of Danger* for a conservative publisher, Henry Regnery and Company. *Out of Debt, Out of Danger* was a slashing attack on the international banking *Insiders*, who profit extensively from Keynesian deficit spending. FDR and his cronies had convinced most Americans that they need not worry about the mounting national debt because "we owe it to ourselves." Voorhis showed that we didn't owe it to ourselves, we owed it to the international bankers. Clearly, Voorhis had to go. He was a Liberal, but he was an anti-international banker Liberal — a variety scarcer than a woman of virtue in a house of ill-fame. Just what role, if any, the international banking clique played in Nixon's race against Voorhis is difficult to prove. It is reported, reliably we believe, that New York banking elements poured funds into the Nixon campaign and provided behind-the-scenes know-how from the Madison Avenue advertising firm of Batten, Barton, Durstine and Osborn, which also operates out of Los Angeles. Voorhis has hinted at this in print and been much more blunt about it in private conversations. William Costello, in his "unauthorized" biography of Nixon, wrote:

> Voorhis intimated later in his book that the Nixon campaign headquarters may not have been quite so impoverished as this story [a magazine story by Mrs. Nixon, which portrayed a shoestring operation] would suggest. The congressman said the representative of a large New York financial house made a trip to California in October 1945, about the time the Committee of One Hundred was picking Nixon, and called on a number of influential people in Southern California. The emissary "bawled them out" for permitting Voorhis, whom he described as "one of the most dangerous men in Washington," to continue to represent a part of California in the House. As a consequence, Voorhis said, "many of the advertisements which ran in the district newspapers advocating my defeat came to the papers from a large advertising agency in Los Angeles [at a time when this now common practice was unheard of], rather than from any source within the Twelfth District. And payment was made by check from that same agency."
>
> Just how much or whether outside interests actually contributed to Nixon's campaign has never been made clear.[8]

It should be noted here that William Costello, a Liberal, portrays Voorhis as simply a champion of the "little man," and says nothing of his *Out of Debt, Out of Danger*, his advocacy of the dismantling of the Federal Reserve, or his opposition to the international banking establishment. Voorhis was much more than just a foe of "big business." He was a foe of "big banking," and there is a difference — a difference that was much larger then than now.

Nixon waged an energetic and aggressive campaign against Voorhis. At first he wore his old Navy uniform while delivering speeches, until it was learned that rank-conscious ex-G.I.'s reacted to this practice with hostility. Nixon's campaign leaflets billed him as the "clean, forthright young American who fought in defense of his country in the stinking mud and jungles of the Solomons" while Voorhis "stayed safely behind the front in Washington." According to biographer Costello:

> . . . Nixon, canvassing the 200,000 voters of the district, introduced himself as a "liberal Republican." He refrained from attacking the New Deal in all its aspects, but he pulled no punches in attacking Voorhis.

As he was to do so successfully in future campaigns, Nixon made a major issue of Communism. He told the Republican kickoff rally in Whittier on August 29, 1946:

> I want you to know that I am your candidate primarily because there are no special strings attached to me. I have no support from any special interest or pressure group. I welcome the opposition of the PAC [the CIO's Political Action Committee], with its Communist principles and huge slush fund.

Later Nixon referred to Voorhis as "the PAC candidate and his Communist friends." The charge was damning, but not true. The PAC was indeed controlled by Communists, but Voorhis had been refused PAC support. Nixon's allegation was based on the fact that a local CIO unit had requested national approval of Voorhis, but it was rejected. The maverick Voorhis was not only anti-international banker, he was also strongly anti-Communist, and while he was a member of the House Committee on Un-American Activities had fought Communist penetration of PAC. The West Coast Communist paper, *People's World*, complained bitterly that "Voorhis is against unity with Communists on any issue under any circumstances."

But Voorhis was extremely vulnerable on the issue of socialism. Over and over candidate Nixon told audiences: "A vote for Nixon is a vote against . . . socialization of free American institutions." Liberals resented, and resent to this day, Nixon's linking of socialism with Communism. In doing so they ignore the fact that Marx made no distinction between the two and that it is a basic tenet of Communist philosophy that a nation must adopt socialism before Communism is possible. It is ironic that as President, Nixon has supported and expanded the very legislation and concepts he used to lash his first political opponent with. In the end, Nixon's aggressive tactics worked, and he was able to pull off one of the major upsets of the year by trouncing Voorhis 64,784 to 49,431.

As a Congressman Nixon carved out a moderately Conservative voting record on domestic issues and a Liberal one on foreign policy. From the beginning Nixon was a supporter of foreign giveaway programs, which have long been demanded by the international socialists and the CFR. Joseph Stalin had stated earlier, concerning the importance of foreign aid to the triumph of socialism:

> . . . It is essential that the proletariat of the advanced countries should render real and prolonged aid to the backward nationalities in their cultural and economic development. Unless such aid is forthcoming, it will be impossible to bring the various nations and peoples within a single world economic system that is so essential to the final triumph of socialism.[9]

Of course, such aid was indeed forthcoming.

In *Nixon and Rockefeller* Stewart Alsop tells us:

> Nixon has also loudly and consistently advocated an adequate foreign-aid program. Indeed, in Nelson Rockefeller's struggle . . . on this issue he was Rockefeller's strongest . . . ally.
>
> * * *
>
> Ever since the Herter committee days . . . he has been a strong advocate of foreign aid, with no visible political profit to himself. He is an internationalist, an activist, an interventionist . . . in foreign policy. [10]

Nixon defended his foreign aid stands on the basis that it was in America's interest to build up the free world so that it could resist Communism. Unfortunately, while examples can be cited in which foreign aid has done just that, in many more instances foreign aid money has been used to socialize countries and to oust anti-Communist leaders and replace them with "neutralists," who usually side with the Iron Curtain countries. Nixon's "internationalist" policies are simply those of the Council on Foreign Relations in its efforts to bring about a world superstate. Nixon's admitted mentor in this area, Christian Herter (CFR), a top *Insider* who later became Secretary of State after Dulles' death, had married into the Standard Oil fortune and served its internationalist interests well.

Nixon accompanied Herter to Europe to compile the reports that became the basis of the $17 billion Marshall Plan. Large amounts of the money were used to rebuild West Germany, where much of the industry had been bombed out during World War II but even more had been given to the Russians. In the aftermath of Yalta, the Bolsheviks had been allowed to cart off to Russia from *West* Germany entire factories, down to the last drill press, nut, and bolt. Nixon never mentioned this as one of the real reasons for the Marshall Plan. The Marshall Plan is usually pointed to as an example of the "success" of the foreign aid program, but it actually was used to promote socialism in Western European countries. Although the program was justified to Americans in the name of "anti-Communism," the Plan had been designed in part by a Russian-born Communist immigrant named Lewis Lorwin, who, according to Congressman Edward Cox, had been an associate of Leon Trotsky in the abortive Communist revolution of 1905. On March 29, 1948, after listing numerous persons in positions making policy for the Marshall Plan whose Far Left and Communist front backgrounds indicated what was happening, Cox told his fellow Congressmen: "To permit pro-Communists, Socialists, or collectivists of any hue to administer this American program, at any level, would be a grave mistake."

Even the name of the program was phony. The Marshall Plan was put together by Herter and his associates, including Communist Lewis Lorwin. Secretary of State George C. Marshall's name was tacked on to the Plan as a signal to Leftist forces around the world that the Plan was controlled by the Left. Marshall (CFR), a man who had been mysteriously promoted over the heads of thirty-four superiors to head the Joint Chiefs of Staff just as he was about to be retired after an unspectacular career, was well known in sophisticated revolutionary circles as one of their own.

Early in his Congressional career Nixon began to develop his reputation among both Liberals and Conservatives as a cynical opportunist. "Almost from the start," writes Costello, "Nixon showed a grasp of the opportunistic art of working one side of the fence while a bill was being amended and perfected, and then switching to the other side or being conveniently absent when the measure came to a final vote." [11] He was also careful to build contacts into both Conservative and Liberal wings of the Republican Party. In those days Nixon was a true pragmatist, interested not in ideology but in building his chosen career. One political observer noted that Nixon could spend one evening with the

"Modern Republicans," convincing them he was their best
ball carrier, and the next evening could convince the backers
of General MacArthur that he was their man. As Nixon
learned the Washington ropes, he became aware, possibly due
to his close association with Herter, that the behind-the-
scenes power in the Republican Party lay with Tom Dewey
(CFR), two-time unsuccessful Republican candidate for the
Presidency. Dewey ran the Eastern Liberal Establishment
wing of the Party for the Rockefeller and related New York
international banking interests. Probably through his connections with Dewey, Nixon became a founder of Republican
Advance, the Republican offshoot of the ADA that was
discussed in the previous chapter. Republican Advance was
established to mitigate the influence of the Taft wing of the
Republican Party and water down its anti-socialist policies. It
was financed by *Insiders* Nelson Rockefeller and Sidney
Weinberg, who wished to make the policies of the Republican
Party a carbon copy of Democrat Party policies. Later,
Republican Advance was to become "Citizens for Eisen-
hower," and to steamroller the outmaneuvered Taft people.

One of the key decisions of Nixon's Congressional career
was to accept a proffered assignment on the House Committee on Un-American Activities. Weighed in the balance was
the fact that the Committee offered an unparalleled opportunity to become widely known in a hurry and to take
advantage of the growing concern of the country over the
advances of Communism. Against this was the fact that the
Committee had been the recipient of a colossal smear job
from Communists, pro-Communists, and woolly-minded Liberals, many of whom had been sucked into Communist fronts
and were not happy about the exposure of their indis-
cretions. After due consideration Nixon decided to accept
the Committee assignment — a decision which started a chain
of events that would eventually put the young lawyer from
Whittier into the White House. The political climax of

Nixon's Congressional career was the Alger Hiss affair. In the short space of 134 days, between August 3 and December 15, 1948, Nixon's name became a household word, and as the two Hiss perjury trials dragged through the courts in 1949, with sensational revelation following sensational revelation, the "fighting Quaker," as Nixon loved to categorize himself, became a national celebrity.

During the summer of 1948, the House Committee called upon Whittaker Chambers, a senior editor at *Time* Magazine, to testify. Nixon recalled later that the witness "made charges which at the time seemed fantastic — that he'd been a Communist, that he had worked with Hiss, [Harry Dexter] White, [John] Abt, [Lee] Pressman, [Nathan] Witt, and a number of other people who were also connected with the government." Hiss had been a very important man in the New Deal, although he was not well known to the man in the street. According to Nixon biographers Mazo and Hess:

> . . . [Hiss] was highly respected in the government, and also in legal and diplomatic circles. Only the year before he had been appointed president of the Carnegie Endowment for International Peace at a salary of $20,000, which was $5,000 more than what was then paid Cabinet members and congressmen. The Carnegie board which hired him was composed of eminent men. Its chairman was John Foster Dulles, the Republican party's foremost expert on foreign affairs . . . . [12]

Hiss seemed beyond reproach. He had been at FDR's side while the ailing and failing President was dealing with the Russians, and he also had been the principal architect of the United Nations Charter. Mazo and Hess continued:

> . . . . Hiss had been principal adviser to the American delegation at the first United Nations General Assembly Session. Before that he had distinguished himself as secretary-general of the conference in San Francisco which created the United Nations. Furthermore, he had accompanied the Roosevelt party

to Yalta and had been executive secretary of the Dumbarton
Oaks Conference in 1944 . . . .

Hiss's was by far the most important name dragged out of
the reluctant Chambers, and Hiss demanded an immediate
hearing to answer Chambers' charges.

On the witness stand Hiss was smooth as glass. Not only
did his confident testimony contrast with the halting and
tortured words of Chambers, but the appearance of the tall,
slim, impeccably dressed Harvard graduate also contrasted
favorably with that of the dumpy and rumpled Chambers.
When Hiss concluded his testimony, the general feeling in
Washington was that the long-controversial House Committee
had just slit its own throat. Almost everyone was convinced
that Chambers had duped the Committee into using it as a
forum from which he could slander people. Congressman
John Rankin, an outspoken segregationist from Mississippi
who was hated by the Liberals with an absolute passion, was
so moved by Hiss's testimony that he left his seat to shake
Hiss's hand. That morning President Truman told a press
conference that Republicans had cooked up spy hearings "as
a red herring."

Legend has it that Nixon, due to his courtroom experience, detected that Hiss's testimony was just a little too
smooth. Later, to explain his "hunch," the California
Congressman called attention to a few lines of testimony that
had seemed to strike a phony note from the first.

> Q. You say you have never seen Mr. Chambers?
> A. The name means absolutely nothing to me.

Nixon, it seemed, perceived that Hiss was not answering
the question. Nixon later explained:

> As I read the testimony later I became convinced that if Hiss
> was lying he was lying in such a way as to avoid perjury, with a

very careful use of phrasing. He never made a categorical statement. He would say, "To the best of my recollection" over and over again. He never said, "I have never known Whittaker Chambers." He constantly reiterated when the question was put to him, "I have never known a man by the name of Whittaker Chambers." In other words, he was too careful in his testimony, too smooth. It was very possibly an act, it seemed to me.

Again, legend has it that, on the basis of these suspicions, Nixon followed up on the case and personally re-interviewed both Chambers and Hiss. This he did do, but not on his own initiative. The material on Hiss was not new in government security circles. Not only had Chambers told other investigators privately about Hiss on previous occasions, but the FBI had also been hot on Hiss's trail. In 1964, Nelson Rockefeller admitted that when he was attending the San Francisco conference as Assistant Secretary of State, he had met with FBI men in his hotel room every morning at 7:30.* According to Rocky, "They came in one morning and said, 'We've got the goods on Alger Hiss.' "[13]

In a TV interview on CBS in 1962, Senator Karl Mundt, who at the time of the Hiss case was chairman of the House Committee on Un-American Activities, revealed that an Assistant Secretary of State named Jack Peurifoy had shown him the State Department's dossier on Hiss, which "Truman would not let House investigators see." According to the Associated Press, "Mundt said his look at the security file on Hiss came before Richard Nixon, then a congressman, had

---

*Why did Rockefeller wait nearly twenty years before revealing this information about fellow CFR member Alger Hiss? Why did Rockefeller not relay this information to his superiors in the State Department? His excuse was that he had the feeling that "maybe this [the FBI] was a fascist organization in our midst." This provides us with a valuable clue as to the esteem in which Rockefeller holds J. Edgar Hoover and the F.B.I. His esteem for the United Nations, on the other hand, is indicated by the fact that, even though the UN Charter had been largely written by Soviet spy Alger Hiss, who was serving as Administrative Secretary General, the Rockefeller family had donated the land upon which the UN building stands.

made up his mind that Hiss was guilty." [14] Mundt was told by Peurifoy, "I know that what you're saying about Alger Hiss is true as I have access to the files of the State Department, which Truman will not let you have."

There were at this time a group of ex-Communists and former FBI agents in Washington who were working diligently to try to get the facts about Communist subversion and infiltration of government made public. This group worked on Nixon for months to try to impress upon him the importance of going after Hiss. One of these men, whose name still cannot be revealed, told the author:

> We had an awful time with Nixon. Nixon was very timid about it [pursuing Hiss]. He didn't want to do it. Some other members of Congress were recruited to apply additional pressure on him. He was anything but a tiger and some of us who helped create the Nixon image have lived to regret it. We didn't realize the extent to which he was chicken. He has been consistent in this particular weakness ever since.

Nixon had reason to fear taking on Hiss, despite the fact that he knew Chambers was telling the truth. Hiss was not only the fair-haired boy of the New Dealers, he was also a member of the Council on Foreign Relations, and John Foster Dulles (CFR), a top *Insider* and Rockefeller relative who had served as an attorney for numerous international banking firms and who was later to be Ike's Secretary of State, had appointed him as president of the Carnegie Endowment for Peace. In taking on Alger Hiss, Nixon was taking on not only the street-bunder-level Communists and their allies and sympathizers, but also his own future partners in the Eastern Liberal Establishment. On the other side of the scales was the opportunity to achieve fame and political advancement on the tide of revulsion against Communism that was rising across the land. Nixon decided to take the chance and the Nixon legend was born.

Commenting on this legend, Martin Dies, for many years chairman of the House Committee on Un-American Activities, wrote:

> ... in the case of Alger Hiss, there are many facts which have never been known by the public. Our people believe, for instance, that the discovery of Hiss was largely the work of Richard Nixon. The truth is that he had very little to do with it . . . . [15]

Dies continued, providing background to the Hiss case:

> . . . . We had known about Hiss for some time. As a matter of fact, Whittaker Chambers had come to my office several times and had told me about Hiss in very general and vague language. I knew what he was talking about because I had the information supplied by the Prime Minister of Canada; but Chambers was not ready to break openly with the Communists and testify. I knew that without his testimony we could not make out a case. I did what I could to persuade Chambers to testify as an act of atonement for his complicity in the theft of our secrets . . . .

Dies went on to explain:

> . . . I quit Congress [for reasons of health and election opposition from his own party leader, FDR] and Chambers began to contact my very able Chief Investigator and Secretary, Robert Stripling. When Whittaker Chambers finally decided to talk, it was to Stripling. Stripling could have given those facts to any member of the Committee and it would have made him famous and guaranteed his promotion to the Senate. He chose to select Richard Nixon, an obscure Congressman from California. The rest is history. It was the "breaking" of this story which put Nixon in the Senate and Vice Presidency. Richard Nixon should have been eternally grateful to Stripling and it was publicized that Stripling would be offered an important post in the Eisenhower Administration. He deserved it and had the ability to fill any post in the government with credit to the Administration.
>
> . . . I always had a feeling that Stripling wanted the recognition he deserved. So far as anyone else knows, he was never offered the opportunity to accept or reject. Nixon was placating

the "Liberals" and the last thing the "Liberals" would have tolerated was Robert Stripling in an important position. Furthermore, Eisenhower was a protégé of Roosevelt. He was implicated with Roosevelt in the stupid blunders which made it possible for Communism to become the greatest menace of all times. Eisenhower shared the views of Roosevelt about the Communists as disclosed by his various public statements which I quoted at length in my book, *Martin Dies' Story*. Nixon dared not displease Ike, and the recommendation of Stripling to an important post would have been very unacceptable to Eisenhower.

Nixon used Robert Stripling, and then ditched him as he has so many others who befriended him during his climb to the political peaks. Once Nixon made the decision that there was more to be gained than lost by going after Hiss, he was persistent. Hiss helped to seal his own doom by suing Chambers for calling him a Communist. Under that pressure, Whittaker Chambers produced a thick envelope containing four pages in Hiss' handwriting and a number of typewritten documents which he said had been copied on Alger Hiss' typewriter. He charged the envelope contained confidential State Department Documents which Hiss had pilfered and passed on to him in the service of the International Communist Conspiracy. Examination showed the papers were in fact copies of authentic top-secret documents; and other testimony established that the transmission to the Russians of verbatim texts of these papers would have enabled the Soviet government to break the State Department's secret code.

So powerful were the Communists in government that even in the face of all of this there was an intimation from the Justice Department that the Hiss-Chambers case would be dropped unless additional evidence could be found. At that point Mr. Nixon performed his penultimate service in the Hiss case. At a private interview with Chambers on the latter's farm in Maryland, Congressman Nixon learned that Chambers had in his possession additional documentary evidence. The next evening, in a cloak-and-dagger scene that fired the national imagination, an agent of the Committee served a subpoena on the ex-Communist; Chambers led him in darkness to a pumpkin in his garden, and from the pumpkin he drew five rolls of microfilm containing photostatic copies of confidential and secret documents stolen from the State Department.

A New York Grand Jury, on the verge of indicting Whittaker Chambers for perjury, reversed itself when Nixon rushed to New York and testified that it must have been Hiss who lied in saying he had not turned official documents over to Chambers. Simultaneously, the FBI was able to establish that the pumpkin papers had been typed on the same Woodstock typewriter as letters from Mrs. Priscilla Hiss. On December fifteenth, the Grand Jury climaxed its investigation by bringing in an indictment for perjury against Alger Hiss, who was later found guilty and jailed.*

For his role in exposing Hiss, Richard Nixon earned the undying hatred of a vast segment of the American Left. Hiss had been a fair-haired boy among the Liberals. Adlai Stevenson (CFR), Felix Frankfurter (CFR), and Dean Acheson (CFR) had served as character witnesses at his trial, and many another super-Liberal had gone out on a limb to defend him. Until Nixon's persistent investigation (actually Stripling's, but Nixon received credit for it) produced the evidence, the dapper and urbane Hiss was on the way to being cleared. Nixon left a lot of Liberal Democrats with egg on their faces as he concluded the experience, a national hero.

To this day many knee-jerk Liberals have never forgiven Nixon for his overrated role in pursuing Hiss, even though it was virtually his last anti-Communist act. Ever since the Hiss

---

*While on trial, Hiss stayed at the home of Helen Lehman Buttenwieser, whose husband, Benjamin J. Buttenwieser (CFR) is a partner in Kuhn, Loeb and Company, the international banking firm that was the major bankroller of the Bolshevik Revolution in Russia and has had close ties with Russia ever since.

case Nixon has worked hard to ingratiate himself with the Establishment Left, and though he continued to flay Communism verbally until 1968, there has been no action since the Hiss case to back up the laudable talk. Nixon, as Dies stated in his book, *Martin Dies' Story,* "was the only Congressman ever to profit by anti-Communist activity, and he profited only because he backed away from it." He parlayed the Hiss case into a Senate seat, the Vice Presidency, and eventually the Presidency. Seldom if ever in American political history has a man wrung so much mileage over so many years from a single act.

Even today, the Nixon-Hiss legend lives on. The ADA type of fuzzy-minded Liberal still goes into contortions when Nixon's name is mentioned. And although it is obvious that Nixon is now in league with the Eastern Liberal Establishment *Insiders* and has accepted their policy of working towards convergence with Communism in a world superstate, among well-meaning Republicans Nixon still benefits from the Hiss case. When it is pointed out that he is following the same CFR policies of appeasing the Communists as did Roosevelt, Truman, Eisenhower, Kennedy, and Johnson, the inevitable retort is: "Yes, but how about the Hiss case?"

The next step on Nixon's ladder to the Presidency was the capture of one of California's Senate seats. The incumbent, Conservative Democrat Sheridan Downey, was challenged in the Democratic primary by ultra-Leftwing Congresswoman Helen Gahagan Douglas. Mrs. Douglas, a former actress and wife of film star Melvyn Douglas, had been a member of two organizations cited by government investigating bodies as Communist fronts, while her husband, in addition to being a member of the ACLU, had joined six cited organizations. Nixon seemed like a long shot until Downey dropped out of the Democratic primary, naming reasons of health. Instead of facing a Conservative incumbent, Nixon now faced the vulnerable Helen Gahagan Douglas.

Those were lean days for many Leftist politicians. The Truman Administration had been rocked by corruption and spy scandals. To top it off, in June of 1950 the Korean "police action" broke out, and those whose voting records indicated they were "soft on Communism" were in trouble.

When Nixon announced his candidacy for Senator he declared that the main issue was "simply the choice between freedom and state socialism."[16] Although Nixon never, but never, uses the word "socialism" any more, when he announced for the Senate he proclaimed: "Call it planned economy, the Fair Deal or social welfare — but it is still the same old Socialist baloney, any way you slice it."[17]

The Nixon-Douglas campaign was one of the bitterest on record. Taking a cue from his friend, Florida Congressman George Smathers, who had knocked off rival Claude Pepper with the well-deserved appellation, "Red Pepper," Nixon dubbed Mrs. Douglas "the Pink Lady." Nixon Red-baited the Pink Lady unmercifully. The Republican candidate told audiences:

> . . . if she had had her way, the Communist conspiracy in the United States would never have been exposed . . . it just so happens that my opponent is a member of a small clique which joins the notorious Communist party-liner, Vito Marcantonio of New York, in voting time after time against measures that are for the security of this country.[18]

Marcantonio was a Congressman from New York City, where he represented the rather openly Communist-controlled American Labor Party. Mrs. Douglas retorted by trying to hang the Marcantonio albatross back around Nixon's neck, citing a couple of bills on which they had voted together. But it did not work against Nixon, who was basing much of his campaign on his exaggerated role in the Hiss case.

Mazo and Hess, among Nixon's most favorable biographers, comment on the reciprocal mud slinging:

An analysis of the Nixon and Douglas campaigns shows that the most notable difference was in the adroitness and calmness with which Nixon and his people executed *their* hyperbole and innuendo. When the Nixon camp questioned her fitness to be even a Democrat, for instance, or bemoaned her inability to judge between what was good for America and what was good for Russia, it was like a team of experienced surgeons performing masterful operations for the benefit of humanity . . . . when compared with the surgeons of the Nixon camp, Mrs. Douglas' operators performed like apprentice butchers . . . . [19]

Nixon's *pièce de résistance* in the campaign was the famous "Pink Sheet," a leaflet printed on pink paper (for obvious reasons), which the candidate's workers distributed by the basketful. Headlined "Douglas-Marcantonio Voting record," it began:

Many persons have requested a comparison of the voting records of Congresswoman Helen Douglas and the notorious Communist party-liner, Congressman Vito Marcantonio of New York.

Mrs. Douglas and Marcantonio have been members of Congress together since January 1, 1945. During that period, Mrs. Douglas voted the same as Marcantonio 354 times. While it should not be expected that a member of the House of Representatives should always vote in opposition to Marcantonio, it is significant to note, not only the *great number of times* which Mrs. Douglas voted in agreement with him, but also the issues on which almost without exception they always saw eye to eye, to-wit: Un-American Activities and Internal Security.

The sheet ended by asserting there was a "Douglas-Marcantonio Axis."

Naturally Liberals went into convulsions over the "Pink Sheet," and the less sophisticated ones still do. Defenders of Mrs. Douglas pointed out that Nixon himself had voted with Marcantonio 112 times during his four years in Congress (vs. Mrs. Douglas's 354 times in six years). The Pink Lady's apologists also pointed out that many Liberals had voted with Marcantonio on domestic issues, but this came off as rather a castigation of Liberals as socialists than a legitimate defense of Mrs. Douglas.

But in his ruthlessness, Nixon had passed over some important differences between Mrs. Douglas and Marcantonio. For one thing, there was no "Douglas-Marcantonio Axis," despite the similarity of their voting records. According to Mazo and Hess:

> In the California election, when Mrs. Douglas was first tied to Marcantonio by her Democratic primary opponent, Marcantonio went to a friend of Nixon's and said, chuckling, "Tell Nicky to get on this thing because it is a good idea." Marcantonio disliked Mrs. Douglas intensely and normally used an obscene five-letter word when referring to her in private conversations. [20]

There were also several key votes concerning Communism where Mrs. Douglas and Marcantonio voted against each other. Although Mrs. Douglas was blind in many ways about Communism (as she remains today) and was used by the Communists, she was not consciously pro-Communist. Mazo and Hess admitted:

> ... she was actually a vigorous foe of the Communist party and had fought Henry Wallace's Progressive party in a congressional district [Beverly Hills] where that took considerable courage. [21]

It was the "Pink Sheet" that led Nixon's opponents in the Democratic Party to label him "Tricky Dick." Later, Republicans who worked closely with him were to learn that the Democrats had assessed Mr. Nixon's character, if not his politics, correctly.

Another Nixon stunt that raised a furor during the Senatorial campaign was literature, mailed to thousands of registered Democrats, that pictured a smiling Nixon and family and greeted readers: "Fellow Democrats!" The excuse was that in those days in California politicians could cross-file and run on both the Republican and Democratic tickets simultaneously in primaries. Nixon had cross-filed in the Senate primary, but to address voters in the general election as "Fellow Democrats" was very tricky business.

As a climax to one of the twentieth century's most undignified campaigns, in the final hours the Nixon forces launched a telephone drive, promising that for anyone who answered the telephone with "Vote for Nixon," there would be:

> PRIZES GALORE!!! Electric Clocks, Silex coffeemakers with heating units — General Electric automatic toasters — silver salt and pepper shakers, sugar and creamer sets, candy and butter dishes, etc., etc. WIN WITH NIXON!

And win Nixon did — by 680,000 votes. At thirty-seven, Richard M. Nixon was a United States Senator from California.

As an epilogue to this contest, in 1957 Nixon was questioned by a British reporter about the campaign against Douglas. With dignified sadness he replied, "I'm sorry about that episode. I was a very young man."

Nixon's Senate career was short, lasting only nineteen months before his Vice Presidential campaign began, and was undistinguished, as one would expect from a freshman Senator. Nixon's voting record was very similar to the one he had achieved in the House, voting Conservative on most domestic issues and Liberal-internationalist on foreign policy. Nixon did, however, take a strong stand against the pulled-punches war in Korea. "Certainly we cannot ask our men to give their lives unless we back them to the hilt . . . " he told the Women's National Republican Club in New York. Nixon was very much a hawk on the Korean conflict, and was a strong supporter of General Douglas MacArthur after the General was fired by Truman for having the temerity to try to win the war. "MacArthur," he said, "was fired simply because he had the good sense and patriotism to ask that the hands of our fighting men in Korea be untied." Nixon pleaded for the avoidance of "tragic appeasement" and promised that the "policies of MacArthur will bring victory and peace in the Pacific . . . . "

On April 11, 1951, Nixon took the floor of the Senate to proclaim: "I believe that rather than follow the advice of those who would appease the Communists . . . we should do what we intended to do when we went into Korea, bring the war to a successful military conclusion . . . . " In order to accomplish this, the junior Senator from California recommended that the United States adopt MacArthur's program of stopping all free-world trade with Red China, bombing enemy bases on Chinese soil, imposing a naval blockade, and using Chiang Kai-shek's troops.

On April 27, Nixon made another speech before the Senate ridiculing the Administration's policy of fighting a land war "instead of using to the fullest extent our naval power and our air power."

"We are using our airplanes only for the purpose of tactical bombing," he said. "We are not using our navy for the purpose of a blockade . . . . We are unable to win a military victory in Korea. We are unable to do so because we are restricted in the use of both strategic bombing and naval power."

On May 1, Nixon expressed his thoughts about the then current peace talks: "I believe the only way we can end this war is not by a ninety-day-long 'peace talk' but by military victories and economic blockades to shut out all foreign trade and smuggling such as now continues to aid Red China. There can be no 'political' settlement."

All of this advice was militarily and politically sound; if it had been followed we would not be wallowing in the current mess in Asia. Moreover, by substituting the word "Vietnam" for the word "Korea," you have a perfect argument against the current policies of the Nixon Administration.

By this time Nixon was an acknowledged "comer" in the Republican Party. He had proved that an orthodox Republican could defeat a Liberal Democrat in an industrial state where one million more Democrats than Republicans were duly registered. Nixon now became the most sought-after Republican, and regularly broke away from his Senatorial duties to preach the gospel of national salvation through Republicanism. Always, the young Senator made a major issue of Communism, as in this statement:

> . . . one thing can be said to our credit which cannot be said for the party in power, that is, that we have never had the support of the Communists in the past. We have never asked for that support. We do not have it now, and we shall never ask for it or accept it in the future. And for that reason a Republican administration, we can be sure, will conduct a thoroughgoing housecleaning of Communists and fellow travelers in the administrative branch of the government because we have no fear of finding any Communist skeletons in our political closets.[22]

There is much mystery surrounding the events that led to Richard Nixon's selection to run on the Eisenhower ticket. We shall never know the whole truth, as we can never find out for sure what goes on in the back room among the boys with the cigars. Any story that is released to reporters is bound to be a heavily censored and edited version. In most cases the decisions which shape history are not put into the history books. As Harold Lavine remarks in his *Smoke Filled Rooms — The Confidential Papers of Robert Humphreys* (Humphreys was a professional staff member of the Republican National Committee):

> Nothing in politics just happens. There is always someone who sets the stage for it, writes the dialog, rehearses the actors, prompts them from the wings. True, sometimes the play takes on

a life of its own; the actors begin to ad-lib, the scenery collapses, the audience joins in the action. [23]

Some surface facts concerning Nixon's rise to the Vice Presidency are known, however. In May 1951, Nixon went to Europe as a member of the U.S. Delegation to the UN's World Health Organization. On June 5, while debating a bill on the floor of the Senate, Nixon mentioned that he had dropped in on Eisenhower at NATO headquarters in Paris. A week before leaving for Europe, Nixon had met in New York with the Eastern Liberal Establishment's powerful king-maker, Thomas E. Dewey.*

According to Mazo and Hess:

> His [Nixon's] New York appearance stood out because of what happened rather than what he said in his speech [at a fund-raising dinner], for Governor Dewey informed Nixon after the dinner that he should be the candidate for Vice President on the Eisenhower ticket. [24]

"The two of us sat around for about an hour or an hour and a half before he took his train," Dewey said. "That was the occasion on which I discussed with him briefly the possibility of him becoming the Vice-President." [25] It was no doubt Dewey who arranged for Nixon to see Eisenhower while he was in Paris. Dewey wasn't pulling an unknown rabbit out of a hat. Although Dewey had never been in the House or the Senate, he nonetheless controlled many Liberal Republicans and, as a political controller for the *Insider* Establishment, was a behind-the-scenes mover and shaker. According to those who know Nixon well, Nixon had become aware of the power and money wielded by Dewey and his New York colleagues, and as a highly ambitious man

---

*One of Dewey's sons, Thomas E. Dewey Jr., is now a partner in the international banking firm of Kuhn, Loeb and Company, the organization that financed Leon Trotsky and the Russian Revolution.

he had gravitated in their direction. This gravitation was tangibly expressed when Nixon became a founding member of the leftist Republican Advance.

Nixon, however, found himself in a sticky position as the nominating convention approached. He could not publicly endorse Eisenhower, because as a member of the California delegation he was pledged *by law* to support Governor Earl Warren as a favorite-son candidate until Warren released the seventy delegates; and Warren was not about to release any delegates, because he was hoping for an Eisenhower-Taft deadlock in which the convention would turn to him. Also, there was already no love lost between Warren and Nixon. Warren, who ran for governor on both Republican and Democratic tickets (thus taking advantage of California's then-existing cross-filing system, as had Nixon in running for the Senate), had never endorsed Nixon for either Congressman or Senator.

Paul Hoffman, as one of Eisenhower's chief lieutenants, had met twice with Nixon before the convention, to try to line up the California delegation for Eisenhower on the second ballot if the General needed only a few more votes to win and Warren's candidacy seemed hopeless. Since California came early in the roll call, a switch of its delegation's votes to Eisenhower could be psychologically crucial. The Eisenhower forces knew that if Warren released the delegation, Eisenhower would receive fifty-two of the votes to eighteen for Taft.

Meanwhile, in early June, Nixon conducted a private poll by mailing 23,000 letters to his 1950 precinct workers, asking them to name not their second choice, but "the strongest candidate the Republicans could nominate for president." It was charged, but never proved, that the Citizens for Eisenhower Committee paid for printing and addressing the survey. When Warren learned of Nixon's straw poll, the feathers hit the fan. Warren's people regarded the canvass as a stab in the back and a deliberate attempt to undermine the governor's position as a favorite-son candidate. If Warren won, it could do nothing to enhance his position; if he lost it would be a crushing psychological blow. Warren's fears were soon confirmed, as news began to "leak" from Nixon's office that Eisenhower was running far in front. Of course, Nixon's people were doing the counting.

Nixon went to Chicago on July 1, several days in advance of the rest of the delegation, as a member of the platform committee. Three days later he flew from Chicago to Denver and boarded the California delegation's convention train there, whereupon chaos ensued. There are numerous versions of what happened, but what had been a gay party disintegrated, and more intrigue took place on that train than on the Orient Express. Nixon began meeting with delegates in the lounge car, claiming that Eisenhower was a cinch on the first ballot (which Nixon could not have thought unless he already knew that many delegates were going to be stolen from Taft), and suggesting that the California delegation jump on the bandwagon so as not to waste its votes. If it did so, argued the Senator, it would be in a position to suggest as a *quid pro quo* the choice of Nixon as veep. Bitterness ran high among the Warren loyalists, who considered Nixon's actions as self-serving and a double-cross of the man he was legally committed to. The Warren people even talked of denying the Senator a berth on the train. By the time the train arrived in Chicago the split in the delegation was wider than the Grand Canyon, and Nixon detrained at a suburban station in order to avoid reporters' questions.

Having nudged the knife into Warren, Nixon now slipped the stiletto into Taft. He joined the move to outflank the Taft supporters by denying credentials to sixty-eight Southern delegates committed to Taft who were being challenged by Eisenhower delegations. It was at this crucial juncture that Nixon showed his hand publicly for the first time. Dashing to the microphone, Nixon addressed the California delegation and accused those who were the victims of theft of being thieves. The non-Machiavellian Taft people were dumbfounded and outflanked. In reply to pleas that the convention should accept the majority opinion of the credentials committee, Nixon proclaimed:

> If we were to feel that we were bound automatically to accept the decisions of our committees here, there would be no reason for us to come to the convention at all. We could leave the nomination entirely up to committees.

Of course, this was a complete *non sequitur*, but in the emotion of the moment it swayed many. The California delegation voted fifty-seven to eight to cast the state's vote for the misnamed "fair play" resolution. As Costello observed: "From that moment the drift toward Eisenhower became a stampede, and Nixon's future was assured."[26]

On July 11, Eisenhower was nominated on the first ballot, and the course of American history was dramatically changed. Future history may show that on that day America lost one of its best opportunities to save the Republic from the International Conspiracy of which Communism is an integral part — but only a part. From that day to this it has been all down hill for America. The Republic still can be saved, but at a much greater price than would have been required had Robert Taft been elected President of the United States.

That same day the first of two caucuses to select the General's running mate took place in Eisenhower's suite at the Blackstone Hotel. At the meetings, those involved went through the motions of considering numerous possibilities before settling on the man who had been pre-selected months in advance by the Dewey clique. Nixon's name was introduced by Dewey, who later recollected:

There were a lot of people with a lot of views. I waited until they had gotten down through the list. I didn't say much about it, until finally they had gotten from the East all the way across to the West. Then I named Nixon as the logical nominee.[27]

No one offered any objections, and Paul Hoffman, as chief spokesman for Citizens for Eisenhower, was invited to put his group on record.

"I told them that everything I had heard about Senator Nixon was good," the Establishment stooge later wrote in *Colliers* magazine. [28] "I looked on him as one of the Republicans who had an enlightened view [i.e., Liberal-internationalist-one world] on foreign affairs, and I thought that a man of his views should run with General Eisenhower."

Hoffman intimated that the Dewey forces were prepared to make a fight for Nixon if necessary, but as it turned out there was no need to do that. Nixon had much to recommend him as the candidate. He was geographically right, had a reputation as a fighter against corruption, subversion, and Communism, and was a vigorous campaigner. He was also regarded as a "bridge" to the alienated Taft people, to keep them from bolting the party in disgust after seeing the nomination stolen from their candidate. This role Nixon filled admirably, even though Stewart Alsop was later to write:

> The admiration for Nixon among the Taft-worshippers is essentially irrational, since Nixon contributed to Taft's last defeat in 1952 and since he has none of Taft's hankering for a simpler past. [29]

At this time in his career, Nixon was by no means a member of the Establishment, although he had doubtless realized that that was where the power lay within the Republican Party and beyond. The *Insiders* needed Nixon to pacify the Taft people and had good reason to believe that a man as inordinately ambitious for power and wealth as was Nixon could be controlled easily enough.

The Taft people should have realized that any man who was the protégé of the likes of Hoffman and Dewey was not a man they could trust.

Taft himself had seen enough of Richard Nixon working behind the scenes to realize that it was not for nothing that he was nicknamed "Tricky Dick." Following the '52 convention he told friend and supporter Joseph Polowasky that Nixon was "a little man in a big hurry." He also noted that the ambitious Californian had a "mean and vindictive streak," a fact that many others in and out of the Republican Party were to discover from firsthand experience. Taft expressed the fervent hope that circumstances would never propel Nixon into the Presidency. [30]

After the cigar smoke lifted from the back rooms at the 1952 convention, this question wafted out onto the breeze: How did Earl Warren, a man totally lacking in judicial experience, become Chief Justice of the Supreme Court? The events leading to his appointment were described by Frank Hanighen in *Human Events* in January 1958:

> By 1952, Warren considered himself the boy most likely to succeed to the top nomination — but, Warren-like, took out insurance to cover his candidacy. The policy was proffered, at the outset of the National Convention in Chicago, by representatives of candidate Dwight D. Eisenhower; they feared the General could not win the nomination unless the convention accepted Ike delegations sent by five Southern states in opposition to Taft delegations chosen by regular party process.
>
> Their proposition to Warren was simple; he could have his choice of Secretary of Labor or Interior when Ike became President, if he only cast California's . . . convention votes for himself on the actual balloting for the nomination, but he was just to vote to seat the Southern Eisenhower men. Warren demurred; the *quid pro quo* was raised to the first Supreme Court

vacancy, a lifetime job. He took it. California voted for the Ike delegations, and Taft's hopes went glimmering.

The payoff came in September 1953, with the untimely death of Chief Justice Fred Vinson. In a few days, Attorney General Herbert Brownell flew to Sacramento to tell Warren that, in compliance with the promise, President Eisenhower would nominate him to be an Associate Justice of the Supreme Court, naming one of the sitting Associates to the presiding chair. No, said Warren firmly; the promise to him was for the first vacancy, and since the first vacancy was the Chief Justiceship, he intended to have it. [31]

Needless to relate, Ike caved in and Warren became Chief Justice. The rest is tragedy.

Nixon's campaign for the Vice Presidency had just begun when one of his six (or more) crises popped up. The *New York Post* hit the streets on September 18 with a front-page story headlined: "Secret Rich Men's Trust Fund Keeps Nixon In Style Beyond His Salary." The story was picked up and blown out of all proportion by pro-Adlai Stevenson newspapers. There was indeed such a fund. It had been put together by Pasadena lawyer Dana Smith, according to Smith, so that Nixon could continue campaigning and selling concepts of free enterprise between formal elections. Nixon could not possibly have done this on his salary of $12,000 per year plus $2,500 for expenses. It would have been difficult to find an elected official in Washington who did not have some such fund; Adlai Stevenson himself had two. Smith had been careful to limit individual contributions to the fund to $500, so as to avoid any inference that "wealthy industrialists" were buying themselves a Senator. However, the *Washington Star* later revealed that Nixon's office had interceded on behalf of Smith himself in a Justice Department case in which a company owned by Smith's family was seeking a tax rebate of more than half a million dollars. Moreover, the legal opinion from the firm hired by the Republican National Committee to research the propriety of the fund acknowledged that, after interviewing "a number of contributors," the researchers had learned that "in two instances the contributor had contacted Nixon to request his assistance in connection with matter pending before a department or agency of the government."[32] In total, the fund had, in a little less than two years, raised $18,000, which was used to finance speaking trips, send Christmas cards to Nixon's 25,000 campaign workers, defray expenses on mail that could not be franked, and pay for long-distance telephone calls. Nixon claimed that "not one cent . . . went to me for my personal use." But he had earlier admitted to columnist Peter Edson that had it not been for the fund, he could not have made the down payment on his house in Washington.[33]

The revelation of the fund was a powerful weapon against the Republicans, who were making a big issue of dishonesty and corruption in the Truman Administration. The Democratic politicians grabbed at it in desperate self-defense, ignoring the fact that most politicians had funds of the same sort. The public, which in general did not know that the economic facts of life in Washington necessitated outside support, was, by and large, extremely upset. Nixon tried to counter by blaming the charges on the Communists. From the observation platform of his campaign train he told audiences:

> You folks know the work that I did investigating Communists in the United States. Ever since I have done that work, the Communists, the left-wingers, have been fighting me with every smear that they have been able to. Even when I received the nomination for the vice-presidency, I want you folks to know — and I'm going to reveal it today for the first time — I was warned that if I continued to attack the Communists and crooks in this government they would continue to smear me, and, believe me, you can expect that they will continue to do so. They started it yesterday — you saw it in the morning papers. They tried to say that I had taken the money, $16,000.
>
> What they didn't point out is this: that what I was doing was saving you money, rather than charging the expenses of my

office, which were in excess of the amounts which were allowed by the taxpayers and allowed under the law, rather than taking that money.

Rather than using the money, the taxpayers' monies for those purposes, what did I do? What I did was to have those expenses paid by the people back home who were interested in seeing that the information concerning what was going on in Washington was spread among the people of their state.

I'll tell you what some of them do. They put their wives on the payroll, taking your money and using it for that purpose. And Pat Nixon has worked in my office night after night after night, and I can say this, and I say it proudly, she has never been on the government payroll since I have been in Washington, D.C.

Point two: What else would you do? Do you want me to go on and do what some of these people are doing? Take fat legal fees on the side? During the time I've been in Washington — and I'm proud of this — I've never taken a legal fee, although as a lawyer I could legally but not ethically have done so, and I'm never going to in the future, because I think that's a violation of a trust which my office has . . . . [34]

Still there was no word from Eisenhower. Agonizing day followed agonizing day for Nixon as he waited for reassurance. Many key Republicans were calling for him to be dropped from the ticket. Dewey contacted Nixon and suggested that he bare his soul on national television. Out of this came the famous "Checkers Speech."

Shortly before going on the air for the "Checkers Speech," Nixon received a call from Dewey, bearing the bad news that most of Ike's advisers favored dumping Nixon. It seemed a hint for the candidate to resign on the air. The emotional strain was immense as Nixon went before the cameras with a hastily written speech scrawled on a note pad. The Senator delivered an emotion-laden speech that detailed the history of the fund, leaving out a point here and there, and adding that someone had also given his family a cocker spaniel, "Checkers," which his children loved, and they weren't going to give it back. Nixon closed his talk, not by resigning, but by putting the decision up to the Republican National Committee and asking the public to voice their sentiments to that body via telegrams.

The speech was described by Stevenson supporters as "soap opera schmaltz and mawkish ooze," but it was one of the most effective political speeches ever delivered. The Republicans received telegrams signed by more than one million citizens, overwhelmingly supporting Nixon. Nixon's political skin had been saved. That weekend he flew to Wheeling, West Virginia, where Eisenhower was on hand to greet him as "my boy."

Throughout the rest of the campaign Nixon worked tirelessly for the ticket, making as many as a dozen speeches a day. His formula was "K-1, C-3" — so-called for Korea, Communism, corruption, and costs. The Democrats were vulnerable on all items, and Nixon did not spare the rhetoric. He began on September 2, 1952, in a speech at Bangor, Maine, with the statement:

> We can anticipate charges of smear . . . if the record itself smears, let it smear. If the dry rot of corruption and Communism which has eaten deep into our body politic during the past seven years can only be chopped out with a hatchet — then let's call for a hatchet.

Some of his speeches showed the flair for alliteration that would help to make Spiro Agnew a household word nearly two decades later. On October 1, 1951, the candidate told assembled loyalists in Alexandria, Virginia:

> The Truman-Stevenson duet is simply designed to bamboozle the American people into continuing in power an Administration steeped in corruption, confusion, compromise and Communist-coddling.

Nixon reminded the public of the vast millions of people who had disappeared behind the Iron and Bamboo Curtains during the reign of the irascible man from Missouri. For this he justifiably blamed the Administration. The folks in Wilkes-Barre, Pennsylvania, heard this from the candidate on October 9:

> Because of recent attempts of Messrs. Truman, Acheson and Stevenson to falsify the record to cover up their failure to deal with the Communist conspiracy or to develop any program for meeting it in the future, I am going to take the case before the American people.

In the same vein, Nixon reiterated the truth to an audience in Utica, New York, on October 18:

> I charge that the buried record will show that Mr. Truman and his associates, either through stupidity or political expedience, were primarily responsible for the unimpeded growth of the Communist conspiracy within the United States. I further charge that Mr. Truman, Dean Acheson and other Administration officials for political reasons covered up this Communist conspiracy and attempted to halt its exposure.

Two of Nixon's favorite targets in these days were Truman's Secretary of State, Dean Acheson, and his policy of "containing" Communism. On October 16, Hoosiers in Evansville heard the candidate proclaim:

> I say, make "containment" read "appeasement." Yet Adlai Stevenson — who carries a Ph.D. from Dean Acheson's cowardly college of Communist containment — approves this disastrous policy.

In those days the Republicans were calling for victory over Communism, not proposing an "era of negotiation." Acheson (CFR) was a particularly juicy target, since he had surrounded himself with Alger Hiss, Owen Lattimore, John Stewart Service, Oliver Clubb, John Carter Vincent, Lauchlin Currie, and their like — all of them either Soviet spies or security risks. Undoubtedly it was just a coincidence, but Joseph Stalin had hired Acheson to be the Soviet Union's personal attorney in the United States prior to the official recognition of the Soviets by FDR. Just how Stalin happened to pick Acheson to serve as the Bolsheviks' barrister has not, to our knowledge, ever been explained. There is of course the possibility that he happened to be browsing through the Yellow Pages and found Acheson's name at the top of the page. During Acheson's tenure as their legal representative, the Communists made tremendous advances throughout the world. Acheson had also been responsible for elevating Hiss to a high position in the State Department, and even after Hiss had been convicted of perjury for lying about his spying for the Soviets, Acheson announced: "I will not turn my back on Alger Hiss." Since Nixon was deeply involved in the Hiss case, and since he and Acheson were such violent enemies, it is truly one of the great ironies of the Nixon Administration that Dean Acheson should be able to an-nounce, as he did on his CBS Special with Walter Cronkite, that he is now a behind-the-scenes advisor to President Nixon. CFR politics makes strange bedfellows. Maybe Nixon too was browsing through the Yellow Pages.

Journalist Clark Mollenhoff, until recently a member of Nixon's staff, disclosed:

> He [Kissinger] has his admirers and detractors.
> Among the former are former Secretary of State Dean Acheson, who believes that our foreign policy is a mess, but that Henry Kissinger's handling of things in the White House is the only reason that the United States is not in more difficulties in the world.[35]

The anti-Communist rhetoric of Nixon in 1952 contrib-uted to Eisenhower's landslide victory, as the victory-starved Elephant Team swept thirty-nine states and corralled 442 electoral votes.

References
1. William Costello, *The Facts About Nixon*, New York, Viking Press, 1960.
2. *Los Angeles Times*, May 10, 1970.
3. Earl Mazo, *Richard Nixon*, New York, Harper & Brothers, 1959.
4. United Press International, November 2, 1970.
5. *Life*, March 27, 1970.
6. United Press International, *loc. cit.*
7. *Los Angeles Mirror*, July 14, 1952.
8. Costello, *op. cit.*, p. 51.
9. Quoted by Under Secretary of State Spruille Braden in the *Dan Smoot Report*, June 22, 1959.
10. Stewart Alsop, *Nixon and Rockefeller*.
11. Costello, *op. cit.*, p. 180.
12. Earl Mazo and Stephen Hess, *Nixon, A Political Portrait*, New York, Harper & Row, Popular Library Edition, 1968, p. 46.
13. *National Review*, January 28, 1964.
14. Associated Press, July 30, 1962.
15. *American Opinion*, May 1964, pp. 66-67 (Martin Dies, "Treason").
16. Mazo, *op. cit.*, p. 65.
17. *Ibid.*, p. 66
18. *Ibid.*, p. 72.
19. *Ibid.*
20. *Ibid.*, p. 74n.
21. *Ibid*, p. 67.
22. *Ibid.*, p. 78.
23. Harold Lavine, *Smoke Filled Rooms – The Confidential Papers of Robert Humphreys*, Englewood Cliffs, N.J., 1970.
24. Mazo, *op. cit.*, p. 77.
25. *Ibid.*, p. 81.
26. Costello, *op. cit.*, p. 88.
27. Mazo, *op. cit.*, p. 86.
28. *Colliers*, October 26, 1956.
29. Alsop, *op. cit.*, p. 29.
30. Costello, *op. cit.*, p. 7.
31. *Human Events*, January 6, 1958.
32. *Washington Star*, September 24, 1952.
33. *Los Angeles Daily News*, September 17, 1952.
34. Mazo, *op. cit.*, pp. 102-103.
35. *Independence Press-Telegram*, March 7, 1971.

CHAPTER VI

Purging The Party Of Patriots

The Eisenhower-Nixon team triumphed in the 1952 election by promising to stem Communist aggression abroad, root out Red infiltrators at home, and reverse the socialistic policies of the New Deal. The party platform promised:

> We shall eliminate from the State Department and from every Federal office, all, wherever they may be found, who share responsibility for the needless predicaments and perils in which we find ourselves. We shall also sever from the public payrolls the hordes of loafers, incompetents and unnecessary employees who clutter the administration of our foreign affairs . . . . The Government of the United States, under Republican leadership, will repudiate all commitments contained in secret understandings such as those of Yalta which aid Communist enslavements . . . . We shall again make liberty into a beacon light of hope that will penetrate the dark places . . . . We shall see to it that no treaty nor agreement with other countries deprives our citizens of the rights guaranteed them by the Federal Constitution . . . . There are no Communists in the Republican party . . . . We never compromise with Communism and we have to expose it and eliminate it in government and American life. A Republican President will appoint only persons of unquestioned loyalty . . . . Reduction of expenditures by the elimination of waste and extravagance so that the budget will be balanced and a general tax reduction can be made.

But all this was not to be. A former assisstant to J. Edgar Hoover, Dan Smoot, has declared:

> If Stevenson had won in 1952, the growing anti-Communist,

165

anti-socialist, anti-world government sentiment of the people would have continued to grow with accelerated speed, because it was apparent that Stevenson meant a continuation of Truman's policies.

But millions thought their revolt had succeeded when Eisenhower and Nixon were elected. Eisenhower and Nixon, riding into office on the crest of a great wave in the swelling anti-communist, anti-socialist movement, destroyed the movement by giving it lip service, while vigorously supporting the very policies they were elected to oppose.[1]

Calling this "the most tragic irony in the history of America," Smoot continued by saying:

... The Eisenhower-Nixon team, elected in 1952 because it was considered strongly anti-communist, broke the back of the anti-communist movement in the United States!

Given Ike's debt to FDR and the *Insiders* around him, this is not surprising. Exactly as George C. Marshall had been elevated to Chief of Staff, Ike was picked by the Roosevelt Administration in 1942 to be Allied Commander in North Africa, over the heads of 366 Army officers who outranked him. To contend that these were both coincidences is to insult all logic. How much Eisenhower owed to the Roosevelt Administration may be seen in the fact that he was only a Lieutenant Colonel at the outset of the war, and his career, like Marshall's, was considered a flop. In 1943, with the same backing that Marshall had, he became Supreme Commander of Allied Forces in Europe.

History has shown that the man who bears the actual title of President of the United States is not always the man who really wields the power. Behind Woodrow Wilson there was Colonel House. Behind FDR was Harry Hopkins. Those who really ran the United States while Eisenhower was on the putting green were Sidney Weinberg, Milton Eisenhower (CFR), Sherman Adams (CFR), John

Foster Dulles (CFR), and Paul Hoffman (CFR), all lifelong devoted Leftists. This group came to be known as the "Palace Guard."

The Hearst newspapers of July 6, 1953, over the byline of their Washington Bureau, said: "The man-behind-the-guns in the Eisenhower Administration is Sidney James Weinberg, Wall Street investment banker." Weinberg, until his recent death, was a partner in the international banking firm of Goldman, Sachs and Company. An article in the *New Yorker* magazine in 1956 pointed out:

> [Weinberg] has been a liaison between Wall Street and the White House ever since the inception of the New Deal. In the early '30's, he was among the few prominent men in big-money circles whom President Roosevelt could count on for support, and during both the 1932 and 1936 Presidential campaigns he was assistant treasurer of the Democratic National Committee.[2]

The same article quotes *Business Week* as calling Weinberg "an ambassador between financiers and politicians," and says that, " . . . though largely unknown to the man in any street but Wall, [Weinberg] is among the nation's most influential citizens. In his role as a power behind the throne, he probably comes as close as Bernard Baruch."[3]

Continuing, the *New Yorker* article observes: "There is hardly a ramification of the money and credit business in which Goldman, Sachs is not active." In FDR's administration Weinberg was one of the organizers of the Business Advisory Council, an unofficial arm of the Council on Foreign Relations created to get the approval of businessmen for the New Deal.

A hallmark of the true *Insider* is that he is equally at home in either political party, since he knows that while the parties talk a slightly different language they are controlled by the same people. In 1940, having supposedly concluded that a third term for FDR was unsound, "Weinberg popped up as a

founder of and diligent fund-raiser for the Democrats for
Willkie."[4]

In 1951, Weinberg became a financial backer of Republican Advance, the ADA of the Republican party.[5] In 1952,
Republican Advance, of which, it will be remembered, Richard Nixon was a charter member, changed its name to Citizens for Eisenhower-Nixon, and Weinberg became its treasurer. Was it very difficult for this super-*Insider* to infiltrate the
Republican Party? Not at all. "The Republicans are not very
bright," observed Weinberg.[6] The *New Yorker* article
informed us:

> When Eisenhower was President-elect, he asked three trusted
> and well-informed agents — [Lucius] Clay [CFR], Sherman
> Adams [CFR] and Herbert Brownell [CFR] — to draw up a list
> of recommendations for the cabinet he would have to appoint.
> These three men, in a sense, were acting as Eisenhower's advisors,
> but in this complex political age even advisors need advisors, and
> among those the trio turned to was, most notably, Weinberg.[7]

Goaded by his mysterious backers, Ike began purging
Conservatives from the Republican Party instead of Commu-
nists from the government. First to feel the wrath of the
"New" Republicans were the followers of Robert Taft. The
Taft-Conservative wing of the party had closed ranks behind
the Eisenhower-Nixon ticket, thanks largely to the work of
Nixon, despite the fact that following the convention
Eisenhower's advisor and intimate, Paul Hoffman, had
returned to Pasadena and held a press conference, at which
he said, in substance, according to a story by Morrie
Ryskind: "The GOP has finally rid itself of the Taft incubus,
and our job now is to get rid of all the Taft adherents."[8]

After helping to defeat Adlai Stevenson handily, Conservatives hoped that Eisenhower would appoint some Taft
supporters to key cabinet positions, to implement the
promises of the Republican Party platform. But the only

Taft supporter to be appointed to the cabinet was Ezra Taft Benson, who served in the post of Secretary of Agriculture.

Former Republican Congressman Howard Buffett explained how cleverly Conservatives were being purged in the Eisenhower Administration:

> During Ike's first weeks in office, a list of Taft Republicans to be purged was prepared at the White House. In this strategy the Modern [Liberal] Republicans did not make Roosevelt's mistake in announcing their aims. Instead they laid their plans secretly and no public exposure of their tactics ever appeared. The frequent disappearance of conservative Republicans from public office and political influence in the following years was mute testimony to the effectiveness of this liquidation policy.[9]

It had not taken Bob Taft long to read the handwriting on the Eisenhower Administration's wall. In the White House on April 30, 1953, before a dozen Congressmen and others, Taft told Eisenhower: "You're taking us right down the same road that Truman traveled. It's a repudiation of everything we promised in the [1952] campaign."[10]

Instead of building his administration around Conservatives and anti-Communists, Eisenhower continued the reign of the CFR members who had controlled the Roosevelt and Truman Administrations. CFR members holding key slots in the Eisenhower Administration included:[11]

President of the United States, Dwight D. Eisenhower;

Vice President of the United States, Richard M. Nixon;

Director of the Central Intelligence Agency, Allen W. Dulles;

Secretary of State, John Foster Dulles;

Secretary of State, Christian A. Herter (succeeding John Foster Dulles);

Secretary of the Treasury, Robert B. Anderson;

Secretary of the Navy, Thomas S. Gates;

Secretary of Labor, James P. Mitchell;

Secretary of Commerce, Lewis L. Strauss;

Under Secretary, Department of Health, Education and Welfare, Nelson A. Rockefeller;

Special Assistant to the President for National Security Affairs, Gordon Gray;

Special Assistant to the President, James R. Killian Jr.;

Staff Secretary to the President, Brig. Gen. A.J. Goodpaster, USA;

Under Secretary of State for Economic Affairs, Douglas Dillon;

Deputy Under Secretary of State for Political Affairs, Robert Murphy;

Assistant Secretary of State for European Affairs, Livingston T. Merchant;

Assistant Secretary of State for African Affairs, Joseph C. Satterthwaite;

Assistant Secretary of State for International Organization Affairs, Francis O. Wilcox;

U.S. Ambassador to the United Nations, Henry Cabot Lodge;

Atomic Energy Commission, John A. McCone; and

U.S. Representative on Disarmament, James J. Wadsworth.

The Republican Party platform of 1952 had stated:

> We shall eliminate from the State Department and from every Federal office, all, wherever they may be found, who share responsibility for the needless predicaments and perils in which we find ourselves.

The "Palace Guard" carried this plank out — and buried it. Instead of eliminating those in the State Department responsible for Yalta, China, and other tragic disasters, the Eisenhower Administration promoted to Secretary of State one of the individuals who were most responsible, John Foster Dulles. Dulles had been a protégé of Colonel House and was a founder of the Council on Foreign Relations. He was also a protégé of Dean Acheson, the Secretary of State on whose record of successive losses for America the Republicans had based much of their campaign against the Democrats. Senator William Jenner of Indiana wrote: "Mr. Dulles is Mr. Acheson's identical twin." Dulles had become officially a right-hand man of Acheson in 1950, and was so completely a part of the Truman foreign policy menagerie that he no longer gave his address to *Who's Who in America* as 48 Wall Street, New York, where his law office was, but as "Department of State, Washington."

Dulles was a strange individual to oversee the promised clean-up of the State Department. The appointment of Dulles as Secretary of State appeared strange and disillusioning even to William F. Buckley Jr., who wrote in *Human Events* of April 18, 1953:

> The principal reason why the Senate and the people should have no confidence in Dulles on matters relating to loyalty and security is his reversal, in February, of the Civil Service Loyalty Board's findings that a "reasonable doubt" does indeed exist as to John Carter Vincent's loyalty. Not only did Dulles overrule this highly cautious board, he also exonerated Vincent on the lesser, looser, laxer score by declaring that neither is there "reasonable doubt" that Vincent is a security risk. Now, the evidence against Vincent, garnered from a study of his career, is very persuasive . . . .
>
> But even apart from Vincent's activities and associations in China, there is the testimony of Louis Budenz, who asserts that he knew Vincent to be a member of the Communist Party . . . . Mr. Dulles in effect declared that there is no reasonable doubt that Louis Budenz is a liar. And this in spite of the fact that on the basis of thousands of pages of secret testimony, corroborating wherever possible, the FBI gives Budenz the highest reliability rating . . . . Mr. Dulles dealt the federal security program . . . . an Achesonian blow.

It was John Foster Dulles, then, who was appointed by Ike, or for Ike, to clean the security risks out of the State Department and to put a termination to the "America last"

CFR foreign policy, as had been promised in the 1952 Republican Party platform. It has been observed of Dulles that he always said the right thing and always did the wrong one. In speeches and public statements, Dulles was always the proponent of the real American position, the man who announced the policies and intentions which the American people wanted to hear and which they recognized as right. The American people for the most part were not aware that he did just the opposite of what he proclaimed. But that, one must remember, is the way the *Insiders* operate.

During World War II Dulles was appointed chairman of the Federal Council of Churches' Inter-Church Commission to Study the Bases of the Just and Durable Peace. In early March of 1942, that organization held a conference at Delaware, Ohio. Chairman John Foster Dulles submitted the report, which had been approved by the members of his committee. It included the following recommendations:

One, ultimately a world government of delegated powers;

Two, complete abandonment of United States isolationism;

Three, strong, immediate limitations on national sovereignty;

Four, international control of all armies and navies;

Five, a universal system of money;

Six, world-wide freedom of immigration;

Seven, progressive elimination of all tariff and quota restrictions on world trade;

Eight, a democratically controlled international bank.

Chairman Dulles, an in-law of the Rockefellers and long-time attorney for the international bankers, placed on the United States much of the blame for the Second World War. His report said:

> It should be a matter of shame and humiliation to us that actually the influences shaping the world have largely been

irresponsible forces. The natural wealth of the world is not evenly distributed. Accordingly, the possession of such natural resources . . . is a grant to be discharged in the general interest.

Time magazine of March 16, 1942, which carried under Dulles' picture the caption, "Shame on U.S.," stated:

Some of the conference's economic opinions are almost as sensational as the extreme internationalism of its political program. It held that a "new order of economic life is both imminent and imperative" — a new order that is sure to come either "through voluntary cooperation within the framework of democracy or through explosive political revolution." Without condemning the profit motive as such, it denounced various defects in the profit system for breeding war, demagogues and dictators, "mass unemployment, widespread dispossession from homes and farms, destitution, lack of opportunity for youth and of security for old age." Instead, "the church must demand economic arrangements measured by human welfare . . . . "

Dulles was a prominent and much publicized member of the first meeting of the World Council of Churches, held in Amsterdam in 1948, at which that body officially declared capitalism to be just as evil as Communism.[12] Dulles neither protested nor disavowed the resolution.

An idea of what John Foster Dulles had in mind in his pursuit of American foreign policy was given in *U.S. News & World Report*, December 28, 1956, where Dulles said: "It is very important that this satellite situation should develop in a way that the Soviet Union is surrounded by friendly countries." Commenting upon an earlier similar statement, Frank Meyer, now of *National Review* magazine, wrote:

Surely if the administration had the faintest sense of reality about the character of the struggle, the tightest possible encirclement of the Soviet Union by the most hostile peoples would be one of our first aims. What is Secretary Dulles saying? That any friends we have in the periphery of the Soviet empire are to be sacrificed to the Russian desire for captive neighbors? How does this differ from the policy of Yalta, the sellout of Poland in 1945?

You will recall that during the 1952 campaign, Nixon had called the Truman-Acheson policy of "containment" of Communism "cowardly." Under Dulles the Eisenhower Administration did not repudiate the Yalta agreements as promised in the platform, but instead repudiated any repudiation of the agreements. Since Dulles was a founder of the Council on Foreign Relations it is not surprising that he was a strong supporter of Atlantic Union, which advocates changing NATO from a defense alliance into a complete political union.[13] The *San Francisco Examiner* of May 4, 1956, called Dulles' program "world government in disguise," and said that Eisenhower "fully supports the 'Dulles plan.'"

Despite the fact that Nixon had achieved great political mileage out of horsewhipping Dean Acheson for his, at best, badly mistaken policies towards Communism, he quickly gravitated toward Acheson's protégé, Dulles. Writing in *Look* magazine, Earl Mazo was to note:

> Only a few have known that the relationship between Nixon and Dulles was perhaps the warmest in the Administration . . . . Dulles was Nixon's behind the scenes adviser in many cases, especially during Eisenhower's illness.

It is not surprising that Nixon would feel an affinity for Dulles. Both possessed the ability to project a public image which ran quite counter to their actions. But sophisticated Washington watchers must have laughed to see the supposedly militant anti-Communist Nixon cozy up to Acheson's sidekick, Dulles. Acheson, in 1971 an unofficial Nixon adviser, was Nixon's favorite target in 1952, with statements like this:

> Stevenson himself hasn't even backbone training, for he is a graduate of Dean Acheson's spineless school of diplomacy which cost the free world six hundred million former allies in the past seven years of Trumanism.[14]

Four days later Nixon again linked Stevenson with Acheson, the man who said he would not turn his back on Alger Hiss after Hiss was convicted of perjury regarding his activities in spying for the USSR: "[Stevenson's] entire record shows that he is incurably afflicted with Acheson color-blindness — a form of pinkeye — toward the Red threat."[15]

While campaigning for the Presidency in 1952, Ike told a Milwaukee audience that Communism had:

> . . . insinuated itself into our schools . . . and our government itself. What did this contamination into government mean? It meant contamination to some degree of virtually every section of our government . . . . We have all had enough, I believe, of those who have sneered at the warnings of men trying to drive Communists from high places — but who themselves have never had the sense or the stamina to take after the Communists themselves . . . .

Eisenhower's Attorney General, Herbert Brownell, started to expose some of the Communist influence in the Truman Administration. One week after Brownell's public revelation about Communist spy Harry Dexter White in 1953, he was silenced. Brownell got the picture. The exposures ceased.

After promising to investigate the Communists in "every department," Eisenhower let stand an order issued by Truman in 1947, prohibiting access by Congress to government files on the loyalty of personnel. Another 1948 directive by Truman forbidding government officials to give information to Congressional committees without White House permission was also left standing by Eisenhower. And on Friday, May 17, 1954, Eisenhower issued an order forbidding government departments to provide any information to investigating committees, which went far beyond the Truman "gag" rule. Chairman Francis Walter of the House Committee on Un-American Activities called the Eisenhower Executive Order "incredibly stupid."[16] No one, apparently, considered that from the standpoint of the *Insiders* the move was *incredibly smart*. Congressional committees were now, for all practical purposes, out of the business of investigating Communists and other subversives in the government — in complete repudiation of Eisenhower's campaign promises. This was also a complete repudiation of the idea that the American public has the right to know what its government is doing. As early as October 18, 1953, after campaigning on promises to clean the Communists out of the government, Eisenhower told a news conference that he hoped the whole security issue of Communists in government would be "a matter of history and memory by the time the next election comes around." He deplored the fear of Communism in government and "the suspicion on the part of the American people that their government services are weak in this regard."[17]

The "great crusade" that Eisenhower during his campaign had promised to lead turned out to be a pied piper's pipe dream. The "Communist threat" disappeared under Eisenhower just as the "missile gap" did right after John F. Kennedy's election. Eisenhower did, however, lead one "crusade": the crusade to "get" Senator Joseph McCarthy of Wisconsin. *Human Events* stated:

> It is now obvious the Administration, striving desperately to down Senator McCarthy, has embarked upon a series of moves which, if successful, will take the nation a long way toward dictatorial government. These moves are depicted as an effort of President Eisenhower to shield himself from a McCarthy "domination" of the Republican party which, of course, is sheer moonshine. Back of these moves are the leftwing groups that have

successfully penetrated the Republican party and who see in Senator McCarthy a chance to build an omnipotent executive who will have the power to hasten the establishment of a Socialist state in America.[18]

McCarthy had been tolerated during the 1952 campaign, even though Eisenhower's backers despised him, because at that time the monumental smear job against him had been largely ineffective. In 1952, McCarthy had more supporters than detractors. In the years since then little has been said in defense of McCarthy, but the Liberal Establishment has continued to defame him to such a point that today there is hardly an American who does not believe that the Wisconsin Senator made outlandish and unprovable charges.

As it became obvious that Acheson's old subordinate, John Foster Dulles, had no intention of carrying out the campaign promises of Eisenhower and Nixon to clean out the State Department, McCarthy began to turn the heat on the Eisenhower administration. The ex-Marine was proving to be disturbingly nonpartisan on the Communist infiltration issue. Nixon was assigned to try to divert McCarthy onto other issues.

The Vice President had been a close friend of McCarthy's, and McCarthy apparently trusted Nixon. For a while he toned down his attacks. Nixon is credited with persuading McCarthy to call off his threat to investigate the Central Intelligence Agency, which the Dulles brothers had been primarily responsible for founding. Nixon also talked McCarthy into firing J.B. Matthews as his chief investigator, after Matthews published a magazine article thoroughly documenting the depth of penetration by Communists of religious bodies, including the National Council of Churches, and the success with which the Communists had enticed tens of thousands of non-Communist, liberal clergymen into joining their fronts. McCarthy was also upset with the Eisenhower Administration's position on relaxing aid and trade restrictions against the Iron Curtain countries. The Wisconsin Senator had written a scathing letter to Eisenhower on the subject, but Nixon persuaded McCarthy to let him intercept the letter before it reached the President.

The Vice President attempted to divert McCarthy's energies to other matters. He told the Wisconsin Senator: "You should not be known as a one-shot Senator."[19] After visiting McCarthy in Florida, Nixon told reporters that McCarthy would turn his attention to Democratic corruption and away from the Communist issue. McCarthy apparently decided that whatever promises had been made to him that the Eisenhower administration would slowly and without fanfare get around to the "subversion in government" issue were not going to be kept. He denounced as a lie Nixon's statement to the press that McCarthy would lay off the Communism issue.

When it became obvious to the "Palace Guard" that Nixon could no longer control McCarthy, a way had to be found to engineer the Senator's downfall. The three most important men in arranging the destruction of McCarthy were William Rogers, then Assistant Attorney General and now Secretary of State; Henry Cabot Lodge, currently Nixon's ambassador to the Vatican; and Ford Foundation official Paul Hoffman. Fulton Lewis Jr. said:

> One man above all others in the White House family hated Joe McCarthy, and that man was Paul G. Hoffman, the President's confidante whom he named to the United Nations . . . . Paul Hoffman, in his hatred, helped to pay for the lawyers who drew up the censure charges which Senator Flanders of Vermont lodged against Senator McCarthy, and which finally — though proven to be false — resulted in McCarthy's censure. [Hoffman was the darling of the United World Federalists, of whom Flanders was one.]
>
> On July 19th of last year, Senator Flanders openly admitted this act on the floor of the United States Senate, at that time he publicly apologized to Senator McCarthy for what he had done.

He said he wished the whole thing could be forgotten, but he did admit that Mr. Hoffman contributed $1,000 for the drafting of those false charges.

Hoffman, who hated Taft, McCarthy and all the anti-Communists with a passion, you will remember, married a Communist. [Hoffman's wife is Anna Rosenberg, who has been the public relations brains behind Nelson Rockefeller's political career.] What the "Palace Guard" was attempting to do was to make the White House into a Bergen with only Charlie McCarthys in Congress, not Joe McCarthys.[20]

In his article for *Colliers* magazine, "How Ike Saved the Republican Party," Hoffman had made it plain that McCarthy and the anti-Communists were to be purged from the party. He said:

[McCarthy and his group were] creating the illusion both at home and abroad that the Republican party was anti-Communist and nothing else, that it had lost its interest in the quest for peace abroad and for human welfare at home. Such a negative image of the Republican party could prove disastrous; if the Republican party were to win, it had to be for something.

The reason the Eisenhower Administration was so eager to get McCarthy was not merely that he was exposing subversives who had infiltrated the government bureaucracy, but that following the trail of the lower echelon conspirators had led him to start knocking at the doors of the upper-level conspirators of the so-called "legitimate world." When McCarthy began making the connection between the Communists and the penthouse conspirators above them, his career was doomed. The same was true of the Reece Committee, which had been investigating foundations until the probe was killed on orders from Eisenhower. Whenever any government investigation gets above the level of exposing the gutter revolutionaries and begins following the trail to the "legitimate world," the investigation is always quashed.

Although the issue of Communist infiltration of government, which the Republicans had used to get elected in 1952, was buried as soon as they assumed office (and McCarthy with it, when he attempted to force the Republicans to carry out their campaign promises), it was resurrected for the 1954 off-year elections. Nixon was used again, as he had been in 1952, as a Judas goat, to lead naive anti-Communist sheep into the "New" Republicans' ideological slaughterhouse. This time Nixon claimed that the Eisenhower Administration had rooted the Reds out of government. In Omaha on September 20, 1954, Nixon stated:

> [The Eisenhower Administration is] kicking Communists, fellow travelers, and bad security risks out of the federal government by the thousands. The Communist conspiracy is being smashed to bits by this administration . . . . Previous Democratic administrations underestimated the Communist danger at home and ignored it. They covered up rather than cleaned up.

A week later at New Bedford, Massachusetts, Nixon again claimed: "We have driven the Communists, the fellow-travelers, and the security risks out of government by the thousands." Soon, Nixon began playing the numbers game as he toured the country campaigning for Republican office seekers. The number of ousted "security risks" escalated from 1,456 to 2,200 to 2,429 to 2,486, and then climaxed at 6,926. Using this figure, Nixon told an audience in Rock Island, Illinois, on October 21:

> The President's security risk program resulted in 6,926 individuals removed from the federal service . . . . The great majority of these individuals were inherited largely from the Truman regime . . . . Included in this number were individuals who were members of the Communist Party and Communist controlled organizations.[21]

These individuals numbered 1,743, according to Nixon.

The Vice President went so far as to assert November 1, in Denver, Colorado, that "96 per cent of the 6,926 Communists, fellow travelers, sex perverts, people with criminal records, dope addicts, drunks, and other security risks removed under the Eisenhower security program were hired by the Truman administration."

Fifteen months later the Eisenhower-appointed Civil Service Chairman Philip Young informed a Senate committee that a subsequent survey showed that 41.2 percent of the dismissed or resigned security risks actually had been hired after Eisenhower had taken over the executive department from the Democrats. [22] Since Eisenhower had been in office for so short a time, it would appear that things were getting worse under Ike than they had been under Truman. Young had earlier testified that he knew of *no single government employee who had been fired by the Eisenhower Administration for being a Communist or fellow traveler!* During Truman's last full year, the administration fired 21,626 for cause. Nixon's claims were clearly fraudulent, but they did make for exciting campaign rhetoric. His boss had made investigation of Communist penetration in government a dead letter by continuing Truman's gag rule.

By the 1956 campaign Nixon was burying the issue entirely. On October 17, Nixon told an audience at Cornell University, according to the Associated Press, that investigations of Communist activities of the kind formerly conducted by McCarthy were no longer needed. He gave credit to the Eisenhower Administration's security policies for taking "this issue . . . out of the political arena."[23] In a sense he was telling the truth. The issue had been taken out of the political arena. The Democrats certainly weren't going to bring it up if the Republicans didn't. Yet seventeen days earlier, in Grand Rapids, Michigan, Nixon had asserted that the GOP would never do what it soon did. According to the Vice President:

> We will never underestimate or pooh-pooh the Communist
> danger, either abroad or in the United States of America.
>   In a political campaign, it is tempting to tell the American
> people that we can get rid of our draft, cut our defenses, find a
> cut-rate way to meet our international obligations, but American
> security must come before any political ambitions.[24]

What made Nixon's burial of the internal subversion issue
all the more ironic was his earlier claim that the Democrats
had buried it, as in this September 21, 1948 statement: "The
full story of Communist espionage will not be told until we
get a Republican President who is not afraid of skeletons in the
closet."[25] Nixon advanced his own career with statements
like the following, made shortly before he ran for the Senate:

> Because they treated Communist infiltration into our Ameri-
> can institutions like any ordinary petty political scandal, the
> [Truman] Administration officials responsible for this failure to
> act against the Communist conspiracy rendered the greatest
> possible disservice to the people of this nation.[26]

This was made all the more significant because Elizabeth
Bentley, who had served as a courier for the Communist
party, had testified that of the many Communist cells in the
U.S. government, only two, the Silvermaster and Perlo cells,
had been partially uncovered. It should be duly noted that
Nixon had full knowledge of the depth and extent of
Communist penetration of the government from his activities
on the House Committee on Un-American Activities and the
Hiss case. To tell the American public that the issue was dead
can only be described as deceitful, although it doubtless
enhanced his stock among the *Insiders*, to whom he was
catering in every possible way.

Another extremely important issue that Nixon used to
sabotage Conservatives and anti-Communists was the Bricker
Amendment. The Bricker Amendment was framed by Ohio
Senator John Bricker, who was concerned that treaties

entered into by the President superseded the Constitution. His argument was based on a statement made by John Foster Dulles before the American Bar Association in Louisville in April 1952. Dulles had discussed the status of treaties in international law and under the Constitution. He pointed out that the Constitution specifically says (Article VI) that approved treaties "shall be the supreme law of the land." He added that such treaties "are indeed more supreme than ordinary laws, for congressional laws are invalid if they do not conform to the Constitution, whereas treaty law can override the Constitution."[27]

The Bricker Amendment forbade the President to enter into any treaty that would supersede the Constitution of the United States and deny to any citizen the rights guaranteed by it. One would assume that no elected official could oppose the Bricker Amendment. The Amendment was specifically aimed at the United Nations Charter, which is a treaty. Bricker feared we were headed for "socialism by treaty" through the United Nations.[28] Under the Bricker Amendment, it would be impossible to surrender our sovereignty to a world government by treaty. Naturally, the Amendment was anathema to all the world government clan, the CFR in particular. It was denounced as an attempt to undermine the treaty-making power of the President — which it was, assuming that the President sought to enter into a treaty that would violate the Constitutional rights of Americans. Eisenhower fought the Bricker Amendment bitterly right down to its hairline defeat on the Senate floor, denouncing its supporters as "nuts and crackpots." The man responsible for the defeat of the Bricker Amendment was Richard M. Nixon.

While in the Senate, Nixon had favored the Amendment, but as a hatchetman for the Eisenhower Administration, he worked for the defeat of this crucially important bill. White House correspondent William Costello wrote:

184 *Richard Nixon*

> The Bricker amendment . . . called for Nixon's best talents. The White House set itself adamantly against the amendment's proposed limitation on the President's treaty-making powers, and it was Nixon who brought the report that sentiment both in and out of Congress was more sympathetic to Bricker than the President had supposed. The Vice President, after first proposing compromise, found himself in loyalty to the White House stalling, placating, instructing, and negotiating and finally joined Eisenhower in opposition to Bricker's demand.[29]

The Bricker Amendment lost in the Senate by a single vote. Some day Americans may realize how crucial that betrayal of the Constitution was.

The Vice President made a convincing "yes man" for the Eisenhower-Dulles version of the Truman-Acheson appeasement of the Communist program. Nixon's support of such anti-anti-Communist programs helped drown resistance to them.

On March 17, 1960, Eisenhower told *Los Angeles Times* reporter Don Shannon: "So far as I know, there has never been a specific difference in our points of view on any important problems in seven years."

Ultra-Liberal columnist Marquis Childs (CFR) quoted Nixon as stating: "My beliefs are very close, as it has turned out, to the philosophy of the Eisenhower Administration on both foreign and domestic policy." Mr. Childs added: "In embracing the Eisenhower philosophy and the 'new Republicanism,' Nixon has gone against his own conservative voting record when he was in the Senate and House."[30] Taking the Vice President at his word, we see that he supported the Eisenhower policies of:

1. Keeping Chiang Kai-shek's troops bottled up on Formosa while settling for an armistice in Korea;

2. Surrendering North Vietnam to Ho chi Minh by refusing to permit an air strike against the Communist armies surrounding the French at Dien Bien Phu;

3. Repudiating the platform promise to repudiate the Yalta betrayal;

4. Turning the Suez Canal over to the Communists;

5. Betraying our promise to help the Hungarians if they revolted;

6. Inviting Khrushchev, the Butcher of Budapest, to visit America just after he had finished slaughtering freedom-seeking Hungarians;

7. Accepting as a policy the Communists' proposal for "peaceful co-existence," which by their own admission means conquering the world by subversion and civil wars; and

8. Allowing a Communist bastion to be established ninety miles from our shore.

All of these events were critical, with long-term implications that still affect us today.

In order to ingratiate himself with the International Left, Nixon did such things as escort the notorious Indonesian Communist Achmed Sukarno around the capital and introduce him to the Senate as the George Washington of Indonesia. He did the same for Fidel Castro. Although our military intelligence, our ambassadors to Cuba and Mexico, and all of South America had known for years that Castro was a Communist and had tried to so inform our government, Nixon did his best to try to keep up the pretense that Castro was just another of those George Washingtons. On April 18, 1959, Vice President Nixon stated: "[The] Cuban people themselves will not tolerate a Communist government or a Communist takeover."[31] Five days later, in an address to newspaper editors, he remarked:

> I mentioned Dr. Castro's visit, and I am looking forward to the opportunity of seeing him tomorrow in my office . . . .
>
> No one can come to the United States, no one can talk to American audiences, no one can talk to the officials of our government, as Dr. Castro will have, without going back convinced that the U.S. government and people share whole-

heartedly the aspirations of the people of Latin America for peaceful existence, for Democratic freedom, for economic progress, and for the strengthening of the institutions of representative government.[32]

Nixon vocally supported extending foreign aid to Communist Poland and the Cultural Exchange Program, despite the fact that J. Edgar Hoover had warned that the latter was a ruse for smuggling spies into the country. Nixon proved to be an excellent tranquilizer for Conservative Republicans while Eisenhower and the "Palace Guard" tugged and hauled the party Leftward.

One of the major themes of the 1952 Eisenhower-Nixon campaign had been a pledge to reverse the onrushing movement towards socialism. In those days Republicans used the word "socialism" to describe the program of the Democrats. Today, since Eisenhower and Nixon adopted the Democrats' programs, the word is as thoroughly taboo among Republicans as it is among Democrats. Pollster Samuel Lubell observes that "to solidify itself permanently in American life the New Deal needed at least one Republican victory . . . [which would] endorse much of the New Deal through the simple device of leaving things untouched." That is exactly what the Eisenhower Administration did. As M. Stanton Evans, editor of the *Indianapolis Star*, has written:

> One result of this was to alienate from the party the new majority which had temporarily surfaced in 1952: the taxpayers and homeowners who looked to the Republicans for relief, and who were rudely disappointed as augmented federal spending and taxes shifted the cost of government more heavily on them than before. In consequence the GOP emerged from the White House with little to show for its eight years' occupancy: a party base more shrunken than ever, repeated defeats in the battles for Congress, and no strategy for reversing things. [33]

In 1950, middle-class Americans paid thirty-three percent of the total tax burden. By 1958, they found themselves paying forty-seven percent of it. By the end of Ike's career the federal government owned three million more acres of land in the continental United States than it had when he was inaugurated.[34] During the Eisenhower years federal employment continued to climb and bureaus to expand. While Ike was getting publicity for paring personnel in one place, he was quietly adding more in other places, resulting in large net gains in federal employment — breaking yet another of his campaign pledges. Eisenhower's proposed budget for 1957-58 called for domestic spending of $31 billion, against the highest figure under Truman, who had the Korean War to finance, of $20 billion.[35]

Under Eisenhower the Department of Health, Education and Welfare was created, a department which Republicans and Conservative Democrats had successfully kept the ADA crowd from creating under either Roosevelt or Truman. HEW has now grown into the most expensive department in the federal government.

During the eight years of the Eisenhower Administration the national debt increased by almost $27 billion. Truman, in seven budgets, had increased the national debt by only $5½ billion, in spite of the fact that he had a full-blown Korean War to deal with. In April 1957, Norman Thomas, six times candidate for President on the Socialist Party ticket, stated: "The United States is making greater strides towards socialism under Eisenhower than even under Roosevelt." [36]

Result of all this; the Republican party was swept under in the 1958 elections, sustaining a defeat second only to the disaster of 1936 in modern Republican history.

Nixon had been, as Paul Hoffman said, a faithful servant of the Eisenhower Administration. His job had been to quash any revolt by the rank and file against Ike's socialism by making strong public statements, just as Vice President Agnew has done for Nixon. When he was out speechifying, Nixon sounded as hard-core as ever. During his campaigning in 1954, he was still castigating the Democratic program as socialism. "A Democratic victory," he said, "will mean a sharp turn to the left, back down the road to socialism." He told a group of the faithful in Van Nuys, California: "When the Eisenhower Administration came to Washington on January 20, 1953, we found in the files a virtual blueprint for socializing America."[37] The Democratic plans, he stated, "call for socialized medicine, socialized housing, socialized agriculture, socialized water and power and perhaps most disturbing of all, socialization of America's greatest source of power, atomic energy." Washington wags have since claimed that Nixon must have dusted off the old blueprint the Administration found in 1953 and reissued it as the "New Federalism."*

The Vice President really became carried away one night and blurted out this statement: " . . . speaking for a unanimous Supreme Court, a great Republican Chief Justice, Earl Warren, has ordered an end to racial segregation in the nation's public schools."[38]

But pacifying grass-roots Republicans with Conservative rhetoric was not Nixon's only job in the Eisenhower Administration. He worked behind the scenes, pushing and shoving recalcitrant Republican Congressmen and Senators into supporting the "New Republicanism" of Ike and his "Palace Guard."

The Council on Foreign Relations and the "Palace Guard" had done their job well. During the entire Eisenhower Administration there was no interruption of "America last" policies abroad and the welfare state at home. The *Insiders* had proved that they could not only control the selection of Republican Presidential candidates, but could actually control a Republican administration.

---

*It later turned out, when reporters quizzed Nixon's press secretary about the "blueprint," that it was a figure of speech and the Vice President was merely referring to the Democrats' general philosophy and proposals.

In one respect the Eisenhower Administration was a monumental success: it was undeniably successful at purging Conservatives from the party. Ike's "confidante," Paul Hoffman in his October 1956 article in *Colliers*, laid out in the very bluntest terms the strategy for purging Conservatives from the Republican party. On February 16, 1957, *Human Events* reported that Hoffman claimed that the White House had suggested the idea of the article and that he "wrote a draft and submitted it to members of the Palace Guard. The latter returned it to him, saying it was not strong enough and urging him to name names. Hoffman acceded to this request and the *Colliers* piece appeared in print in a new and tougher version, with the names." Hoffman admitted that, when Eisenhower was elected, only "thirty percent of the local and county leaders of the party — and less than twenty percent of the Congressmen and Senators" within the Republican Party supported Eisenhower's Liberal foreign and domestic policies. Eisenhower was upset, Hoffman said, because even as leader of the ticket he could not control all Republicans. He stated:

> What Eisenhower did not grasp was the entrenched power of some of the greater figures on Capitol Hill and how deep and firm were the rusty, old-fashioned convictions in which they believed.

If you wanted to make progress within the new Republican establishment, you had to sell out and go Liberal. Hoffman quoted Charles Halleck as shaking his head and saying: "I had to swallow hard two or three times because the boss believes in things I don't, but he's the boss . . . . " Halleck soon got the picture. "You have to go along to get along," as the politicians say. Hoffman wrote: "By now, I should add, Charlie Halleck has turned out to be a tower of strength for the Eisenhower program . . . . "

Hoffman admitted in the *Colliers* article that during the Eisenhower regime Conservative Republicans were moved out and Liberals in. He said:

Forty-two new state chairmen of the Republican party are new, solid, Eisenhower men. Eighty-five of the one hundred forty-six members of the national committee in 1952, have been replaced by new faces. In state after state the young men and women [many of them Democrats] first brought into politics through the Citizens for Eisenhower have begun to occupy commanding posts in the regular structure. There are, to be sure, areas where the old guard still retains its control . . . . But by and large, the nature of the party in 1956, is almost totally different from what it was in 1952 — either in personalities, or in philosophy of Republican stalwarts. We have come to accept Eisenhower leadership wholeheartedly.

Hoffman continued:

Eisenhower's overriding political directive to Leonard Hall, our national chairman, is to find young people, new people of the Citizens for Eisenhower stripe and bring them into the organization. This fall, in New York and Wisconsin, bitter intra-party fights for the Republican Senatorial nomination in these great states have been won by two distinguished liberals, [Communist Party protégé] Jacob Javits and Alexander Wiley — both of them 100% Eisenhower men — over opposition from the right wing.

"This is not to say that the battle to remake the Republican Party is entirely won," wrote Hoffman. There still remains . . . the Senate, where years of power built up men whose entrenched positions still let them resist the philosophy of the Twentieth Century," he said.

Then Hoffman continued:

In the Senate, there are too many Republican Senators claiming the label Republican who embrace none or very little of the Eisenhower program and philosophy.

This group can be divided into two splinters. One splinter contains men like Senator Joseph McCarthy of Wisconsin, Senator William Jenner of Indiana, Senator Herman Welker of Idaho, Senator George Malone of Nevada, who can be called the unappeasables. I shall not try to stigmatize the dangerous thinking and reckless conduct of these men except to say that, in my opinion, they have little place in the new Republican party.

The other splinter within the dissident third [the conservative, anti-Communist one-third] consists of what I consider the "faint-hope" group: men like Senator Henry Dworshak of Idaho, Senator Andrew Schoeppel of Kansas, Senator Barry Goldwater of Arizona. This splinter has been unable to demonstrate, conclusively and permanently, that it accepts the modern America with its needs of social security or balanced labor-management relations, or government partnership and guardian-ship of our complex economy. Nor, being still wedded to the old-fashioned idea of fortress-America-isolated-in-space, can it accept America's role as the chief champion of peace and decency in active international relations.

All of the Senators except Goldwater soon met their political Waterloo. Is it rational to believe that this article would have appeared in *Colliers* magazine without the prior approval of Eisenhower and the "Palace Guard?" Could Hoffman's message have been any clearer? There is no room in the "modern" Republican Party for Conservatives. All the "modern" Republicans want from Conservatives is their vote on election day.

In the same article, however, Hoffman did have praise for one Republican:

> In the Senate, from the very beginning, the President's program has had the unqualified and vigorous support of Vice President Nixon. Some liberal Republicans are still unconvinced as to the Vice President's attitude, holding that he had supported the program only out of personal loyalty to the President, and that his original ultra-conservative views are unchanged. Based on what Nixon has said both publicly and privately, it is my view that he genuinely and deeply believes — that the Eisenhower program is best for the country.

On September 15, 1954, *Human Events* had charged that no administration in history had so strikingly disregarded party loyalty in job appointments, many key positions having gone to CFR Democrats. Eisenhower also succeeded in destroying a coalition of Southern Conservative Democrats and Northern Republicans that had blocked much socialist legislation. Now Republicans were put in the position of being traitors if they did not support the Eisenhower Administration's programs. The *Chicago Tribune* of January 1, 1958, commented editorially:

> The fact is that the Republican party, as it has developed, or, more properly, degenerated under Mr. Eisenhower and his Palace Guard, now stands for pretty nearly everything that can be found in unadulterated form under a Democratic wrapper. The great achievement of the occupant of the White House, if such it can be called, is to have destroyed the Republican party as a repository for any recognizable body of orthodox doctrine.

The elections of 1954, 1956, and 1958 were Republican debacles, except for Eisenhower's personal success in 1956. As Theodore White observed:

> Divorced from the personal curing power of his great name, in each measurable off-year Congressional election under his administration, the Republican party lost ground . . . . With the Democratic triumph in the election of 1958, the fortunes of the Republican party, as a party, had sunk to their lowest ebb since the zenith of the New Deal in 1936.

While Republican candidates were being defeated, Eisenhower never campaigned for any other Republican, with the exception of the ultra-ultra-Liberal Clifford Case (CFR), when he ran for the Senate in 1954. So successful was Ike at purging Conservatives from the GOP that at the end of the 1958 elections Harold Lavine, senior editor of *Newsweek*, wrote:

> Eisenhower has succeeded where Roosevelt and Truman failed . . . . The Republican party is a thoroughly demoralized body . . . . Republican morale has been able to sustain five

successive defeats, but it has crumbled completely as a result of Eisenhower's two great victories.[39]

Eisenhower made no bones about the fact that there were no ideological differences, as far as he was concerned, between the two parties. Since he was really a Liberal Democrat who became a Liberal Republican only in order to run for the Presidency, this is not surprising. Writing in the *Saturday Evening Post*, Eisenhower stated his philosophy that the Republican party had a better delivery system for socialism:

> The difference between parties is, in most instances, a matter of approach to problems and programs. We Republicans want our government at appropriate levels to be responsive to our needs, but *not* to invade our individual rights, liberties, and responsibilities. Though we have many of the same ultimate goals as the Democrats, we disagree with them on methods and in their application, believing that ours are safer and more effective in preserving individual rights, responsibilities, and initiatives, which, after all, are the basis of self-government.[40]

Conservative strength at the national level of the Republican party was decimated by the Eisenhower-Nixon Administration, so that when the grass-roots Conservative groundswell of the 1960's developed, it was strictly at the local level, with little support within the national party machinery.

The result of eight years of Eisenhower-Nixon was that the New Deal had not only been saved from threatened extinction, but had been expanded. William F. Buckley Jr. wrote in 1958:

> ... The passion to federalize social and economic functions is as ardent today as it was in 1952, and beyond a few ritualistic rhetorical dampeners, Mr. Eisenhower has done nothing to check it. The problem of internal security, on the way to a solution when Mr. Eisenhower was elected, has, by his inattention, relapsed to a state worse than that under Mr. Truman. The labor

barons, who posed in 1952 an acute problem understood by Senator Taft, have waxed stronger in five years, and have got virtual guarantees of noninterference from the Eisenhower Administration: for to interfere with them would mean to dig in and take a stand, and Eisenhower does not take stands, except against McCarthy and the Bricker Amendment . . . .[41]

It is important to note from Mr. Buckley's concluding sentence that Mr. Eisenhower could be extremely tough and resolute when he wanted to be. Yet Mr. Buckley attributed Eisenhower's disastrous policies with regard to Communism to lack of understanding and will. Buckley wrote:

There is no other intelligible explanation for Eisenhower's movements in the past five years than that he does not take the Communists at their word as to the aims of Communism. What man who knows Communism would have gone to Geneva to act as a sounding board for Communist propaganda? What man, having made the mistake of going, would have declared, the whole world breathless at his feet, that he believed the Communists — as he put it — "want peace as much as we do"? Where is the man who understands Communism who would say, as Eisenhower did at a press conference last summer, that " . . . I was very hard put to it when [Marshal Zhukov] insisted that [the Communist] system appealed to the idealistic, and we completely to the materialistic, and I had a very tough time trying to defend our position . . . "? Who except a man incapable of understanding Communism could, after so many demonstrations that the Communists mean exactly what their high priests say, permit the national policy to bog down one more time over so palpable a ruse as Marshal Bulganin's call for the one-millionth conference at which to "reconcile the world's differences"? . . . . The tranquil world of Mr. Eisenhower is the world in which the Communists are thriving.[42]

Mr. Buckley described the effect admirably and ignored the cause, i.e., that Dwight Eisenhower was the creation of the CFR and the men behind it, and was their willing tool if not their partner. Instead of being in retreat after eight years of

"Republican" leadership, the world Communist movement was stronger than ever. It even had a foothold on our own doorstep in Cuba, thanks to brother Milton Eisenhower and the uncleansed State Department, which ignored reports that Castro was a long-time Communist. The "crusade" that had been promised was never launched. Instead, it was business as usual, with a new group of operators running the same show for the same *Insiders* behind the scenes.

References
1. *Dan Smoot Report*, May 30, 1960.
2. E.J. Kahn Jr., "Profiles," *The New Yorker*, September 15, 1956, p. 49.
3. *Ibid.*
4. *Ibid.*
5. Rose L. Martin, *Fabian Freeway*, Belmont, Mass., Western Islands, 1968, p. 402.
6. Kahn, *loc. cit.*
7. *Ibid.*
8. Morrie Ryskind, *Los Angeles Times*, March 22, 1963.
9. *Human Events*, April 29, 1959.
10. Phyllis Schlafly, *A Choice Not An Echo*, Alton, Ill., Pere Marquette Press, 1964.
11. Phoebe Courtney, *Nixon and the C.F.R.*, New Orleans, Free Men Speak Inc., 1970, p. 7.
12. Edgar C. Bundy, *Collectivism in the Churches*, New York, Devin-Adair Co., 1958, p. 209.
13. *New York Times*, November 25, 1953.
14. "Whistlestopping, Western Pennsylvania," *The Almanack of Poor Richard Nixon*, Cleveland, World Publishing Co., 1968, p. 56.
15, *Ibid.*, p. 57.
16. *Dan Smoot Report*, July 13, 1956.
17. William Costello, *The Facts About Nixon*, New York, Viking Press, 1960, p. 120.
18. *Human Events*, June 2, 1954.
19. *Look*, September 3, 1957.
20. Fulton Lewis Jr., *Newsletter*, May 3, 1957.
21. Associated Press, October 21, 1954.
22. Earl Mazo and Stephen Hess, *Nixon, A Political Portrait*, New York, Harper & Row, Popular Library Edition, 1968, p. 142n.
23. Associated Press, October 17, 1956.
24. *The Almanack of Poor Richard Nixon*, October 1, 1956, p. 83.
25. *Ibid.*
26. *Ibid.*, January 26, 1950, House of Representatives, p. 67.
27. Dwight D. Eisenhower, *Mandate for Change, 1953-1956*, Garden City, N.Y., Doubleday & Co., 1963, p. 279.
28. *Ibid.*, p. 278.
29. Costello, *op. cit.*, p. 277.
30. *Pasadena Star News*, September 25, 1956.
31. *The Almanack of Poor Richard Nixon*, p. 133.

32. *Congressional Record*, April 23, 1959.
33. M. Stanton Evans, *The Future of Conservatism*, p. 223.
34. "Report from Washington," *Southern States Industrial Bulletin*, August 15, 1957, p. 3.
35. *Wall Street Journal*, March 8, 1957.
36. *Harvard Times-Republican*, April 18, 1957, report of speech on Harvard campus.
37. *The Almanack of Poor Richard Nixon*, p. 68.
38. *Ibid.*, p. 167.
39. "Commentary," October 1958, quoted in *Human Events*, December 22, 1958.
40. *Saturday Evening Post*, January 30, 1965.
41. *National Review*, January 18, 1958.
42. *Ibid.*

CHAPTER VII

"We Are Not
Going To Be Outbid"

By 1960, Richard Nixon had undergone eight years of solid apprenticeship for the Presidency. He had performed well. His pragmatic principles had proven sufficiently flexible to contort to any particular position that might be required by the President or his New York bosses. Richard Nixon was like the little boy in the fourth grade who wanted to be in the fifth graders' club. He wasn't quite sure what the club was all about or just who-all were in it, but nonetheless he had done everything possible to please the big boys in the hope that he might himself be initiated.

Part of Nixon's frustration stemmed from the fact that he had never been accepted or trusted by Eisenhower. This distrust dated from the "Checkers speech." Shortly before Nixon went on the air, he received a phone call from Dewey telling him that Ike's advisers, and therefore obviously Ike, wanted him to end his TV program by offering his resignation to Ike. Dewey also asked Nixon to have telegrams of "Yea" or "Nay" in response to Nixon's plea sent to Los Angeles. The "Checkers speech" was really a behind-the-scenes duel between Nixon and Eisenhower. Nixon didn't offer his resignation, but he ended the program by asking listeners to send their telegrams to the Republican National Committee in Washington, and said that he would leave to the Committee the decision as to whether or not he would stay on the ticket. Nixon was showing Ike and his backers that when it came to political in-fighting he had not come to town on a load of pumpkins with straw hanging out of his ears. The Republican National Committee was in the hands of party regulars and not Eisenhower people. Had the telegrams been sent to Los Angeles, as Dewey requested, the decision as to whether to keep Nixon on the ticket would still have been in Eisenhower's hands. Through this maneuver, Nixon saved his position on the ticket, and therefore his political career, but he paid a high price for it. Throughout the eight years of the Eisenhower Administration, Eisenhower treated Nixon like a lowly clerk and an expendable errand boy. Although Nixon sat in on high-level strategy meetings, his advice was never sought. He was also deliberately left out of Ike's social life, and there were rooms in the White House that Nixon had never seen until LBJ gave him a tour in late 1968.*[1]

During his years in the Vice Presidency, Nixon obviously had not been taken into the conspiratorial apparatus, although he certainly recognized its existence. His following of the Eisenhower program with its purging of Conservatives from the higher echelons of the party was doubtless pragmatic and opportun-

*Many people have tried to condone Eisenhower's sins by contending that he was too dumb to know what he was really doing, citing the tongue-tangled syntax he displayed at press conferences. Not so, says Garry Wills in his highly readable (but in spots very misleading) book, *Nixon Agonistes*. Wills writes: "Eisenhower was not a political sophisticate; he was a political genius." Behind that infectious smile there resided a cold and calculating mind. Although Eisenhower did not do well scholastically at West Point, he scored extremely high at the even more competitive General Staff School. He was an excellent bridge player and turned poker into an extremely profitable pastime. More important, says Wills, Eisenhower's army career was largely built on his ability as a writer of manuals and ghost writer of speeches, and he was regarded as an excellent editor, with dogmatic insistence on precise syntax. The fumbling and bumbling and the garbled circumlocutions were so much show biz. This was a conscious strategy of Eisenhower's to avoid answering questions in detail. For example, Wills reports during the Quemoy-Matsu crisis, the President's press secretary, James Hagerty, advised him to take a "no comment" position on the whole issue. "Don't worry, Jim . . . . If that question comes up, I'll just confuse them," replied Eisenhower. It takes superior intelligence to be able to deliberately double-talk one's way out of tough situations. The President's speech writer, Emmett John Hughes, acknowledged that Eisenhower "made not one politically significant verbal blunder throughout eight years of press conferences and public addresses."

istic, an attempt to convince the *Insiders* that he could be trusted and would play their game. Some, as Paul Hoffman observed, still did not trust him. He had to fend off a movement headed by Harold Stassen (CFR) to remove him from the number two slot on the ticket in 1956. Ike had already suffered a heart attack, and there was a chance that if Ike died and Nixon became President, he might revert to the position of his anti-Communist days. The Stassen coterie wanted as veep, just in case, either Presidential assistant Sherman Adams (CFR) or Nixon's old tutor, Christian Herter (CFR), both of whom were known to be trustworthy.

For a time, Ike seemed to be wavering, and he offered Nixon a cabinet post — any one he wanted, "except the State Department, which was reserved for Dulles."[2] (You'd better believe it was!) But the faction of *Insiders* supporting Nixon was stronger than the clique attempting to oust him. The Vice President's supporters included "Leonard Hall [CFR], Dr. Milton Eisenhower [CFR], Dewey [CFR], and Sidney J. Weinberg [BAC*]."[3] In fact Weinberg, reportedly Eisenhower's boss — possibly acting for staunch Eisenhower supporter and top Democrat Bernard Baruch — told Eisenhower, "I am for Dick Nixon 100%."[4] Weinberg had supported Nixon for the number two spot on the ticket in 1952 and was an advisor to Nixon in his 1960 Presidential race.[5] (Strangely, after supporting Nixon for so many years, Weinberg turned up as Hubert Humphrey's chief money raiser in 1968. This certainly dispels any idea that Weinberg had become more Conservative since his days of enlisting business support for FDR. Since party labels mean nothing to *Insiders* like Weinberg, he could jump from one CFR candidate to another with the ease of a gazelle hurdling a mud puddle. Weinberg's place on the Nixon team was reportedly taken, after his defection, by Kuhn, Loeb and Company partner Lewis L. Strauss [CFR].)

---

*The Business Advisory Council was virtually an affiliate of the CFR.

As 1960 neared, more and more was heard of the "new" Nixon. The "new" Nixon was not the shoddy Red baiter, the shrill campaigner of yore who resorted to sneaky debater's tricks, but a matured, statesman-like man sobered by his experiences in the Vice Presidency. Stewart Alsop commented:

> He wanted to be President very much, and he knew that he had a chance, perhaps a good chance, to become President. But he also knew — for he is anything but a fool — that a reputation as an extremist and partisan would sharply reduce that chance. Hence his change of political style.
>
> A man's motives are always mixed, and no doubt it is true that Nixon changed his political style after 1954 in part for purely practical political reasons. But does the change go deeper than that?[6]

It certainly was not shallow opportunism that led to the birth of the "new" Nixon. It was a very deep-seated opportunism, as Nixon gained more and more knowledge concerning the power of the *Insiders* both inside and outside the Republican party.

There were times when he slipped back into old Nixonisms, as in this statement before an audience in Cleveland in January 1958:

> If we have nothing to offer other than a pale carbon copy of the New Deal, if our only purpose is to gain and retain power, the Republican Party no longer has any reason to exist, and it ought to go out of business.

But after the 1958 mid-term elections such rhetoric disappeared from Nixon's verbal ammunition stockpile. Now, the strategy was to publicize just how Liberal the "new" Nixon, the "real" Nixon, really was. During the latter years of the Eisenhower administration, sophisticated Liberals knew he was in their camp. Richard Wilson, chief of *Look* magazine's

Washington Bureau, telegraphed this in a feature article for
Look titled "The Big Change in Richard Nixon." Wilson
raved on and on about the "new Nixon," declaring:

> *He has made a distinct turn to the left. When the choice has*
> *been between the Republican right and the Republican left,*
> *Nixon has sided with the Republican left . . . .*
>
> The years, then, are building up in Nixon a set of convictions
> he did not have four years ago. As he grows with these
> convictions, and becomes better known, voters will find a basis to
> judge his political readiness to go beyond his training stage — and
> into the White House. [Emphasis added.][7]

Nixon himself was beginning to adjust his image with the
rank and file. Biographer William Costello mentions:

> In another departure from party orthodoxy, he argued in favor
> of making liberals as well as conservatives feel at home in
> Republican ranks; he told a Philadelphia breakfast rally there was
> need for both conservative and liberal points of view in a healthy
> party . . . . [8]

The *New York Times* reported that Nixon had begun "a
quiet courtship of Republican liberals and moderates."[9] The
theme was picked up by the *Wall Street Journal*, which duly
noted:

> On foreign policy, he called himself "a liberal rather than a
> conservative because I have an international view rather than an
> isolationist view on foreign policy . . . . " On economic matters he
> is " . . . trying to avoid getting obsessed with the idea (of
> balancing the budget)."[10]

The very Liberal *Chicago Sun Times*, on December 31, 1959,
did its bit toward debunking the idea that Nixon was still a
Conservative:

> . . . The Democrats have stepped up their campaign to label

Vice President Nixon as the darling of that reactionary fringe of the GOP known as the Old Guard.

This is political hokum.

The Old Guard — or what little is left of it — notoriously stands for isolationism and against social reform.

Nixon is an internationalist in the tradition of Wendell Willkie, for whom he campaigned in 1940. He is an outspoken champion of the United Nations, of a stronger world court even at the cost of modifying U.S. sovereignty, of generous foreign aid . . . .

As part of his presidential build-up, Nixon arranged for a trip to Russia in the summer of 1959. He went strictly on his own hook, as Eisenhower refused to give him any mission, but merely told him what subjects to avoid so as not to muddy the waters for the negotiations that were already going on behind the scenes. Ostensibly he was to "probe for areas of possible East-West agreement . . . and impress the Soviets with America's sincere desire for peace . . . . "[11] Of course, anyone who knew as much about Communism as Nixon did was aware of the fact that the Communists had been cynically using "America's sincere desire for peace" to their advantage ever since FDR agreed to recognize the Soviet Union in 1933. The idea that the Kremlin believes that we are really warmongers, and that therefore we must prove *our* good faith over and over while never requiring any positive acts of good faith from the Communists, is so much hogwash.

Once Nixon was in Moscow, Khrushchev quickly put him on the defensive by becoming highly irate about Congress' having passed a resolution commemorating "Captive Nations Week," which demanded that the United States "continue" [*sic*] its efforts to win the release of the millions of peoples held in the Soviet prison camp of nations. Nixon told Khrushchev, "This was a foolish resolution." "Do you mean to say that the members of Congress are fools?" Khrushchev asked. "This is just a private conversation," Nixon cleverly countered.[12]

In another dazzling display of verbal brilliance, the Vice President told the lovable Butcher of Budapest:

> There are some instances where you may be ahead of us — for example, in the development of the thrust of your rockets for the investigation of outer space; there may be some instances in which we are ahead of you — in color television, for instance.[13]

Khrushchev reportedly was polite and did not burst out laughing. Nixon, however, got even the next day when the two visited the American National Exhibition, a sort of county fair, which was being shown in Moscow. While in an exhibit of a typical American kitchen, the famous "kitchen debate" occurred, in which Nixon was graciously permitted to shake his finger in the Soviet tyrant's face for the benefit of press cameramen. That shot may have been worth a million votes.

As the Republican National Convention approached, it became obvious that Nixon had the nomination sewed up tight. For nine years he had been stumping nearly every town and hamlet in the country for the Republican party and all of its candidates. His years on the creamed chicken circuit may have been responsible for considerable indigestion, but in their course Nixon had collected a bushel-basketful of political I.O.U.'s. The Republican National Convention was foreclosure time for the Californian. As early as the previous March, polls showed that the Vice President was the favorite of 64 per cent of the country's Republicans, so there seemed to be little to worry about as convention time neared. Yet in mid-May, Nelson Rockefeller, newly elected governor of New York, tried to stick his nose into the Presidential tent. Rockefeller had no chance of getting the nomination, yet Rocky's mere entrance onto the scene seems to have earned him a bargaining position with Nixon. When Rockefeller found he could not lay claim to the actual nomination, he moved to dictate policy from behind the scenes. A meeting was thus arranged between Nixon and Rockefeller for the Saturday before the Republican Convention opened in Chicago.

In *The Making of the President, 1960*, Theodore White noted that Nixon accepted all the Rockefeller terms for this meeting, including provisions "that Nixon telephone Rockefeller personally with his request for a meeting; that they meet at the Rockefeller apartment . . . that their meeting be secret and later be announced in a press release from the Governor, not Nixon; that the meeting be clearly announced as taking place at the Vice President's request; that the statement of policy issuing from it be long, detailed, inclusive, not a summary communiqué.[14]

As a result of the meeting, a four-way telephone circuit was set up linking Rockefeller protégé Charles Percy (chairman of the Republican Platform Committee and a board member of Rockefeller's Chase Manhattan Bank), a second Rockefeller deputy in Chicago, Nixon, and Rockefeller. What finally emerged was the fourteen points of the famous Compact of Fifth Avenue.

The Republican Platform Committee had been meeting in Chicago for an entire week, laboriously pounding out a platform reflecting the views of Republicans from all fifty states. Now the Platform Committee was handed the Rockefeller-Nixon orders: Forget the effort and the time you have spent to come to Chicago at your own expense, hear witnesses, and draft a document to submit to the Convention — throw it all out and accept the Rockefeller-Nixon platform worked out, in secret, eight hundred and thirty miles from the Convention site. The Liberals were ecstatic; here was their kind of democracy in action!

The *Wall Street Journal* of July 25, 1960, claimed that the Fifth Avenue meeting was not a Rockefeller coup but a Nixon victory; that Nixon had needed a rationalization for dumping the party Conservatives. As a result of the meeting, the *Journal* stated:

. . . a little band of conservatives within the party, of whom Senator Goldwater is symbol and spokesman, are shoved to the sidelines . . . . First impressions to the contrary, Mr. Nixon has achieved all this without giving Mr. Rockefeller a single important concession he did not want to make.

This is not to deny that the fourteen points are very liberal indeed; they comprise a platform akin in many ways to the Democratic platform and they are a far cry from the things that conservative men think the Republican party ought to stand for . . . .

But as you go down the fourteen points, one by one, it's clear they reflect the Nixon brand of liberalism . . . .

Actually Mr. Nixon has rather skillfully used the Rockefeller meeting to get a few liberal planks into the platform which he already wanted but which he was having trouble getting through the platform committee . . . .

Thus it is that in one burst of speed Richard Nixon has accomplished three maneuvers — defied the conservative wing of the party, cut loose from President Eisenhower and neatly outflanked his major opponent within the party . . . . Mr. Nixon's risk is that conservative voters will be outraged enough to stay away from the polls and that his liberal gesture will not in fact gain any liberal votes from the Democrats . . . .

In doing so he has moved the Republican party a little more to the left on the political spectrum, a thing that is bound to be sad not only to men of conservative mind, but also to those who would like to see the philosophic differences that divide the country sharpened into clear political issues. Once more we are going to be deprived of that kind of a choice in a presidential election.

As a matter of tactics, Mr. Nixon with this platform abandons the deep South and conservatives everywhere to whatever they can make of the Democratic platform.

Another *Wall Street Journal* article of the same day concluded that the Rockefeller-Nixon agreement "brings the spotlight shining once more on a facet of his public image he has long labored to eradicate; that of 'Tricky Dick,' the politician who sacrifices principle to expediency."

The *Chicago Tribune* headlined its editorial on the Nixon-Rockefeller meeting, "Grant Surrenders to Lee." The welfare platform dictated by Rockefeller and Nixon, which included an endorsement of the objectives of Communist-inspired sit-ins in the South, was called by Senator Goldwater "the Munich of the Republican Party."

Republicans everywhere understood the meaning and significance of the new Rockefeller-Nixon alliance. Nixon had purged himself of his independence to become acceptable to the *Insiders* of the International Left. As Theodore White put it:

> Never had the quadrennial liberal swoop of the regulars been more nakedly dramatized than by the open compact of Fifth Avenue. Whatever honor they might have been able to carry from their services on the platform committee had been wiped out. A single night's meeting of the two men in a millionaire's triplex apartment in Babylon-by-the-Hudson, eight hundred and thirty miles away, was about to overrule them; they were exposed as clowns for all the world to see.[15]

Nixon confirmed the alliance by accepting as his running mate one of the foremost darlings of the international clique, a discredited instigator of the smear-Taft maneuver of 1952 and of the anti-McCarthy smear of 1954, Henry Cabot Lodge. Lodge then proceeded to virtually sit out the campaign. *Newsweek* of March 23, 1964, phrased it more delicately: "His laziness became legend."

The Rockefeller-Nixon meeting certainly made it plain that Nixon was willing to pay the price Taft had been unwilling to pay. But the significance of the meeting may go much deeper than that. Rockefeller represented much more than a mere political rival. He was acting as a political power broker not just for himself, but for brother David of the mammoth Chase Manhattan Bank and the coterie of international bankers who form the nucleus of the *Insiders'* Council on Foreign Relations. It is very possible, though we shall never find out for sure, that at this time Nixon was initiated into one of the outer circles of the conspiracy. For the truth is that there was no need to crawl to

Rockefeller. Nixon had the nomination in the bag regardless of what Rockefeller did. Rockefeller's influence in the Republican party is immense at the apex and quite small at the grassroots base. He is like the owner of a professional football team who cannot make the team he owns. Though Rockefeller would doubtless trade his left ear lobe for the Presidency, he is forced to operate through others at the Presidential level. Nixon is perfect for this. Nixon can deliver the grass roots and Rockefeller can deliver the CFR Establishment. The two men may dislike each other intensely, but they need each other. It may be that they are not even as great personal enemies as they appear to be. Nixon and Rockefeller were close friends during the Eisenhower Administration and Rocky sent Nixon this telegram in 1956: " . . . Under you and the President the Republican party is now emerging, at home and abroad, as the great liberal party of the future."[16] Stewart Alsop (CFR) indicates in his book *Nixon and Rockefeller* that the two men are really Leftwing birds of a feather:

> There are in fact, it should be noted, no sharp ideological differences between Rockefeller and Nixon, as there were between Dewey and Taft and Eisenhower and Taft. When Rockefeller worked in Washington for the first Eisenhower administration, he often found an ally in Nixon on such issues as foreign aid. The difference is really a difference of style and background and approach to politics – above all, the difference between a professional, partisan politician, a "regular," and a seeming amateur with an air of being above partisanship. It is a choice which has confronted the Republican party before, although in different form.[17]

From a political standpoint, the most that Rockefeller could offer was the delivery of New York State in the election, and it was extremely doubtful that he could deliver that. To top it off, after receiving credit for dictating the Republican platform, Rockefeller, for all practical purposes, sat out the election, thus helping to ensure Nixon's defeat. Rockefeller may have figured that if Nixon were defeated in 1960, he, Rockefeller, would have the inside shot at the nomination in 1964.

But there can be little doubt that Nixon knew what he was doing. Although it appeared to the man in the street that he had made a foolish bargain and had sold out for a mess of pottage, actually Nixon had insured his long-run political career. Of course, Mr. Nixon could have chosen to fight the conspiracy, but having seen the depth of its power during the Eisenhower administration, he apparently figured it was much easier to join the conspirators than to fight them. Otherwise his actions in 1960 make little sense, and whatever he is, Nixon is a shrewd politician.

That there was a deal of monstrous proportions is beyond question. In analyzing Nixon's acceptance speech at the Republican Convention, the *Wall Street Journal* of August 1, 1960, noted:

> He does not reject any particular Federal activity — whether it be Federal medical help for the aged, Federal aid to education, or Federal foreign aid — on the ideological ground that it is something the central government has no right to do.

Of course, Nixon did throw a bone to the dejected Conservatives, proclaiming in his acceptance speech: "The only answer to a strategy of victory for the Communist world is the strategy of victory for the free world." But, as the *Journal* commented, "Exactly what Mr. Nixon has in mind in this regard will have to await clarification." That clarification never came.

In the 1960 campaign Nixon attempted a feat more difficult than passing a camel through the eye of a needle. He tried to outpromise the Democrats. *Newsweek* of July 11, 1960 quoted him as saying:

> We are not going to be outbid .... We can reach goals the

so-called economic liberals of the Galbraith-Schlesinger school can never reach. We can show that we can produce better schools, hospitals, health, higher living standards.

And Nixon knew what he was doing. He was now advocating *more* of the very same policies he had once denounced so vociferously as socialist and Communist. On July 29, 1960, the *Wall Street Journal* even headlined an article, "Nixon Aims to Wed Fiscal Responsibility to Welfare State." As the *Journal* explained:

> ... the Republican party this year stands on a platform that borrows much from this modern liberalism. In the area of civil rights, and welfare legislation, in the acceptance of big Government spending, the Republican party is once more seeking to meet the Democratic party on its own ground . . . .
>
> Mr. Nixon is going to completely ignore any distinction between conservatives and liberals in wide political areas . . . .
>
> He will accept it as proper for the Government to intervene in the nation's business, to take on for the people some of the obligations which were once left to them individually — the path is straight from social security to socialized medical care. In that sense the Roosevelt revolution is complete; Mr. Nixon, if elected, will not dismantle the welfare state.

The only difference the *Journal* could find between the Democrats and Republicans was that the Democrats promised socialism through deficit spending, while the Nixon Republicans promised socialism with balanced budgets. Either way, America was to be the loser.

Before the campaign even started, Nixon had announced that internal subversion was a dead issue, stating:

> Domestic Communism is no longer a political issue. The danger has receded a great deal in the last few years, domestically, mainly because we have become increasingly aware of it. The Communists used to fool an awful lot of well meaning people who were not Communists. There is still a group, a small group that can be fooled.[18]

And, as if to make sure that nobody missed how completely he had joined the socialist team, candidate Nixon added:

> If we have to choose in allocating funds between military programs and economic, information, and other non-military programs, I would put the emphasis on the non-military programs, and take a gamble on the military programs.

In a book put out for the campaign, biographer Earl Mazo reported that Richard Nixon personally "considers himself a 'radical' when it comes to the goals he would set for the country (his definition of 'radical' being the 'opposite of conservative')."

In his campaign against fellow CFR member Senator John Kennedy, Richard Nixon regularly pulled his punches. Who will ever forget Nixon's "I agree with Mr. Kennedy . . ." statements on the TV debates? He never discussed what informed Republicans considered to be his best issue: the Senate records of Kennedy and Johnson — including Senator Kennedy's sponsorship of legislation to repeal the loyalty oath provision of the National Defense Education Act, his vigorous support of Communist revolutionaries in Algeria, and his backing of the repeal of the Battle Act provision, which prohibited the sending of strategic materials to Iron Curtain countries. And Nixon never even mentioned Mr. Johnson's killing of the bill to restore to the states the right to punish subversion.

Instead, like Willkie and Dewey before him, Richard Nixon conducted a campaign using the orthodox "New York strategy," concentrating his efforts on the big cities at the expense of rural areas, the West, and the South. Nixon failed as Willkie and Dewey had failed before him because he simply could not force the Liberal East and Conservative West into a single phalanx. The principal irony of Mr. Nixon's campaign was that he could very probably have won every state he did win without any effort to project a "new

Nixon." And had he not turned Left, he might have picked up in the South the votes he needed to become President in 1960.

Yes, it was very ironic.

It had, indeed, been a strange campaign — especially considering that it was waged by one whose long suit was two-fisted campaigning. Gone were the thumb-in-the-eye, ear-biting, shin-kicking campaigns of yore. Nixon had suddenly become dignified. No more rolling in the dirt. Now it was tea and crumpets with the opponent. Republicans kept waiting for Nixon "to take the gloves off." But Nixon had traded his boxing gloves for the white fawnskin variety. An exasperated Brent Bozell wrote in his *National Review* column:

> M-moment, that point in future time when Richard Nixon throws off the camouflage and hauls up his true conservative colors, moves steadily forward along its inexorable path to infinity. Nixon's Moment of Truth was scheduled for early 1960 when he would become an "avowed" candidate and in that capacity would speak his "real" mind. When spring turned to summer and not much had happened besides the avowal, the deadline was set ahead to the Republican convention. Then the Vice President would step forward: Since his official status as party standard-bearer would take precedence over the inhibiting responsibilities of his present office, Nixon would at last be free to elaborate on his differences with the [Eisenhower] administration. Now these differences have begun to emerge and they all point the wrong way. Conservatives have steeled themselves, accordingly, to yet another postponement — we will be patient through the campaign, but watch the smoke after Inauguration Day!
>
> Many conservatives were telling themselves that last week, but very few of them believed it.[19]

On election day Kennedy edged Nixon by an eyelash — and that with the aid of many of the dear departed in Texas and in Cook County, Illinois, who returned from the hereafter to vote the straight Democratic ticket. With Texas and Illinois in the Republican column, Nixon would have been elected President.

The *New York Times'* very liberal Tom Wicker made a noteworthy point regarding vote frauds:

> A shift of only 4,480 popular votes from Kennedy to Nixon in Illinois, where there were highly plausible charges of fraud, and 4,491 in Missouri would have given neither man an electoral majority and thrown the decision into the House of Representatives. If an additional 1,148 votes had been counted for Nixon in New Mexico, 58 from Hawaii, and 1,247 in Nevada he would have won an outright majority in the electoral college . . . . Any experienced reporter or politician knows that that few votes can easily be "swung" in any state by fraud or honest error.[20]

In a post-election report following the Kennedy-Nixon race, Richard Wilson, the veteran Washington correspondent and columnist, wrote in *Look* magazine, in an article entitled "How To Steal An Election":

> For the first time, many thousands of Americans suddenly realized that elections can be stolen. They only half-believed it before 1960, as part of our historical lore . . . . Many, many thousands of voters and civic-minded people in several leading states no longer take the easygoing attitude toward election frauds.

The thievery in Texas, where such things were traditional whenever Lyndon Johnson was involved in a race, was so blatant that Texas political reporters were screaming for some national media representative to pick up the story. At least 100,000 votes had been stolen and the Kennedy-Johnson ticket carried the state by only 46,000. *New York Herald Tribune* reporter Earl Mazo did a four-part article detailing how the election was stolen. Nixon invited Mazo over to his office and Mazo assumed Nixon was finally going to call for a federal investigation. Instead, to Mazo's shock,

Nixon told him: "Earl, those are interesting articles you are writing — but no one steals the presidency of the United States." Mazo states: "I thought he might be kidding. But never was a man more deadly serious ... he enumerated potential international crises that could be dealt with only by the President of a united country, and not a nation torn by the kind of partisan bitterness and chaos that inevitably would result from an official challenge of the election result." Nixon claimed: "Our country can't afford the agony of a constitutional crisis — and I damn well will not be a party to creating one just to become President or anything else."[21]

Nixon pleaded with Mazo to cancel the eight remaining articles he had prepared on how the election was stolen. It is obvious from Mazo's statements that he was sure Nixon had been defrauded. But Nixon apparently was willing to reward the thieves. He was strangely magnanimous, for a man who for years had moved heaven and earth to claw his way to the top of the political heap.

This odd behavior from a man who had earned a well-justified reputation for political ruthlessness naturally triggered a bevy of rumors. Most of them centered on widely circulated unconfirmed stories that Kennedy had information about a large Caribbean gambling debt Nixon had run up, a real estate scandal in California, or strange actions by Nixon's closest friend, "Sweet Bebe" Rebozo.

More plausible is the theory that Nixon knew the timing was not right for him and that the *Insiders* wanted Kennedy. Nixon wanted to be President all right, and expected to be. But he was farsighted enough in 1961 to realize that his way of helping the *Insiders* to advance, by posing as an anti-Communist who continuously had to yield to Communist pressures to avoid worse results — which had been the formula during the Eisenhower years — was not going to be the formula preferred by the top *Insiders* for the next eight-year stretch, 1961 through 1968.

For the last thirty years the *Insiders* have been carrying out this strategy in America by alternating swings of the pendulum. In 1961 they were ready for another eight-year period of driving this country down the road to Communism by direct measures, carried out under a President whose political strength depended on his open support of Communism disguised as Liberalism. Nixon did not fit that picture, and knew it well. The last thing he wanted was, as President, to be bucking *Insider* plans; or, alternatively, to lose his own political following by failing to do so. It was going to be 1969 before those bosses would want another Eisenhower in the White House. And Nixon was by no means reluctant to wait.

The next episode in the strange political career of Richard Nixon, following his eyelash defeat (if that is what it was) by JFK, was his strange quest for the governorship of California. This undertaking is still shrouded in mystery and, as with so many other important stories, the men who know are not about to talk. What we do know is that Nixon's decision to run for the governorship of the Smog State was tied in with the political ambitions of two other men, former California Assemblyman Joe Shell and Nelson Rockefeller. Shell, a former captain of the USC football team, was a hard-nosed Conservative with political ambitions; and at this time (the early '60's) Rockefeller had not undergone a divorce and his aspirations to be President were much more realistic than they were later to become.

In early 1962, Shell contacted Nixon, who was then practicing law in Beverly Hills, to see if the former Vice President had any intention of seeking the governorship. Shell was realistic enough to know that he would have no chance against the universally known Nixon in a primary fight for the Republican nomination, and he did not propose to waste time and money in trying. Nixon assured Shell that under no circumstances would he become a candidate for the governorship. Based on Nixon's unqualified declaration that he was not interested, Shell filed for the governorship in the primary.

Some weeks later Shell received a "courtesy" phone call from Nelson Rockefeller. After an exchange of pleasantries, Rockefeller asked Shell where he would stand if he were elected governor and thereby became the leader of the California delegation to the 1964 Republican nominating convention. Shell replied that he was sorry to have to say that he would not be in Rockefeller's corner. This rather abruptly terminated the "courtesy" call. One week later to the day, a Friday, Rockefeller's secretary called Shell's secretary and announced that Richard Nixon would be entering the California gubernatorial race.

We can only speculate on just what kind of hold Rockefeller had over Nixon, or what kind of deal Rockefeller had made with Nixon either personally or as a member of the *Insider* Establishment. Jules Witcover, in his recent book *The Resurrection of Richard Nixon*, reveals:

> It has been widely assumed that Nixon ran for governor in 1962 because he was unable to resist local and state pressures from important Republicans in California. Although it is true such pressures were great, the strongest persuasion came not from California but from Republican powers and friends in the East . . . . [22]

Later, Witcover adds:

> There were many others, though, who thought Nixon needed it [the California governorship] if he hoped to make another serious try at the Presidency. They were the same members of "the Eastern Establishment" — that rather formless collection of Republican moderates best symbolized by the last Republican Presidential loser, Thomas E. Dewey of New York — who had masterminded Dwight D. Eisenhower's two party nominations and had helped Nixon nail down the Republican nomination in

1960. Several times in early and mid-1961, Nixon and Finch traveled back to New York and Washington to confer with Dewey, Herbert Brownell, Jr., William P. Rogers, Clifford Folger, the old Eisenhower and Nixon finance man, Leonard W. Hall, General Eisenhower's campaign manager . . . .[23]

Harold "Butch" Powers, who had also entered the primary, bowed out with this statement:

> The kingmakers, whoever they may be and wherever they live, have decreed in effect that California Republicans shall take a discard from the rubble heap of national politics . . .[24]

It has been claimed that Nixon had to run if he was to retain any semblance of national party leadership, and that the California governorship was a forum for such leadership. Subsequent happenings have proved this was not true.

Nixon defeated Shell handily in the primary and appeared to be a shoo-in against Democrat incumbent Edmund G. Brown. Under Brown, known as "Pat" to his friends and "Bumbles" to his critics, taxes had skyrocketed, while everything else seemed to be disintegrating. In addition, "Bumbles," referred to by *Time* Magazine as "a tower of jelly," had a penchant for inserting his foot in his mouth and was not particularly popular with rank and file Democrats. Also, unlike the Presidential race in which Nixon had had to defend the administration, this one found him free to attack, to exploit the numerous weak spots in Brown's record.

Reflecting all these factors, early summer polls showed Nixon leading Brown by 53 to 37 per cent, with 10 per cent undecided. Even if he lost all of the undecided vote, he would still win handily. Yet somehow Nixon managed to blow the election in the state he had carried comfortably in his 1960 Presidential race.

Nixon, the man famed for his slick, hard-hitting campaigns, proceeded to conduct a stumbling, amateurish campaign that left his supporters aghast. The campaign seemed to be dogged by bad luck from the beginning. An airliner crashed, killing Richard Jones (CFR), who was carrying a valise with $65,000 in cash, widely reported to be funds from the Establishment for the Nixon campaign. Another problem was the $205,000 loan made to Richard Nixon's mother, Hannah, in 1951, by the Hughes Tool Company. Every time the subject was brought up, Nixon would say how happy he was that someone had asked him that question. You can imagine how happy he was. Nixon always prefaces his "answer" to a tough question by telling you how ecstatic he is that you are trying to nail him. Next, he says that he wants to make himself "perfectly clear," and then you know the double talk is about to begin — but it will be the most *sincere* double talk you have ever heard.

In this case Nixon explained that his mother had put up a piece of property as collateral for the loan, and that the lot meant a great deal to his mother. This, of course, did not answer the question of whether it is moral or ethical for a politician in high office to permit his family to receive a secret loan from a major defense contractor.

Nixon's brother, Donald, not Hannah Nixon, was the recipient of the $205,000. He never paid it back, but instead went through bankruptcy, and the Hughes Tool Company wound up with the property.

Another embarrassing matter that was brought up during the gubernatorial campaign was the fact that Nixon, who had always been a strong champion of civil rights and who was a member of the NAACP, had bought a home in Washington, D.C., the deed to which contained a restrictive clause forbidding its sale to Negroes.[25] Lawsa mercy, that *was* embarrassing.

Nixon had won fame as a campaigner by always being on the attack. But in 1962, he ran a strangely defensive campaign. "Bumbles" Brown was not only subject to attack because of his incompetence; he also was more vulnerable to "Red-baiting" than the "Pink Lady," Helen Gahagan Douglas, had been. Pat Brown had been president of the Northern California chapter of the National Lawyers Guild, cited by the House Committee on Un-American Activities as "the foremost legal bulwark of the Communist Party." But Nixon never mentioned that.

Brown was also closely tied to the California Democratic Council (CDC), which, according to a former FBI undercover operative, had been formed with the help of the Communist Party. The CDC's stand on virtually all issues was unbelievably identical with the official Communist Party line as set down in Party publications. Not only did Nixon not broach this serious issue, he actually took steps against Republican Conservatives who wished to make an issue of Brown's strange bedfellows.

And then there was Proposition 24, the Francis Amendment, to outlaw the Communist Party. Half a million voters signed petitions to put this anti-subversive measure on the ballot. William F. Knowland's *Oakland Tribune* editorial on October 29, 1962, stated:

> Every such law, even if perfectly written, is challenged and subjected to court test . . . . This will undoubtedly happen again, and if Proposition 24 has faulty sections, they will be eliminated by court action . . . . On the other hand, the measure contains certain provisions that are vitally needed.

The Communists were all against Proposition 24. Pat Brown and his CDC cohorts were against it, the entire Leftist claque was against it, and so was Richard Nixon. Nixon claimed that the proposed law was unconstitutional, although the measure had been carefully drawn up by a battery of constitutional attorneys to avoid the very pitfalls Nixon claimed were in the bill. Strangely, Nixon spent much of his effort in attacking Proposition 24 instead of Pat Brown.

Even more strangely, Nixon devoted much time to attacking incumbent Republican Congressman John Rousselot and Edgar Hiestand because of their membership in The John Birch Society. Richard Nixon, the man with the reputation of being "the great unifier" of Party factions, the man who could support such ultra-Leftists as Clifford "Hopeless" Case (CFR) and Jacob Javits (CFR), was now reading two incumbent Conservatives out of the party. This despite Nixon's pre-primary pledge of full support for the entire state GOP slate.[26] In retrospect, it appears quite obvious that Nixon pursued this suicidal course under orders from headquarters — New York. Nixon alienated Conservatives in both parties, and many of them either did not vote for any gubernatorial candidate in the election, or voted for an unknown dentist who was running for governor as a patriotic Conservative, on the Prohibition Party ticket. The Nixon-Brown race drove many people to the "dry" candidate.

The result was a debacle. Forced to run on a campaign format dictated by Establishment *Insiders*, Nixon's former 53 per cent lead evaporated into a defeat by 300,000 votes. At the same time Dr. Max Rafferty was running for State Superintendent of Education on a Conservative platform, and even with the all-out opposition of all Liberal-labor forces, he wound up winning by more than 210,000 votes. Rafferty received over 500,000 more votes than Nixon.

Operating under the conditions imposed on him by Rockefeller and the Establishment was undoubtedly a particularly frustrating experience. Losing to JFK by a hairbreadth was certainly no disgrace, but losing (or, in essence, being forced to take a dive) to Brown was humiliating. The morning after his defeat Nixon made his famous farewell to politics speech ("You don't have Nixon to kick around any more"), in which he lambasted the media for their bias. The whole thing had been a nightmare, and on that morning

Nixon probably believed that his political career was deader than the mahjongg craze.

Among those factors contributing to Nixon's defeat was the widely held suspicion that Nixon wanted the California governorship as a stepping stone to a second try for the Presidency. This belief was given impetus on election eve, when Nixon inadvertently referred to himself on television as the prospective "Governor of the United States."[27] But this was not actually the case. By this time Nixon knew full well that the strategy of the *Insiders* called for eight years of rather overt moves toward building an all-powerful socialist state, and that his time had not yet come. And he also knew that his patience would be rewarded. Jules Witcover in *The Resurrection of Richard Nixon*, revealed some facts concerning Nixon's California race:

> Nixon was not seeking a stepping-stone to a 1964 rematch against John F. Kennedy; he was seeking a sanctuary from it. Far from wanting to use the state-house in Sacramento to launch another Presidential bid in 1964, as Brown successfully charged in the 1962 campaign, Nixon actually had hoped to use it as a four-year hiding place, from which he could avoid making another losing race against Kennedy. Inherent in his decision to run for governor was a Presidential timetable not of 1964, but of 1968, when he finally did make his second try. Thus, though he lost in California in 1962, the gubernatorial contest in the end served the political purposes intended at the start — to keep Nixon off the national ballot in 1964 and to make him the Republican Party's logical choice in 1968! The circumstances that produced both these results never of course were anticipated. But because Richard Nixon did not win in California in 1962 and did not run for President in 1964, he was able to emerge again in 1968, when his party found itself with a rare opportunity for victory, but facing a leadership vacuum.[28]

Following the disastrous loss to Brown, Nixon picked up his family and shuffled off to New York to join the Wall Street law firm of Mudge, Rose, Guthrie, Alexander and Mitchell.* The deal was reportedly arranged by Nixon's old friend, Elmer Bobst, of Warner Lambert Pharmaceutical Co. The firm did not seek Nixon. Nixon moved into Nelson Rockefeller's apartment building at 810 Fifth Avenue, into the same apartment where Nixon and Rockefeller had arranged the infamous "Compact of Fifth Avenue" in 1960. After Rockefeller re-married he had moved into an apartment on the other side of the building. Thus, all during Nixon's stay in New York he and Rocky were neighbors.[29] It does seem unusual that one would buy an apartment from and become a neighbor of someone who is supposed to be one's political arch-enemy. Just how this, and Nixon's joining a New York law firm, fit in with his consenting to be Rocky's hatchet man against Joe Shell, we cannot tell. Those who know the story behind this story are not talking, and it is a line of questioning that most reporters do not care to follow.

While Nixon's job with Mudge, Rose, Guthrie, Alexander and Mitchell was reputedly arranged by Elmer Bobst and not Rockefeller, the Mitchell of the firm was John Mitchell, now the Attorney General, who was Rockefeller's personal attorney. Furthermore, columnist Leonard Lyons, on September 6, 1968, reported that the firm handles much of Chase Manhattan's (Rockefeller's) trust business. Bobst is listed as a member of the highly secret Pilgrim Society, which is even closer to the inner circle of the conspiracy than the CFR.

When Nixon left Washington, he reportedly had little more than an old Oldsmobile automobile, Pat's respectable Republican cloth coat, and a government pension. While in law practice Nixon had an income of $200,000 per year, of which more than half went to pay for the apartment in Rocky's building. By 1968, he reported his net worth as $515,830, while assigning a value of only $45,000 to his partnership in his increasingly flourishing law firm. Nixon

*A former partner in the firm had been notorious Communist-fronter Roger Baldwin, a founder of the A.C.L.U.

listed total assets of $858,190 and liabilities of $342,360. Most of his assets represented Florida and New York real estate. All of this reveals a remarkable use of capital, considering that income taxes on $200,000 are substantial. Nixon was reportedly paying $70,000 a year in income taxes, and $109,500 a year in payments and taxes on his coopera- tive apartment, which alone would eat up $180,000 of his $200,000 salary. In addition, there was the unknown cost of his limousine and chaffeur and his constant traveling all over the country and the world, plus the normal costs of first-class living in New York City.

During this time Nixon was also moving up in social circles. Theodore White informs us:

> He himself [Nixon] belonged uptown to the Links Club, the most Establishment of New York's Establishment clubs. Down- town, he belonged to the Recess Club and India House . . . .[30]

Nixon also joined three exclusive and expensive golf clubs.

It may be that the frugal Mr. Nixon acquired the investment capital that mushroomed into $858,190 in assets by faithfully plugging his change into a piggy bank. Then again, it may have been part of Nixon's deal with Rockefeller and the *Insiders* that Mr. Nixon's personal poverty problems should be solved.

It was while Nixon was studying for the New York bar examination and enjoying his newly acquired life of luxury that the phenomenon known as the Goldwater Movement was burgeoning across the land.

References

1. Garry Wills, *Nixon Agonistes*, Boston, Houghton-Mifflin Co., 1970, pp. 123-125.
2. Earl Mazo and Stephen Hess, *Nixon, A Political Portrait*, Popular Library Edition, New York, Harper & Row, 1968, p. 145.
3. William Costello, *The Facts About Nixon*, New York, Viking Press, 1960, p. 148.
4. Mazo and Hess, *op. cit.*, p. 168.
5. New York Times News Service, *Arizona Republic*, April 30, 1968.
6. Stewart Alsop, *Nixon and Rockefeller*, p. 155.
7. *Look*, September 3, 1957.
8. Costello, *op. cit.*, p. 168.
9. *New York Times*, March 24, 1959.
10. *Wall Street Journal*, April 27, 1959.
11. Mazo and Hess, *op. cit.*, p. 188.
12. *Vallejo News Chronicle*, October 15, 1963.
13. *Almanack of Poor Richard Nixon*, Cleveland, World Publishing Co., 1968, p. 143.
14. Theodore White Jr., *The Making of the President, 1960*, New York, Atheneum Publishers, 1961, p. 196.
15. *Ibid.*
16. Earl Mazo, *Richard Nixon, A Political and Personal Portrait*, New York, Harper & Brothers, 1959, p. 186.
17. Alsop, *op. cit.*, p. 9.
18. Mazo, *op. cit.*, p. 70.
19. *National Review*, October 8, 1960.
20. Mazo and Hess, *op. cit.*, p. 246.
21. *Ibid.*, p. 249.
22. Jules Witcover, *The Resurrection of Richard Nixon*, New York, G.P. Putnam's Sons, 1970, pp. 25-26.
23. *Ibid.*, p. 27.
24. *Montrose Ledger*, March 8, 1962.
25. *Ebony*, April 1962.
26. *Los Angeles Times*, November 9, 1961.
27. *New York Times*, Western Edition, November 12, 1962.
28. Witcover, *op. cit.*, p. 25.
29. *This Week*, May 26, 1968.
30. White, *op. cit.*, p. 48.

CHAPTER VIII

Goldwater Over The Dam

After seven futile tries, in 1964 the Conservatives, those who formed the vast majority of the grass roots of the party, finally succeeded in nominating one of their own to run for the Presidency. The impetus for the Goldwater nomination came from the Conservative movement that had mushroomed following the election of John Kennedy. It was primarily a young movement and a grass-roots movement. The new Conservative forces came not from the top down, as the stereotype put out by Theodore White and other authors would suggest, but from the bottom up. The Goldwater drive was as far from the "boss" image as it is possible to get; it was a rare occasion of spontaneous ideological fervor imposing its energies on a reluctant candidate.

It was the personal commitment of people who believed their efforts made a difference that fueled the Goldwater effort, from the primary battles, to the delegate contest in state conventions, to the floor of San Francisco's Cow Palace. The Goldwater people had a "secret weapon" – the Conservative movement and the profound commitment of its partisans. Campaign director Cliff White found in the legions of the movement the people who would go out and make the personal contacts, ring the doorbells, and sit through the precinct meetings. He found people who were motivated by the philosophy of Conservatism. In November 1964, of course, this motivation was not sufficient to overcome the many handicaps under which Goldwater operated. But without the commitment Goldwater would not have been in the race in the first place. In ten primaries Goldwater got 2,148,000 votes, or 48 per cent of the total. His nearest rival, Nelson Rockefeller, got 1,163,000, or 28 per cent.

If the little people liked Goldwater, the big people, and particularly the Establishment *Insiders*, certainly did not. Big business, which is supposed to be Conservative and usually is not, recognized Goldwater as a man it could not control and jumped out of the Republican boat to huddle with Lyndon Johnson, a man who is known to be a pretty shrewd financier himself.

In no campaign had the prejudice of the press expressed itself so clearly as in the legendary distortions of Goldwater's stands.[1]

The true ideological colors of Huntley-Brinkley, *Life, Look, Time, Newsweek, et al.*, have never been more glaringly obvious than in the treatment given Goldwater in his campaign. From a public relations standpoint Goldwater was a most promotable item, and could easily have been given the same charisma that has been created for Lindsay, Rockefeller, and Percy. A sort of modern Thomas Jefferson, Goldwater was a chronic gadgeteer, a jet plane pilot, a sports car fancier, a ham radio operator, an expert on western lore, and an honorary member of an Indian tribe. He was dashing in appearance and laced his public remarks with humor and colloquialisms (which were magnificently twisted by the press). But Goldwater was a threat to the CFR one-party system, and all the big guns of the American communications and publishing industry were turned on him in an attempt to destroy not merely the man, but the movement behind him.

But nowhere was Goldwater attacked as viciously and ferociously as he was by members of his own party, including many for whom Goldwater had made personal campaign efforts in the past. The Liberals loosed upon Goldwater a storm of accusation and innuendo that made their assaults upon the late Senator Taft in 1952 look like warm endorsements. Nelson Rockefeller and Henry Cabot Lodge appeared before 40,000 Negro demonstrators in the streets of San Francisco during the convention, openly inciting them against the candidacy of the man about to be chosen to head their own party ticket. Scranton camp followers spread incredible tales, suggesting that Goldwater was perhaps in league with neo-Fascists in Germany — this about a man whose own father was Jewish. During the California primary Rockefeller had mailed out a million reprints of *Look* magazine's smear on Goldwater, and Rocky insinuated that Goldwater supporters used "Communist and Nazi methods." At the convention the Liberals tried to insert in the platform a repudiation of "extremist groups such as the Communists, the Ku Klux Klan, [and] The John Birch Society." The technique was obvious: to lump a patriotic organization together with two anti-American subversive groups (the albatross technique), and dump them all into the lap of Goldwater — and this from the very Liberals who used to scream loudest about "guilt by association" when it was accurately applied to Communists and fellow travelers. The entire tenor of the '64 convention was to brand Goldwater as a madman and an extremist. The Liberals denounced Goldwater's supporters as extremists but were unwilling to denounce the ADA, the ACLU, the Fair Play for Cuba Committee, CORE, or any of the radical leftwing societies that are influential in the Democratic Party.

The image of Goldwater as a bomb-crazed maniac — fastened on him, as Theodore White observed, "first by Rockefeller, then by Scranton, then by Johnson" — was decisive. The result was that Goldwater wound up running his campaign "not only against Lyndon Johnson and the Democratic record, but against fear itself." [2] Up through the primaries and the convention, both Rockefeller and Scranton strove to argue that they, not Goldwater, were true "Conservatives." Goldwater was portrayed as a "radical" who wanted to defoliate everything, including downtown New York. Robert Donovan observed that:

> The fear that a Goldwater administration might somehow lead to war was the most powerful single factor Johnson had on his side. Everywhere reporters and poll-takers found voters worried about what Goldwater would do abroad . . . . This worry was undoubtedly the main reason why many men and women who might otherwise have been expected to vote Republican deserted Goldwater.[3]

The climax of the liberal Republican attack on Goldwater was contained in the infamous Scranton "letter," which is an excellent example of how immoderate moderates can be when dealing with Conservatives. The letter to Goldwater, which was distributed to every convention delegate, stated:

> Your supporters . . . admit that you are a minority candidate, but feel they have bought, beaten and compromised enough delegate support to make the result a foregone conclusion.
>
> With open contempt for the dignity, integrity and common sense of the convention, your managers say in effect that the delegates are little more than a flock of chickens whose necks will be wrung at will . . . .
>
> You have too often casually prescribed nuclear war as a solution to a troubled world.
>
> You have too often allowed the radical extremists to use you.
>
> You have too often stood for irresponsibility in the serious question of racial holocaust . . . .
>
> In short, Goldwaterism has come to stand for a whole crazy-quilt collection of absurd and dangerous positions that would be soundly repudiated by the American people in November.

When Scranton issued his various statements, of which the "letter" was merely the last of a series, he had no realistic chance for the nomination. The question had been settled before he entered the race. The only purpose that would be served by this eleventh hour harangue was to destroy Goldwater's slender chance of election in the fall. Describing Scranton's frame of mind when he jumped into the race, Theodore White tells us in *The Making of the President, 1964*: "It was his party: and if, to save it, he had to punish Goldwater, an old friend, and destroy, in 1964 the value of his nomination, then so it had to be." After Scranton had done his dirty work he faded away like an old political soldier. White states that the strategy of the "letter":

> ... had made the Republican convention the stage for the destruction of the leading Republican candidate. What Rockefeller had begun in the spring, Scranton finished in June and at the convention: the painting for the American people of a half-crazed leader indifferent to the needs of American society at home and eager to plunge the nation into war abroad .... Rockefeller and Scranton had drawn up the indictment, Lyndon Johnson was the prosecutor. Goldwater was cast as the defendant.[4]

The hatchet job was done by Liberal Republicans. The Democrats were just the clean-up committee.

Of course, it would be ludicrously false to maintain that Goldwater was headed for a smashing victory in November 1964 until he was stabbed in the back by members of his own party. All polls showed that Goldwater's popularity had peaked out just prior to the tragic assassination of President Kennedy in November 1963. Even though the President was shot down by an avowed Marxist who had spent several years in Russia, and who following his arrest gave the Communist clenched fist salute and called for John J. Abt, the chief defense attorney for the Communist party, to serve as his lawyer, the American media blamed the President's assassination on "the climate of hate." Strong implications were made that Conservative activists were somehow to blame for the assassination of the President. The New England Liberal, who according to all the polls was losing popularity, was replaced by a man variously regarded as a Southerner or Westerner, who was believed, mistakenly, to be quite Conservative. During the campaign LBJ delivered a number of speeches that would have won him a standing ovation at a DAR convention. The issue of Conservatism versus Liberalism, which was to have been the focal point of the 1964 campaign, never succeeded in getting discussed after the death of Kennedy.

Robert Donovan noted that: "Millions of voters regarded Johnson as a middle-of-the-road conservative and Goldwater as a radical extremist."

Stanton Evans has asked why it was that, if the Conservative position is as politically disastrous as we are told, the Liberals, confronted with the first Conservative presidential candidate in thirty years, labored so hard to demonstrate that he was not a Conservative. If the American consensus is overwhelmingly Liberal, the best possible strategy against a Conservative candidate would seem to be to prove that he *is* a Conservative, while the best possible strategy for a Liberal candidate would of course be to present himself in full ADA regalia. Yet the Republican Liberals, Johnson, and their supporters in the media resolutely avoided the confrontation. They stuck to the technique of personal attack, promoting the idea that Goldwater was an untrustworthy individual, a "radical," and that Johnson was a stable, prudent person who could be trusted as Goldwater could not. The Johnson campaign avoided throughout any effort to ballyhoo the explicit ADA-style Liberalism at the heart of the Great Society programs. It is no debate of Liberal-Conservative issues, after all, to cry "nuclear death" when serious issues of foreign policy are raised, when the merits of the Test Ban Treaty are discussed, or when the complex question is broached of what kind of delegated authority should exist in regard to tactical nuclear weapons in the event of a massive Communist attack.

The day after the election, Liberals in and out of the Republican party were gleeful. James Reston (CFR) wrote in the *New York Times* of November 4th:

> Barry Goldwater has not only lost the Presidential election yesterday, but the conservative cause as well. He has wrecked his party for a long time to come and is not even likely to control the wreckage.

Jacob Javits (CFR), who, like the other Republican "moderates," had taken a vacation during the campaign, said:

> The election of 1964 should have settled this question for a long time to come. The overriding issue posed by the Goldwater-Miller ticket which was clear to the American people was a call for de-centralization — to shift to the state and local levels of government certain important federal functions and responsibilities. The size of the defeat cannot be seen other than as a repudiation of this concept.[5]

Having done everything they possibly could to sabotage Goldwater and magnify the extent of his defeat, the party's Liberals piously maintained that Conservatism had been repudiated and that the party must move leftward in the future. Having promoted the desertion of the party by many of its own members, the Liberal clique blamed the debacle on Goldwater. Having made the Goldwater defeat as large as they possibly could, the Liberal Republicans proceeded to read the Conservatives out of the positions of power in the party. That Goldwater's poor showing was in large measure attributable to the successful effort to brand him as an irresponsible radical is seen by a comparison of his electoral performance with that of Republican Congressmen in Conservative areas, men who were just as Conservative as Goldwater himself, but who uniformly ran ahead of him. The only

significant difference between these candidates and Goldwater was that they were not subjected to the nonstop smear
job that was his daily lot. H.R. Gross of Iowa, Richard
Roudebush of Indiana, and John Ashbrook of Ohio, all
strong Conservatives, ran far ahead of Goldwater in their
respective districts. If Goldwater's Conservative ideology had
been the reason for his poor showing, these Congressmen
would have run more or less even with him, since their
ideological position was, on all major points, virtually
identical with his. But they, in fact, gained votes from many
people who marked their ballots against Goldwater. These
results made it clear that not only did Goldwater fail to
receive a routine Republican vote; he did not even receive a
routine Conservative vote.

Congressional and other losses suffered by the GOP in
1964 are cited by the Liberals as final proof that a
Conservative Republican "can't win." It is therefore interesting to compare the outcome of the Goldwater campaign
with the last election conducted explicitly in the "Eisenhower mainstream." In 1958, the Republican party sustained
a net loss of forty-eight House seats, compared with
thirty-eight in 1964. The party in 1958 lost a total of
thirteen Senate seats, compared with two in 1964. In
gubernatorial races, the 1958 GOP suffered a net loss of five
governorships; in 1964 the party actually made a net gain of
one. In 1958, the party lost 686 state legislative seats, while
in 1964 it lost 541. The truth is, then, the performance was
uniformly worse in 1958 than it was in 1964.[6]

The Liberals in the GOP have brought about their own
debacles in Presidential years. In 1948, for example, when
Dewey was supposed to win hands down, the GOP lost a
staggering total of seventy-five seats in the House of
Representatives, nine seats in the Senate, and seven governorships — in each case a much higher aggregate loss than was
sustained in 1964. The 1964 election was then, in fact, a

lesser calamity, not a greater one, than was suffered in either 1948 or 1958. The fact is that the charges hurled at the head of Goldwater, and the implication that "modern" Republicans alone know how to build the national party and win elections, simply are not true. Far from being able to win, the Liberal Republicans hold championship marks for engineering GOP defeats.

Nineteen sixty-four is also pointed to by Liberal Republicans as proof that their "New York strategy," which seeks to win elections by appealing to bloc votes in the large cities of key industrial states, is superior to Goldwater's "Southwest strategy," which seeks to weld the traditionally Conservative mid-West to the South-Southwest-West. In truth, this strategy was not tested in 1964, since Goldwater was running not against a New Englander, as would have been the case had JFK not been assassinated, but against a man who was also a Southerner and a Westerner. It should also be pointed out that the New York strategy has worked only twice since 1936, and in both of those cases a highly popular war hero defeated an unappealing egghead.

There were positive aspects to the 1964 calamity. Grassroots participation in Republican politics reached an all-time high; Goldwater received contributions from almost 1,500,000 individuals, whereas Nixon received contributions from only 40,000 individuals. (This is further proof, however, that the "fat cats" who had supported Nixon and other Republican candidates in the past abandoned Goldwater.) Leftwing groups saw in this rise of grass-roots Conservatism a harbinger of the future. Group Research Incorporated, which kept an eye on free-enterprise-oriented groups and individuals for the late Walter Reuther, in a year-end report for 1965 disclosed that Conservative performance since the Goldwater defeat, rather than diminishing, had experienced a marked upward movement and staked out new positions of political strength.[7] The Anti-Defamation League expressed the opinion that:

The real accomplishment of the radical right [Conservatism]
in the 1964 campaign was in the exposure of millions of
Americans to its message, and new recruits to its membership,
and in the reservoir of potential recruits being built up . . .
through their efforts in the Goldwater campaign.[8]

By 1964 the Conservative movement had come so far
that Conservatives were able to accomplish what Taft, on
three different occasions, had failed to do — win the
nomination. The movement, however, was not yet large
enough to win the election. The campaign nonetheless
succeeded, albeit in strangled tones, in getting before the
people some important issues — crime in the streets was the
most obvious — which subsequently became grade A topics
for all respectable politicians. During 1964 the Conservatives
at least got their foot in the political door.

The real tragedy of the Goldwater campaign was that its
leader gave up the crusade when he was defeated at the polls.
On November 4, 1964, there were two kinds of Conservatives
in America: sad ones and mad ones. Some were ready to
crawl into their hole, resigned to the triumph of collectivism.
The mad Conservatives wanted to carry on the crusade.
Goldwater's cardinal sins were two: first, that following the
nominating convention he lost the initiative and went on the
defensive; secondly, following his defeat he handed the party
machinery, which the Conservatives had acquired through
four years of blood, sweat, and tears, back to the Liberals. In
U.S. News & World Report of December 21, 1964, Goldwater was asked how he viewed his future role in the
Republican party. He stated that it was his intention to:
" . . . continue to be a working member of the Republican
party — not trying to dictate anything, just putting my
shoulder to the wheel." Thus did Goldwater in one sentence
"telegraph" to his twenty-seven million supporters that he
did not intend to fight for Conservative principles at the

January meeting of the Republican National Committee in Chicago. The Goldwater abdication in January 1965 did more to hurt the Conservative cause and re-establish one-party government in the United States than did the November 1964 election defeat. Out went Dean Burch and in came Ray Bliss, "Mr. Pragmatist." Ralph de Toledano wrote in his nationally syndicated column of June 29, 1965:

> Like other Liberal Leftist Republicans, Mr. Bliss had made no secret of the fact that he cares not a whit about the sensibilities of the Conservatives who make up the bulk of the party's workers. Conservatives, he contended, have nowhere else to go.

Goldwater was a reluctant candidate in the first place. He had no lust for the power of the Presidency, as had Richard Nixon, nor for the incredible amount of work that goes with it. The Conservative movement fell in love with Goldwater's ghostwriters, who turned out his columns, speeches, and books. Unfortunately Goldwater was not his ghost writers. He was propelled into candidacy by the zeal of the grass-roots Conservatives, which he did not fully share. He had no desire to capitalize on the great depth of exuberance and loyalty felt by his hard-core supporters all over the country. Instead of continuing the crusade Goldwater went back to his ham radio. The '64 election was water over the dam — Goldwater over the dam.

The Liberal Republicans, believing that 1964 was a lost cause anyway, were willing to let the Conservatives have their fling, knowing that it would be disastrous. In its January 24, 1967 issue, *Look* Magazine stated editorially concerning the Republicans:

> In 1964 the overall mood of the convention's professionals was that it didn't really matter who was nominated, because no available Republican could beat President Johnson. The polls showed a bare 35% for Goldwater against Johnson, the same for Nixon, and even less for Governors Nelson A. Rockefeller of New

238 *Richard Nixon*

York and William W. Scranton of Pennsylvania. Also, Goldwater had knocked himself out raising money for the party and had won the big California primary. The conservatives, furthermore, were screaming for "a choice not an echo," and the moderates — correctly assessing the middle-road temper of the country (which is now almost universally recognized) [*sic*] but squabbling over who their leader should be — decided to let the conservatives fall on their faces.

The strategy couldn't have been smarter. Had the Liberal Republicans in 1964 engineered another minority coup, the Conservatives, particularly after Phyllis Schlafly's book, *A Choice Not An Echo*, would have left the Republican party en masse. The smartest thing for the Liberals to do was to let the Conservatives have a year, knowing that they could not win and that their defeat could be blamed on the Conservative philosophy, setting the stage for the re-establishment of a middle-of-the-road Republican party.

The man who benefited most from the Goldwater debacle was Richard Nixon. Obviously, Goldwater or someone equally conservative could not be nominated in 1968, and GOP Conservatives would just as obviously not support any of the Liberal Republicans who had put the knife in their candidate's back. Richard Nixon became the only possible candidate acceptable to both wings of the party.

As the 1964 Republican convention approached, Nixon, like an old firehorse, and apparently against his better judgment, again began to smell smoke. He had lain low, bided his time, and avoided the stop-Goldwater movement until late in the game. He had made it "perfectly clear" that he was not taking sides in the Goldwater vs. Rockefeller primaries. Then, as Stephen Hess and David Broder recall in their book, *The Republican Establishment*:

Just as suddenly, Nixon switched sides and became the self-appointed leader of the stop-Goldwater forces. A week after California had voted, on June 9th, he flew to Cleveland for the

national Governors' Conference .... Nixon ... astounded everyone by attacking Goldwater at a press conference. Citing the
Senator's view of the United Nations and Soviet-American
relations, his suggestion that social security be made voluntary,
that the Tennessee Valley Authority be sold to private interests,
and civil rights enforcement be left to the states, and a national
right-to-work law be enacted, Nixon said, "It would be a tragedy
for the Republican party in the event that Senator Goldwater's
views, as previously stated, were not challenged and repudiated."[9]

Nixon was trying, according to Hess and Broder, to set up
Romney as a stalking horse in a last desperate effort to
produce a convention deadlock from which he, Nixon, would
emerge as the nominee.

On June 15, 1964, the *Herald Tribune* News Service
reported this repudiation by Nixon of his June 9th statement
that Goldwater's views would be a "tragedy" for the party:

> Richard M. Nixon did everything possible Tuesday to join the
> Goldwater camp here except put on a Goldwater cowboy hat for
> the benefit of photographers .... [Nixon] declared that the
> Senator from Arizona really is "mainstream" of the party now
> that "he has become a national rather than a regional candidate."

Hess and Broder explain Nixon's broken field running this
way:

> ... privately, the last two weeks of June, 1964, Nixon began
> to readjust his sights from the 1964 nomination to the
> 1968 .... Nixon evolved a new role for himself: the apostle of
> party unity who would campaign doggedly for the ticket in 1964
> and for all Republican candidates in 1966, as a way of rebuilding
> his political capital for 1968.[10]

It could be that Nixon really did not want a stalemate at
the convention that would cause it to turn to him with the
nomination. He had known since 1960 that his time was
1968, not 1964. His brief flurry of anti-Goldwaterism may

have been a show to keep his credentials in order with party
Liberals. Nixon knew that Goldwater was "doomed to
defeat," but Nixon nevertheless campaigned tirelessly for the
Arizonan, knowing that he would thus become the only
possible candidate who would not divide the party in 1968,
since most other Republican leaders were sitting out the
campaign.

One week after the '64 election, Nixon told Warren Duffee
of UPI that the Republican Party had "gone too far right,"
and now "most of all needs some discipline." Nixon
continued: "The Republican party's national position must
represent the responsible right and the responsible ultra-
liberal." The future position of the GOP, Nixon said, "must
be the center . . . . The formula [for victory] should be the
Eisenhower-Nixon formula, not because it is more to the left,
but because it is the right position . . . . " Nixon placed
himself squarely in the "center," but failed to comment on
the fact that the middle of the road had been moving
Leftward for thirty-five years. He did, however, state: "I will
discourage − I will not tolerate − any activity on behalf of
myself by anyone else for 1968." [11] Sure, sure. But when
Goldwater dropped the leadership torch, Nixon was Johnny-
on-the-spot to pick it up. In an article in the *New York Times*
of February 14, 1965, the following comment was made:

> When Barry Goldwater consented to the removal of the man
> of his choice as Republican National Chairman and renounced his
> own Presidential aspirations, the leadership of the Republican
> party lay there for the taking.
>
> But not for long. Richard M. Nixon has firmly grasped the
> leadership role, which being unofficial, can become anything he
> wants to make it. He intends, apparently, to make much of it.

References

1. Lionel Locos, *Hysteria, 1964,* New Rochelle, N.Y., Arlington House, 1966.
2. M. Stanton Evans, *The Future of Conservatism: From Taft to Reagan and Beyond,* New York, Holt, Rinehart & Winston, 1968, p. 197.
3. *Ibid.,* p. 196.
4. *Ibid.,* p. 192.
5. *Ibid.,* p. 33.
6. *Ibid.,* pp. 221-222.
7. *Ibid.,* p. 138.
8. *Ibid.,* p. 135.
9. Stephen Hess and David Broder, *The Republican Establishment,* New York, Harper & Row, 1967, pp. 168-169.
10. *Ibid.,* p. 170.
11. *Oakland Tribune,* November 10, 1964.

CHAPTER IX

Be Sincere
Whether You Mean It Or Not

With the 1964 elections now history, the Nixon Express began to build up steam while its engineer carefully studied its 1968 timetable. Nixon's law firm allowed him seemingly unlimited time for world travel to keep up his reputation as an expert on foreign affairs, and for campaigning on behalf of GOP candidates. Hess and Broder observed:

> For major chunks of each year he circles the globe . . . on personal fact-finding junkets . . . . For other parts of each year he circles the United States . . . restoring his credentials as a political leader.[1]

During the 1966 Congressional elections, Nixon made appearances in thirty-five states for eighty-six Republican nominees. In addition he raised large sums of money to fill candidates' campaign coffers.

Although Nixon was campaigning for others, he made LBJ — the man most likely to be his opponent two years hence — the target of his assault. Typical was this Nixon statement:

> Every time a housewife goes into a supermarket today, she is faced with the High Cost of Johnson . . . . Every time a businessman tries to make a loan that would produce more jobs, he runs into interest rates that are really the High Cost of Johnson . . . . Every time a young couple tries to buy a home these days, the door is slammed in their faces by the High Cost of Johnson.[2]

Ironically, the Democrats will probably make "the High Cost of Nixon" a major campaign theme in 1972.

In the off-year elections the Republicans picked up forty-seven seats in the House of Representatives, three Senate seats, eight governorships, and 540 seats in state legislatures. The Elephant that everybody had been ready to consign to the graveyard two years before was back in fettle and optimistically looking forward to the '68 jousting match with the rival Donkey. And Richard Nixon received much of the credit for the comeback. Candidates for whom he campaigned ran much better, statistically, than those for whom he did not appear. What is more, Nixon, the old master poker player, acquired more IOUs than a riverboat gambler. These political IOUs all had a 1968 due date.

Nixon had to do well in the primaries, as he admitted, to remove the "loser" image which dogged him. His main opposition in the New Hampshire kickoff primary was George Romney, who conveniently cut his own political throat by telling newspapermen he had been brainwashed on the Vietnam question. Polls showed Romney doing so miserably that he dropped out of the New Hampshire primary, leaving the field to Nixon. The unopposed victory was just the psychological boost the Nixon campaign needed. After that it was all downhill to Miami.

In his quest for the 1968 nomination Nixon assumed the Conservatives had nowhere else to go, and courted the Left. By attending the funeral of civil rights agitator Martin Luther King, Jr. along with virtually every other presidential office seeker and black nationalist, Nixon made it clear that he was willing to crawl for the Negro bloc vote. Certainly Nixon with his contacts had access to the information in the FBI file on King, which reveals King's close association with Communists.

Nixon, who had called the Civil Rights Bill of 1964, described by two former presidents of the American Bar Association as ten per cent civil rights and ninety per cent government control, a "great step forward,"[3] capitalized on the hysteria following King's death to push another civil rights bill through Congress. According to the *Los Angeles Times* of March 24, 1968, NAACP member Nixon had been working behind the scenes to support a forced housing bill before the King assassination. According to *Human Events*, Nixon played a strategic role in getting Congress to adopt the hastily drawn 1968 Civil Rights Act. He not only pressed for adoption of the "open housing" section, which had never undergone proper committee hearings, but he had been urging House Republicans to accept the Senate version of the Civil Rights Bill without any alterations. Such Nixon lieutenants as Representative Clark MacGregor of Minnesota helped to persuade House Republicans to accept the Senate amendments *in toto*. Nixon's telephone call to Representative John Anderson of Illinois, swing man on the important House Rules Committee, turned out to be crucial to the fate of the Senate bill:

> The rules committee had appeared deadlocked over whether to send the Senate bill to a Senate-House conference, where House members could rework the legislation, or to send the bill to the House floor for a vote with a gag rule that would prevent any amendment whatsoever. Nixon phoned Anderson and urged him to send the bill to the House floor for a quick vote. Under pressure from Nixon and the tense conditions in the country following the murder of King, Anderson buckled.[4]

The *Insiders* and their puppets know that during the psychological shock of a disaster the public is willing to accept legislation that would not otherwise be adopted.

In order to capture Negro support in his 1968 quest for the Presidential nomination, Nixon formed an alliance with the revolutionary black power fanatics of CORE. CORE has adopted the forty-year old Communist cry for a separate Black Nation, and CORE's retiring chairman, Floyd McKissick, the violent leftwing Socialist who has repudiated nonviolence, advocated not welfare for Negroes but a complete redistribution of the wealth, beginning with government subsidization of Negro-owned businesses. This has been mislabeled "black capitalism," and is a subtle perversion of the only true answer to the Negroes' economic plight, namely, the genuine free enterprise system. Liberal columnists Evans and Novak reported:

> In recent days, Nixon has been in contact with CORE leaders Floyd McKissick and Roy Innis [McKissick's successor] through intermediaries. Thus, their surprising agreement on economic black power could turn out to be Nixon's first real breakthrough into the Negro leadership.[5]

CORE then came out in praise of Nixon for having seen "the relevance of black power," and claimed that Nixon is the "only Presidential candidate who is moving in the direction of CORE's program."[6] What Nixon and CORE advocate is not the channeling of private capital into Negro-owned or Negro-managed businesses, but nonprofit co-ops financed by government loans. Tax-free, nonprofit co-ops, financed by the taxpayers, do not constitute capitalism. What Nixon mistakenly calls "Black Capitalism" is in reality black communes or Black Soviets.

In a further quest to attract support of the bloc vote of Liberal Negroes, *Parade* Magazine of June 16, 1968, revealed that Nixon considered Edward Brooke of Massachusetts as his running mate. However, Brooke had decided to throw in his lot with Nelson Rockefeller. Liberal columnist Carl Rowan, who served in high appointive capacities in the Kennedy and Johnson Administrations, reported that leftward forces in Massachusetts:

> . . . regard Brooke as one of their own — infiltrating the enemy camp — and making them like it. They regard the Massachusetts Senate race as a contest to see whether an ideological Democrat can go all the way to the top in a Republican masquerade.[7]

The great puppet show of 1968 was the Nixon-Rockefeller contest. Many an astute observer believes that Rockefeller may have entered the Presidential race at a time when he had little chance of winning, solely to bring some badly needed publicity to the Republican party's race and to solidify Conservative backing for Nixon. Rocky and Richard were not the enemies they were pictured as being. ADA member Stewart Alsop wrote in his book, *Nixon and Rockefeller*:

> There are in fact, it should be noted, *no sharp ideological differences between Rockefeller and Nixon*, as there were between Dewey and Taft and Eisenhower and Taft. When Rockefeller worked in Washington for the first Eisenhower Administration, he often found an ally in Nixon on such issues as foreign aid. The difference is really a difference of style and background and approach to politics . . . . [Emphasis added.] [8]

Nixon's friendly biographer, Earl Mazo, says that in Washington "Nixon and Rockefeller became good friends and supported each other consistently . . . ."[9] After the 1956 election Rockefeller wrote Nixon on November 7th: " . . . under you and the President the Republican party is now emerging, at home and abroad, as the great liberal party of the future."[10] Joseph Alsop, brother of Stewart and also a member of the ADA, wrote in a 1963 column on the then upcoming election:

> What the Republican politicians call the "old New York crowd" will almost certainly stick by Nelson Rockefeller as long as propriety and good manners require them to do so. But it is a very good guess that men like former Governor Thomas E. Dewey, and the financial leaders who used to work with Dewey, are already thinking hard about where they can go if Rockefeller does not make the grade. And it is an equally good guess that they are thinking about going to Nixon.[11]

Then there was the little matter of Nixon moving into

Rocky's apartment house and going to work for the law firm used by Chase Manhattan for its trust accounts.

Rockefeller may have held some hope that he could actually wrest the candidacy from his own puppet, but as the *Wall Street Journal's* Vermont Royster observed:

> Indeed, Mr. Rockefeller's initial half-hearted campaign seemed only to demonstrate that he expected to lose to Mr. Nixon. The governor drifted along almost aimlessly while his vaunted staff became disorganized. Meanwhile, Mr. Nixon sailed on serenely, making no mistakes that could give the New Yorker an opening . . . .
>
> It was only after Sen. Robert Kennedy's assassination June 5 that Mr. Rockefeller's campaign got rolling. By then, only a slim chance existed of stopping Nixon, but Rocky spared nothing — spending millions for national advertising, and pushing himself through a frenetic cross-country campaign . . . . [12]

The Rockefeller campaign suggested from the beginning that the New York governor was acting as a stalking horse for his ostensible opponent, Richard Nixon. First there was his reluctance to become a candidate at a date when he had time to forge a successful campaign. Then, when he did begin to flirt with the idea of getting in, he soon backed off, claiming that his old ardor for the Presidency was no longer there and that the rank and file wanted Nixon. He would not, he said, divide the party. Only after the primaries had come and gone, and Nixon had the nomination sewed up, did Rocky enter the race, spending money like a Rockefeller and keeping the Republicans in the headlines.

It was an eloquent performance. Nixon had to have an enemy on the Left to make him a salable commodity to the Conservatives. The *Insiders* knew very well that if Nelson Rockefeller came out against Hell, many Conservatives would begin to find redeeming qualities in Satan. Thus, if Rocky didn't like Nixon's Conservatism, it must be a very good brand of Conservatism indeed. Republican Conservatives began to salivate after Nixon as if he were to the Right of Barry Goldwater.

At Miami the country was treated to the picture of a superconfident Richard Nixon who seemed not to have a worry in the world. He didn't. And the biggest tip-off was the sight of Nixon's supercompetent professional staff competing with Rocky's bumbling amateurs — a group crawling with just the sort of high-pressure New Left types guaranteed to offend the delegates. There may be some who really believe that Nelson Rockefeller couldn't put together a team of first-rate professionals, but they must be political kindergartners.

As the Elephant Herd assembled in Miami Beach for the quadrennial ceremonial nominating dance, Richard Nixon knew he had the prize in the bag. Relaxing before the festivities started, Nixon called a press conference in which he repudiated his past anti-Communist stands. A mere two weeks before the rape of Czecho-Slovakia by the Soviets and their henchmen, *New York Times* headlines blared: "Nixon Says He Has Eased Views On Communist Bloc Since 1960." Mr. Nixon explained to the newsmen at Miami that the Communist Conspiracy was no longer an unyielding, monolithic force. In 1960, the candidate maintained, "the Communist world was a monolithic world. Today it is a split world, schizophrenic, with very great diversity."

As Americans died in Vietnam, Nixon even said he believed that the "era of confrontation" with the Communist world had ended, ushering in a new "era of *negotiations* with the Soviet Union . . . and . . . the leaders of the next superpower, Communist China . . . . "

In subscribing to the new myths and ignoring the old realities, Richard Nixon announced that the harsh words he had for the Communists in his 1960 acceptance speech are today "irrelevant." And, he added, "as the facts change, any intelligent man does change his approaches to the problems.

It does not mean that he is an opportunist. It means only that he is a pragmatist."

At the convention the Nixonites grabbed Conservative issues lock, stock, and barrel. Unfortunately they did not adopt Conservative solutions, only the issues. But Conservative Republicans who should have known better loved it. The object, however, was to propagandize the Conservative wing of the Party, quietly pat its wounded ego, and sell it a gilded brick. That brick was labeled *Party Unity*.

The way the script was written, the disunity of 1964 was no longer the fault of those disloyal "Liberals" who betrayed and sabotaged Barry Goldwater, but that of the twenty-seven million ideological dervishes who had run screaming onto the swords of Lyndon's legions, believing that their sacrifice would somehow help to re-establish our Constitution and the American system of free enterprise. Now, with a Liberal candidate in prospect, it was the turncoats of 1964 who were leading the cry for unity and pragmatism. With Wallace in the race, the Liberals realized that they must have Conservative support to win. "Pragmatism!" they cried. And Conservative Republicans echoed: "Pragmatism!"

It was all very cordial. Liberals even permitted the former Conservative spokesman, a fellow named Goldwater, to support their plea for unity before the convention. It was like calling the victim of a mugging as a character witness for his assailants — not so much offering proof of the victim's compassion as providing evidence that when the muggers struck they hit the man in the head harder than anyone had realized at the time. Conservatives were now welcomed back into the Republican Party. It was like being met at the door of your own home by a hospitable burglar and invited to come in for a drink. Curiously, Republican Conservatives seemed elated by such courtly treatment from Party Liberals, and gratefully accepted the incredible invitation. Thus, the Republican Right was forgiven for the "crime of 1964" and its sins were washed away in the soothing waters of Party Unity. It was quite a trick to get the Conservative lambs to lie down with the Liberal lions while their cage was being constructed, but that was precisely what happened. As the *Insiders* scripted a soothing of Party Conservatives to keep them away from the Wallace campaign, they also moved to keep the Party's non-Establishment Liberals (who also take these conventions seriously) from committing hara-kiri at the thought that the Republican Party might campaign on Conservative principles. Indeed, the scenario called for monumental staging.

The cast of this pragmatic extravaganza contained a protagonist on the Left (for the Liberals to cheer and the Conservatives to hiss), a Rightist knight of the silver screen (to make Conservative hearts go pitter-pat and to horrify unsophisticated Liberals), and a centrist (an experienced and highly competent professional, skilled at uniting the Party in a shotgun marriage to last until the second week in November). The centrist, as you know, got the girl in the end.

At Miami, Mr. Nixon was *the one*, on the first ballot. And his acceptance speech proved a masterpiece of pragmatism — superbly eloquent and totally noncommittal. He sounded to the casual listener like a combination of Billy Graham calling for a crusade against sin, John Wayne delivering a Fourth of July speech to the American Legion, Pat O'Brien exhorting Notre Dame to "win one for the Gipper," George Wallace at his ironic best, and Martin Luther King ascending the mountain. The speech was delivered in terms that drew positive reactions from both Liberals and Conservatives without offending either. Such an accomplishment is more difficult than passing an elephant through the eye of a donkey, and one must admire Mr. Nixon's oratorical expertise if not his anti-ideology. The speech was amazing. Mr.

Nixon said that to the "new" Republican Party the enemy of liberty is not collectivism itself, but the mismanagement of collectivism. Generalities abounded. Although the address was far different in tone from Nixon's acceptance speech of 1960, in which he had attempted to outpromise the Democrats in detail, the theme was the same. The *Wall Street Journal* had dubbed the 1960 acceptance a wedding of the "Welfare State to fiscal responsibility." That theme was repeated in 1968 — but this time Nixon hedged his bet by attacking the consequences of the very collectivism he proposed.

Richard Nixon knew that in 1968 the mood of the nation had become increasingly Conservative; Americans were sick of court decisions handcuffing the police, of the scandal-ridden "War on Poverty," of jogging inflation, and of the looting and burning of our cities by psychotic Black Nationalists and revolutionary delinquents. As America's pre-eminent reader of trends, he devoted his 1968 acceptance speech to an attempt to steal a march on these issues — all raised by George Wallace — just as he had attempted in 1960 to steal a march on the issues raised by John Kennedy. The difference, as always with Mr. Nixon, was a matter of solutions: This time he was arguing that his alchemists could cook up a totally new brand of federal collectivism guaranteed to cure welfare problems, racial hostility, violence in the streets, and probably warts.

Richard Nixon did say many of the right things in that speech — and he said them beautifully. He talked of the American Revolution being the only true and continuing revolution, and of what private initiative has done for our country. He spoke of law and order and America's declining world position. But by reading the address, rather than merely listening to it, one discovers that he conveyed many illusory impressions. The speech implied that we would recapture the *Pueblo* and free its crew, but made no specific commitment. It sounded as if Nixon would stop the war in Vietnam, but it said nothing about winning it. It dwelt on law and order, but promised only a war on "organized crime . . . loan sharks . . . numbers racketeers . . . filth peddlers and the narcotics peddlers . . . . " with no mention of the Communists and their Black Nationalist comrades, who are making good their promises of guerrilla warfare. It also seemed to say that Nixon would cut federal spending and taxes; but again, this was only an implication made by the tone of the rhetoric.

Here was a candidate who even seemed to be promising an end to foreign aid — the very man who had said in his article of October 1967 in the Council on Foreign Relations' magazine, *Foreign Affairs*, that he sought a new Marshall Plan to dump even vaster sums of foreign aid into bottomless Asia.

The Republican platform committee labored mightily and brought forth an ideological mouse. It was the perfect platform for Nixon to stand on. One wag remarked that anyone from Mao Tse-tung to Attila the Hun could comfortably run on it. It made virtually no commitments. It did courageously declare the Party for good and against evil, but it was very hazy about how to tell which is which. Certainly the platform tended to be far more Liberal than even Nixon's acceptance speech, and the Party "moderates" called it highly "progressive." James Reston of the *New York Times*, gloating over the platform's abandonment of Conservatism, wrote:

> . . . [the Republicans] have learned from their disastrous campaign of 1964. Nobody is putting party ideology above party unity, not even Goldwater. In fact, Goldwater, Reagan, Nixon and Rockefeller have all accepted the objectives of a party platform that Humphrey or even McCarthy could accept.

Ah yes, and Mao and Attila too.

Following Miami, Nixon shifted gears into the smoothest,

most professional, most public relations-oriented campaign ever conducted. One of the developments in modern political life that has concerned both Democrats and Republicans is the rise of public relations firms and their brainchild, television campaigning. TV, it is generally felt, puts a premium on wit and good looks at the expense of intellectual depth and the discussion of issues. Ugly old Abe Lincoln, it is often noted, would be at a distinct disadvantage against one of today's slick Madison Avenue products. Now, everything is charisma — that undefinable "it" that JFK had and HHH and RMN don't.

Whether you approve or disapprove of TV as a political weapon depends upon how well your candidate uses the medium. The Republicans loved it in 1952 and 1956 when "father-image" Eisenhower's "sincerity" came across better than Baby Dumpling Stevenson's egghead intellect. In 1960, however, the tables were turned as the Nixon-Kennedy TV debates turned out looking like robust and suntanned Charles Atlas versus a pale and puny Count Dracula in need of a shave.

In 1968, Nixon realized that he must learn how to turn TV into an asset or face another defeat. In Oregon Nixon was asked what he thought of artificially created political images. He replied:

> People are much less impressed with image arguments than are columnists, commentators, and pollsters. And I for one rejected the advice of the public relations experts who say that I've got to sit by the hour and watch myself. The American people may not like my face but they're going to listen to what I have to say.

With that he prepared to launch the most expensive public relations-and-TV-dominated campaign in the history of American elections.

Law partner Leonard Garment put together Nixon's staff of high-powered image builders. They included Harry

Treleaven, who had run ideas up the J. Walter Thompson flagpole for eighteen years for such clients as Pan American, RCA, and Ford; Frank Shakespeare, who had spent a like number of years at CBS; and Paul Keyes, a producer of "Laugh-In," who was supposed to convey the impression that Nixon had a sense of humor.* The make-up man from the Johnny Carson show was hired to make sure that Nixon never again went before the cameras looking like a baggy-eyed Count Dracula with insomnia.

With TV, the image is everything. And the image of the man need have no relation to the real man. The candidate becomes a product to be peddled like soap or instant mashed potatoes. The bright-colored box may belie what is within. Raymond Price, a Nixon speechwriter and TV advisor, was very blunt about this in a memo to Nixon:

> It's not what's there that counts, it's what's projected — and carrying it one step further, it's not what he projects, but rather what the voter receives. It's not the man we have to change, but rather the received impression. And this impression often depends more on the medium and its use than it does on the candidate himself.[13]

Probably the most fascinating account of the Nixon-Humphrey campaign yet produced is *The Selling of the President 1968,* by Joe McGinniss of the *Philadelphia Inquirer* (until recently owned by Nixon's close friend and appointee as Ambassador to the Court of St. James', Walter Annenberg).[14] The book jacket describes McGinniss' mission:

> Wondering if a presidential candidate could be advertised and sold like a car or a can of peas, Joe McGinniss informally joined the Nixon forces at the very early stages of the campaign. Around the clock, day-to-day, he lived with the technicians, ghost writers, experts, and pollsters.

---

*Treleaven's private opinion of Nixon, quoted by Joe McGinness in his *The Selling of the President 1968*, page 56, was: ". . he comes across as such an utter bore. I don't think the man has had an original observation in his life."

Whether it was an advertising concept meeting, a television
taping, a panel selection, an "ethnic specialists'" discussion;
whether at a hysterical moment of anticipated triumph, or a
quiet moment of misgiving and self-doubt, Joe McGinniss was
there, listening, asking — eliciting some of the most candid,
truly human disclosures and insights ever made about our
electoral process.

It seems incredible, but apparently nobody on the Nixon
staff made any attempt to discover whether McGinniss was
friendly or hostile before admitting him into the inner
sanctum. They know now; McGinniss's book was on top of
the best-seller list for many months running, and it presents a
most unflattering picture of Nixon and his campaign team.
McGinniss, it turned out, was a very nasty Liberal, a Eugene
McCarthyite, and quite possibly a spy for the Humphrey
campaign. But despite his foaming-at-the-mouth Liberalism,
McGinniss' book contains some gems of conversations he sat
in on that reveal the total cynicism of the Nixon campaign.

In preparing for the all-important part that TV would play
in the campaign, Harry Treleaven wrote:

> There'll be few opportunities for logical persuasion, which is all
> right — because probably more people vote for irrational,
> emotional reasons than professional politicians suspect.[15]

"I am not going to barricade myself into a television studio
and make this an antiseptic campaign," Nixon told a press
conference shortly after his nomination, as he prepared to do
just that. Six months earlier, Nixon had said, "We're going to
build this whole campaign around television. You fellows [his
TV advisors] just tell me what you want me to do and I'll do
it."[16] The Nixon campaign relied heavily on ten one-hour
specials, spread around the country, that featured an audience of shills from the local Republican clubs. They were
coached to scream like crazy every time Nixon answered a
question and then to mob him at the end of the show to give

the viewers the impression that the candidate was just oozing
with charisma. Reporters were never allowed in the studio
lest they report that the shows were staged. Staff members
cynically referred to the shills as "the applause machine."
The semi-shills who fed Nixon the questions always included
one Negro (two might be offensive and not to have one was
unthinkable), a housewife, a businessman, a Liberal, and a
working man. In most cases all went smoothly because Nixon
had well-rehearsed answers to all the standard questions,
which he had answered hundreds of times since New
Hampshire. In fact, Nixon did turn himself into a veritable
human computer, with stored answers for the most common
questions, such as: "Is there a 'new' Nixon?" Response: "My
answer is yes, there is a new Nixon, if you are talking in
terms of new ideas for the new world and the America we
live in." Garry Wills described the Nixon human computer
process:

> . . . . The tapes were sent to Washington, where computers
> typed "personalized" answers — one paragraph per concern,
> dialed out of a bank of 70 stock answers to the most common
> questions. That dialing process was a perfect extension of the
> man we watched on television. Bud Wilkinson would ask the
> same questions, or a panel would, over and over. There would
> be a pause (the internal dialing), a signaled mechanical frown of
> concern and "personalized" typing (print-out on the face — still
> fuzzy, that machine has never been perfected), and Nixon
> would finally deliver, in his tight resonant voice — like Disney's
> Audio-Animatronic figure of Lincoln, improvising Gettysburg
> Addresses to a ballet of programmed gestures — one of the 70
> paragraphs stored in this walking memory bank. [17]

But something went awry in Philadelphia, where local call-in
show host Jack McKinney, a non-shill, was accidentally asked
to be one of the questioners. McGinniss describes the
repartee:

Jack McKinney did not lead with his right but he threw a much stiffer jab than Nixon had been expecting: Why are you so reluctant to comment on Vietnam this year when in 1952, faced with a similar issue in Korea, you were so free with your partisan remarks?

Not a crippling question, but there was an undertone of unfriendliness to it. Worse, it had been put to him in professional form. Nixon had been expecting, maybe, a request for comment on the war, to which he would have given the standard With-Peace-Negotiations-At-Such-A-Delicate-Stage reply. But here was a question which assumed that reply and requested that it be defended, in light of a seeming contradiction. Nixon stepped back, a bit off balance. This sort of thing threatened the stability of the whole format; the basis being the hypothesis that Nixon could appear to risk all by going live while in fact risking nothing by facing the loose syntax and predictable, sloppy thrusts of amateurs.

Nixon threw up an evasive flurry. But the grin was gone from his face. Not only did he know now that he would have to be careful of McKinney, he was forced to wonder, for the first time, what he might encounter from the others.[18]

After Nixon had easily fielded standard questions from the Negro, the businessman, the housewife, etc., McKinney got his second shot:

It was McKinney's turn again: Why was Nixon refusing to appear on any of the news confrontation shows such as Meet the Press? Why would he face the public only in staged settings such as this, where the questions were almost certain to be worded generally enough to allow him any vague sort of answer he wanted to give? Where the presence of the cheering studio audience was sure to intimidate any questioner who contemplated true engagement? Where Nixon moved so quickly from one questioner to the next that he eliminated any possibility of follow-up, any chance for true discussion . . . ?

"I've done those quiz shows, Mr. McKinney. I've done them until they were running out of my ears." There was no question on one point: Richard Nixon was upset.

Staring hard at McKinney, he grumbled something about why

there should be more fuss about Hubert Humphrey not having press conferences and less about him and Meet the Press.

... The audience cheered. Suddenly, Nixon, perhaps sensing a weakness in McKinney where he had feared that none existed, perhaps realizing he had no choice, surely buoyed up by the cheers, decided to slug it out.

"Go ahead," he said, gesturing, "I want you to follow up."

McKinney came back creditably, using the word "amorphous" and complaining that viewers were being asked to support Nixon for President on the basis of "nothing but a wink and a smile" particularly in regard to Vietnam.

"Now, Mr. McKinney, maybe I haven't been as specific . . . . " and Nixon was off on a thorough rephrasing of his Vietnam nonposition, which, while it contained no substance — hence, could not accommodate anything new — sounded, to uninitiates, like a public step forward. The audience was ecstatic. Outnumbered, two hundred forty-one to one, McKinney could do nothing but smile and shake his head. [19]

The big telethon on the Sunday before the election was even more rigged. A battery of girls were brought in to accept questions by phone, but the questions Nixon was to answer had been selected and rehearsed in advance. Questions from callers approximating the pre-selected questions were then matched so that emcee Bud Wilkinson could say something like: Mr. Nixon, Mrs. J.J. Jones of Pompano Beach, Florida, would like to know what you intend to do about pensions for starving winos. Then Mr. Nixon could reply: "I'm glad you asked that question, Mrs. Jones. [You bet he was — after spending all that time rehearsing.] Let me make it perfectly clear blah, blah, blah the usual doubletalk."[20] It all sounded very spontaneous, although it was a complete show biz fraud. Anyway, the campaign fraud only cost $25 million and that was given voluntarily. The cost to taxpayers in broken campaign promises has been considerably higher.

Part way through the campaign the image makers began to doubt that they were successfully creating an image of the "new Nixon" as warm and personable. They decided on a

new format for TV spots that featured Nixon's voice behind
a series of still pictures rapidly flashing on the screen.
McGinniss describes the new strategy:

> The words would be the same ones Nixon always used – the
> words of the acceptance speech. But they would all seem fresh
> and lively because a series of still pictures would flash on the
> screen while Nixon spoke. If it were done right, it would permit
> Treleaven to create a Nixon image that was entirely independent
> of the words. Nixon would say his same old tiresome things but
> no one would have to listen. The words would become Muzak.
> Something pleasant and lulling in the background. The flashing
> pictures would be carefully selected to create the impression that
> somehow Nixon represented competence, respect for tradition,
> serenity, faith that the American people were better than people
> anywhere else, and that all these problems others shouted about
> meant nothing in a land blessed with the tallest buildings,
> strongest armies, biggest factories, cutest children, and rosiest
> sunsets in the world. Even better: through association with the
> pictures, Richard Nixon could *become* these very things. [21]

Eugene Jones, the man who created these ads with the
laughing, playing children and the glorious sunsets and
Richard Nixon, told McGinniss that he was leaving the
country after the election because he didn't think this was
any place to raise children.

The cynicism of building a phony TV image was matched
by the hypocrisy of Nixon's stand on the issues. Long
regarded as America's number one political weathervane,
Nixon constantly promised "new leadership" while at the
same time using polls to decide which positions were the
most popular. In a column titled "Nixon Reborn – In A
Poll's Image," Joseph Alsop wrote:

> In this year's lurid presidential campaign, one of the most
> important figures behind the scenes has certainly been Joseph
> Bachelder of Princeton, N.J.
>   Bachelder is a poller with a small planning-and-analysis staff of

his own. He also has access, by contract, to Dr. George Gallup's
nationwide polling apparatus and to the Gallup machinery for
sorting and computation in Princeton. Long ago, Bachelder
became Richard M. Nixon's personal poller, and Bachelder has
since been taking polls for Nixon, almost nonstop, in depth and
on a very big scale.

The results that Bachelder has passed on to Nixon are among
the most closely guarded secrets of the Republican candidate. Yet
it is transparently obvious that the former Vice President's
campaign strategy is heavily poll-dominated.

In order to see why this is so, you have only to glance at the
published results of other, less secretive pollers, such as Louis
Harris. There is a near-perfect fit between Harris's most recent
findings about the mood of the country and the things that
Nixon and Spiro T. Agnew have been saying and doing since they
took the stump.

Another example of the Nixon campaign cynicism was the
candidate's making Attorney General Ramsey Clark a main
target for his campaign rehetoric on law and order. Of course
Clark deserved every brickbat and more, but privately Nixon
thought very highly of him. Richard Harris wrote in the *New
Yorker*:

> Apparently Nixon himself did not enjoy his attacks on the
> Attorney General. "Ramsey Clark is really a fine fellow," he said
> to his closest associates during the campaign. "And he's done a
> good job." In view of one of the candidate's top advisers, the
> candidate had felt compelled to use this "simplistic approach" to
> stir up the voters.

The two CFR candidates, Richard Nixon and Hubert
Humphrey, were remarkably alike in their views, despite the
"image" of being poles apart ideologically. Neither deviated
from the official CFR foreign policy of "internationalism,"
by which America is committed to opposing Communism
with so-called Democratic Socialism. Both Nixon and
Humphrey prided themselves on being staunch supporters of

large foreign aid giveaways. This is the cornerstone of the foreign policy of the CFR, as it pours money into the coffers of the international bankers and their law firms.

Both candidates have always gone right down the line in support of the infamous "House that Hiss Built," the United Nations. Both Nixon and Humphrey have advocated the establishment of a UN army that would supersede our own. Both RMN and HHH have supported United World Federalists and Atlantic Union world government schemes.

While Nixon in the past had talked a hard line against Communism, in his press conference at the outset of the Miami convention, he had reversed this stand. This brought him into a position similar to Humphrey's on resistance to Communism.

Hubert Humphrey has been a leading advocate of the welfare state at home, which Nixon at one time opposed. But by 1960, Nixon had done an about-face on the welfare state, though he still paid lip service to the free enterprise system. Nixon justifies the welfare state in Conservative terms while Humphrey does it in Liberalese.

Humphrey and Nixon have both supported all civil rights bills, both the good ones and the bad ones. It was ironic to see NAACP member Nixon campaign through the South as a champion of home rule and a staunch opponent of school busing.

Given these close parallels in their records, how is it that Nixon is widely believed to be a moderate Conservative, while Humphrey is considered a quite radical Liberal? Much of it goes back to their earlier political careers, when these labels had a great deal more validity. Many ardent supporters of both men remember them as they were, not as they are. Humphrey has tailored his appeal to suit labor union and minority elements. Nixon's target has always been "middle America," now generally known as "the silent majority." Therefore, both men have often said substantially the same thing, but they have couched it in very different language. A Nixon campaign speech and a Humphrey campaign speech were as different as winter and summer. In general, so were the audiences. But when George Wallace claimed that there wasn't a dime's worth of difference between the two candidates, he was more accurate than he realized. Wallace was referring to the two parties' stands on forced integration, but that was not the real story. The real story lay in the CFR control over both candidates. Rhetoric aside, they stood for virtually the same thing and both were run by the same bosses in New York. One was working the Liberal side of the street and the other was working the Conservative side of the same street.

While the Establishment *Insiders* had everything to gain and nothing to lose, no matter which candidate won, it was obvious in 1968 that Humphrey was only a foil for Nixon (although he almost beat him). The "big money" went behind Nixon the Republican just as it had gone behind Johnson the Democrat four years earlier. The March 1970 issue of *Fortune* (page 104) disclosed:

> After Nixon's nomination, national-level Republican commit-
> tees spent nearly $25 million on the presidential campaign, while
> comparable post-convention expenditures by the hard-pressed
> Democrats came to less than half of that — about $10,600,000.
> Third-party candidate George C. Wallace reported spending
> $6,985,455.
>
> * * *
>
> But it was the Republican revival among large contributors,
> especially businessmen, that really paid the G.O.P.'s way in 1968.
> Large contributors, traditionally Republican, who had deserted
> Goldwater to support Lyndon Johnson, returned to the fold
> more openhanded than ever before.
>
> * * *
>
> Nowhere is the return to the Republicans more apparent than
> in the pattern of contributions by members of the Business
> Council [a virtual subsidiary of the CFR], an elite group of men

who own, finance, or manage the country's major enterprises.
... Business Council contributions, predominantly Democratic
in 1964, were once again overwhelmingly Republican in 1968, by
better than three to one. One Business Council member who went
full circle was C. Douglas Dillon, Under Secretary of State in the
Eisenhower Administration and Secretary of the Treasury under
Presidents Kennedy and Johnson. In 1960, Dillon gave $26,550
to Republicans and nothing to Democrats. Four years later he put
up $42,000 for Johnson, nothing for Goldwater. But in 1968,
Dillon contributed only to Republicans ($9,000) . . . .

* * *

George Wallace, who notably failed to win support among
industrialists, received nothing.

Guess who was not the Establishment's candidate!

Another indication as to where the Establishment stood on
Nixon was the stand taken by its key literary spokesman. In a
last gasp before hanging up his typewriter, Walter Lippmann,
a CFR founder who was for years known as "the official
voice of the Establishment," pontificated from Mt. Olympus:

> . . . It has become painfully clear that the Democratic party is
> too disorganized to run the country . . . .
>
> This leaves us with Nixon as the one and only candidate who
> can be elected and shows the promise, like it or not, of being able
> to put together an administration to run the government . . . .
>
> I do not shrink from the prospect of Nixon as president. He is
> a very much better man today than he was 10 years ago, and I
> have lived too long myself to think that men are what they are
> forever and ever . . . .
>
> All in all we cannot deny that the near future will be difficult,
> and I have come to think that on the central issue of an organized
> government, to deal with it Nixon is the only one who may be
> able to produce a government that can govern. [22]

Lippmann's apparent successor, James Reston (CFR), re-
frained from making a direct recommendation, but made it
quite clear that the ideological differences popularly believed
to exist between the two candidates were ephemeral. Reston

admitted that in voting for Nixon the voters were casting their ballots for something they would not receive. According to Reston:

> He [the voter] has no clear ideological choice this year, as the voters had in 1964 . . . .
> The voters want a change. They are clearly leading the nation toward what they suppose to be — probably quite inaccurately — a quite conservative Nixon administration . . . .
> Richard Nixon and Hubert Humphrey do not differ about goals. They both accept the two related principles [internationalism and the welfare state] that have guided American [i.e., CFR] policy over the last generation . . . . [23]

A third professional Liberal who surprisingly (to most Republicans) endorsed Richard Nixon was Stewart Alsop of the Fabian-Socialist Americans for Democratic Action. Alsop's recommendation in *Newsweek* was totally through the back door, as he turned on one of the founders of his own ADA organization:

> There is a compelling, if rather negative, case to be made for the proposition that the national interest urgently demands the election of Richard M. Nixon as President of the United States. The case rests largely on the mounting evidence that the election of Hubert H. Humphrey would be a national disaster . . . .
> A stalemate between the White House and Capitol Hill existed when John F. Kennedy was murdered. But poor Hubert Humphrey has been deserted by virtually all the liberal Democrats and the imaginative intellectuals who helped to make Kennedy's brief rule exciting and productive despite the stalemate. [24]

Presumably, Nixon would do much of what the "imaginative intellectuals" might recommend, though most of them would always dislike Nixon personally. The major reason given by Alsop for supporting Nixon was that he could pull off a staged surrender in Vietnam. Alsop continued:

.... Nixon could negotiate without major political damage a
Vietnam settlement that might get Humphrey impeached. Nixon
is an able man with other qualifications for the Presidency, but
this is the heart of the case for Nixon ....

Lippmann, Reston, and Alsop, all certified Establishment
spokesmen and all extreme Liberals, support Republicans
about every third blue moon, but in 1968 they obviously
realized that there was an excellent opportunity to advance
Leftward with Richard Nixon simply because he would
disguise his programs in a Conservative costume.

On November 5, Richard Nixon made good his remarkable
comeback, although the finish was much closer than most
people had predicted, and Nixon appeared to be losing
strength as the campaign progressed. Richard Nixon had
achieved the goal he had sought so covetously for many
years. The question was: What price did he have to pay to get
to the pinnacle of the political heap? Here was a man who
was down and out both politically and financially in 1962.
He was taken to New York, given a cushy partnership in a law
firm, bought a cooperative apartment he could not afford,
joined the finest clubs, lived the life of a millionaire, acquired
nearly a million dollars in assets, traveled the world several
times, spent his time politicking, and was made President of
the United States. Somebody up there liked Richard Nixon.
That somebody was the Establishment *Insiders*. Nixon was
willing to pay their price, as Taft was not, and so, as Taft had
not been able to do, Nixon became President of the United
States.

References

1. Stephen Hess and David Broder, *The Republican Establishment*, New York, Harper & Row, 1967, pp. 162-163.
2. Earl Mazo and Stephen Hess, *Nixon: A Political Portrait*, Popular Library Edition, New York, Harper & Row, 1968, p. 301.
3. Hess and Broder, *op. cit.*, p. 168.
4. *Human Events*, May 18, 1968.
5. *Los Angeles Times*, May 29, 1968.
6. *Human Events, loc. cit.*
7. M. Stanton Evans, *The Future of Conservatism: From Taft to Reagan and Beyond*, New York, Holt, Rinehart & Winston, 1968, p. 209.
8. Stewart Alsop, *Nixon and Rockefeller*, p. 9.
9. Earl Mazo, *Richard Nixon, A Political and Personal Portrait*, New York, Harper & Brothers, 1959, p. 5.
10. *Ibid.*, p. 186.
11. *San Francisco Examiner*, November 29, 1963.
12. *Wall Street Journal*, August 9, 1968.
13. *Ibid.*, August 24, 1970 ("The Real Nixon Is Better Than the Mask," by Douglas L. Hallett).
14. Joe McGinniss, *The Selling of the President, 1968*, New York, Trident Press, 1969.
15. *Ibid.*, pp. 44-45.
16. *Ibid.*, p. 81.
17. Garry Wills, "The Enigma of President Nixon," *Saturday Evening Post*, January 25, 1969.
18. McGinniss, *op. cit.*, pp. 106-107.
19. *Ibid.*, pp. 108-109.
20. *Ibid.*, pp. 149-159.
21. *Ibid.*, p. 85.
22. *Los Angeles Times*, October 6, 1968.
23. *San Francisco Chronicle*, September 29, 1968.
24. *Newsweek*, September 30, 1968.

CHAPTER X

Sincere Advice
From The Unsilent Minority

Following Nixon's hairbreadth election the pundits of the Liberal media disgorged tons of advice to the President-elect. The tone was set by the CFR's Joseph Kraft in an article titled "Nixon's First Job: To Gain Unity Through Coalition." Exercising his typically involuted Kraftmanship, the ultra-Liberal columnist opined that the President-elect must abandon " . . . partisanship for a genuine move toward coalition with major elements of what is still the major party in the country — the Democrats."[1]

Former adviser to President Eisenhower Arthur Larson urged the President to move the Republican party Leftward:

> There are two kinds of bringing-together or coalition possible. One, which is the source of genuine concern to Nixon's opponents, would be to fall back upon the familiar conservative coalition of Republicans with the most conservative Southern Democrats. The other would be to attract to a central core of moderate Republicans a whole range of dissatisfied moderate and liberal Democrats and independents, young people, Negroes, opponents of the Vietnam war and of the draft, and urban residents suffering from the myriad ailments of the cities.
>
> The surest way [for Nixon] to "blow it" would be to adopt the first course.
>
> . . . It has been observed before that the role of the Republican party, like that of the Conservative Party in England, has sometimes seemed to be to come along after a burst of innovative legislation, and contribute a talent for consolidation and efficient administration . . . .
>
> Since the key to success in the Nixon Administration will be

administration, not legislation, the place to launch the coalition is in the staffing of the Executive Branch and of the operating programs at all levels. That is why the importance of an unusually generous allocation of responsible jobs to Democrats, independents, and dissenters was never higher than now .... what would be a more auspicious beginning than to call in Daniel P. Moynihan, who in his approach to these problems combines genuine compassion with unblinking realism and professional expertise?[2]

For far-Left "Republican" Arthur Larson, not even Leftish Democrats were far enough to port. Larson wrote:

Although it is reassuring to see Nixon and Humphrey pledging unity, the "coalition" must reach even further than this — to those disaffected liberals, blacks, students, intellectuals, and urbanites who supported neither Nixon nor Humphrey ....

For seven years I observed at close range Nixon the elected Vice President. On the strength of that observation I can testify that Nixon is quite capable of developing a brand of Republicanism broad enough to bring into a working relation the disparate elements I have mentioned.

It is curious that the Liberals who had called John F. Kennedy's microscopic victory over Nixon in 1960 a "mandate" were now calling Nixon a minority president and screaming for a coalition with the Left. Nothing could have been more illogical. Actually, if Nixon's vote was added to that received by former Alabama Governor George Wallace, the repudiation of the Democrats' welfare-state-at-home, no-win-war-abroad policies was overwhelming. But no one was advocating that Nixon form a coalition government with the disaffected ten million who cast their votes for George Corley Wallace. They were apparently third-class citizens who did not deserve a voice, even though much of Nixon's campaign rhetoric was lifted lock, stock and cracker barrel from Wallace, whose campaign speeches attracted huge crowds around the country.

The *Los Angeles Times'* Washington correspondent, Robert J. Donovan, was not as strident as other Liberals who demanded a coalition with the Left. Donovan wrote: "The sum and substance of a Nixon Administration will be the defense of the political center in America against assault from the right and left."[4]

Nixon had himself stressed many times that he was not a Conservative but a centrist. "America needs to hear the voices of the broad and vital center. The center is under savage attack. It must be held at all cost," the President-elect stated.[5] During his campaign Nixon had played down the ideological differences that will determine whether the country shall continue to head left or shall swerve back toward the traditional stand of a free enterprise Republic. "The old quarrels between management and labor, between Democrat and Republican, between liberal and conservative must be put on the back burner until we decide together if society itself is going to survive," the President-elect said.[6]

Donovan crowed that while Conservatives would be given some baubles, they would be hollow ones. "As a reward for past services – and maybe his only reward – Sen. Strom Thurmond (R-S.C.) will be invited to state dinners – and will love every minute of them." Donovan predicted that, ignoring the Conservatives who put him in office, the President would make a pitch to Liberal intellectuals: " . . . the new President, having seen his predecessor mangled by the intellectuals, will set out to show that, in his fashion, he is as hospitable to them as President John F. Kennedy was."[7]

Donovan also predicted that the campaign promises to eliminate waste and government spending would never sprout wings. Wrote Donovan:

> . . . He will espouse the "new economics" – the doctrine that the government shall use its taxing and spending powers to maintain a healthy economy . . . .
> A continued rise in government spending [is assured], partly as

a result of military requirements and of built-in increases in existing programs. Including everything, Nixon estimates an annual increase of $10.8 billion [in spending] . . . .
. . . . It is not for nothing that Nixon calls himself a pragmatist.[8]

Many Conservatives were confident, however, that the Nixon administration would at least partially repudiate the policies of those he had so caustically derided on occasion during his campaign. An optimistic Russell Kirk wrote:

> Obligated to no powerful interests [*sic*] for his election, he [Nixon] is free to act defensively for our common good, and the good of the world . . . .
> Mr. Nixon owes nothing to the Republican liberals, who bitterly opposed his nomination and contributed little to his election. He is free from the slogans of yesteryear.
> Mr. Nixon owes nothing to the men of big business, who supported and cajoled President Johnson so long as that policy served their turn. He is free to act on behalf of the forgotten American.
> If ever a President was free to lead the people, unfettered by promises to special interests, Richard Nixon is that man.[9]

Vacationing in San Juan, Puerto Rico, columnist James Jackson Kilpatrick was confident that Nixon would ignore the pleas from the Left. Kilpatrick observed:

> The word that washes ashore on this sun-drenched island is that Richard Nixon is getting tons of bad advice these days: He is being urged to turn to the left in his policies and appointments, with a view towards recapturing the lost legions of the great northeast.
> The word comes in part from Robert Novak, the pundit, who has been roughing it here for the past few days. He is suggesting that Nixon "may go far leftward by Eisenhower standards." He expects the new cabinet "to be speckled with left-of-center Republicans."

*   *   *

Why in the world should Nixon turn to the left? What's the left done for him lately? And how is it conceived that he owes some "debt" to Nelson Rockefeller?

* * * *

Nixon will blunder — and blunder badly if he veers to port in forming his administration and framing his program . . . .

But the greatest argument against any turn to the left by Nixon lies in the nature of the man. Nixon could not opt for newer and gaudier programs of public welfare, or for giddy flights of federal innovation, without abandoning the whole tenor of his fall campaign. He would then be fairly chargeable with hypocrisy, double-dealing, bad faith, and all the rest. He would be untrue to himself; and that he will not do. Of course, Nixon will go generally to the right. His own deepest instincts will not let him go anywhere else.[10]

Although the observations of Kirk and Kilpatrick are perfectly logical if one ignores Nixon's long-time connections with the CFR, the fact remains that he lived in Nelson Rockefeller's apartment house as Rockefeller's neighbor in New York City and used Nelson Rockefeller's personal attorney, John Mitchell, as his campaign manager. The President soon made it clear that he was listening to the Krafts and Larsons and not to the Kirks and Kilpatricks. He announced that he would solicit "fresh ideas, new ideas, dissenting ideas, from many segments of the U.S. public. The intellectual community will not be reached by creating "a little office" in the White House to recruit brains, Nixon said, "because if we are not worthy of support from the intellectual community [i.e., the academic Left] we are not going to get it . . . . I consider myself an intellectual . . . we want to have a continuing relationship with the best brains in this country, with the colleges, universities, foundations, business organizations," Nixon said.[11]

Many wishful-thinking Conservative Republicans rationalized away Nixon's actions during his eight years as Veep in the Eisenhower administration, and his often Liberal statements during his own two Presidential campaigns, by saying, in essence, "Just wait until he gets into office. Then he can be his own man. The real Nixon is a staunch Conservative."

References

1. *Los Angeles Times*, November 8, 1968.
2. *Ibid.*, November 17, 1968.
3. *Ibid.*
4. *Ibid.*, November 7, 1968.
5. *Ibid.*
6. *Ibid.*
7. *Ibid.*
8. *Ibid.*
9. *Santa Ana Register*, November 10, 1968.
10. Washington Star News Service, November 25, 1968.
11. *Los Angeles Times*, January 13, 1969.

CHAPTER XI

The Pachyderms Return

During the election campaign many influential Conservatives were approached by Nixon emissaries and told in knowing confidential tones that, after "Dick" was elected, "for every Liberal brought in the front door, seven Conservatives would be brought in the back door." Most Conservatives hopefully accepted this promise, many, because of past experience, against their better judgment. In reality the reverse has proven to be true. While a few Conservative advisers are dangled (like so many charms on a bracelet) before the increasingly incredulous Americanists, the *status quo* has prevailed over the Liberal bureaucracy, while Nixon's "good grey men" dutifully attempt to apply the same type of business efficiency to socialism that their counterparts in Germany applied to Hitler's concentration camps. And, we might add, the same morality applies in both cases.

Shortly after his election Richard Nixon assembled a brain trust to staff the new Republican administration. The ideological make-up of the brain trusters was to be reflected in the appointments they made.

One of the key men working behind the scenes for Nixon on the selection of talent to staff the new administration was Joseph E. Johnson, a member of the board of directors of the Council on Foreign Relations and president of the grossly misnamed Carnegie Endowment for International *Peace*. Johnson is a former chief assistant to, and close friend of, Soviet spy Alger Hiss. When he was indicted, Hiss was president of the Carnegie Endowment for International Peace; he was succeeded by Joseph E. Johnson.

According to internationally respected journalist Edward Hunter, Johnson was "actively engaged in preparing alternative Republican personalities to replace top Democratic party officials," in a Nixon reorganization "to bring in precisely those Republicans as successors who are most similar to those being displaced." Since Richard Nixon was partially responsible for the unmasking of Hiss, it is incredibly ironic that he should pick Hiss's successor to help staff a Republican administration.

Johnson was chairman of a conference held in the State Department on November 14-15, 1968, by the American Foreign Service Association. Hunter stated: "The theme underlying the two days of speeches and private discussions was the retention of power through personal selection." Those attending the conference included such familiar Establishmentarians as Adam Yarmolinsky, Herman Kahn, Doak Barnett, Arthur Larson, R. Richard Rubottom Jr., and Charles E. ("Chip") Bohlen. Nicholas Katzenbach, who at that time had announced his resignation but was later retained, attended as representative of Secretary of State Rusk. A laugh greeted Katzenbach's salutation to "fellow officers and fellow Republicans." Former Young Communist Leaguer Adam Yarmolinsky, who, according to *U.S. News & World Report,* had been responsible for securing the appointment of Robert Strange McNamara to the position of Secretary of Defense, discussed the retention of a class of appointees developed by the Kennedys called the "In-and-Outers." Yarmolinsky pointed out that a procedure must be assured by which these persons could continue to move between official government posts and related jobs outside, as in graduate schools and "think factories."

On December 7, 1968, the AP noted that another of Mr. Nixon's chief talent scouts was Dr. Glenn Olds, who (said

Human Events on November 23, 1969) conferred over appointments for the Administration with Adam Yarmolinsky. Yarmolinsky, the son of two well-known comrades and a key figure in the Kennedy administration, is now a professor at Harvard, where he once led the Young Communist League. No doubt Yarmolinsky had some fascinating suggestions for Olds. *Human Events* lamented:

> Dr. Glenn Olds, a chief talent scout for the Nixon Administration, continues his liberal ways. Having previously suggested that Nixon tap LBJ rejects Robert McNamara and Arthur Goldberg for the Cabinet, Olds has also recommended that the President-elect bring George Ball back into the government.

Dr. Olds says he "was involved in helping to get the Peace Corps going"; he also worked with Sargent Shriver in setting up VISTA. Just how he became a Nixon talent scout is a mystery. Old's own explanation was rather hazy: "Mr. Nixon said, 'Glenn, I don't want you to be concerned with political partisanship.' "

The man in charge of top Nixon appointments was an international banker named Peter Flanigan. Stuart Loory noted of him, in the *Los Angeles Times* of March 3, 1969:

> The keeper of the document known in the Nixon Administration as "the Plumb Book," one of the most powerful men in the capital during these early days of the new presidency, has no official title, draws no salary and is preparing to leave town as quietly as he came.
>
> He is Peter M. Flanigan, the man who has directed the talent search for all the top-level positions — cabinet officers, their deputies and the occupants of slots on all the important boards and commissions in Washington.

Instead of leaving town, Flanigan joined the White House staff. He is a senior partner in the international banking firm of Dillon, Reed & Co., where he works for JFK's Secretary of the Treasury, C. Douglas Dillon, a member of the board of directors of the Council on Foreign Relations.

In the 1960 campaign Flanigan was chairman of the Citizens for Nixon organization. Wrote Loory:

> While he worked for Nixon last year, a more senior partner in his firm, former Treasury Secretary C. Douglas Dillon, worked hard promoting the candidacy of New York Governor Nelson A. Rockefeller for the Republican nomination.

Columnist Loory's description of Flanigan suggested that he was playing Colonel House to Nixon's Woodrow Wilson:

> He was never appointed to a government position. Yet his office can be reached quickly by calling the White House switchboard. One White House official calls Flanigan's relationship to the White House "the Czar" and says objections to it were raised shortly after the inauguration. The objections were considered and rejected, however . . . .
>
> And along with submitting a sampling of evaluations by others to the President, Flanigan also expresses his own opinion on each applicant. And as an aide said, "His power of suggestion is considerable."

Flanigan did not exactly lean over backwards to bring Conservatives into the administration. A year and a half later Ralph de Toledano noted:

> In fact, a quick look around official Washington shows that, with a few exceptions, the people who laid it on the line for Mr. Nixon over the last two decades are conspicuously absent. It could, of course, be that these old battlers for Nixon lack the qualifications for White House positions — or that Peter Magnus Flanigan, the patronage-and-knife-wielder in residence, has discovered that they all have political bad breath.
>
> However, the absence of the old Nixon stalwarts goes beyond these personal considerations. For they represent, ideologically speaking, the millions of Americans who put Mr. Nixon in office and who are expected in November to give him a Republican

Senate and House. These Americans made Mr. Nixon, but they
have, in effect, lost their franchise.[1]

Yet another of the President's top procurers of talent for
the administration was Leonard Garment, a former Nixon
law partner, who, according to the *Wall Street Journal* of
August 12, 1968, " . . . considered himself a very liberal
Democrat — until his conversion to the Nixon candidacy."
Garment's job was to recruit non-Republican Leftists into the
administration. Evans and Novak wrote in the *Washington
Post* on November 8, 1968:

> Nixon aide Leonard Garment, a political liberal in Nixon's law
> firm, has been exploring the ranks of liberal Democrats and some
> New-Left thinkers to cull ideas and size up personalities . . . .

The *Los Angeles Times* of May 24, 1969, in an article
titled "Outsider with Inside Ties," said of Leonard Garment:

> There are times in the White House when the discussion among
> President Nixon's staff reaches a point where someone will say:
> "What does Len think about this?"
> So someone will pick up a phone, dial 298-5970, and get
> Leonard Garment . . . and, if necessary, Garment can get from his
> desk chair across the street and through the south-west gate of
> the White House (where he is not likely to be spotted entering)
> within a few minutes to render his advice in person.
> Garment's name appears on no White House roster. He is not
> on federal salary. Yet he is one of the key men in the Nixon
> Administration.
> He needs no clearance to get through the gate. He wears no
> Secret Service badge as other visitors must . . . .
> Garment studiously avoids interviews, preferring to stay as far
> behind the scenes as possible . . . .
> After the election, he stayed on in a small office at campaign
> headquarters helping put the new administration together . . . .

That half-block walk must have been getting to be too

much. According to columnist Victor Riesel in the *Indian-apolis Star* of July 21, 1969, Garment, after returning from the Moscow Film Festival, moved into the White House and, said *U.S. News & World Report*, was regarded as Nixon's "No. 1 idea man." "Officially," wrote Riesel, "Garment is special counsel to the President on the arts, volunteerism and minorities — reminiscent of a [Franklin] Rooseveltian aide, Dave Niles." (David K. Niles was a White House contact man for Soviet agents.) Leonard Garment has been called Nixon's Harry Hopkins — since Hopkins was for all practical purposes a Soviet agent. Garment is currently in charge of the Washington branch of Nixon's law firm, but none of the Liberals who opposed Judge Haynsworth's confirmation to the Supreme Court bench have said anything about Garment's flagrant conflict of interest.

James Reston (CFR) inadvertently revealed that Robert Anderson (CFR), Ike's Secretary of the Treasury, a member of the Business Advisory Council — which comprises the hierarchy of the CFR — and a partner of the *Insider* international banking firm of Carl M. Loeb, Rhoades and Co., was sneaking in and out of Nixon's apartment, obviously wanting not to be seen. Reston wrote:

> It is a fascinating parade — from old-fashioned Chippendale Republicans like Everett McKinley Dirksen to functional modern Democratic types like Patrick Moynihan of M.I.T. Most of them [those attending sessions at which appointments are discussed] come out of Nixon's quarters saying that it was all very interesting, and some of them, like Robert Anderson, slip down the freight elevator out of sight . . . . [2]

Two other advisers from the campaign believed to have played a part in staffing the Nixon administration are J. Irwin Miller (CFR), head of Cummins Engine Co., and Kingman Brewster (CFR), president of Yale University.[3] Miller was the first layman to ascend to the presidency of the politically-powerful National Council of Churches and was called by *Esquire* magazine the man most qualified to be President of the United States. He was a backer of the "poor people's army" that invaded Washington during 1968. Miller, who has always been a Rockefeller man, served as chairman of a special presidential panel that recommended liberalization of U.S. trade with the Communists. Both Miller and Brewster have ties with the Ford Foundation: Miller is a member of its board of trustees, and Brewster — who made headlines in the spring of 1970, when he said that Black Panther Bobby Seale could not get a fair trial in this country on a charge of murdering a police informant — has served on a special committee for the Ford Foundation.[4]

The screening of thousands of prospects for rank-and-file jobs with the Nixon administration was handled by Harry Flemming, age 28. He is the son of the radical Arthur Flemming, Leftist president of the National Council of Churches and head of the Department of Health, Education, and Welfare under President Eisenhower. *Human Events* of December 14, 1968, reported that Flemming's friends said he was "an out-and-out liberal who actually preferred Rockefeller to Nixon."

Young Flemming, who might be thought hardly experienced enough at 28 to be an authority on national talent, sent letters to all 70,000 persons listed in *Who's Who in America*, soliciting suggestions for presidential appointments. (The editors of this volume have exhibited a marked bias in listings to favor the Left.) He said that neither party nor ideology would be a barrier to selection, and many Republicans complained about the large number of jobs Flemming was handing out to "Liberal" Democrats. So bad was the situation that Senator Robert Dole of Kansas, half in jest and wholly in earnest, urged Republican lawmakers to include this line in any letters of recommendation for a Nixon appointment: "Even though Zilch is a Republican, he's highly qualified for the job."

Battle Line, the publication of the American Conservative Union, in its February-March 1969 issue, had this to say:

> Slowly but surely it has finally dawned on Republican party regulars across the nation that they have been taken. First there was the hoaked-up post-election business about a "great talent hunt" by the aides of the President-elect Nixon among thousands of Americans who might be qualified to serve in Washington. The GOP pols, ready, willing and Republican, did not understand why their applications for jobs carried no more weight than a listing in *Who's Who*. After all, how many of the thousands of citizens listed in the 2287 pages between Messrs. Aagaard and Zugger had actually worked for the election of Richard Nixon . . . ?

The column of Liberals Evans and Novak in the *Los Angeles Times* of February 13, 1969, reported:

> Thus the Nixon Administration . . . is running badly afoul of its own party over jobs and patronage. Some such trouble is inevitable in any new administration, but what sets the Nixon Administration apart is the unprecedented decision not to clean house.
>
> To the contrary, Republican politicians are convinced that Mr. Nixon is so concerned about getting along with the Democrats, who still control Congress, that the promised bureaucratic housecleaning is indefinitely postponed.
>
> That may help Mr. Nixon with the Democrats. But it's a far cry from the party-building operation Republicans were absolutely certain Mr. Nixon would put into sweeping effect if he ever entered the White House.

Like many other Republicans, Mrs. Phyllis Schlafly, who had done much to achieve Nixon's election by organizing Republican womens' groups, was extremely upset by the Nixon policy. In an article for the May 10, 1969 *Human Events* titled "Patronage Is the Name of the Game," Mrs. Schlafly proclaimed:

> Ever since Richard Nixon won the Presidency in November 1968, the press has been filled with variations on the principal

theme: President Nixon can only fill 1,500 to 3,000 federal jobs — the rest of the federal employees are locked in by Civil Service.

This claim is preposterous and Republicans at every level should call the bluff of the Democrats and the liberals who are trying to put it over.

The Democrats have never permitted Civil Service to impede their political objectives. Presidents Roosevelt, Truman, Kennedy and Johnson ruthlessly got rid of Republican holdovers — Civil Service to the contrary notwithstanding — and used every possible tactic to put Democrats on the payroll and keep them there. No holds were barred in their purge of Republicans and payroll padding with Democrats.

The elimination of this payroll padding would be a fulfillment of Republican campaign promises and a service to the over-burdened American taxpayers . . . .

This failure to use federal patronage [during the Eisenhower Administration] is also probably a principal reason why, in every subsequent year of the Eisenhower Administration, the Republican party steadily lost ground and more of its candidates were defeated . . . . There are hundreds of thousands of jobs which must be turned over to Republicans if we are to accomplish policy changes . . . .

There should be thousands of Republicans flooding into federal offices from every state in the union — especially from the states which contributed substantially to Nixon's victory. This is the only way we can secure the change for which the American people voted.

Candidate Nixon admitted publicly, when he spoke to Republican delegates in caucus at Miami Beach during the convention in 1968, that one of the greatest failures of the Eisenhower administration was the complete lack of White House action in building up the Republican Party organization.[5] It appears that GOP history not only repeats itself, it stutters badly.

As the months dragged on it became more and more obvious to dismayed Republicans that there would be no housecleaning of the federal bureaucracy, which by its very nature is overwhelmingly Liberal. In an article in the *Long*

Beach (Calif.) *Press Telegram* titled "Where's the New Broom?" Nixon partisan James Jackson Kilpatrick lamented:

> Out with it: Mr. Nixon, thus far, disappoints . . . . Where is the new broom of our autumn exertions?
> Mr. Nixon has not cleaned house. To be sure, a new cabinet is in office, but what of that? Bureaucracy is a kind of root vegetable: What counts is underground. It is at the third and fourth levels that memorandums are drafted, regulations enforced, speeches prepared, and policies shaped. If Mr. Nixon fails to dig down to these levels, and to put in new men with new ideas, he will harvest the same old thing . . . .

Human Events added on May 10, 1969: " . . . while Republicans occupy the highest-paying jobs, Democrats remain entrenched in the second-level jobs where policy is often set." Nixon's friendly biographer Ralph de Toledano commented:

> . . . Mr. Nixon [has] forgotten the prime rule of politics, so well applied by Franklin D. Roosevelt and Harry S. Truman: Reward your friends and punish your enemies. The opposite has been true in this administration . . . .[6]

Given the debts to the *Insiders* of the Eastern Liberal Establishment run up by Mr. Nixon in order to become President, and the men who picked the appointees to the new administration, it is no wonder that Conservatives fared so poorly. Again we cite Mr. de Toledano:

> The "conservatives" won the election for Richard Nixon — and they are losing the election to him. It can no longer be denied that those to the right of center who carried the election for Nixon have gotten less than the back of his hand for their efforts.
> Obviously, the spoils are going to those who did their worst, or best, to see Nixon's opponents triumph . . . . [7]

This being the case, it is interesting and instructive to

reflect on the men who did receive appointments from the new president.

While stumping the hustings during the campaign, Mr. Nixon had given this description of the men he would appoint to high positions if elected: "I don't want a government of yes men in which high officials are asked to dance like puppets on a presidential string."[8]

Following the election, rumors as to who would be picked for the cabinet positions were of course rife. Evans and Novak hopefully forecast that "he [Nixon] may go far leftward by Eisenhower standards."[9] The *Christian Science Monitor* reported that Nixon was "giving serious thought" to the selection of Nelson Rockefeller as Secretary of Defense — a possibility that received the approval of none other than William F. Buckley Jr. It was also pointed out that Rockefeller would fit in as Secretary of State. The names of other prominent Republican Liberals were bandied about like so many ping-pong balls. However, the jobs did not go to Rockefeller or any of the other big-name Eastern Establishment Republicans, but instead went primarily to old Nixon confidants and second-echelon Establishment men. Rockefeller was apparently content to operate through lieutenants rather than stir up a hornets' nest by taking a job himself. *U.S. News & World Report* observed in its March 17, 1969 issue: "Some 'conservative' Republicans are complaining that too many appointments by the Nixon Administration have been influenced by Governor Nelson Rockefeller . . . ."

The *New York Times'* Tom Wicker, a literary spokesman for the elite snobs, wrote that "one of the notable events of the transition period was the collective sigh of relief that went up from the liberal Eastern Establishment" when Nixon made his appointments.[10] The Liberal press was mildly enthusiastic. "The quality of pragmatism, may indeed, best sum up the basic characteristic of Nixon's incoming cabinet."

The *New York Times* itself sniffed, on December 12, 1968: "As a group Mr. Nixon's men bear a much closer resemblance to the Kennedy-Johnson team they replace than to the Eisenhower Republican team from which they are theoretically descended."

On the same date the hysterically Leftist *Washington Post* gave its approval:

> The Nixon Cabinet, and that small part of the supporting cast which was unveiled earlier, has a look of careful practical-mindedness, a sense of purposefulness, and an air of competence, taken in the main . . . .
> . . . it is enough to say that Mr. Nixon has begun well, by collecting around him the sort of competent men that are the prerequisite to a competent Government.[11]

Even LBJ said he had a "good opinion" of cabinet appointees he knew.[12] Democratic National Chairman Lawrence F. O'Brien described them as "a group of distinguished men with fine backgrounds." All the Liberals seemed relieved.

The American Conservative Union's *Battle Line* wasn't quite so thrilled. It rhetorically asked in February 1969: "Who ever heard of most of these men, much less ever having seen them at a Republican Lincoln Day dinner anywhere . . .?"

Most observers concluded that the Cabinet was made up of "good gray men" who were unlikely to steal any of Nixon's thunder but were hardly what Nixon had promised — "a Cabinet made up of the ablest men in America, leaders in their own right and not merely by virtue of appointment."[13]

In fact, the appointees very much resembled the "yes men" whom Nixon had said during the campaign that he did not want. And on closer inspection, some of the "good gray men" don't appear quite so gray.

Some of these appointees are personal friends and associates or political cronies of the President — men like, for instance, Robert Finch of California, an old intimate, who was first Nixon's Secretary of Health, Education, and Welfare and is now Presidential Advisor; John N. Mitchell, Attorney-General, who was Nixon's campaign manager in spite of the fact that he has close ties with Nelson Rockefeller; and William P. Rogers, Secretary of State, an old and close friend of the President since his Vice-Presidential campaign, who as Eisenhower's Attorney-General had spearheaded the move to destroy Senator Joseph McCarthy and had also played a major role in the drafting of the Civil Rights Act of 1957. Other appointees are ideological Liberals, Democrats or theoretical ex-Democrats, CFR members, and other types of strange bedfellows for an allegedly Conservative Republican President — for example, Henry A. Kissinger (CFR), Special Assistant for National Security Affairs and the most important man in the Nixon Administration, bar none; Arthur Burns, now chairman of the extremely powerful Federal Reserve Board, who was a New Deal Democrat before he turned "modern Republican" and was appointed to President Eisenhower's Council of Economic Advisors; Jacob Beam (CFR), now American Ambassador to Russia, who as Eisenhower's Ambassador to Poland had been involved in the Warsaw sex and spy scandals and had resigned his post under mysterious circumstances, only to be appointed director of the U.S. Arms Control and Disarmament Agency and later, under LBJ, Ambassador to Czecho-Slovakia; and Presidential Counselor Daniel Patrick Moynihan, self-professed "Liberal radical" who salvaged — expensively — the Great Society under the Nixon administration.

References
1. *Anaheim Bulletin*, June 27, 1970.
2. *Long Beach Press-Telegram*, December 11, 1968.
3. *Newsweek*, October 7, 1968.
4. *Independent American*, September 1968.
5. *Battle Line*, February-March 1969.
6. *Houston Tribune*, June 4, 1970.
7. *Indianapolis News*, February 26, 1969.
8. North American Newspaper Alliance, *Santa Ana Register,* July 3, 1969.
9. *Washington Post*, November 8, 1968.
10. *Indianapolis News*, December 18, 1968.
11. *Ibid*.
12. United Press International, December 13, 1968.
13. *The New Republic*, December 21, 1968.

CHAPTER XII

President Of The Universe

The ultimate goal of the *Insider* conspirators is an all-powerful World Superstate, which they will control. The cartelists and monopolists will then be able to parcel out franchises on the world's natural resources, transportation, finance, and commerce to their own clique of oligarchs. The *Insiders* won't have to worry about pesky upstart competitors, because there won't be any competitors. You won't be able to be in business without a license from the monolithic World Superstate. This explains the seeming contradiction of so many of the super-rich advocating a world socialist government. There will be only two classes — the *Insiders* with their managerial elite and their enforcers at the top, and the other 99 per cent of the population, made up of slave-drones, at the bottom. These are the same conditions that prevail today in the Communist countries, where, contrary to Communist philosophy, some are much more equal than others. Even Red China provides Rolls Royces for its high mucky-mucks, or did, while the workers in that proletarian paradise are fortunate if they own bicycles. Marxists have always worked to eliminate the middle class, and Marxism is the tool of the superwealthy *Insiders*.

Speaking for the *Insiders*, James Warburg, whose father was primarily responsible for the creation of the Federal Reserve System and whose relatives financed the Communist Revolution in Russia, told a Senate Committee on February

17, 1950: "We shall have world government whether or not you like it – conquest or consent."

Selling the American people the idea of world government has not been an easy task. The aftermath of World War I, during which all of the secret treaties and double-dealings surfaced at Versailles, convinced isolation-inclined America that foreign entanglements were to be avoided. Only the growth of international Communism, always carefully nurtured by what would appear to be its arch-enemy, the super-rich international bankers, has altered America's attitude toward foreign entanglements. But while Americans have accepted defense alliances, they are still wary of world government, because they realize that, with 5 per cent of the world's people and 50 per cent of the world's wealth, we would literally be looted to pay the taxes for the world superstate.

The Liberal media have created an image of those who oppose "internationalism" or the "America last" foreign policy as rabid chauvinists who despise everything and everyone that is not American. Those who believe we should mind our own business and let other countries mind theirs have been given the name "isolationists," a term that has been made synonymous with bigotry and backwardness. In truth, for almost one hundred and fifty years Americans had traded with the rest of the world, importing and exporting goods and carrying on normal diplomatic relations with all legitimate governments. But America had stayed strictly neutral in all foreign wars and had neither tried to set the policies of foreign governments nor let them establish ours. Prejudice, hatred, and provincialism had nothing to do with it. In his Farewell Address, George Washington had warned: "Against the insidious wiles of foreign influence, the jealousy of a free people ought to be constantly awake; since history and experience prove that foreign influence is one of the most baneful foes of Republican government." Since abandoning this philosophy America has been involved in a perpetual war for perpetual peace in which we fight one foreign war after another, each one propagandized as the war that will lead to permanent peace.

Ever ready to play both sides of the street, the Ultra-Left has now largely become "neo-isolationist," by which is meant favoring the termination of even the semblance of resistance to the advance of Communism. This perverted isolationism applies only to the military, as the "neo-isolationists" would actually step up foreign aid to socialist and Communist countries.

Leftists have always advocated centralization of power in government. When there is only one central government to infiltrate and take over, instead of thousands of local governments, the job is infinitely simplified for the would-be totalitarian dictators. Karl Marx's *Communist Manifesto* clearly implied the eventual establishment of a single world socialist state – a world government. In 1915, in No. 40 of the Russian organ, *The Socialist Democrat,* Nicolai Lenin proposed a "United States of the world." The program of the Communist International of 1936 says that world dictatorship "can be established only by the victory of socialism in different countries or groups of countries, after which the Proletariat Republics would unite on federal lines with those already in existence, and this system would expand . . . at length forming the world union of Soviet Socialist Republics."

Joseph Stalin divided his plan for achievement of this Communist world federalism into three stages:

(1) Socialize the economies of all nations, particularly the Western capitalistic democracies; (2) bring about federal union of various groupings of these socialized nations; and (3) amalgamate all of the federal unions into one world-wide union of socialist states.

World government has a strong emotional appeal for Americans, based on their universal desire for world peace.

The *Insiders* have the Communists rattling their sabers with one hand and dangling the olive branch with the other. Naturally everyone gravitates towards the olive branch, not realizing that the olive branch is controlled by another arm of the entity that is rattling the sabers.

There are basically two tightly interlocked groups promoting world government. The first, the United World Federalists, proposes turning the UN into a world government that would include the Communists. The other, the Atlantic Unionists, would form a new nation, the United States of Atlantica, built around the NATO countries, as a supposed deterrent to Communism. The *Insiders* manipulating the world government movement work both sides of the street, taking advantage of those who wish to appease Communism and those who wish to oppose it. Richard Nixon has been associated with both factions of the world government pincers movement.

In the October 1949 issue of their magazine, *World Government News*, the United World Federalists stated: "The Movement, while supporting the efforts of the United Nations, shall work to transform it by fundamental amendment into a world federal government."

The United World Federalists organization was born in 1947, when three hundred assorted Liberals, socialists, and Communists from a number of one-world groups met at Asheville, North Carolina, and combined into a single group. The UWF is an affiliate of the World Movement for World Federal Government, which was established in Switzerland in 1946. UWF is the largest world government group in the United States (except for the Communists), and the most vigorously active in its propaganda. UWF wants a "world government" that will make world law and enforce it directly upon individuals, who will thereafter be "world citizens" — no longer citizens of their respective nations. This movement has attracted more persons influential in business life than any other, and has branches in fifteen countries. In its "Beliefs, Purposes and Policies" (revised November 1–2, 1947), the UWF stated:

> . . . World peace can be created and maintained only under a world federal government, universal and strong enough to prevent armed conflict between nations, and having direct jurisdiction over the individual and those matters within its authority.

To accomplish this, UWF leader Grenville Clark stated:

> The manufacture of all war weapons would be prohibited to the member nations. Such manufacture would be confined to those arms required by the world police force and would be conducted solely in arsenals owned and operated by the United Nations.[1]

In an effort to bring about the world police force, the UWF is very active in lobbying for various disarmament bills, gloating, for example, in its official newspaper, *The Federalists*, in November 1963, "Perhaps the Test Ban Treaty didn't introduce the millennium, but it put an end to yesterday."

In September of 1952, at a conference held in London by the World Association of Parliamentarians for World Government, representatives of the United World Federalists worked with members of that organization in the preparation of a plan for a world police force and occupation armies to enforce "peace."

The Plan established that after they had succeeded in revising the U.N. Charter (at some future date) and converting the United Nations into a world government, these conspirators would deploy "peace-keeping" forces around the globe. According to this formally prepared scheme, there would be a "World Dictator," the eight "Zone Directors," and fifty-one "Regional Directors," none of whom would ever be allowed to serve in their respective countries. That, of course, would ensure "impartiality."

The Plan, exposed by Colonel Eugene Pomeroy and the internationally famous journalist Douglas Reed, provided that no American troops of the "Peace" force would ever be stationed in or even *near* the United States, but our nation and Canada would be occupied by armies from Russia, Mongolia, and probably East Germany. Red troops from other countries as well would be scattered over the rest of the six regions into which it was decided to divide North America, in order to enforce the authority of the new world government and prevent Americans from engaging in the "crime" of "sheltering behind national allegiance."

Because of their tremendous populations, the Chinese Communists and their Soviet Comrades would dominate the World Parliament of such a government. If this chilling plan is allowed to reach fruition — as the conspirators intend that it shall — America is dead.

Since UWF advocates "union now" with the Communists, it is not surprising that it also strongly backs aid and trade with the enemy.

UWF sponsored resolutions in the various state legislatures calling for world government. By 1953 the resolution had passed twenty-three states, but in that year California rescinded its approval and sixteen other states thereafter followed California. The world government forces, however, did not give up. They simply changed their tactics. Direct action through legislation having been blocked, they now turned their propaganda assault to the "strengthening" of the United Nations Charter.

We could, literally, list for a hundred pages the Communist and Leftist front affiliations of those who founded the United World Federalists. Even our necessarily limited file of Senate and House Committee documents shows seven hundred forty affiliations of the forty-two key founders of the United World Federalists with officially cited Communist fronts and projects. And, going just a step further, we find from a similar scanning of the public records of some one hundred eighty officials and members — one-sixth of whom are members of the CFR — that a total of one hundred sixteen have somehow managed to amass at least 1,250 affiliations with Communist fronts and publications.

While most members of the UWF are Democrats, the organization also has strong support from modern Republicans. In a message to the United World Federalists in May 1963, former President Eisenhower stated: "The United World Federalists, adhering to common standards of justice and international conduct, requires the continued support of all those dedicated to freedom."

Also supporting the UWF is Modern Republican Jacob Javits, who sent this message to the one-worlders:

> I want to commend the World Federalists for their continued fine efforts on behalf of world peace under a world rule of law, for your outstanding contribution on behalf of the United Nations, and your spirited tradition of service.[3]

In September of 1968, candidates for public office received a letter from the United World Federalists that stated:

> Our organization has been endorsed and commended by all U.S. presidents in the last 20 years and by the current nominees for the presidency. As examples we quote as follows:
>
> Richard Nixon: "Your organization can perform an important service by continuing to emphasize that world peace can only come thru world law. Our goal is world peace. Our instrument for achieving peace will be law and justice. If we concentrate our energies toward these ends, I am hopeful that real progress can be made."
>
> Hubert H. Humphrey: "Every one of us is committed to brotherhood among all nations, but no one pursues these goals with more dignity and dedication than the United World Federalists."

There really was not a dime's worth of difference. Voters were given the choice between CFR world government advocate Nixon and CFR world government advocate Humphrey. Only the rhetoric was changed to fool the public.

Richard Nixon is, of course, far too clever to actually join the UWF, but he has supported their legislative program since his early days in Congress. In the October 1948 issue of the UWF publication *World Government News*, on page 14, there appears the following announcement: "Richard Nixon: Introduced world government resolution (HCR 68) 1947, and ABC (World Government) resolution 1948."

Of special interest to the UWF throughout its history has been its campaign to repeal the Connally Reservation, whereby the United States has reserved to itself the power to decide what matters are essentially within the domestic jurisdiction of the U.S. and may not be brought under the jurisdiction of the World Court. The UWF wants repeal of the Connally Reservation, which would mean that the United States would accept "as binding the rulings of the International Court of Justice [World Court] on disarmament, on interpretation of the U.N. Charter and laws, and of international treaties." The abolition of the Connally Reservation would leave us at the mercy of the Afro-Asian and Iron Curtain blocs that dominate the U.N. It would be tantamount to surrendering the sovereignty of the U.S. to its enemies, and would thus be a gross violation of the Presidential oath to "preserve, protect and defend the Constitution of the United States." Yet Richard Nixon for many years has advocated the repeal of the Connally Reservation. Incredulous patriots who wrote Nixon about his advocacy of its repeal were sent a copy of a letter dated April 14, 1960, from Richard Nixon to Eugene Pulliam, publisher of the *Phoenix Republic and Gazette*, in which Nixon flatly stated that he favored repeal. In the letter Nixon said: "I believe . . . that the intervening years have shown that our so-called 'self-judging reservation' is no longer necessary."

Actually, the intervening years − during which the U.N. has expanded to take in the Afro-Asian mini-states, whose common denominator is a hatred of the United States and a desire to get their hands on our wealth − have shown that the protection of the Connally Reservation is more necessary than ever.

President Nixon actually goes far beyond mere repeal of the amendment embodying the reservation, to advocate "world rule through world law" − the official slogan of the UWF − in which the World Court is to be made the Supreme Court of the World. (Mr. Nixon does not mention whether Earl Warren should be made its Chief Justice.) The *New York Times* of April 14, 1959, commenting on a speech made by Mr. Nixon the day before, stated:

> An important and far-reaching proposal for realizing the guiding ideal of both the United States and the United Nations was made by Vice President Nixon in his speech before the Academy of Political Science.
>
> The ideal, long proclaimed by American statesmen, in particular President Eisenhower, and embodied in the United Nations Charter, is to establish a peaceful world in which the rule of force will be replaced by the rule of law.
>
> To that end Mr. Nixon proposes to elevate the International Court of Justice at The Hague to a real Supreme Court of the world with far wider jurisdiction and employment in international disputes and with the power to make binding decisions especially in cases involving differing interpretations of international treaties and agreements that have been a dominant element in the conflict between the free world and the Communist bloc . . . .
>
> Mr. Nixon characterized his proposal as still unofficial. But he has wide Administration backing for it and, in line with President Eisenhower's State of the Union message, forecast Administration recommendations to Congress to give effect to it by modifying American reservations [the Connally Reservation] as to the court's jurisdiction which set a pattern for other nations.
>
> . . . Mr. Nixon's proposal deserves both study and support.

Giving the World Court power over America and Americans has been a long-time UWF goal. And Mr. Nixon is in the process of revitalizing the court. According to the *Los Angeles Times* of May 3, 1970:

> Among those interested are Secretary of State William P. Rogers and his undersecretary, Elliot Richardson, who have both made recent speeches urging revival and extension of the court; an assortment of high federal judges; a bipartisan group of congressmen led by Rep. Paul Findley (R.-Ill.); U.N. Secretary General U Thant — and, somewhere in the wings, President Nixon . . . .
> It is not accident, then, that certain State Department leaders are already hard at work trying to scrape up some cases from dusty files to take to the court . . . .

The other major world government movement is the Atlantic Union group, which believes that getting half a loaf is half way to getting a whole loaf. Like Stalin, they believe that circumstances necessitate a nation's going through a regional government set-up before going on to world government. Although the UWF seeks immediate amalgamation with the Communist countries, that idea is often hard to sell; so the *Insiders* have Atlantic Union, which is ostensibly anti-Communist. And indeed, there are some sincere, if naive, anti-Communists in the Atlantic Union movement who support abolishing the United States and forming, with the countries of Western Europe, a new nation, the United States of Atlantica. Most members of Atlantic Union, however, are extreme Liberals from whom seldom is heard an anti-Communist word, except when they are urging the necessity of joining in a United States of Europe to guard against the advance of Communism.

The idea of Atlantic Union is not new. In fact, it had its origin in the fertile brain of an Englishman named Cecil Rhodes, whose idea was to reconquer the United States and make it an integral part of the British Empire. To this end he established the Rhodes Foundation, providing for the education in England of bright young Americans. Andrew Carnegie, the steel magnate, in return for the promise of a dukedom in his native Scotland, was persuaded to assist in the plan, and in 1910 the Carnegie Endowment for International Peace was established.

In 1939, a Rhodes Scholar and old-time one-worlder by the name of Clarence Streit wrote a book called *Union Now*, which advocated a gradual approach to final world union by way of regional unions, starting with the union between the U.S. and Britain. According to the *Carnegie Year Book of 1940*, the Carnegie Endowment for International Peace financed the placing of four hundred copies of the Streit book in libraries of the United States and sent over one thousand copies to carefully selected editors, newspapers, and journalists in the United States and Canada. Committees were set up all over America, and Mr. Streit reported that over two million Americans had signed petitions asking for union with Britain. In *Union Now*, Streit, who has been a close associate of Communists and socialists all his adult life, had said that the more complex the world becomes, "the more urgent [is] its need for world government." On page 256 of his book he stated:

> Into this world came Union Now, challenging the dogma of absolute national sovereignty and asserting that a world organization not only was necessary, but must be stronger than the League of Nations, must be based upon different principles, on citizenship rather than national sovereignty. It [Union Now] proclaimed the need of world government and insisted that no country needed this more urgently than the United States.

In Streit's own words (page 257), Atlantic Union was the first step towards complete world government: "Union Now held the formation of a free federal government to be the eventual goal and urges the first step towards its Union Now of the democracies . . . "

In 1941, Streit published another book, entitled *Union Now with Britain*, in which he claimed that the union he advocated would be a step toward the formation of a free world government; but the book itself made it clear that by joining a union with other nations, America would be amalgamated with the socialist and Communist systems that existed in these other nations.

In the *Washington Evening Star* of January 5, 1942, an ad appeared under the heading: "In Union Now Lies the Power to Win the War and the Peace — a Petition." The petition said:

> We gain from the fact that all the Soviet Republics are now united in one government, as also are all the Chinese-speaking peoples once so divided. Surely we and they must agree that union now of the democracies wherever possible is equally to the general advantage. Let us begin now a world United States.

A resolution urged a federal union with common citizenship, direct taxation of citizens, responsibility for law enforcement, authority to coin and borrow money, a monopoly of armed forces, and the ability to admit new members. At one time Streit's organization favored including the Russians.

On April 27, 1942, the board of directors of Federal Union adopted a new policy statement, which said:

> We believe that we can best preserve and extend those basic freedoms which are the heritage of western civilization by forming now . . . a federal union with those peoples with whom we have compelling natural ties . . . . We believe that the world imperatively needs an all-inclusive international organization in which the United States . . . Russia . . . and other powers known as the United Nations should take the lead.

Following World War II, when the idea of forming a union

with Russia became unpalatable to the American public, Streit, showing the agility possessed by all one-worlders, reversed his field and announced that Union Now would be a bulwark against world Communism!

Streit, who may have gotten his ideas on Atlantic Union from various tracts on the subject published by the Fabian Socialist Society in England, clearly has no hostility towards collectivism. He said in *Union Now*: "Democracy not only allows mankind to choose freely between capitalism and collectivism, but it includes Marxist governments."

In his pamphlets Streit asks the question: "Does the rise of socialism in some Western European democracies prevent our federating with them?" He answers with an emphatic "No!"

Streit's organization to promote Union Now was called Federal Union, and was financed by grants from the Carnegie Endowment for International Peace, of which Communist spy Alger Hiss was later to become president.

In March 1949, Federal Union set up a political action unit called the Atlantic Union Committee. The first president of this Committee was former Supreme Court Justice Owen J. Roberts, who testified before the Senate Foreign Relations Subcommittee in 1950 that joining Union Now would mean the United States government would have to surrender its rights and power to coin money, levy taxes and tariffs, regulate immigration, enact citizenship laws, declare war, and maintain standing armies. Roberts has said he considers national sovereignty a "silly shibboleth" and believes that U.S. and Western European union "must be built on a common citizenship."[4]

The *Los Angeles Examiner* on February 8, 1951, described what Atlantic Union meant to America:

What Senator Kefauver actually is proposing is that the United States summon the nations of Western Europe and offer to abolish itself as a nation, surrendering its sovereign powers to those nations.

They would impose their socialism in place of our republican self-government, extract taxes from us as they pleased, draft our men for their armies and our women for their factories, appropriate the bulk of our productive wealth for their own enrichment.

How can any Senator or Representative elected to represent the people of the United States bring himself to advocate so clear a policy of national self-destruction?

How can any adult American even consider such an idea?

Yet less than a dozen years after its founding the Atlantic Union Committee had grown to eight hundred seventy-one wealthy and influential members, one hundred seven of whom were members of the CFR, and thirty, members of the United World Federalists.

Elmo Roper (CFR and UWF), the pollster, formerly President of the Atlantic Union Committee, in his book, *The Goal Is Government of All the World*, betrayed how Atlantic Union fits into the world government scheme:

> Some of us who have been interested in World Government for several years now have come together to form the Atlantic Union Committee. Our objective in this committee is to have the Congress pass a resolution supporting the call of a Constitutional Convention of at least the Atlantic Pact nations.

Under the subtitle "How Federal Union Will Work," Mr. Roper stated:

> Such a union would have the right to conduct foreign relations, maintain armed forces, issue currency, regulate commerce and communications between states in the union and grant citizenship. The union must have the power to tax . . . . There would be nothing, there must be nothing, in such a union which would be out of consonance with the aims and objectives of the United Nations.

A resolution calling for an Atlantic Union Convention was introduced into Congress in 1949. Senator Estes Kefauver of Tennessee took the lead in pushing the resolution, which had the support of Senators William Fulbright (CFR), Hubert Humphrey (CFR), Jacob Javits (CFR), Herbert Lehman (CFR), and Richard Nixon. Others in and out of Congress who supported this or succeeding bipartisan bills included William Benton (CFR), John Foster Dulles (CFR), Milton Eisenhower (CFR), Thomas Finletter (CFR), Henry Ford II (CFR), William C. Foster (CFR), Clark Kerr (CFR), Mr. Nixon's *alter ego*, Henry Kissinger (CFR), John V. Lindsay (CFR), George C. Marshall (CFR), Eugene McCarthy (CFR), Charles S. Rhyne (CFR), Arthur Schlesinger Jr. (CFR), Adlai Stevenson (CFR), and Thomas Watson (CFR). The bill has never passed Congress, although it has been introduced again and again by world government promoters, some calling themselves Democrats and some, Republicans. In February 1951, *World Government News*, the official publication of the United World Federalists (pages 8 and 9), hailed Richard Nixon for sponsoring the Atlantic Union Resolution the second time it was introduced into the Senate.

The one-world advocates never give up. John Foster Dulles, two days after he had been selected by President Eisenhower to be our Secretary of State, wired the Second Congress of the Atlantic Union Committee, which was meeting in Buffalo (November 22, 1952), expressing his support of their idea and suggesting that NATO be converted into a federal union. The NATO Treaty had been ratified in 1949, under Truman, as a military alliance to protect the free world against expanding Communism. Many had ideas of expanding this into a federal union.

In an article on world government, *U.S. News & World Report* of February 24, 1956, stated:

Among Republicans, President Eisenhower has endorsed the

idea of some form of union. Vice-President Richard Nixon and
Governor Christian Herter of Massachusetts, as members of the
Senate and the House a few years ago, introduced resolutions
calling for conventions to study the question of unity. Secretary
of State John Foster Dulles has endorsed such a study.

Not all Republicans, however, bought the globaloney. *U.S.
News & World Report* quoted Senator Bricker of Ohio as
calling the bill to set up an Atlantic Union convention an
"exploration of the desirability of junking the American
Declaration of Independence." Bricker regarded the plan as
one under which "the United States would become a vassal
province in a regional superstate evolving out of NATO," and
the American Bill of Rights would go down the drain.[5]
Streit and his organization are undaunted by the fact that
they have yet to force their plan past Congress, despite strong
bipartisan support, and they continue to push and gain
momentum. A report from Atlantic Union on the "Remarkable Advance of the Atlantic Federal Union Concept in
1966" boasted that Atlanticans had strong potential Presidential support. *Freedom and Union* magazine of March
1966 listed as backers who had endorsed the Atlantic Union
Delegation Barry Goldwater, Mark Hatfield, Richard Nixon,
Nelson Rockefeller, George Romney, and William Scranton.
Congressman Paul Findley (R.-Ill.), who introduced the latest
Atlantic Union bill in Congress, stated:

> Based on these endorsements, I predict that the next Repub-
> lican President will work to achieve Atlantic union . . . . Virtually
> all the presidential level leadership of the Republican party thus
> supports the most promising proposal for uniting free people
> since the American Revolution, 1776-89.

Richard Nixon, in his letter of endorsement to Findley,
said: "As Clarence Streit probably told you I have supported
this resolution for many years and I wish you every success in

your efforts." [6] During 1964 Nixon had taken time off from his campaign to send the committee this statement, dated September 1: "It is fitting that the United States, the world's first truly federal government, should be a main force behind the effort to find a basis for a broad federation of the Atlantica nations." The message forthrightly concluded: "The Atlantic Union Resolution is a forward-looking proposal which acknowledges the depth and breadth of the incredible change which is going on in the world around us. I urge its adoption."

Nixon was merely echoing the beliefs and aims of Nelson Rockefeller. The same issue of *Freedom and Union* magazine quoted Rockefeller as maintaining:

> Our generation is called on for ... political creativity and economic construction – on an inter-continental basis .... I have followed with sympathy and interest the development of the joint resolution [for an Atlantic Union Convention] and deeply believe that its enactment would be an historic milestone in the annals of human freedom and world peace.

All this bipartisan support elated Streit, who gloated:

> In the past, the main support for Atlantic Union resolutions came from the Democrats; the Republicans – with notable exceptions – were indifferent or hostile. This year the proposal, without losing its Democratic backing, gained leadership at the presidential level. It also gained a higher percentage of support from Republican and Democratic membership in the House despite this being an election year. This advance is highly important for it insures full bi-partisan support should the President decide to lead toward Atlantic Union ....

Whenever Mr. Nixon has been queried on his support of dissolving the United States into the new nation of Atlantica, he has vociferously denied that Atlantic Union has anything to do with mouse-trapping America into a world superstate, and his verbiage is designed to make it appear that anyone who intimates such a thing is guilty of a monstrous unfounded slander against him. Only those who have actually taken time to study the facts know who is doing the truth-twisting. Atlantic Union, which has a great deal of dual membership with UWF, makes no bones about the fact that it is the halfway house to world government. On the twenty-fifth anniversary of Atlantic Union in 1964, Clarence Streit admitted, once again, his organization's one world ambitions:

> The Atlantic Union it means to see constituted now will be but a nucleus designed to grow in peace through generations to come, until the Federation of the Free embraces the whole race of mortal man.

Since becoming President, Mr. Nixon has remained very quiet about the Atlantic Union movement. No doubt, any move in this direction is being saved until after 1972. Atlantic Union, however, has not forgotten Mr. Nixon. At Federal Union's Award Dinner in Washington, D.C., on November 20, 1970, founder Clarence Streit presented the Atlantic Union Pioneer Award to Richard Nixon for eighteen years of championing the cause of establishing "the United States of Atlantica." The award bears this inscription:

> RICHARD M. NIXON, President of the United States. Far-seeing Senator, he Cosponsored in 1951 the Original Atlantic Union Resolution. As Vice President, his Bold Action Led to the 1962 Atlantic Convention in Paris. Alone among Presidential Aspirants, he Wrote the 1966 House Hearing, Urging a Stronger Bill — Still Pending — With these Words that History will Remember: "The United States should be a Main Force" for a "Federation of Free Atlantic Nations . . . In the Age of the Rocket, Dreams become Reality with a Speed Difficult to Imagine. The Atlantic Union Resolution . . . a Forward-looking Proposal . . . Acknowledges the . . . Incredible Change Going on Around Us. I Urge its Adoption."

Mr. Nixon has taken a major step toward surrendering American sovereignty with his advocacy of Senate ratification of the United Nations' Genocide Convention. This treaty is so Leftist-oriented and so dangerous that no President in twenty-one years has succeeded in shoving it through the Senate. The Genocide Convention was first submitted to the Senate by President Truman in 1950. Public opposition caused it to be bottled up in the Senate Foreign Relations Committee, where it has lain dormant ever since. In 1953 President Eisenhower tried to get the treaty revivified and ratified, but opposition was too great and the attempt was abandoned. The same thing happened under President Johnson in 1966. Now President Nixon has put the prestige and pressure of his administration solidly behind the effort to obtain ratification, despite the fact that the American Bar Association has all along been on record as strongly opposing this giveaway of American rights and sovereignty. Liberal Democrats Truman, Kennedy, and Johnson could not achieve passage of this misnamed treaty, but Nixon may well succeed where others have failed, simply because most Americans accept the Madison Avenue image of Mr. Nixon as a staunch defender against the Left.

The convention was adopted by the U.N. in 1948, and since then some seventy-five nations have ratified the instrument, among them the Soviet Union — a sponsor of the treaty. Columnist James J. Kilpatrick comments:

> And if it seems remarkable that the masters of the Kremlin should have signed this document, wiping their hands still stained with the blood of Katyn, it is because the Genocide Convention does not apply to political or revolutionary groups. It applies only to "national, ethnical, racial or religious groups," and the Kremlin hardly ever seeks to eliminate them as such. The camps of Siberia house nothing but bums.[7]

Kilpatrick continues:

> The Soviet Union's ratification of the treaty has this impor-
> tance only: It is being used by proponents of the convention as a
> club for beating on the Senate. The Russians, we are told, are
> ashamed of the United States. How could we fail to embrace a
> treaty so enlightened and humane?

Yes, how could we fail to be suckered into this trap? Who
could be opposed to a treaty outlawing the killing of human
beings? The *Washington Post* has called our failure to
ratify the treaty an "unsightly stain on the good name" of
the U.S.A. Also demanding passage are such Leftist organizations as the American Civil Liberties Union (ACLU), the American Humanist Committee, Americans for Democratic Action
(ADA), the League for Industrial Democracy (LID), the
Unitarian-Universalist Association, the United Auto Workers,
the National Council of Churches, and the Communist Party.
William Loeb, publisher of the *Manchester* (N.H.) *Union
Leader*, commented:

> . . . the genocide treaty is actually an old Communist trick:
> Put a nice label on something – like "home or mother" – and
> you can count on the customers (or the voters) not reading the
> fine print. It is in the fine print where the Communists hook you.
> The genocide treaty, if passed, would go far towards destroying
> freedom of speech for every American, it would put weapons in
> the hands of the state which could make it very easy to imprison
> almost any individual.

The dangers in the United States' ratifying of the U.N.'s
Genocide Convention were spelled out by Kilpatrick:

> One of the forbidden acts [of the Genocide Convention] is
> "causing serious bodily or mental harm to members of the
> group." Either "mental harm" means something, or it means
> nothing. It means, we must suppose, whatever it may some day
> be construed to mean by judges, foreign or domestic, presiding at
> the trial of some public official or private person charged with
> this gauzy crime.

Another forbidden act is "deliberately inflicting on the group conditions of life calculated to bring about its physical destruction in whole or in part." Criminal statutes, we are taught, must be strictly construed. Who can construe this clause? What is meant, at another point, by "public incitement?" What is meant by "complicity in genocide?" Who knows?[8]

The treaty also provides for an "international penal tribunal" to have jurisdiction in such cases. This group would have the power to yank Americans before it and try them for the crime of causing "mental harm" to some minority group. We have had plenty of experience with civil rights groups seeing "racism" under every bed, and one can imagine that they would go hog-wild if they could haul any person or group against whom they have a gripe, real or imaginary, before a sympathetic group of international magistrates. This could conceivably lead to secret seizures, deportations, and trials. Americans would be stripped of the protections guaranteed them by the Constitution. Mr. Nixon made sure of this when as Vice President he worked behind the scenes to engineer the defeat of the Bricker Amendment, which would have guaranteed that no treaty could supersede the Constitution's protections. (See Chapter VI.)

Columnist Holmes Alexander, in writing of Nixon's recommendation to the Senate (which, incidentally, has the backing of "Conservative" Attorney General John N. Mitchell), says, in effect, that the President is only kidding. Nixon, Alexander says, knows the tenor of the Senate and that it would not ratify so monstrous a thing. So, he writes, we shouldn't worry about Nixon's recommendation, no matter how dangerous it might be. As columnist John Synon remarked:

> How cynical. That's like saying not to worry about handing a loaded gun to a nitwit. The United States Senate, I'm here to tell you, is capable of ratifying anything, genocide, homicide, or suicide.

The Senate will succeed in ratifying it only if a number of weak-kneed Republicans who would normally oppose it submit to threats, arm twisting, and promises of pork barrel projects for their home states.

If Mr. Nixon has been only kidding about his devotion to forging the links in the chain of the World Superstate that is to be welded around America's wrists, then he is a consummate hypocrite. But his commitment to world government goes back nearly a quarter of a century, and indeed he would not now be in the White House if he were not committed to this ultimate goal of the *Insiders.* It is Mr. Alexander and the millions of other complacent Republicans who are fooling themselves by rationalizing that Mr. Nixon does not mean business every step of the way to world government.

For those who can read between the lines, Mr. Nixon's devotion to world government is quite obvious. However, he never uses the term "world government," which would produce a strong reaction, but rather the euphemistic standard code words of the world government addicts, "world order." Mr. Nixon often speaks of "building a new world order," but that phrase is meaningless to all but a few. If the *Insiders* are successful, the "new world order" will probably be built, ultimately, on the existing U.N. structure. President Nixon has long been a U.N. enthusiast, despite the fact that, of all people, he knows best that the primary author of the U.N. Charter, Alger Hiss, was a Soviet spy — for he helped to convict him. Although the United Nations has lost much of its luster for the public, it has still been the beneficiary of the greatest propaganda build-up in history, despite the fact that its creation had the full support of the Communists. The Communists knew they could manipulate it, and *Political Affairs*, the official theoretical journal of the Communist Party, U.S.A., in its April 1945 issue told the comrades:

> Great popular support and enthusiasm for the United Nations
> policies should be built up, well organized, and articulate. But it
> is necessary to do more than that. The opposition must be
> rendered so impotent that it will be unable to gather any
> significant support in the Senate against the United Nations
> Charter *and the treaties which are to follow.* [Emphasis added.]

Shortly after his election President Nixon and his Secretary of State-designate William Rogers visited "the house that
Hiss built" (on land donated by the Rockefeller family), "so
that by this visit," Nixon said, "we could indicate our
continuing support of the United Nations and our intention
in these years ahead to do everything that we can to
strengthen this organization as it works in the cause of peace
throughout the world."[9]

All of this really should not be surprising. The President
was quoted in a favorable biography, *Nixon*, by Earl Mazo
and Stephen Hess, as saying: "Am I a conservative or a
liberal? My answer is that I'm an internationalist." [10] An
internationalist is one who is not a nationalist. He is one who
puts other nations, or the world, ahead of his own country.
He is one who advocates peace by yoking America in an
organization with the world's most murderous warmakers. He
is one who believes that sovereignty over the United States
should reside outside the United States. This may seem like a
rather curious position for one who has taken an oath to
uphold the Constitution of the United States, which set up a
sovereign nation, but Mr. Nixon is not alone in this
contradiction. It is the Liberal position, and Mr. Nixon has
stated unequivocally numerous times: "I'm a liberal on
foreign policy." [11] But most people are not aware of this
statement. They are only aware of his campaign oratory, in
which he has denounced in the strongest possible terms the
architects of disaster who have led America in stumbling
from one foreign policy disaster to another for over

twenty-five years. Once in office he followed the same pro-Communist policies as his predecessors. As ultra-Liberal Dr. Lincoln P. Bloomfield has explained: "If the communist dynamic was greatly abated the west might lose whatever incentive it has for world government." The reason that Mr. Nixon has followed the same policies, and even kept the same "architects" in positions of power, is that he is committed to these policies. If he were not, he would today be a prosperous lawyer in California, but a political has-been.

Rather than a political has-been, Richard Nixon today is President of the United States. The *Insiders* reward well those who are willing to play their game. Many students of the *Insiders'* conspiracy believe that they intend to establish their totalitarian world superstate during Mr. Nixon's second term. It would doubtless come about through a series of precipitated and manipulated crises involving a world-wide monetary debacle, a major depression in America, major moves around the world by the Soviets, and possibly war in the Mid-East. World government would come as a savior, promising world peace and an end to the Communist threat. Most Americans would not realize until it is too late that the problems were created in order that world government might be accepted as a solution.

A world government by its very nature must be a socialist government. The planners want to extend their plans over the entire world. The *Insiders* want to control the economy of the whole planet. A world government requires a world supreme court, and Mr. Nixon is on record in favor of a world supreme court. And a world government must have a world police force to enforce the laws of the World Superstate and keep the slaves from rebelling. The *Los Angeles Examiner* of October 28, 1950, reported that Congressman Richard Nixon had introduced a "resolution calling for the establishment of a United Nations police force . . . . " So we know where Mr. Nixon stands on that one! But why would Mr. Nixon want to see the United States sucked into the world government trap? Could it be that the *Insiders* have promised him that he will be the organization's first president? You must admit it beats being an attorney in bucolic Whittier.

References

1. *Plan for Peace*, New York, Institute for International Order, 1954.
2. Quoted from United World Federalists pamphlet, "We Believe in World Peace Through World Law."
3. *Ibid.*
4. *Human Events*, March 5, 1955.
5. *U.S. News & World Report*, February 24, 1956, p. 82.
6. *Freedom and Union*, March 1966, p. 9.
7. *Los Angeles Times*, May 12, 1970.
8. *Ibid.*
9. *Indianapolis Star*, December 18, 1968.
10. Quoted in *Indianapolis News*, August 11, 1968.
11. *Ibid.*

CHAPTER XIII

The More It Changes

The cornerstone of Richard Nixon's rise to political power was staunch opposition to both Communism and Socialism. In fact Nixon often equated Communism and Socialism; that was one of his traits that most infuriated Liberals. Nixon knew that Karl Marx in his *Communist Manifesto* of 1848 had used the words interchangeably. It is not for nothing that Russia calls itself the Union of Soviet *Socialist* Republics. As Nixon so eloquently stated it in 1952:

> There's one difference between the Reds and Pinks. The Pinks want to socialize America. The Reds want to socialize the world and make Moscow the world capital. Their paths are similar; they have the same Bible — the teachings of Karl Marx.[1]

The basis of socialism is "big government" — bureaucracy, controls, deficit spending, and inflation. Socialism is the road to total government. When you get there you have Communism. Nixon once remarked, " . . . I don't want any part of any road — middle, right or left — which eventually leads to total government."[2]

In a pamphlet entitled "The Nixon Stand," Nixon said: "If I were to pick one major issue in this 1968 election in which the candidates have a basic disagreement, it is with regard to the role of government. There are some who believe the way to a better society is for government to get bigger and bigger — which means the rights and responsibilities of people will get smaller and smaller . . . . "[3]

315

"The choice we face today," he maintained at one point in the campaign, "very simply is this: Do we continue down a road that leads to big government and little people, or do we take a new road, one that taps the energies of the greatest engine of productivity the world has ever seen — the engine of American industry and American private enterprise? . . . Private enterprise, far more efficiently than the government, can provide the jobs, train the unemployed, build the homes, offer the new opportunities which will produce progress — not promises — in solving the problems of America."[4]

In opposing "big government" Nixon was not only doing what was morally right, he was doing what was politically right. An August 1968 Gallup Poll showed that 46 per cent of Americans felt that "big government" was the "biggest threat to the country." This was contrasted to only 14 per cent who felt that way in 1959. Gallup commented: "Although big government has been a favorite Republican target for many years, rank and file Democrats are nearly as critical of growing Federal power as are Republicans."[5]

However, a clue as to what would actually happen during the Nixon administration was given in the February 3, 1969 issue of the *Wall Street Journal*:

> A trio of Nixon Administration Cabinet officials gave a partial picture of how "Great Society" programs will fare under the Republicans.
> There won't be any attempt to dismantle the Johnson Administration programs, nor will there be a major effort to expand public spending for them.
> Instead, there will be a general tidying up through much Governmental reorganization, a minimum of new legislation and a major effort to involve private industry, voluntary agencies and other nongovernmental entities in the cause of social change.[6]

And NEA columnist Bruce Biossat revealed that despite all the "very sincere" campaign rhetoric:

No one in the top Nixon entourage really imagines that the federal government is going to be reduced in size. Its bigness in a big and growing country is accepted as inescapable.

The task is to make the bigness work and, critically, to persuade the American people that federal actions — and the lesser actions of state and local governments — really end up getting things done which affect people who have problems they need to have solved.[7]

In other words, the Nixon administration gave up on fulfilling that campaign promise even before Inauguration Day. This might lead one to believe that Nixon and his cohorts were never very sincere about doing battle with the Democrat-instituted welfare state in the first place. There was a time when Richard Nixon denounced such "me-tooism" in no uncertain terms. He told a Los Angeles crowd on April 20, 1949:

There are some who believe that the only way we can win is to go down the road with the Democratic Party on a me-too basis, except that we should go them one better. It is true that such a program might win for us, but in winning this way, we would be abdicating our responsibilities to the people.[8]

But it was obvious by Nixon's appointment of such welfare-staters as Robert Finch and George Romney that the Great Society was home safe. We were going to have efficiently administered socialism under the Elephant Brigade. Surely anybody could run a bureaucracy more efficiently than the spendocrat donkeys. After taking office, however, the GOP found that trying to make socialism efficient was like trying to make the Pacific dry. The Nixon administration abandoned its solemn pledge to fight big government, and began expanding it on all fronts. This move was indicated in the staccato-style "Newsgram" in *U.S. News & World Report* of February 2, 1970:

As *Mr. Nixon's plans*, sketched in his state-of-the-union speech, take hold: Washington will move even *deeper into people's lives.* For example —

Education, over the long haul, will be financed more by Washington. School districts are showing they want additional U.S. money to save local taxes.

Welfare, under the program drawn up by Mr. Nixon, is to be based on more uniform standards set in Washington, money paid out by Washington.

Housing, once a local matter, is to rely further on federal decisions. Much the same goes for *health.* The drift forecast by high officials is toward some sort of national health-payment arrangement eventually.

"Consumerism," as it begins to work, is seen as pointing toward additional federally set standards for goods used by nearly everybody.

It's to be federal money that pays for many new local *police* facilities.

"New Federalism," as conceived by Mr. Nixon, is based on returning more money collected by Washington to the States. But it is to be Congress and the President who decide on the tax rates that produce the money.

What *the nation* seems to be approaching is *general agreement* that big problems are to be handled via Washington. *Reform movements* in this country almost always follow that path. Mr. Nixon's is no exception.

That thinking will accelerate as the nation becomes *more* populous, urban areas sprawl across State lines, business and communications ties tighten.

States are seen to be hunting a *new role*, not really sovereign.

"Conservatives" will object. *"Liberals"* will complain Mr. Nixon isn't moving fast enough. But *the President* will try to please *the center* majority.

Traditional pump priming — very easy money, big Government spending — would risk a new burst of inflation, it is reasoned. Planning, instead, is emphasizing Government *training programs* for the jobless.

Next step would be new methods of inducing companies to hire the newly trained. *Tax incentives*, Government *subsidies* will be mulled.

The day when Government guarantees *everyone a job* may not be far off.

When it comes to the *federal budget*, about to be unveiled, note this:

Seeds being planted now by Mr. Nixon and Congress point to *bigger spending* in years beyond 1971. Specifics are beginning to take shape.

The idea that, because the country is getting bigger or we have more technology, the government is forced to become Big Brother is fallacious. Actually, the bigger the country, the less able the central government is to govern efficiently.

During the 1960's, the size of the federal government, and of federal spending, fairly exploded. Roger Freeman, a scholar at the Hoover Institute at Stanford University and a former member of the White House staff, pointed out:

More than half of the $129 billion increase in federal expenditures between fiscal 1953 and 1971 was applied to social purposes, less than one-fifth to defense. Defense meanwhile shrank from 64 percent of the federal budget to 36 percent, from 13.6 percent of the Gross National Product to about 7.2 percent.

In other words, the share of federal revenues and of the Gross National Product allocated to national defense has been cut almost in half since 1953. Most of the huge savings were applied to social purposes, with education one of the main gainers.

Columnist Paul Scott revealed that under Nixon defense spending is shrinking, while spending on social welfare programs is expanding:

While everybody has been talking about the need for reordering national priorities, a dramatic change in government spending already has taken place.

For the first time since World War II, federal expenditures this year for health, education, welfare and labor programs will exceed defense expenditures.

This highly significant change in national priorities was highlighted by the recent passage in the House of appropriation bills for the Departments of Labor, and Health, Education & Welfare.

These giant money bills, the largest in history, contain an estimated $74.3 billion for social programs. This compares with the $73.6 national defense spending budget now pending before Congress and which is expected to be reduced further. In 1953, federal expenditures for national defense totaled $49.4 billion as compared to $7.1 billion for the government's social programs. [9]

Some diligent soul who made a count of the number of federal administrative agencies came up with more than 2,400 — most of them, probably, un-Constitutional. Congressman William Roth (R.-Del.) assigned to staff members the task of calculating the number of federal aid programs in existence, and the total came to 1,315 as of September 1969, 225 more than the previous year. According to Congressman Wright Patman there are nearly 1,600 advisory committees and commissions in the executive branch alone. By early in his administration, Richard Nixon had added forty to the total.

Of these 5,315 programs, bureaus, and commissions, Mr. Nixon announced that he had found fifty-seven that could be dispensed with. For example, Mr. Nixon believed that the Republic could survive without a bureau of tea tasters. But, alas, at last report, most of the fifty-seven bureaus, including the doughty tea tasters, had survived the axe, proving once again that old bureaus never die, and they seldom even fade away. It is not as if there were not plentiful targets for Mr. Nixon's scalpel in the budget and the bureaucracy if he were sincerely interested. But Richard Nixon came to Washington not to bury big government, but to multiply it.

The major cause of the phenomenal mushrooming of big government has been the fantastic expansion of "Welfare" in all its forms and guises. During his successful quest for the Presidency, Republican candidate Richard Nixon told the National Alliance of Businessmen:

> As we look through the ages — and welfare is not new — we have found that inevitably when such programs continue and escalate in any society, welfare tends to destroy those who have received it and to corrupt those who dispense it.

It was sixteen months later, as President-elect, that Mr. Nixon again addressed himself to the subject of "Welfare." This time he was speaking before an assembly of the nation's Governors at Colorado Springs:

> We confronted the fact that in the past five years the Federal Government alone spent more than a quarter of a trillion dollars on social programs — more than $250 billion. Yet far from solving our problems, these expenditures had reaped a harvest of dissatisfaction, frustration and bitter division.
>
> Never in human history has so much been spent by so many for such a negative result . . . .

Mr. Nixon was not exaggerating. *U.S. News & World Report* for January 13, 1969, revealed that the number of Americans receiving "Welfare" had jumped over 50 per cent during a decade of unparalleled prosperity, and by the end of 1968 it totaled nearly 10 million persons. The *Washington Evening Star* informed us that "Welfare" rolls across the country were proliferating at the astonishing rate of 200,000 per month. In its issue of February 3, 1969, *U.S. News* added:

> In the past eight years, federal spending for education, old-age pensions, health, handouts to the poor and all other "social welfare" has jumped to 61 billions a year. Add the more than 51 billions spent by State and local governments for similar aid, and the bill exceeds 112 billions a year.
>
> . . . It is 40 percent more than the U.S. spends annually for defense, including war in Vietnam.

In addition to the $112.4 billion spent by government at all levels for "social programs," private welfare outlays amount to another $50.7 billion — a total of $163.1 billion. This, said *U.S. News & World Report*, accounts for almost 20 per cent of the entire U.S. output of goods and services. The same source informs us that 36 per cent of all federal spending, and 44 per cent of all state spending, now falls within the category of "social welfare." This makes expenditure for such handouts second only to that for national defense.

Yet, *U.S. News* noted, despite these absolutely staggering figures, "all ideas with official backing seem to point in only one direction: toward bigger, costlier relief experiments." At the federal level alone there are now 112 poverty aid programs, handled by eleven separate agencies; sixty-nine vocational programs, operated by eight different federal agencies; and forty-three separate programs for children, administered by five different agencies.

While millions of jobs go begging, the number of those on "Welfare" is increasing nationally at an annual rate of 10 per cent compounded. Yet the *Wall Street Journal* reported on April 24, 1969:

> President Nixon has asked his top domestic policy experts to explore a deeply perplexing social phenomenon . . . . In short, the Great Society enlarged the demand for welfare and also increased its supply.
>
> "My main conclusion is that the increase in the caseload is a *good* thing. More eligible families are getting assistance, so the system is in this sense working better," sums up one White House welfare specialist. This judgment is shared by many other Nixon Administration officials . . . .

Assuming that President Nixon's figure of $50 billion per year for "Welfare" over the past five years was approximately accurate, the average American family pays about $1,250 per year in direct and indirect taxes to support those who can't or won't support themselves. This means the average productive American has during the last half-decade paid out $6,250, and worked approximately 3,000 hours, to support these programs. Yet, assuming that there are approximately four million families in America living in poverty, every one of these families could have had a tax-free income of $12,500 per year with the amount of money *already* being spent. Probably as much as one-half to three-fourths of this money goes for overhead and salaries for the povertycrats, with probably less than 25 per cent of "Welfare" expenditures ever reaching the hands of the poor. Even so, although figures vary from state to state and according to the size of the family and other circumstances, monthly direct cash payments to "Welfare" recipients in industrial states now average $250 to $300 per family unit — more income than is provided by the Congress for many of our military families.

In addition, according to *U.S. News & World Report* of April 28, 1969, a total of 3.8 million Americans each year now receive from the taxpayers some 24.7 pounds of free food per month — including flour, canned meat, raisins, butter, lard, and seventeen other staples.

The federal Food Stamp Program (which has been greatly expanded) provides food at a discount of roughly 33 per cent to 2.9 million Americans who have been enticed onto the dole. In addition, 2.3 million children receive free school lunches from the government and an additional 16.7 million get subsidized lunches, while 200,000 youngsters receive free breakfasts under a recently initiated program. Most of these giveaway schemes have received Congressional appropriations for expansion approximately 25 per cent during the coming year.

It has been estimated by *U.S. News & World Report* that in order to equal the value of cash, food, medical and

recreational services available without charge and tax-free to
those who find it convenient to live idly on "Welfare" at the
expense of their working fellows, the average taxpayer would
have to earn in excess of $7,000 per year. The difference is
the 2,000 hours of toil which the working taxpayer must put
in each year to earn a living, while the "Welfare" people sit
fatly on their government checks.

Exactly one year from the day the Republican Party
nominated him for President, Richard Nixon summarily
preempted national television time to spell out "his" revolutionary new "Welfare" program. The President damned the
current system in the strongest terms and proposed that the
variegated state welfare programs be replaced by a federal
minimum floor for "Welfare" recipients in every state *plus*
subsidies to the "working poor" and a gigantic job-training
program. The President's scheme was described in *U.S. News
& World Report* for August 25, 1969:

> If enacted by Congress, the Nixon proposal would more than
> double the number of people on relief, triple the number of
> children receiving assistance and add almost 4 billion dollars to
> the federal costs of welfare in the first full year of operation. At
> that time, according to Administration estimates, there would be
> at least 22.4 million people receiving Government aid, or 1 out of
> every 9 Americans . . . .
>
> Relief recipients in the nation would then exceed the total
> population of such a large State as California – 19.3 million – or
> New York – 18.1 million. Total cost to taxpayers would run
> around 15 billion dollars a year in federal, State and local funds.*

According to Ted Lewis of the *New York Daily News*,
much of the philosophy behind Nixon's proposals came from

---

*After Nixon presented his "New Federalism" [the name apparently taken from a
book by that title written by Nelson Rockefeller] to assembled Governors in
Colorado Springs a month later, the Governors demanded that the federal
government take over *all* "Welfare" financing. The lone dissenting voice was that
of Lester Maddox of Georgia.

Lyndon Johnson's Secretary of Health, Education and Welfare, John Gardner — a key *Insider* and member of the Council on Foreign Relations, who has recently organized "Common Cause," a grass-roots lobbying organization aimed at establishing a total Marxist state through federal legislation. According to Lewis, Mr. Nixon sent the following note to HEW Secretary Finch:

> "John Gardner's Godkin lectures (attached) express better than anything I have yet read what I hope will serve as the basic philosophy of this administration. I commend them for your weekend reading. Sincerely, RMN."
>
> * * *
>
> The lectures referred to were delivered at Harvard College by LBJ's onetime HEW Secretary Gardner, who quit the Johnson cabinet in a dispute over welfare methods . . . .
>
> None of the significant tasks can be accomplished, said Gardner, "if we are unwilling to tax ourselves."

Then Presidential Assistant Daniel P. Moynihan, a Liberal Democrat and member of the board of directors of the socialist ADA, who was largely responsible for drafting the Nixon "Welfare" program, commented:

> What the President really has done is make an historic and fundamental assertion of national responsibility to provide minimum incomes to poor people, stop taxing them, start supplementing their incomes and help the states find enough resources to do this.

The response from the Left to the President's Family Assistance Plan (FAP) proposal was nearly unanimous approval. Republican *Battle Line* quoted a Democratic leader: "If this plan goes through, Richard Nixon will take over Hubert Humphrey's constituency and George Wallace's too." Writing in the *Chicago Tribune* for August 17, 1969, Walter Trohan quoted another top Democrat: " 'I wish we had

thought of it,' a top economic advisor for Lyndon B.
Johnson told this commentator. 'It's a marvelous vote
catcher.' " The *New York Times'* James Reston, spokesman-
apparent for the Establishment now that Walter Lippmann
has hung up his typewriter, was even more effusive:

> . . . . He [Nixon] has been denouncing the "welfare state" for
> 20 years, but he is now saying that poverty in America in the
> midst of spectacular prosperity is intolerable and must be wiped
> out . . . .
>
> A Republican president has condemned the word "welfare,"
> emphasized "work" and "training" as conditions of public
> assistance, suggested that the states and the cities be given more
> federal money to deal with their social and economic problems,
> but still comes out in the end with a policy of spending more
> money for relief of more poor people than the welfare state
> Democrats ever dared to propose in the past.
>
> This is beginning to be the story of American politics . . . .
>
> . . . And now on the most controversial question of domestic
> policy, he changes the rhetoric, the philosophy and the admini-
> stration, but proposes more welfare, more people on public
> assistance, which will take more federal funds than any other
> president in the history of the Republic . . . .
>
> Nevertheless, Nixon has taken a great step forward. He has
> cloaked a remarkably progressive [*sic*] welfare policy in conserva-
> tive language . . . .
>
> . . . He has repudiated his own party's record on social policy
> at home and even his own hawkish attitudes abroad, and this tells
> us something both about the President and the country.
>
> For he has obviously concluded that the American people are
> for peace abroad and for a more decent distribution of wealth at
> home, and the chances are that this will prove to be both good
> policy and good politics.

A week later Reston crowed that Nixon was "zig-zagging
to the left."

The *New Republic's* T.R.B. also formally welcomed Nixon
into the Fabian underworld with a column titled "Nixon
Outsmarting Democrats":

Most important, for the first time in U.S. history he accepted the idea of a national minimum income for all Americans. It would cover not merely the poor-who-get-aid but the previously excluded "working poor." We have waited for it all these years. This is a new ball game; it's here and it's irreversible.

... The disparity between the haves and have-nots is so great that no random plan can deal with it, we think, and it can only yield to a national, comprehensive plan. Mr. Nixon may not realize it, but that's what he has started ....

... And the plan does provide a platform to build on. This is the first national minimum income program for all Americans. It's the start of systematic income maintenance. Every sign points to the direction in which the country will go.

The socialist *New Republic* was not shy about calling a shovel a shovel. It cheered that the President's proposals amount to "creeping socialism." One read with a gasp: "It must have been quite a scene, the Camp David cabinet meeting at which President Nixon informed the Neanderthal men that he had accepted and would assert creeping socialism, the principle of the Federal Government guaranteeing a minimum income to all disadvantaged Americans."

The *Washington Post's* Roscoe Drummond went even further, commenting:

Whatever happened to conservative Richard Nixon?

Here he is in the lead for the most far-ranging, ground-breaking, daring, social-welfare reform since the early years of the New Deal ....

Strange to contemplate but the time may come when people will think of Richard M. Nixon as the Republican Franklin D. Roosevelt of the 1970s!

Newsweek also called the plan "Nixon's New Deal" and quoted elated Leftists in praise of the proposals:

"I'm both amazed and pleased," applauded Walter Heller, John Kennedy's chief economic advisor and pioneer advocate of

Federal welfare minimums . . . . Some Johnson Administration veterans stared enviously at plans thought too radical in their time. Campaign supporters of Robert Kennedy and Eugene McCarthy spotted causes that their own candidates had championed . . . . It was the finest hour in a much-buffeted six months for Pat Moynihan and HEW's Secretary Robert Finch . . . . Richard Nixon . . . confided to a friend his conviction that [referring to Disraeli] "Tory men with liberal principles are what has enlarged democracy in this world."

It is ironic that Richard Nixon should quote the man who started England on the road from empire to mini-state, if less so that RMN should be praised for his Liberalism and compared with FDR.

Of course, it is the "forgotten Americans," to whom Nixon appealed so successfully during his campaign, who will have to pay for what will amount to 20 million additional drones on the "Welfare" rolls. In its issue of August 25, 1969, *U.S. News & World Report* noted:

Once on the books, programs are rarely, if ever, cut back . . . .
Experts are already talking about 30 to 40 billion dollars a year as eventual cost for a fully developed system of minimum income for all.

Frank S. Meyer, the remaining hard-line Conservative on the staff of *National Review*, characterized the President's plan in these words:

The Nixon welfare program is a program for progressive pauperization of an increasing section of the American people. It was just such pauperization that was one of the outstanding causes and symptoms of the decay of Rome. For "bread and circuses," substitute a federal dole and a television set in every welfare home.

Marxists have long cherished dreams of a federally guaranteed annual income for America. Previously Nixon had staunchly opposed the Marxist guaranteed annual income. "Nixon's the One" who said, while campaigning on May 15, 1968:

> One of the reasons I do not accept . . . a guaranteed annual income or a negative income tax is because of my conviction that doing so, first, would not end poverty, and second, while it might be a substitute for welfare, it would have a very detrimental effect on the productive capacity of the American people . . . that is why I take a dim view of these programs.[10]

The American Conservative Union noted:

> Despite his flat denial that he was proposing a guaranteed annual income, President Nixon's "family assistance plan" is just that. Numerous welfare experts noted that this principle is central to Nixon's plans, and conservatives fear this will open the door to even higher minimum incomes guaranteed for all. Public opinion polls have shown the great majority of Americans opposed to such a scheme because of what liberals sneeringly call "the Puritan Ethic," the popularly supported theory that every man should work for an income.

A year later Nixonites were admitting that the FAP was a guaranteed annual income, a tacit confession that earlier they had been prevaricating.[11]

While the Nixon scheme would replace the much criticized Aid for Dependent Children, it would only increase the incentive for reliefers to produce more children. Let us inspect the consequences of Mr. Nixon's breed-and-feed program.

Suppose a man and a "Welfare mother," who may be absolute strangers, decide to spend the night together communing with their natures. For his moments with this Venus, the man may pay by spending two months with Mercury, but the taxpayers will pay for that evening of pleasure for at least the next twenty-one years, and probably for the next seventy-five. In addition, the chances are great that the first illicit offspring will be the starting point for another geometric progression of "Welfare" recipients whose status will thereafter be "guaranteed."

What is the original father's responsibility? From a practical standpoint, none. To the mother, the child is a guaranteed annual meal ticket. What is your responsibility? We are told by Mr. Nixon that it is your responsibility over the lifetime of that child to labor thousands of hours, and to deny the fruits of your labor to your own children, in order to support the offspring of such brood-mothers. This is euphemistically called "having a social conscience." It has a more accurate name but, alas, that name is inappropriate for repetition here.

We are told that birth control will be introduced into the Nixon program at some point, but of course birth control tablets and devices are readily available now. It is not because of ignorance or poverty that they are not used. While the brood-mothers may be school dropouts, they are graduates *cum laude* of the university of the street, and are anything but ignorant when it comes to sex. They are simply in the baby business for fun and profit. And some of them are brazen enough to be proud of it.

In the best Orwellian fashion, Richard Nixon berated the centralization of power in Washington over the past thirty years, and then proposed to nationalize "Welfare" under Mr. Rockefeller's misnomer, "the New Federalism." Those already familiar with the result of federal intervention in public schools, labor disputes, legislative redistricting, and alleged job discrimination can hardly applaud now what they have opposed for so long.

Yet even as Mr. Nixon was beguiling the Governors with offers of federal money with no strings attached, John Price, a former leader of the Leftist "Republican" Ripon Society, now on the staff of Daniel P. Moynihan, was telling editors in

Chicago on August twelfth that if the states refused to go along with federal "Welfare" standards, the Administration would have to "blackjack the states" by withholding funds until they complied.

The part of Mr. Nixon's plan that was most appealing to the public was the tying of "Welfare" funds to jobs or job-training programs. Yet this idea has more holes than Swiss cheese. As *Human Events* pointed out:

> The President himself left a large loophole for those who don't want to accept work by stressing that any job must be "suitable." Who will determine the "suitability" of a job? . . .
>
> What assurances, moreover, does the taxpayer have that those eligible for work will actually be forced to find work or seek job training? Will the Administration set up some tough enforcement machinery or, as is likely, permit soft-hearted social agencies to monitor this most important task? . . .

Want to bet?

The President's "reform" invites even more cheating and fraud than is presently found in the "Welfare" system. *Human Events* reminded us:

> Moreover, the entire program could become a bonanza for chiselers and loafers — just as have many welfare schemes in the past. Applicants for family allowances, for instance, would not be subject to much scrutiny. To receive a government check, all they would have to do would be to fill out a simple statement of need, saying what they expect their income to be in the benefit year. Monthly amounts would be mailed directly to recipients from a central federal agency, without preliminary investigation . . . .

Most Conservatives have concluded that the President's proposed reforms are no reforms at all. As with the war in Vietnam, Americans are offered a choice between false alternatives. Everything Mr. Nixon has said in indicting the current "Welfare" system is true, but his proposals for reform originated with the same Fabian Socialists who put the country into the current "Welfare" quagmire. It's an escalation of more of the same.

Regardless of the good intentions of many legislators, the only real solution to this nightmare − a salvation from the fate which befell Rome − is to take "Welfare" out of the hands of the politicians and social workers. After all, according to *U.S. News & World Report*, Americans voluntarily give $55 billion a year in private charity, and would give much more to truly good causes if they were relieved of the enormous current tax burden.

The alternative to phasing our current system into a private one is to go the route of Rome and be overrun by armies of the poor demanding bread and circuses while threatening revolution. As taxes go higher and higher to support ever higher and higher "Welfare" benefits, more and more Americans, either by choice or because of circumstances, will desert to the ranks of the parasite class. Eventually the remnant of the American middle-class will be caught in a vise between the Fabians above and the proletarian army below.

The second major ingredient of the President's "New Federalism" is revenue sharing with the states. Although the first part of the "New Federalism" involves a large step towards centralization and nationalization of welfare, "revenue sharing" is promoted as a major step toward decentralization. As part of the propaganda to sell this program Nixon has stated:

> A third of a century of centralizing power and responsibility in Washington has produced a burocratic monstrosity, cumbersome, unresponsive, ineffective. ... After a third of a century of power flowing from the people and the states to Washington it is time for a new federalism in which power, funds, and responsibility will flow from Washington to the states and the people.[12]

As usual, Nixon promotes more socialism, but describes the problems in very Conservative terms. Machiavelli and Orwell would have been proud of him. Theoretically, the grants to the states and local governments are to have "no strings attached," just as were Federal Aid to Education grants. But Nixon's aides privately admit the grants are just bait to further centralize power in the federal government. Even Mr. Nixon hinted at this when he made his proposals:

> Consider for a moment the name of this nation: the United States of America. We establish minimum national standards because we are united; we encourage local supplements because we are a federation of States, and we care for the unfortunate because this is America. [13]

Only the most politically naive could believe that the Nixon program would actually decentralize power. As James J. Kilpatrick remarked: " . . . this power to control follows the Federal dollar as surely as that famous lamb accompanied little Mary." Nixon's revenue-sharing program actually centralizes the power it pretends to decentralize. The Supreme Court has ruled, in this instance quite logically, that whatever the federal government finances it can control. As soon as the states and local governments get hooked on the federal funds, the controls will be put on just as they were in education, agriculture, and every other field the government has attempted to take over by first subsidizing it. No political institution of any kind, at any time in history, ever gave away anything on a no-strings-attached basis. You can't decentralize government by centralizing the tax collections.

House Ways and Means Chairman Wilbur Mills has called the revenue-sharing plan a "trap" that "could become a massive weapon against the independence of state and local government." The plan, said Mills, "goes in the direction of centralized government." [14]

The Administration, for instance, does not propose to

simultaneously phase out other programs while phasing in revenue sharing. Not at all. The revenue-sharing proposal will be just one more layer of programs piled onto the thousands that already exist.

The plan would not reduce state or local taxes, but merely add on to federal taxes. Indeed, according to Dr. Arthur Burns, it could raise state and local taxes. Republican *Battle Line* reported:

> Indeed, the revenue-sharing provision of the Nixon Plan might lead to even higher state taxes, admitted presidential aide Dr. Arthur Burns, because the Federal share paid to each state would be based on the state's matching taxes; the higher the state tax, the more they would get back from Washington.[15]

Human Events added:

> There are other drawbacks as well. Some officials have admitted to a haunting fear of tax sharing because so many existing federal aid programs are "open-end." The cost to the U.S. government is limited only by the ability and willingness of states to come up with matching funds. What would happen, it is asked, if states were to use their tax-sharing money to match federal grants under old programs? Says one official: "They could bleed the Treasury white with its own money."[16]

Representative John Byrnes (R.-Wis.), the ranking Republican on Ways and Means, also looks at revenue sharing with a jaundiced eye. Speaking to a legislative committee of the Appleton City Council in Appleton, Wisconsin, Byrnes said:

> In the first place, there just isn't any federal revenue to share. We had a federal funds deficit of $10 billion in the 1970 fiscal year; the way Congress is spending money now we are looking at another deficit for this year at least as great and probably much higher. The federal government has nothing to share with the states except a federal debt of $380 billion . . . .
>
> The crucial error in revenue sharing is that it encourages

irresponsible spending. It does so by removing from one set of legislators the onus of levying taxes to pay for the spending they authorize, thus eliminating the best restraint we have against unjustifiable spending . . . .

The first path to wisdom is to recognize that all levels of government are squeezing blood from the same turnip — the American taxpayer, and that no gimmick, such as revenue sharing, to disguise which level is putting on the pressure, is going to make it any easier for him.[17]

Revenue sharing is another way of passing the buck — figuratively and literally. The real problem is to keep government from spending so much money in the first place, not to find new ways to filch revenues from other government levels. If Richard Nixon were really interested in "returning power to the people," he would simply cut federal spending instead of escalating it as he has done. In the Nixon scheme of things, "power to the people" is really a sleight-of-hand procedure resulting in "power to the President."

While he is looking around for places to slice the budget, Mr. Nixon might consider the foreign aid program. Richard Nixon has always been a super-staunch supporter of foreign aid, since this is a CFR sacred cow. But during his campaign he implied (though, of course, he never actually stated) that foreign aid would be slashed during a Nixon administration. He told audiences that "the whole foreign-aid program needs a complete reevaluation," and let his hearers come to their own conclusions as to what he really meant by the statement. On another occasion during the campaign Nixon proclaimed:

> . . . All of America's foreign commitments must be reappraised. Over the past 25 years America has provided more than 150 billion dollars in foreign aid . . . I say the time has come for other nations of the free world to bear their fair share of the burden.[18]

Naturally that implication was music to taxpayers' ears. Behind the scenes Nixon was taking a typically equivocal and cynical stand on the subject of foreign aid. *Time* magazine of July 26, 1968, reported that Nixon, at a breakfast of GOP Congressmen, gave this answer to a question on how to vote on the foreign aid bill: "If I came from a tight district, I'd vote against it. If I did not − and it would not defeat me − I'd vote for it . . . ." This was the type of leadership, morality, and integrity that the nation's voters were being asked to rally behind. *Time* admitted: "Some Republicans were dismayed by Nixon's advice." It has long troubled Nixon supporters who worked closely with him that on many issues he had two opinions, a private one and a public stand that differed from it. This is why many of his strongest supporters from the early days have abandoned him. They could not take the two-faced actions any more. Some have gone beyond referring to him as "Tricky Dick" and have hung the appellation "Mr. Conniver" on him.

Once in office, Nixon asked for foreign aid to be raised by $900 million, declaring: U.S. assistance [to foreign nations] is essential to express and achieve our national goals in the international community − a world order of peace and justice.[19] Note the phrases "international community" and "world order" − typical code words for "world government," with which Nixon always laces his foreign policy speeches. He has said:

> Foreign aid must be seen for what it is − not a burden, but an opportunity to help others to fulfill their aspirations for justice, dignity, and a better life. No more than at home can peace be achieved and maintained without vigorous efforts to meet the needs of the less fortunate.[20]

We can carry the world on our backs, but we cannot stand alone. If we really wanted to help the rest of the world we would encourage them to cure their backwardness the same way we did — by replacing feudalism and socialism with the free enterprise system. Meanwhile, starving savages are not about to overrun the United States. Massed bodies are no substitute for technology.

At the same time he was announcing more foreign giveaways to further socialize the ninety-nine countries that receive our aid (including Communist countries), Mr. Nixon was also raising the national debt limit. But his request for $2.6 billion was just the tip of the foreign aid iceberg. According to Congressman Otto Passman, the bases for backing $1 billion from the foreign aid budget are summed up in three telling arguments:

—The actual over-all total of "new requests for foreign assistance" for the fiscal year starting July 1, 1970, is $12.133 billion, not merely $2.2 billion. The latter is only one item in a long list of proposed foreign aid expenditures scattered through the President's full budget.

— Approximately $20 billion "in accumulated unexpended funds voted by Congress in prior years" is piled up in the various government agencies engaged in foreign aid spending.

— Some 50 per cent of the $375 billion national debt represents money borrowed by the Treasury to be disbursed abroad in grants and loans. Over-all cost of foreign aid from 1946 through fiscal 1970 is in excess of $190 billion — including the interest on borrowed funds.

"The interest on our staggering federal debt for this fiscal year is $15.958 billion," said Passman. "One-half of this immense amount is due to our foreign aid expenditures plus interest. During this worldwide spending spree, our gold holdings have been reduced from nearly $23 billion to less than $11 billion. Further, our balance-of-payments situation has become serious.

"It is an old strategem of the bureaucrats," Passman declared, "to fragment foreign aid programs by scattering them throughout the budget under different titles. In that way they hide them in order to cover up the real scope and immense cost of foreign aid. It took me many hours of digging and poring to put together this highly revealing list."[21]

Vigorously opposing Nixon's proposed hike in foreign aid, Congressman H.R. Gross on June 11, 1969, declared:

> With the Federal debt at around $375 billion, requiring the appropriation of more than $17 billion this year just to pay the interest on the debt, with inflation chewing up the dollar, I am utterly amazed that demands should be made for another multi-billion dollar foreign giveaway program.[22]

Typical of the impact of the Nixon administration on Republican Congressmen who in the past have steadfastly fought against the financing of socialism at home and abroad was their reaction to the Nixon foreign aid program. "I am bleeding over this thing," Congressman E. Ross Adair (R.-Ind.) said. His record showed that he had never voted for foreign aid during his eighteen years in Congress. But with a Republican president he admitted that he was under great pressure to go along with the new bill.[23]

In September 1970, Nixon revealed what the "reforms" in foreign aid would be that he had talked about during the campaign. The idea, he explained, was to channel our foreign aid money through United Nations agencies so that the recipients would not feel compromised by living on our money.[24] This "reform," advocated by Liberals for years, is another step toward the day when the amount of foreign aid money to be spent will be determined by the U.N. and not by Congress. Turning over foreign aid to the U.N. will be a giant step toward Mr. Nixon's "world order."

One of the most scandal-ridden boondoggles in the history of the nation is the misnamed War on Poverty. Numerous investigations have shown that it is not only a cornucopia for crooks but, worse, has systematically been a source of funds for revolutionary militants. It is hard to find a major U.S. black militant, from Stokely Carmichael to Rap Brown to Huey Newton, who has not at some time been on the War on Poverty payroll. Republicans in Congress, with few exceptions, vigorously opposed the establishment of the War on Poverty, and many have called for its abolishment as various official and unofficial investigations have disclosed the anti-American attitudes of many of its employees. During his campaign, Nixon was full of derogatory remarks about the War on Poverty and strongly implied that under his "new leadership" administration this monstrosity would be abolished. On one occasion he declared:

> A current poverty program that should be eliminated is the Job Corps. This is one program that has been a failure. It sounds good, but it costs $10,000 a year to train a man for a job that may not even exist.

But, as he has done with so many of his campaign promises, once Richard Nixon assumed office he reversed himself on the War on Poverty issue. The *New York Times'* super-Liberal Tom Wicker acknowledged:

> The President also has moved to extend the life of the Johnson-created Office of Economic Opportunity for another year, an even further departure from the Nixon campaign line. This appears to reflect a judgment — as Pat Moynihan puts it — that the poverty program's "goals are valid and this Administration wishes to embrace them as its own goals."[25]

In a special message to Congress on February 19, 1969, the President asserted: "From the experience of OEO, we have learned the value of having in the Federal Government an agency whose special concern is the poor." He then called for a one-year extension of the Office of Economic Opportunity, stating that "the OEO has been a valuable fount of ideas and enthusiasm . . . . "

On June 2, 1969, the *Washington Post* reported:

President Nixon yesterday broadened his commitment to the Nation's war on poverty agency by asking Congress to extend its life for two years, instead of one year as originally intended.

This was followed on June 13 by a *Washington Post* report that:

Donald Rumsfeld [Director of O.E.O.], far from presiding over the liquidation of the Office of Economic Opportunity, has moved in his first 18 days on the job to revive it as the dominant innovative force on most aspects of domestic policy.[26]

A disgusted *Indianapolis News* commented:

The Nixon administration covered itself with confusion this month when it forced through a continuation of the scandal-ridden "war on poverty" on its present footing.

Despite the fact that Nixon campaigned against the jerry-built "poverty" set-up in the 1968 election, his regime lobbied strenuously to prevent needed changes in the program and torpedoed an amendment for which there appeared to be ample support in the U.S. House of Representatives . . . .

The net result of this is that the Nixon administration has salvaged one of the most discredited of liberal Democratic programs intact in obvious contradiction to the rhetoric which brought the administration to office. The "mess" that the new regime was supposed to clean up in this area goes on as before, with no structural changes other than a change of personnel at the top. This is an implicit violation of the trust reposed in the new regime by the voting public . . . .

As Rep. Edith Green, D-Ore., comments, the approach favored by Rumsfeld "did not have a single change − not a single change in the . . . program in terms of administration − in terms of structure − in terms of all the abuses that have occurred − and in terms of what I think are outright violations by [the Office of

Economic Opportunity] of congressional intent .... The only
change in the bill was to say to the OEO, 'We will give you an
additional $295 million to spend in the way you want to spend
it.' "[27]

Yes the "Conservative" Nixon administration asked for
$295 million more than the Liberal Johnson administration
had been spending. Then, under the guise of "reforms," parts
of the War on Poverty were transferred to other departments
where they could be hidden more easily in bigger budgets.

In keeping the War on Poverty, the Nixon administration
surrendered to blackmail. A column by Joseph Alsop of
March 2, 1969, discussed the reason why Nixon has not
abolished the Community Action programs under the Office
Economic Opportunity. The Community Action programs
employ about 29,000 non-professionals on a full-time basis.
According to Alsop, a substantial majority of these people
come from the urban ghettos, and the non-professional
employees in the ghettos now constitute a new and powerful
vested interest. Alsop then went on to say:

> The reason the vested interest was not tackled head on, which
> is freely admitted by the highest Nixon policymakers, was that
> "they would have burned the place down, if we'd terminated the
> programs just like that."

The Nixon administration has also made little or no
attempt to clean the militants out. According to *Human
Events*:

> *Human Events* also has it on unimpeachable authority that the
> OEO is still funding the Blackstone Rangers gang in Chicago and
> is supporting leaders of US, the paramilitary, black racist group
> headed by California's Ron Karenga. Karenga's group is con-
> sidered one of the most dangerous black "Mafia" groups in
> existence.
> While Rumsfeld was unaware of it, OEO militants distributed

numerous copies of an inflammatory "training" manual to every
OEO regional office in the country. Called "Trainer's Manual for
Community Action Agency Boards," the booklet stressed that
recourse to rioting is a legitimate means for gaining proper
community action.

That the OEO employees have not changed under Rumsfeld
was dramatically underscored last week when 1,000 community
action leaders from across the country gathered at a three-day
conference of the National Association for Community Development in Maryland.

When OEO Director Rumsfeld asked the nation's community
action leaders to avoid "tactics of confrontation," he was
promptly denounced from the floor. The conferees, in fact,
quickly adopted a position paper that accused the Nixon
Administration of being the "enemy of the poor" and urged all
Americans to join "the army of dissenters."

In brief, the OEO does not look much better under Nixon than
it did under Johnson. [28]

We could go on for pages listing the federal programs
formerly denounced by Republicans as boondoggles, that the
Nixon administration has expanded. The Nixonites have
made no overall attempt to squeeze the water out of bloated
government budgets. Certainly there have been some instances in which the President, with great hoopla and fanfare,
has threatened to veto a particular budget request, and a
couple of instances in which he has actually done so. But
these were so much "show biz." Even the budgets that
replaced the vetoed budgets were higher than the LBJ
appropriations that candidate Nixon so accurately denounced. This type of hoax is good for one's political image,
and in the Nixon administration, image is all-important.
Under Nixon, the welfare state marches on and on and on,
becoming an ever bigger burden to the taxpayers who must
carry the load. As a dejected *Chicago Tribune* admitted, "The
more it changes, the more it remains the same."

References

1. *Almanack of Poor Richard Nixon*, Cleveland, World Publishing Co., August 21, 1952.
2. *Congressional Record*, July 1, 1965.
3. *Human Events*, September 28, 1968.
4. *Ibid.*, January 24, 1970.
5. *Battle Line*, August 1969.
6. *Wall Street Journal*, February 3, 1969.
7. *Long Beach Press-Telegram*, February 13, 1969.
8. *Almanack of Poor Richard Nixon*, Los Angeles, April 20, 1949.
9. *Yakima Eagle*, July 30, 1970.
10. *Santa Ana Register*, February 27, 1971 (Tom Anderson column).
11. *Human Events*, January 2, 1971.
12. Richard Nixon, Welfare Reform address, August 8, 1969.
13. *U.S. News & World Report*, September 15, 1969.
14. *Houston Tribune*, March 11, 1971.
15. *Battle Line*, August 1969.
16. *Human Events*, September 5, 1970.
17. *Ibid.*
18. *Election Guide*, 1968.
19. *Watch Washington*, June 27, 1969.
20. United Press International, *Santa Ana Register*, September 15, 1970.
21. *Santa Ana Register*, April 26, 1970 (Allen-Goldsmith column).
22. *Tax Fax* No. 99, July 1, 1969.
23. *Washington Star*, May 28, 1969.
24. *Indianapolis Star*, October 18, 1970.
25. *Long Beach Press-Telegram*, February 21, 1969.
26. *The Review Of The News*, September 3, 1969.
27. *Indianapolis News*, editorial, December 30, 1969.
28. *Human Events*, October 25, 1969.

CHAPTER XIV

The Great Socialist Revival

One of the most startling articles ever printed in an American magazine appeared in the September 21, 1970 issue of *New York* (not to be confused with *The New Yorker*) Magazine. It is entitled "Richard Nixon and the Great Socialist Revival." The theme of the article is that Richard Nixon is a secret Marxist, working with the giant foundations and international bankers, mouthing platitudes in praise of free enterprise while quietly socializing the country through deeds. The art work graphically illustrates the point; it shows the famous (in Communist circles anyway) poster of Mao Tse-tung with his little Mao beanie and collarless Red Chinese uniform triumphantly waving a huge blood-red Communist flag — except that the face in *New York* Magazine is not Chairman Mao's, but Richard Milhous Nixon's. Subsequent pages show workers giving the Communist clenched-fist revolutionary salute, and the final panel shows a worker giving the salute with the Federal Reserve building in the background. If one read the article without noting the name of the author, one might well conclude that someone had somehow spirited a manuscript out of the editorial offices of *American Opinion* in the dead of night and *New York* Magazine had run it just for fun. On closer scrutiny, however, certain features of the article give away the fact that its author is an *Insider* on the Left. As is indeed the case. The man behind the typewriter for this amazing literary revelation is none other than Harvard

345

Professor John Kenneth Galbraith, the Peck's bad boy of the *Insider* Establishment.

Before reading the article one is tempted to think that Galbraith may be writing satire. But a closer look discloses that he is writing only half in jest, and wholly in earnest. Such a tactic leaves a convenient back door to slip out of in case the situation gets sticky. This ploy was used some years ago by another ultra-Leftist *Insider*, Richard Rovere, in an article for *Esquire* titled "The American Establishment." In detailing the existence and workings of the Establishment, Rovere, with tongue inserted part way in cheek, gave an excellent description of the Council on Foreign Relations, its satellites, and the chief personalities involved. Rovere stated: "The directors of the Council on Foreign Relations make up a sort of Presidium for that part of the Establishment that guides our destiny as a nation." Galbraith is a member of the CFR, and the subject of his revealing article, Richard Nixon, has also been a member of the CFR, and during his 1968 Presidential campaign wrote an article for the official CFR organ, *Foreign Affairs* (which differs from its "underground" counterpart, *Political Affairs*, only in style and sophistication). At last count more than one hundred members of the CFR had been appointed to key positions in the Nixon administration. Both Nixon and Galbraith, then, are members of the same ruling elite, composed of men from the government, foundations, big business, and international banking – all under the CFR umbrella.

For Galbraith, to pronounce the President a socialist is not an accusation, but a compliment. He wants his own Democratic Party to quit pussyfooting around and proclaim its adherence to socialism. The Cambridge sage writes in his latest book, *Who Needs The Democrats?**: ". . . The Demo-

---

*This paperback contains seventy-one pages of text and sells for $1. Socialist Galbraith is apparently a filthy, greedy capitalist when it comes to his own royalties.

cratic Party must henceforth use the word socialism. It describes what is needed . . . ." At least Galbraith is frank; most of his fellow socialists hide behind the euphemistic term, *Liberalism*. As *U.S. News & World Report* recently noted: "The 'liberal' movement in America dates back to the rise of socialism and trade-unionism around the turn of the twentieth century."

Socialists had a difficult time selling their ideology until they stole the honorable word "Liberalism," whose meaning was once the opposite of what it is today. Today's Liberalism is derived from socialism, whose father is Karl Marx; and Marx made no distinction between socialism and Communism in his *Communist Manifesto*. If Galbraith really wanted to be brutally honest he would use the terms Marxism and Communism as well as socialism. Lenin believed that socialism would come to backward countries like Russia by revolution and to industrial nations like Great Britain or America by the creeping method, via the ballot box. Therefore, all Communists work for socialism. They understand what the naive and well-meaning amateur Liberal (as distinguished from the professional Liberal like Galbraith) does not — that the difference between "democratic" socialism as practiced in England or Sweden, and the openly totalitarian socialism practiced in Russia and China, is one not of degree but of time.*

Galbraith was a founder, and has served as chairman, of the 60,000-member Fabian-socialist Americans for Demo-

---

*Of course, virtually all American Liberals and most socialists consider themselves loyal Americans and have no idea that they are unwitting members of a world-wide conspiratorial movement that takes many forms. They become extremely angry when Liberalism is equated with socialism, which is in turn equated with Communism, because they are, in most cases, sincerely opposed to totalitarianism. America can be saved from plunging into the midnight morass of totalitarianism only when a sufficient number of sincere and honest Liberals are educated by knowledgeable (and compassionate) Conservatives to understand the nature and the interlocking structure of the World Revolutionary Movement, headed by its small clique of *Insiders*.

cratic Action (ADA). He has also been affiliated with the avowedly socialist League for Industrial Democracy, which spawned the bomb-throwing Students for a Democratic Society (SDS). Galbraith has never been accused of being anti-Communist. He contends of the Soviets that "they are basically just like us." Whom does he mean by "us"?

Galbraith is probably best known for his book *The Affluent Society*, which propounded the theory that government and its services are being scandalously starved while the private consumer lives in luxury. His solution: Tax the latter more heavily to support the former more generously.

The exploit for which Galbraith is least known is probably his participation in preparing a sinister Orwellian plan published as the "Report From Iron Mountain on the Possibility and Desirability of Peace."* The jacket on the Delta edition of this opus states:

> Report From Iron Mountain [taken from the site of the first meeting] unveils a hitherto top-secret report of a government commission that was requested to explore the consequences of lasting peace on American society. The shocking results of the study, as revealed in this report, led the government to conceal [and subsequently deny] the existence of the commission − they had found that, among other things, peace may never be possible; that even if it were, it would probably be undesirable; that "defending the national interest" is not the real purpose of war; that war is necessary; that war deaths should be planned and budgeted.

The report is a blueprint for the "perpetual war for perpetual peace" technique being used by the *Insiders* in Vietnam, which is doubtless destined to be used soon in other parts of the world. According to the Iron Mountain Boys, "social change" (read socialism) can best be brought about during wartime. People will accept a greater degree of control and

---

*The report was prepared at Herman Kahn's (CFR) Hudson Institute.

taxation when they come in the guise of national defense. Galbraith admits in the *New York* article:

> In the past the war power has been notoriously a cover for socialist experiment and, feeling that the end justifies the means, socialists have not hesitated, on occasion, to stretch the law.

This strategy also allows the revolutionaries from below — students, minorities, and "the poor" — to demand "peace" and "social justice."

While visiting in England, Galbraith admitted that he was indeed one of the report's authors. The Associated Press picked up the admission, but few papers printed it — many undoubtedly not understanding how monstrous was the boast, or the confession (whichever it was). In America, however, Galbraith is a leader of the "peace" movement and feigns sympathy with the young men who are sent to their deaths in wars that are not meant to be won. On the cover of the Delta Press edition, Galbraith (with tongue wholly inserted in cheek) denounces the report as something that might have emanated from the twisted mind of Dean Rusk (who like JKG himself is a member of the CFR, the father of no-win wars). Thus, Galbraith denounces Galbraith. War is peace. Slavery is freedom. The incredibly devious Galbraith is also reported to have written a favorable review of "The Report From Iron Mountain" that appeared under a pseudonym. Such deceitfulness is beyond the comprehension of most people. But in order to be a conspirator, one must be a liar — for no conspiracy can succeed unless its existence is concealed by lies.

Galbraith began his *New York* article by proclaiming:

> Certainly the least predicted development under the Nixon Administration was this great new thrust to socialism. One encounters people who still aren't aware of it. Others must be rubbing their eyes, for certainly the portents seemed all to the

contrary. As an opponent of socialism, Mr. Nixon seemed
steadfast . . . .

It is true that the reality of Richard Nixon is in sharp
conflict with the image he has carefully projected for the
past twenty years. The public's memory is notoriously
short, but those who have watched Nixon's deeds (in
contrast to his words) over the past two decades know that
Galbraith was right. Nixon actually began moving Left well
before he became Vice President in 1952, and by the end
of Ike's second term, sophisticated Liberals knew he was in
their camp. Richard Wilson, Chief of *Look's* Washington
Bureau, acted as a transmission belt for the *Insiders* when
he wrote a feature article in *Look* of September 3, 1957,
titled "The Big Change in Richard Nixon." In this story,
which contained virtually unqualified praise for the "new
Nixon," Wilson wrote: "He has made a distinct turn to the
left. When the choice has been between the Republican
right and the Republican left, Nixon has sided with the
Republican left."

The Galbraith article in *New York* magazine admits that
the economic philosophies of the late lavender lecher, John
Maynard Keynes, promote socialism. Keynes, who tried to
turn the British Fabian Society into a sort of Roaring
Twenties Gay Liberation Front, has been the economic
patron saint of Franklin D. Roosevelt, Benito Mussolini,
Adolf Hitler, John Fitzgerald Kennedy, Lyndon Baines
Johnson, and last but not least, Richard Nixon.* That Nixon
subscribes to Keynesian Economics, we have abundant
evidence. The *Wall Street Journal* noted on December 5,
1968:

It's clear, too, that the President-elect wants the Government

---

*No student of political science, economics, or conspiracy should fail to read and
study the Veritas Foundation's *Keynes At Harvard,* by Zygmund Dobbs.

to use fiscal and monetary policy to urge the nation along a safe
economic course. To that extent he accepts the "New Economics" pursued by the Kennedy and Johnson Administrations . . . .

The *Journal's* Richard Janssen had written even before the
election, on October 21:

> In fact, the Nixon camp is stressing that it's no less committed
> to the basic principle of Government-guided economic growth
> than the Johnson-Kennedy Administrations have been. Mr. Nixon
> has labeled himself a "new economist," aides note, a tag
> customarily attached to such Democratic seers as Walter W.
> Heller, Gardner Ackley and Arthur Okun, the current chairman
> of President Johnson's Council of Economic Advisers . . . .

Presidential economic adviser Herbert Stein even wrote a
book titled *Conservatives Are Keynesian, Too*, the theme of
which was described by *Business Week* of May 3, 1969 (page
88), as follows:

> The great fiscal revolution in America . . . was not the exclusive
> product of Keynesian economists and Democratic politicians.
> Rather it was an event for which Republicans, conservatives, and
> businessmen are entitled to an almost equal share of the credit.
> And that alone should lay to rest any worry that the Nixon
> Administration will revert to antediluvian attitudes if the going
> gets rough in the war against inflation.

Former Harvard Professor Seymour Harris, a top Keynesian and a member of the Fabian-socialist ADA, wrote:

> Current pronouncements by leaders of the Nixon Administra-
> tion sound like those of the able economic advisers of 1961-68.
> This is not surprising since the new economists in the Nixon
> Administration, for the most part, have learned their economics
> under the same influences as the Kennedy-Johnson econo-
> mists . . . .
> Harvard turned out the largest number of the new economists

who in turn moved to Washington to work for the Kennedy-Johnson administrations. Now Nixon offers us Paul McCracken, Henry Wallich and Hendrik Houthakker, the first two Harvard trained, the last a Harvard teacher. They also mobilized John Dunlop and Gottfried Haberler, both distinguished economists of long standing at Harvard, to chair committees to investigate important problems . . . .

Are there then no differences between President Nixon's economics and those of his predecessors? Indeed, there are; but on the fundamentals the objectives and means of achieving them are strikingly similar. It is fortunate for the country that Mr. Nixon has abandoned his attacks on "growthmanship" and on governmental responsibility for the functioning of a healthy economy. For he will need the help of government to maximize output and minimize instability. That is what the New Economics is all about . . . .

It is not surprising that he embraces fiscal policy, as the Democrats do.[2]

The GOP has been railing against Keynesian deficit spending for nearly four decades, but nationally syndicated columnist J.F. Ter Horst observed in the *Indianapolis Star* of October 30, 1968:

Even Nixon, interestingly, has discarded the old GOP axiom of balancing every Federal budget every year. His emphasis now is on "the intelligent balancing of the economy over the business cycle" — which is the philosophy of the New Economics which has dominated budgetary policy the last eight years.

Fabian-socialist Keynes boasted to a friend that his system would be the "euthanasia of capitalism" and would destroy free enterprise under the guise of saving it. Keynesian "New Economics" is but a euphemism for Fabian-socialist economics. The only honest description of the New Economics (socialism) is "Communist economics," since Marx, the father of modern socialism, as we have said, used the words interchangeably. The fifth plank of Marx's *Communist*

Manifesto is "centralization of credit in the hands of the state . . . ." As a celebrated Keynesian himself, Galbraith cannot have been very much surprised at what he calls "the new socialism" under Nixon, even though the public is increasingly flabbergasted.

Galbraith does, however, seem to have been somewhat surprised to see Nixon moving towards socialism in ways other than Keynesian monkeying with government spending to "boost" the economy. The Wizard of Harvard (which is the real land of Oz) proclaimed in his article:

> In an intelligently plural economy, a certain number of industries should be publicly owned. Elementary considerations of public convenience require it. For moving and housing people at moderate cost, private enterprise does not serve. But I had come reluctantly to the conclusion that socialism, even in this modest design, was something I would never see. Now I am being rescued by this new socialist upsurge promoted, of all things, by socialists not on the left but on the right. And they have the blessing, and conceivably much more, of a Republican Administration.

Professor Galbraith contends that the "new socialism" is the basis of the "Nixon Game Plan," based on the successful Fabian-socialist conspiracy in England. Galbraith refers to it as "the doctrine of the commanding heights":

> The new socialism also shows an acute sense of strategy. In the years after World War II in Britain, where socialism had a fair run, British socialists developed the doctrine of the commanding heights. The state would not take over the entire economy. It would aim for that part which was so strategic that its loss destroyed capitalist power, shattered its morale and so secured social control over the rest. The new conservative socialism in the United States has taken over the strategy of the commanding heights with a vengeance.

And Mr. Nixon appears to be beginning where the British, according to Professor Galbraith, also began:

... the first of the heights which the British socialists marked out for capture after World War II was the railroad system. It had great symbolic value. More than textiles, water transport or steel, this was the industry where modern large-scale capitalism began. So, pro tanto, it was where socialism should begin. To be astride the transportation system carried also the impression if not the reality of power.

The railroads were similarly marked out by the new American socialism for its first offensive. This was concentrated on the biggest of the systems, indeed the biggest transportation company in the United States, the Penn Central. The attack was not led by the passengers and shippers, the two groups which had been most aggressively abused by private capitalism in this industry. Nor did the workers, once the big battalions of socialism, react. The socialist thrust against the Penn Central was led by the executives of the railroad — by the agents and instruments of the capitalists themselves.

This is an admission that socialism is not a movement of downtrodden masses but a tool of the power-hungry intellectual and financial elite. The socialists would have us accept the theory that government ownership and control over the means of production of goods and services is the road to sharing the wealth. Socialism is not a share-the-wealth program, but is in reality a consolidate-and-control-the-wealth program aimed at making serfs out of the upstart middle class. This explains the participation of many of the super-rich in socialist movements. If they were merely suffering from a guilt complex because of inherited wealth (which doubtless is a reason in some cases), the super-rich could assuage their consciences by giving away their mansions, airplanes, and yachts and joining the rest of us peasants with our $20,000 mortgages. Instead these *Insiders* hide (and compound) their wealth inside tax-free foundations and avoid taxes by purchasing and selling stocks through Swiss banks.

As Dr. Galbraith notes, when the Penn Central Railroad

faced bankruptcy, it ran (with the urging of seventy-seven banks) to the government, inviting the U.S. to invest $200 million in Penn Central as a first step. The Nixon administration welcomed it with open arms. This dramatic rush to socialism won the initial approval of the Republican administration. Everything, indeed, seemed greased and ready to go, says Galbraith. By this we assume that Dr. Galbraith refers to the fact that Penn Central had hired the legal services of Randolph Guthrie of Nixon's "former" law firm of Mudge, Rose, Guthrie and Alexander. But the move was blocked by Rep. Wright Patman, Chairman of the House Banking and Currency Committee. Galbraith comments:

> But it seems likely that the setback is only temporary. Other railroads are known to want government participation in their capital structure. There is no chance that the Penn Central will get through receivership, much less escape from it, without public capital. Even if he feels strongly about defending private enterprise, Mr. Patman cannot stand up against this kind of pressure forever.

The handwriting is on the wall. Most railroads are very shaky, caught between a business slow-down, labor demands, inflation, and the Interstate Commerce Commission, which controls rates. The chief causes of the railroads' problems were summarized by Professor Michael Conant, writing in the *Wall Street Journal* of September 17, 1970:

> The Federal legislation which inhibits successful management is of three main types. The minimum rate regulation keeps railroads from lowering many rates for commodities in which railroads compete with highway and water carriers. The effect is to increase the nation's investment in trucks which pollute the countryside while railroads could do a more efficient job of carrying most commodities for distances over 250 miles.
> The second group of statutes are railway labor laws, which put so much power in the unions that they force the employment of

large numbers of unneeded workers. Featherbedding in the railroad industry is real and the political power of railway unions prevents the enactment of laws to foster its termination.

The third group of statutes prevents the disinvestment in plant that can be operated only at a net loss. These are the laws relating to pooling of operations, trackage rights and abandonments. The many parallel railroads and thousands of branch lines were built before the days of the hard road, the motor truck and the airplane. The present great excess capacity in railroad lines and yards can only become an increasing source of losses as real estate taxes and costs of maintenance of way increase . . . .

Railroad managements would like the public treasury to give them short-run financial aid. In light of the facts outlined above, however, no reasonable taxpayer can support public loans to failing railroads, the proposal now before the Congress. Until the three groups of Federal statutes are amended, such "loans" would merely be subsidies to inefficiency while railroad losses and bankruptcies continued to increase. The American taxpayers must not be so foolish as to throw money down this bottomless pit.

The only real solution to the Railroads' bevy of dilemmas was proposed by Professor Oscar Cooley in the *Anaheim Bulletin* of July 20, 1970:

> The Interstate Commerce Commission should be abolished. The competition of substitute methods of transportation — trucks, waterways, pipelines, airplanes — not to mention the very real competition between the rail companies themselves, is amply protecting the customers.
>
> The railroad companies should be set free to fix their own rates, provide such services as they choose to provide — after all, they must serve the public if they are to make a profit, and in every respect to run their own business.

But Richard Nixon, for all his campaign talk about how government controls produce stagnation, has not even suggested this possibility. Doubtless nationalization will proceed through a series of steps involving subsidies and loan guarantees. The President did not push plans for infusing money into the Penn Central during the campaign, but the *Wall Street Journal* reported on September 14, 1970: "Some sources believe that large amounts of funds for the Penn Central will be forthcoming after the November elections . . . ." Now the plan can be promoted as giving a badly needed "boost to the economy." In the meantime a bill has passed Congress and been signed by the President to establish a $340 million federally chartered National Railroad Passenger Corporation. This bill, which the October 20, 1970 *Wall Street Journal* dubbed "semi-nationalization," provides for government takeover of passenger service.

Nixon's Secretary of Transportation John Volpe gave us a clue to the thinking of the New Leadership Team: "The only option for keeping service intact — the only one we could think of — is take-over by the Government."[3]

And the Establishment media have indeed started to beat the bongo drums for a government takeover of railroads. *Times* magazine editorialized: "Washington seems to be the only power that has the potential, at least, of building a rational, balanced national rail system."

We must not lose sight of the fact that the sixth plank of Marx's *Communist Manifesto* calls for "centralization of the means of communication and transport in the hands of the state." This is exactly what the *Insiders* have in mind. They will doubtless be bailed out of their Penn Central investments at a handsome profit. The truth is, we don't know who controls the Penn Central behind the scenes (assuming they do still control the Penn Central as they controlled the Pennsylvania).

But now, Galbraith gets down to the real nitty-gritty in his article:

> Important as they are, however, the railroads . . . are not the ultimate goal of the new socialism. The ultimate target is Wall

Street. This is as it should be, and here it is making its greatest
move — one that for drama and a kind of sanguinary gall would
be appreciated even by such a master of these arts as the young
Leon Trotsky himself.

The allusion to Trotsky is interesting, since Trotsky was
financed by the Wall Street firm of Kuhn, Loeb and
Company, and the largest fund raiser for Nixon's 1968
campaign is reported to have been Kuhn, Loeb partner Lewis
Strauss. Galbraith continues:

> The Wall Street objective is nothing less than the New York
> Stock Exchange itself, the very heart of American, even world
> capitalism, the Everest of the commanding heights. The opportu-
> nity arises, as ever, from economic crisis. A known, appreciable
> but undisclosed number of members of the Stock Exchange have
> been hit by falling revenues, high costs and the slump in the stock
> market and thus in the value of the securities they own. In
> consequence of this and their own inefficiency, their capital is
> impaired, the chances for repair are poor and, a miracle apart,
> they cannot make good to their customers the money and
> securities left with them for speculative use . . . .

It is significant that in his article Galbraith nowhere
advocated the elimination of all Wall Street firms. Obviously
the *Insider* firms will survive the violent drops in the stock
market caused by changes in Federal Reserve policies which
they control or to which they are privy.* Los Angeles stock
broker John Weber reports that he was told by a very high
official in the mutual fund industry that a top Securities and
Exchange Commission official admitted to him in 1964 that
what SEC wanted to see within a decade was a consolidation
and elimination of brokerage firms until only ten Wall Street
firms survived. Galbraith, however, believes (or claims to)

---

*See this author's articles, "The Bankers" and "The Federal Reserve," in
American Opinion, March and April 1970 respectively; also available from
American Opinion as a single combined reprint.

that the federal government will eventually dominate all of Wall Street. Galbraith writes:

> The Wall Street vehicle of the new socialism is the proposed Securities Investor Protection Corporation [*sic*], or SIPC, a fund created by the Stock Exchange which is to be guaranteed by the government to the extent of a billion dollars. This will pay off the customers, creditors and victims of the failed houses. Because of some residual opposition to socialism in Wall Street, SIPC is being billed, rather imaginatively, as an insurance fund. Since the firms to be rescued are already in deep trouble, it is the first insurance fund in some time to insure against accidents that have already occurred — to place a policy on barns which have already burned down. But this is a detail. As the new socialists see the prospect (one may assume), several of the larger stock exchange houses will eventually fail. The government will step in to conserve their assets against the claims it has paid. There will be strong pressure to minimize hardship and unemployment by keeping firms going. The government will oblige — the familiar yielding to pressure again. Presently other firms will fail and the government will find itself in a dominant position on the Street and in the Exchange.

The result of this ploy would be that a handful of *Insider* firms would have a monopoly on Wall Street, with government capital to use to acquire whatever they might want. Galbraith in his article says of this plan:

> . . . no old-fashioned socialist ever had a better idea for getting a foothold on Wall Street. Their hats should be off to the new man. Friedrich Engels, a rich and gentlemanly businessman who loved fox-hunting, would, one senses, especially approve.

The Harvard seer concludes his amazingly revealing article with a discussion of "Nixon Game Plan" strategy. He begins by observing that:

> Mr. Nixon is probably not a great reader of Marx, but Drs.

Burns, Shultz and McCracken are excellent scholars who know
him well and could have brought the President abreast . . . .*

Galbraith says of Dr. Burns, a fellow member of the CFR
"Presidium" who has moved from a position of adviser to
Nixon to head the all-powerful Federal Reserve Board:

> A conspiracy theory of history is always too tempting. Dr.
> Arthur Burns as the Kerensky of this revolution, the Federal
> Reserve Building as its Smolny, tight money rather than oratory
> as its weapon, forces unleashed which, as in the case of Kerensky,
> no man can control — these thoughts are almost irresistibly
> attractive.

Mixing fact with what he certainly must know to be
fiction Galbraith describes the "Game Plan":

> . . . it is beyond denying that the crisis that aided the rush into
> socialism was engineered by the Administration. Money was
> deliberately made tight. The budget was deliberately made
> restrictive. The effect of these actions in raising interest rates and
> depressing the economy was firmly acclaimed as the Nixon Game
> Plan. The difficulties of Penn Central, Lockheed and the member
> firms of the NYSE were part of the same game — and socialism,
> as we have seen, is the name of the game. Cause and consequence
> were never closer; cause could not have been more deliberately
> contrived.
>
> And suspicion is deepened by the sensational silence of
> conservatives.

As Galbraith is fully aware, it was the Federal Reserve
Board and not Nixon that moved to tighten money. It is the

---

*It should be noted that Galbraith serves with Arthur Burns as a trustee for the
Twentieth Century Fund, founded in 1919 by a wealthy Boston merchant,
Edward A. Filene, who was affiliated with pro-Communist organizations. The
Twentieth Century Fund has financed Fabian-socialist activities in the U.S. for
half a century. Among the officials of the Fund have been such people as Arthur
Schlesinger Jr., Julius Robert Oppenheimer (self-confessed to have been at one
time a financial contributor to the Communists), and Evans Clark (another friend
of the Soviets).

Federal Reserve Board and not the administration that controls the money faucet. Economist Dr. Milton Friedman wrote before Nixon's inauguration: "Since fiscal policy does not matter, and monetary policy is controlled by the independent 'Fed,' the administration will not really have control over economic policy." [4] Burns himself stated on November 11, 1969:

> The responsibility of the Fed is to supervise monetary policy . . . .The FRB's autonomy was conceived for purposes of maintaining the integrity of the currency. I think it's quite proper that money authority be independent of political authority.

Asked, in an interview reported in the May 5, 1969 issue of *U.S. News & World Report*, "Do you approve of the latest credit-tightening moves?" Nixon's Secretary of the Treasury, David Kennedy, told the interviewer: "It's not my job to approve or disapprove. It is the action of the Federal Reserve."

This does not mean that the FRB is not part of the conspiracy of which Galbraith writes. If the Federal Reserve was created in 1913 for the reasons its defenders claim, i.e., to establish economic stability by putting an end to boom-and-bust cycles, it has been an enormous failure. If, on the other hand, it was created by the *Insiders* to produce inflationary booms followed by depressions or recessions in which the stock market falls out of bed, allowing *Insiders* to accumulate enormous profits from both boom and bust, then the "Fed" has been a tremendous success. Since the creation of the "Fed," which Liberals guaranteed would end depressions forever, we have had the worst depression in the history of the country, and severe recessions in 1920, 1936-37, 1948, 1953, 1956-57, 1960, 1966, and 1970. If you have advance knowledge of Federal Reserve policies you can make a killing whether the stock market is going up or down, and if you control the men who make these policies you can control the timing of the boom and the bust. The FRB inflated wildly (i.e. increased the money supply, thus bidding up prices) during LBJ's second term. During Nixon's first year in office the "Fed" had to stop inflating or face runaway inflation.* The time had come to shear the sheep. Between December 1968 and July 1970, the stock market lost 35 per cent of its value.

Since the same *Insiders* who control the Federal Reserve also control Nixon, Galbraith's statement about tight money in his discussion of the Nixon Game Plan is true in essence if not from a technical standpoint.† And Nixon's fiscal policies (taxing and spending) worked hand in glove with the "Fed's" temporary halting of money expansion. During the campaign Nixon talked of tax-cutting:

> My administration will be one in which we are going to do what is necessary but with less money. That policy, directed toward achieving a balanced budget, will stop the rise in prices and lead to a reduction in taxes.[5]

He specifically promised on numerous occasions to end the 10 per cent surtax on income. Then, said *U.S. News & World Report,* "After taking office, President Nixon in March asked Congress to extend the surtax for another year."

The President's excuse was that the surtax was needed to control inflation. This was absurd. Congressman H.R. Gross,

---

*The term "inflation" is used commonly to mean the wage-price spiral. This is incorrect. It is physically impossible to have a sustained and general wage-price spiral unless the government is increasing the money supply. You can't fill a quart jar with a pint of water.

†Since the Federal Reserve has absolute control (directly or indirectly) over the crucial money supply faucet, one would assume that appointments to the Board would attract great national attention and be subjected to the very closest scrutiny from Congress. But can you name one other member of the Board besides Burns?... Neither can anyone else you know. To the best of our knowledge, Congress has never rejected a single appointment to the Board, despite the fact that as Prof. Hans Sennholz tells us, the views of the appointees on monetary policy have ranged between inflationary and hyper-inflationary.

on June 11, 1969, stated that the 10 per cent surtax on income, which extracts from the taxpayers some $12 billion a year, "hasn't worked because the Government has simply taken the money and spent it."[6] Congressman John Rarick added:

> There is something patently asinine about the theory that it is inflationary for the man who earned the dollar to spend it on his family — but that it is not inflationary for the Government to take the dollar away from him and give it to someone else to spend.

In fact, it is less inflationary to let the man who has earned the money keep it, because he will save at least a part of it, whereas the government will spend every last penny and more. Taxes further feed the wage-price spiral, because they are a cost of production and must be added on to the price of a product at every level. Therefore, the selling price of the product is increased by all of the additional taxes on its ingredients. The *Indianapolis Star* editorialized on July 13, 1969:

> Last year the House approved the tax surcharges by demanding a $6 billion cut in expenditures by the government and a cut of 240,000 employees from the payroll. There was no cut in spending — it increased. There was no cut in the payroll. It increased. The taxpayers were double-crossed.

The President, however, was adamant. He made the surtax vote a loyalty test and threatened conscience-stricken Congressmen with cuts in federal spending in their home districts. Washington correspondent Paul Scott reported in the *Yakima Eagle* of July 3, 1969:

> An estimated forty Republicans dropped their opposition to the controversial tax proposal after the President laid down his loyalty gauntlet during his weekly White House conference with GOP House Leaders.

In a half-hour table-pounding session, the President told the
GOP leaders that the surtax must be extended or "my whole
inflation control program could go down the drain."

"Republican members of Congress," the President told the
leaders, "should be made to understand that I regard their vote
on the tax bill as a party loyalty test."

The President stressed that "I will be watching the vote closely
and future administration actions to help members will be guided
by the way they vote."

Scott's report was confirmed by the vote, as described in
Newsweek of July 14, 1969:

As the hour of reckoning neared, not all the Administration's
minions were being so discreet. Rep. William L. Scott, a Virginia
Republican, complained angrily that a GOP colleague had warned
him that his district would lose a long-scheduled dam if he didn't
vote aye on the surtax; later, he shouted his no "a little louder
than normal."

But the liberals were not to be appeased; they stood their
ground in the kind of solid front they have rarely been able to
forge. After the second call of the roll, the nays had it, 201-194.
Then the Administration began committing its surprise reserves —
conservative Republicans who had promised their votes only if
absolutely necessary. Behind the House rail, a small knot of
congressmen huddled together drawing straws. Short straw men
trudged disconsolately down to the well to switch sides or
withdraw their nays. The final tally: 210 ayes, 205 nays. Only 56
Democrats, most of them tied to the leadership, joined the
winning combination.

The President's next gambit in his socialist conspiracy was
the repeal of the 7 per cent tax credit for capital investment.
Economist Henry Hazlitt commented in the February 1970
issue of *Battle Line*:

Even more ill-advised [than continuing the surtax] was Mr.
Nixon's call for repeal of the 7 per cent corporation investment
tax credit. This was done for two reasons: to raise more revenue,

and to reduce or remove the supposed "inflationary impact" of investment in new plant and equipment. The effect is to increase the tax burden still further on the corporations — precisely on the key productive element on which the whole nation's income and economic growth depend. The anti-inflationary argument is a complete fallacy. It is only government deficits and consequent money creation that cause inflation. The repeal of the tax credit merely means that a larger percentage of private spending will go into current luxury consumption and a smaller percentage into improving the competitiveness, efficiency and productivity of America's industrial plant.

A disillusioned Pierre Rinfret, who had been a Nixon economic advisor during the campaign, contended that "you lick inflation by increasing capacity and not by holding it back." Rinfret claimed the tax credit repeal "has destroyed the only real hope for resolving inflation".[7] But this obviously, was the whole "Game Plan" idea — to restrict money for the private sector, not for the government. Penn Central, Lockheed, and hundreds of other American corporations were put in a financial vise just as Galbraith indicates.

The third trick-or-treat scheme the President pulled from his Machiavellian bag of tricks was the deceitful "tax reform." "Reform" is so much kinder a word than "raise." The National Taxpayers Union pointed out:

> Recently Congress passed new tax legislation. Reform legislation some call it — but it actually raised taxes by 3 billion dollars.
> Senator John Williams, one of the most respected members of the Senate, said:
> "The 'tax reform' bill is a hodgepodge of what seems on the surface to be politically 'popular' but in reality could be repudiated in the next election if the voters are given the real truth about the causes of higher and higher prices and the curtailment of the purchasing power of the dollar."

The spending policies of the master Machiavellian in the White House have been anything but restrictive except by the standard of a crazed Keynesian like Galbraith. The reckless deficit spending of the Johnson years had resulted in huge increases in the money supply, which bid up wages and prices. During his campaign for the Presidency, Mr. Nixon made much of this fiscal irresponsibility. In his acceptance speech at the Republican Convention on August 8, 1968, Candidate Nixon said: "It is time to quit pouring billions of dollars into programs that have failed. We are on the wrong road − it is time to take a new road . . . ." Later, in a position paper on the economy, the candidate stated: "In less than five years the Johnson-Humphrey Administration has squandered the inheritance of a decade's solvency . . . ."[8] He also proclaimed: "The entire budget needs exhaustive review . . . . Some programs. . . must accept less than maximum funding; non-essentials . . . must await easier times; every major program . . . must be scoured for economies."[9] Again, in his position paper, Candidate Nixon blasted the profligacy of the Democrats:

> . . . for five years this Administration has refused to keep federal spending within federal means.
> The total deficit run up in the budgets of the Johnson-Humphrey years will amount to more than $55 billion. This massive deficit has wracked and dislocated the economy . . . .
> There is nothing the matter with the engine of free enterprise that cannot be corrected by placing a prudent and sober engineer at the throttle.
> The old politics of spend and elect have not only worked an injustice on the American people, they have denied America much of its flexibility in dealing with onrushing change . . . .

Over and over again the campaigning Nixon called for LBJ to slash the federal budget, as when he claimed that every day President Johnson put off cutting the budget "places in greater jeopardy the entire international monetary structure."[10] Broadcasting over CBS radio on April 25, 1968, Mr.

Nixon claimed that "only by cutting the federal budget can we avert an economic disaster . . . ."[11] In Dallas on October 11, 1968, he declared that "America cannot afford four years of Hubert Humphrey in the White House," because Humphrey had pushed for programs which would have caused "a spending spree that would have bankrupted this nation."[12]

After the election, all of the laudable rhetoric and soulful promises were conveniently tossed into the memory hole. The fiscal mismanagement of which candidate Nixon had spoken so articulately was truly monumental. LBJ's last budget of $183.7 billion represented an increase of 88 per cent during the Kennedy-Johnson years. LBJ boasted as he prepared to leave office:

> Outlays for major social programs will have risen by $37.4 billion, more than doubling since 1964. This is twice the rate of increase of outlays for any other category of Government programs.[13]

According to columnist Charles Bartlett, JFK and LBJ had expanded the number of the government's domestic spending programs from 40 to 473. Most Republicans had resisted every one of the 433 added socialistic programs. "Reckless spending," shouted Republican Congressmen; "dangerous fiscal madness," echoed Republican Senators. During the waning days of 1968, LBJ prepared a well-padded fiscal 1970 budget to be handed to Nixon. In its January 25, 1969 issue, an angry *Human Events* lamented:

> To make things more difficult for Nixon on the domestic front, LBJ has tried to spread the myth that Nixon somehow has a moral commitment to carry out the programs of the "Great Society."
> As a gesture of bad will, Johnson whipped up a $195.3-billion "exciting" budget for fiscal 1970, with spectacular increases

called for in such things as model cities, housing, foreign aid and the almost totally discredited anti-poverty programs . . . .

Charles Zwick, LBJ's Budget Director, said of the budget prepared for Nixon: "We've tried to keep the momentum in key social programs." The *Wall Street Journal* of January 16, 1969, described Mr. Johnson's budgetary bequest to Mr. Nixon:

> Altogether, Mr. Johnson's budget slates an $11.6 billion rise in outlays, more than twice as large as the $4.8 billion increase that's expected to bring the current year's spending total to $183.7 billion. The major changes reflect his own priorities, White House aides say.

LBJ's priorities became Mr. Nixon's priorities. Nixon originally cut the budget to $192.9 billion, which was still $8.1 billion more than the budget for fiscal 1969, $14 billion more than Johnson spent in fiscal 1968, $34.5 billion more than he spent in 1967, $58.2 billion more than he spent in 1966, and over $100 billion more than the Eisenhower administration had spent in 1960.[14]

The $8 billion increase (which by the end of the year was closer to $15 billion) was touted as "budget cutting," on the basis that it was slightly less than what LBJ had proposed. (And LBJ could have proposed anything he wished, since he was leaving office.) In the end Nixon's budget turned out to be bigger than LBJ's proposals. Now, with the frugal Republicans controlling the White House, last year's profligate expenditures became this year's bare-bones budget. It all depends on whose gang of socialists is doing the spending. The *Indianapolis News* on January 17, 1969, said that references to the budget as tight

> . . . would no doubt bring tears of laughter to the eyes of American taxpayers if they were not already shedding tears of pain.

In point of fact, the budget is a monument to waste and to the spending psychosis which has hit Americans with high and rising taxes and inflicted on them a spiral of increasing prices that keeps everyone running at top speed to stay where he is.

This budget should not only be cut, it should be chopped to the bone . . . . .

For all the oratorical bunkum during the campaign about cutting spending, RMN and his advisors never intended to roll back the Great Society programs that were causing the problems. Richard Janssen wrote in the *Wall Street Journal* on October 21, 1968:

Progress toward budget balance could be much faster if Mr. Nixon would rapidly dismantle many Great Society spending programs, but his advisers vow this won't happen. "There's no concept of undoing anything — it's part of the fabric and leave it be," Mr. [Pierre] Rinfret stresses . . . .

In fact, the GOP could hardly wait to expand the Great Society. On July 16, 1969, the *Wall Street Journal's* Alan Otten revealed:

Only Vietnam-induced budget pressures seem to be deterring the Nixon Administration from proposing still larger Social Security benefits, far more spending on education and health, a far more sweeping war against hunger. Even the most conservative approach now being considered at the White House for new welfare legislation represents a major expansion of existing Government programs . . . .

And super-Liberal columnist Clayton Fritchey, a former Democratic Party official, gasped in the September 1, 1969 *Washington Star*:

Despite talk and pledges of economizing, budget-cutting, and curtailing the federal government, the Nixon administration is, in fact, headed for the greatest spending spree in the history of our country. The planned expenditures are on such a vast and unprecedented scale that nobody, including the Budget Bureau, can presently make a reliable estimate of what they will add up to before President Nixon completes his term in 1973.

It's the Great Society (a slogan borrowed from the title of a book by English Fabian-socialist Graham Wallas) in elephant's clothing.

Keep in mind that these gigantic increases are coming from an enormous base in which per capita taxation is already $975 per annum. [15] The average working man labors two hours and forty-three minutes a day all year just to pay direct and hidden taxes. [16]

The President was not going overboard to set an example. One of his first acts was to accept a $100,000 pay increase, doubling his salary. Congressman H.R. Gross observed: "I don't see how we can increase the President's salary by 100 per cent and claim to be setting a goal of austerity and frugality . . . ." [17] The President was not in dire need of money. In addition to a $50,000 tax-exempt expense account, the President already received operating expenses for White House entertainment, the cost of his plane, travel expenses, and so forth from a special contingency fund. And at the same time Congressman Robert Taft told his fellow legislators: "Until we move toward a tax reduction and a truly balanced budget, we shouldn't even talk of congressional pay increases." But the President did not veto either the generous raises Congress voted for itself or his own pay increase.

The *Wall Street Journal* on March 10, 1970, revealed that spending by the White House had doubled from $70 million under LBJ — never known as Mr. Frugal — to $140 million under RMN. According to the *Indianapolis Star* of April 29 the same year:

Seasoned observers believe that Mr. Nixon has the most expensive White House staff arrangement in history.

In the new budget presentation, the President's traveling

expenses are up 87 per cent, travel and transportation of staff is triple this year's, communications and utilities are up 43 per cent, printing and reproduction has more than doubled and supplies and materials are almost double.

The total number of permanent positions on the White House staff listed for the new fiscal year is 548. The estimate for this year was 250 — the same number that served the last six months of President Johnson's term and the first six of President Nixon's.

The Budget . . . does not account for a tripling of the National Security Council budget, pay for service personnel who tend the grounds, military assistants, presidential aircraft, including helicopters; the biggest part of the communications operation, the White House police and Secret Service staff, Coast Guard patrols off the vacation White Houses, General Services Administration housekeeping, and printing done by other departments.

Congressman Sam Gibbons ticked off some of the President's more lavish expenditures:

> The people may begin to wonder why he did not say "No" to an $830,000 expenditure of tax money to plush up his airplane, already the plushest plane in the world. The people may also wonder why he did not say "No" to the construction of a $350,000 helicopter pad on his Key Biscayne property.
>
> They may wonder why he did not say "No" to the cost of the taxpayers footing the bill for a $60,000 windscreen around his swimming pool at the San Clemente retreat. They may wonder why he did not say "No" to the expenditure of an admitted $250,000 for extra facilities and another $100,000 annually just to maintain them at San Clemente.
>
> They may wonder why he did not say "No" to the $1½ million spent on plush White House offices for the largest Presidential staff in history, and "No" to thousands of dollars for silly gilded uniforms for White House guards. They may wonder why he did not say "No" to the additional $4 million for that staff, many of whom devote time almost solely to partisan political activities in behalf of Republican candidates.
>
> When they look at the life style of this so-called economy-minded administration, the people will not be surprised at a

Cabinet member who redecorated his office at a cost of $40,000 to the taxpayers — including an $1,800 desk and carpeting priced at more than $56 per square yard.

The people cannot be fooled forever. They know who the "big spenders" really are. [18]

Congressman Arnold Olson mentioned the pay increase for the White House staff, up from $3.9 million to $8.5 million, and the $350,000 of government money spent on the Western White House, plus the $100,000 a year in operating costs. Olson commented:

At a time of combined inflation and recession, when the President talks about combating high costs in Government, one wonders about the frugality of maintaining three White Houses — in Washington, San Clemente, and Key Biscayne, not to mention Camp David. What of the tremendous cost of communications to link them all?

Certainly no one begrudges a busy President a rest retreat and our President deserves the finest facilities. But . . . if he wants to project the frugal image for political reasons — for that is the reason — then let him look to the same frugality in his own office.

"Inflation fighter" Nixon also asked for $1.1 million to operate the residence portion of the White House — an increase of $182,000 over the requirements of spendthrift LBJ. He spent $574,000 to turn the swimming pool at the White House into a press room. [19] And he has turned out to be the most lavish party thrower since Perle Mesta. According to *U.S. News & World Report*:

The Nixons have been entertaining guests at the rate of 45,000 per year.

According to White House aides, that is about 10 times as many guests as the Dwight Eisenhowers entertained in a year, and "many times more" than the John Kennedys entertained. It eclipses even the 26,000-guests-per-year pace set by the gregarious Lyndon Johnsons. [20]

The President was forced to ask that an extra $119,000 be added to the White House entertainment budget out of his stringent, bare-bones, austere, economy budget.

At first Nixon claimed that his budget would produce a $5.8 billion surplus that would "speak louder than any words" of his determination to fight inflation, and said:

> ...we believe we have made a necessary and significant beginning toward bringing the Federal budget under a closer Presidential control [and] brought to an end the era of the chronic budget deficit ....[21]

As expenditures rose and revenues shrank (due to the recession that diminished the government's tax take), the $5.8 billion surplus soon became a token surplus of $1.4 billion, which was nevertheless highly praiseworthy, according to the administration. By the end of the fiscal year the surplus had turned into a $2.9 billion deficit. According to UPI on July 29, 1970:

> George P. Shultz, the director of the Office of Management and Budget, said this was a good sign because it showed that the economy was stabilized and poised for an upward thrust.

"Actions speak louder than words," Nixon had said in projecting his surplus. With the pink elephants, surpluses are fine but deficits are even better.

Mr. Nixon's 1971 budget, the first one over which he had total control, was an expansion of the 1970 budget. Mr. Nixon proposed a $200.8 billion budget with a projected $1.3 billion surplus. The budget was hailed by Liberals because, as the President remarked, for the first time in twenty years:

> ...the federal government is spending more on human resource programs than on national defense. This year we are spending $1.7 billion less on defense than we were a year ago; in

the coming year we plan to spend $5.2 billion less. This is more than a redirection of resources; this is an historic reordering of our national priorities.[22]

However, former Nixon adviser Dr. Roger Freeman was aghast:

Since that time (that is, between 1953 and fiscal year 1971 as proposed by the President), defense expenditures increased 49 per cent — approximately equal to the simultaneous rate of price rise. Spending for health, education, welfare and labor increased 944 per cent . . . .

More than half of the $129-billion increase in federal expenditures between 1953 and 1971 was applied to social purposes, less than one-fifth to defense. Defense meanwhile shrank from 64 per cent of the federal budget to 36 per cent, from 13.6 per cent of gross national product to about 7.2 per cent.

In other words, the share of federal revenues and of the gross national product allocated to national defense has been cut almost in half since 1953. Most of the huge savings were applied to social purposes, with education one of the main gainers. [23]

While Mr. Nixon is "reordering our national priorities," the Communists grow increasingly hostile and expand their strategic armaments. "More for life than war," gloated the *Washington Post's* Murray Seeger. To the Liberals and Mr. Nixon, our national defense, the legitimate field of the federal government, is not a "human need." While restricting military spending and expanding most Great Society programs, the President introduced, according to the February 1970 *Battle Line*, "no less than seven major areas of new spending which will cost $3 billion more the first year and perhaps $18 billion annually as quickly as four years from now." The stressing of welfare spending over defense was a far cry from campaign days. The *New York Times* of May 15, 1966, stated:

Mr. Nixon called for heavy cuts in non-military spending at

home and a substantial cut in foreign aid except for that
directly related to the military or such things as the famine in
India."

The highly respected Washington correspondent emeritus
of the *Chicago Tribune*, Walter Trohan, wrote of the Nixon
program on October 29, 1970:

> . . . many Republicans have betrayed "conservatism" and have
> been as socialistic as many Democrats, if not more so. Betrayal of
> conservatism has been something of a fashion for 38 years.
>
> Some weeks ago, President Nixon assailed Congress for its
> failure to pass his legislative program. The curious part of his
> criticism was that the program was hardly "conservative," but
> one which any recent Democratic President might have offered.

After introducing a $200.8 billion budget, the President,
as Republican *Battle Line* put it, threw "caution to the
wind." Added expense came in the form of postal pay
increases, veterans' benefits, construction loans, and government employee pay increases, and in a host of other areas. It
now appears that spending for the year will be around $210
billion instead of $200.8 billion.

Yet through all this Nixon has managed to keep a public
image as Mr. Scrooge, the miserly, penny-pinching budget
slasher. During the 1970 midterm election campaign, economy in government was the number two theme of the
Republicans behind "law and order." Some of the President's
rhetoric warmed the hearts of Conservatives, as when he
proclaimed: "No Federal program is above scrutiny." [24]
Later he stated, "Personal freedom will be increased when
there is more economy in government and less government in
the economy." [25] But *Human Events* noted on January 31,
1970, following one of Mr. Nixon's economy speeches:

> But this conservative rhetoric was marred by the harsh fact
> that the President then proceeded to push for, or propose,

expensive programs that would further propel the federal government into the very debt he had just deplored.

Even if we could finally be convinced that gargantuan government programs were necessary to eliminate certain evils that plague the country, we would expect a Republican President to simultaneously call for the *elimination* of dozens of other programs that have outlived their usefulness .... We are still waiting for the day when the President wages as vigorous a fight to eradicate billions of dollars in entrenched programs as he does to put new programs on the books.

The Nixon technique is to substantially increase a budget and then send it to Congress, where the Democrats up the bid even further. Next the President denounces the Democrats as "big spenders" threatening "the future of the American economy." Occasionally the President even vetoes an appropriation, as described in the *Indianapolis Star* of May 26, 1970:

The failure of Mr. Nixon's "strict controls" is shown by the $19.7 billion bill appropriating funds for the Labor and Health, Education and Welfare departments for fiscal 1970 which he vetoed as inflationary last January. In his veto message, the President said bravely: "These increases (in the bill) are excessive in a period of serious inflationary pressures. We must draw the line and stick to it if we are to stabilize the economy."

What happened? Congress nudged the bill down to $19.4 billion, whereupon the President promptly signed it. Where were the strict controls? Where was the drawing of the line and the sticking to it? Could it be said that any real effort was made to cut expenses significantly? Obviously not.

But this subterfuge allows Mr. Nixon to constantly increase spending and still project the image of a budget-cutting inflation fighter. No matter how much Mr. Nixon increases the budget, he knows that the Liberal Democrats, compulsive spenders of taxpayers' money that they are, will always hike the ante, so the ploy always works.

In February Mr. Nixon said: "I have pledged to the American people a balanced budget." [26] But by October black had become white. The *Wall Street Journal* reported on October 13:

> The new Nixon has bought the "new economics" — or at least the part that condones budgetary red ink at times like now.
>
> In a fundamental break from his old stance on fiscal responsibility, the President has squarely committed himself to a theory that holds a multi-billion-dollar budget deficit is perfectly proper to bolster today's wobbly economy.

On November 17, 1970, House Ways and Means Committee chairman Wilbur Mills announced that unless spending was suddenly curtailed drastically, Mr. Nixon's 1971 budget, which started out projecting a $1.3 billion surplus, was actually going to run an astounding $24 billion in the red — almost as much as LBJ's fantastic $25 billion deficit for 1968, which triggered our current wage-price spiral. Mills also declared that the deficits of the 1960's are the root cause of the inflationary problems of the 1970's.

Few Americans are aware that the deficits are understated. UPI, reporting a statement by Rep. George Mahon, chairman of the House Appropriations Committee, said:

> Mahon, chairman of the House Appropriations Committee, said the fact is that budgets for the current year and the previous year, also pictured as "in the black," ran in the red. The total added deficit for the three-year period, Mahon said, runs about $19.9 billion.
>
> Mahon said the apparent small surplus in Nixon's budget for fiscal 1971 [now a huge deficit] and that for the two previous years — results from a new accounting system under which income and expenditures by government trust funds, such as Social Security, are lumped together with other government revenue.
>
> In recent years, the trust funds have run substantial surpluses that were borrowed by other government funds and included in the national debt.

During 1968, LBJ's last year in office, the debt was $365 billion, up from $293 billion in 1967, Nixon had to ask Congress to raise this, first to $377 billion, and later, in May 1970, to an astonishing $395 billion. That is an $18 billion raise during a period of allegedly balanced budgets! By the time you read this the rise will be significantly higher. Over $17 billion per year is required just to service the debt; this amounts to more than one million dollars an hour. The annual interest on the debt is now the third largest item in the budget. No wonder Nixon's international banking friends like deficit spending: much of the interest is payable to them.

Within a week after Congress voted to double Mr. Nixon's salary, he had to ask for the first debt ceiling hike. But he included a gimmick to make it look as if he were actually lowering the debt. This was described in the *Wall Street Journal* of February 25, 1969:

> In a special message signed before his departure for Europe, Mr. Nixon asked that the ceiling be reduced to $300 billion from $365 billion but that Congress simultaneously exclude from the ceiling's coverage more than $80 billion of Federal securities held by Federal trust funds for Social Security and other purposes.
>
> Thus, only securities that the Federal Government sells to the public would be covered, a change that Mr. Nixon said would make the ceiling "conform fully" to the unified budget format that's currently in its second year. The unified system shows a deficit only when the overall U.S. establishment (including trust funds) is paying out more to the public than it's collecting in taxes.

Congressman H.R. Gross denounced this as "more financial gimmickry of the Lyndon Johnson variety," and Congress refused to allow the President to get away with it. Consequently, following the 1970 midterm elections, Mr. Nixon had to face a national debt of $395 billion with an impending deficit of $24 billion.

And it looks as if this will be small potatoes compared to

what is in store for coming years. A 5.6 per cent unemployment rate hurt the Republicans badly in the 1970 elections. In an article titled "Nixon Signals for Left Turn," Peter Lisagor announced in the *Chicago Daily News* of November 11, 1970:

> Administration officials have indicated that the White House likely will follow its drive for a liberal welfare-reform measure with new "strategies" in the field of health and education of a progressive nature.
>
> They also point to a tentative administration acceptance of a full-employment policy, which in the present state of the economy means deficit financing, a hallmark of the liberal approach in a situation of rising joblessness.
>
> With these goals in mind, the political railbirds conclude that the President's recent meetings with conservative columnists at the White House and leaders of New York's Conservative Party at his Florida retreat reflected his desire to disarm or immobilize potential critics on the right as he tilts toward the left.

Nixon's strategy of moving Left is borne out by his budget for fiscal 1972. According to *Time* of November 16, 1970:

> Aides say that he will send to Congress a fiscal 1972 budget with a planned deficit — amount uncertain — to follow the unplanned deficit of about $15 billion that the Government is likely to run this fiscal year . . . .
>
> Administration officials are bandying about ideas for making the deficit look smaller than they expect it really to be . . . .
>
> . . . the President has begun to distract attention from the forthcoming deficit by stressing an idea known as the "full-employment budget." This is a theoretical measure that, instead of calculating actual Government income, figures how much the U.S. would have taken in if there were full employment. Thus, a deficit under ordinary accounting might well turn out to be a surplus in the full-employment budget. Example: In this fiscal year, the Government stands to spend about $210 billion and collect roughly $195 billion, thus running a deficit of $15 billion or so. But under full-employment accounting, the U.S. would show a surplus — because it would have taken in well over $210 billion if the optimum number of people had jobs.

The October 13, 1970 issue of the *Wall Street Journal* said of the "full-employment" budget:

> ... the concept is comforting to the Nixon regime. "After blasting the Democrats, it is pretty hard to turn around and convince people that our deficits are good ones," confesses a Republican strategist. But the full-employment approach, he contends, helps show that "in fact, there's a world of difference."

This is as if you felt that you could have earned $20,000 this year, but you only earned $15,000, so you go out and borrow $5,000 in order to keep up a $20,000 style of living. *Time* of November 16, 1970, defended this LSD-trip type of economics:

> While this fiddling with figures may seem like another bit of political gimmickry, it is economically sound. The full-employment budget is a fairly reliable gauge for determining whether the amount of Government spending is restraining or stimulating the economy. To stimulate the current slack economy, a fairly large full-employment deficit is called for.

This is the very type of hocus-pocus Nixon and the Republicans used to scream about — and with good cause. The *Wall Street Journal* reported on October 13, 1970:

> Although President Nixon doesn't use the "full-employment budget" term, this is what he means, aides explain, when he says that his "basic guideline" for the budget is that, except in emergencies, "expenditures must never be allowed to outrun the revenues that the tax system would produce at reasonably full employment." In recent days this has clearly become the party line, popping up in every speech by high economic officials, including David Kennedy and Paul McCracken.

This is Tricky-Dickmanship at its best — or worst! According to *Time* of November 16:

> The key figure in Nixon's current discussions of full-

employment budgeting is close to $230 billion. This is what present tax rates probably would bring in during fiscal 1972 at full employment. Nixon's dilemma is whether to hold federal spending to about that level or let outlays go still higher. So far, his aides have been passing word to department heads that spending is to be held to $225 billion. That strategy would allow Nixon to claim, correctly, that a planned deficit in the official budget would not be inflationary. But it would hold out little hope of lifting the economy toward full employment by mid-1972.

Nixon thus will be sorely tempted to shift policy and give an extra boost to production, profits and jobs by allowing Government spending to rise still higher. Some Administration officials think that such a course would risk starting again the price spiral that the U.S. has only begun to curb, but they are frankly afraid that the boss will do it . . . .

The President has concluded that elections are lost on unemployment and recession, not inflation. The June 22, 1970 *U.S. News & World Report* quoted an unnamed aide to the President as saying:

> "Mr. Nixon told me that no major party ever lost an election on inflation, but they have on recession. If he has anything to say, everything will be done to see there is no recession."

Nixon hopes to postpone much of the inflation until after the 1972 elections. There is a time-lapse factor between the time the government injects the deficit-spending dollars into the economy and the time it takes for the new money to percolate through the economy, bidding up wages and prices. In the late '60's the Democrats benefited from the spending and left most of the problems to the Republicans. The Democrats enjoyed the drunken binge and the Republicans got the hangover. Now, reported *Time* in mid-November 1970:

> Nixon and his advisers, says one Administration economist, "discovered that inflation started slowing down after the econo-

382 *Richard Nixon*

my slowed down. Now they may do the reverse: speed up the
economy and let the inflation come afterward — after the 1972
elections."

So we have come full circle from the beginning of the
Johnson inflation, through a half-hearted attempt at defla-
tion with the consequences described by Galbraith, and back
to Johnsonian "stimulation." We are going to try the hair of
the dog that bit us as a cure. If boom-and-bust policies are
good enough for the Fabian-socialist Democrats, they are
good enough for the Fabian-socialist Republicans. As Galbraith says, Nixon has a Game Plan and the "name of the
game is socialism." LBJ may turn out to have been a piker.
LBJ's 1967 budget was $158 billion — and it was roundly
denounced by the Republicans; Nixon's 1972 budget may
run $230 billion — an increase of $72 billion in five years.
And LBJ's deficits, once considered enormous, may be
dwarfed by Nixon's.

Before the 1968 election Mr. Nixon called inflation "the
cruelest tax of all." He added: ". . . it quietly picks your
pocket, steals your savings, robs your paycheck. To check
inflation the government must cut down on unnecessary
federal spending . . . ."[27]

In 1969 alone, inflation robbed Americans of $60 billion
of their savings in banks and life insurance, as the cost of
living went up an official 6.1 per cent during Mr. Nixon's first
year in office. In March 1970, the President told a news
conference that his administration's economic policies had
"taken the fire out of inflation" and would steer the nation
clear of it. [28] Actually, the administration has killed prosperity, but not inflation. Production is down, unemployment is
up — but prices are again rising: officially, the rate was 6 per
cent during 1970. (The official rate is loaded; the true rate is
estimated at 10 per cent by many economists.) This means
that Americans have paid an additional hidden tax of $120
billion in the past two years.

Now, in order to cure the non-existent recession, the administration is prepared to hyperinflate. And the Federal Reserve Board is obviously willing to go along with the Game Plan. Board Chairman Arthur Burns, "the Kerensky of this revolution," has promised that "there will be enough money and credit to meet future needs, and that the orderly expansion of the economy will not be endangered by a lack of liquidity." He has also said he is willing to increase the money supply at a "temporarily excessive speed." In layman's language this means, "The printing presses are oiled and ready to roll." (At swank Washington soirées Nixon men have been seen dancing the Samba to the strains of "Brazil.") *Space-Time-Forecasting* said of this venture:

> It's an illusion that government can make or break prosperity at will by manipulating money supply. It's tragic that men surrounding recent administrations hold this belief, in spite of historical evidence that it's never been successful — very much the contrary. .... It is obvious from statements made in the past that Nixon knows better.*

Nixon inflation will produce the same chaos as Johnson inflation. Inflation is harmful to an economy under any circumstances. If Mr. Nixon had really wanted to cure the Johnson inflation and return to stability, he would have taken a course exactly opposite to the one he has taken. The best way to avoid the effects of inflation is to increase productivity and produce your way out of it. This means drastically cut government spending, balanced budgets, and then tax cuts to give businessmen an incentive to produce, and consumers money with which to buy their products and

---

*Nixon stated in the October 1968 issue of *Fortune* magazine: "The accelerated rise in prices in recent years has resulted primarily from an excessively expanding money supply that in turn had been fed by the monetization of federal government deficits. The way to stop the inflation is to reverse the irresponsible fiscal policies which produce it . . . . ."

services. Instead, Mr. Nixon has instituted the *economics of scarcity* (as noted by Galbraith), expanding the welfare state with a consequent boost in government spending and increased taxes. This is the Game Plan, and as Galbraith observes, "the name of the game is socialism."

In 1965, Nixon declared:

> This administration [LBJ's] has adopted a completely contradictory policy in dealing with the threat of inflation. It has tried to replace the market law of supply and demand with Johnson's law of comply and expand — business complies and government expands.
>
> A policy that requires business to slam on the price brakes while government steps on its spending accelerator will in the end only produce a collision — and the family budget will be the casualty.[29]

In order to postpone the worst of the increases in the cost of living until after the '72 election, the administration will have to resort to "jawboning," "guidelines," and plain old-fashioned arm twisting. Ultimately, wage and price controls will be instituted, as the Socialist Game Plan nears completion, but if possible this will be delayed until after the '72 election. If the cost of living gets completely out of hand, controls may have to be instituted even before the elections. The President has the power to do this, as is made clear in the August 12, 1970 newsletter of Congressman John G. Schmitz:

> On the last day of July, Congress held an unusual Friday session to spend several hours in a most peculiar debate on a bill establishing new cost accounting standards for defense contracting, onto which had been tacked a "rider" empowering the President, by executive order, "to stabilize prices, rents, wages, interest rates, and salaries at levels not less than those prevailing on May 25, 1970" — the date the bill was introduced. This would authorize full price and wage controls.
>
> After a day of bewildering maneuvers, the bill was finally

passed by the astonishingly one-sided vote of 257 to 19, with six other Congressmen also "paired" against it. Thus only 25 members of the House registered their disapproval of price and wage controls.

The redoubtable Congressman H.R. Gross stated bluntly:

> . . . no President should be delegated the awful power to take over the economy and finances of this Nation without having declared an emergency and the reasons therefor. And no Congress should delegate to the President such untrammeled power without requiring such a declaration.

Instead of vetoing it, Mr. Nixon signed the bill — reluctantly, of course. Again, Galbraith's "yielding to pressure." Congressman Schmitz remarked:

> Price and wage controls will not work in a free country. But to a considerable extent they will work in a slave state like Communist Russia. If this is the only way we can think of to fight inflation, that could be its result . . . .

Wage controls, price controls, money controls are really people controls — and that is what a socialist dictatorship is all about.

In December 1969, Congress, in a hurry to adjourn for Christmas, almost clandestinely passed the Credit Control Bill under circumstances closely paralleling the establishing of the Federal Reserve System some fifty years ago. Not one one-hundredth of one per cent of the American people know anything about the existence or the significance of this blueprint for complete economic tyranny. Yet it is on the books, ready to be used whenever the administration feels the time is ripe. Congressman H.R. Gross wrote:

> During the past week, President Nixon has signed the legislation into law. He did so, "reluctantly," he said, asserting that such controls, if used, could "take the nation a long step

toward a directly controlled economy and . . . we can weaken the will for needed fiscal and financial discipline."

Here we have the spectacle of President Nixon, recognizing that this is power no government should have except in the event of a dire emergency — a power that could well mean outright government control of the nation's economy — yet he gave it his blessing by his signature making it the law of the land.

This member of Congress has warned for years that the nation was rushing headlong into financial trouble; that the price of spending insanity would be regimentation through unholy, dictatorial controls from Washington . . . and I am deeply disappointed that President Nixon, recognizing the danger, did not have the courage to veto it.

The legislation provided that without the declaration of an emergency or any other kind of a declaration, President NIxon could turn over to the Federal Reserve, a privately operated financial institution, not only the absolute authority to fix interest rates, but the untrammeled power to fix by regulation all the "terms and conditions of any extension of credit."

It is almost impossible to believe, but the legislation provides that no citizen could lend another any amount of money unless the lender was either registered or licensed to do so. A violation of this or any other provision of the legislation would subject the lender to a year in jail and a $1,000 fine. THIS IS THE STUFF OF WHICH DICTATORS ARE MADE.

Socialism requires a dictator, and with Mr. Nixon, as Dr. Galbraith reminds us, "socialism is the name of the game."*

It is obvious that we are on our way to another inflation-promoting tax increase in the name of fighting inflation. In speaking of projected deficits, the President has stated that if government spending, "in spite of the strict controls I have placed on it, were to exceed the potential yield of the tax system, I would not hesitate to ask the Congress for further increases in taxes . . . ."[30] It is widely reported that Mr. Nixon is "intrigued" (as *Time* put it) by a "value added tax," which is in effect a national sales tax of the kind becoming standard in the Common Market countries.[31] The tax is hidden, but as UPI noted on February 13,

1970, "ultimately, the tax is passed along to the consumer in the form of higher prices." If at all possible, the President will wait until after the '72 elections to saddle the peasants with a tax hike.

Mr. Nixon's program of "re-inflation" to end what has been termed "stagflation" (economic stagnation accompanied by inflation) has international economic implications.

According to *Barron's* Financial Weekly of November 16, 1970, it "is apt to be the dollar's last hurrah." It is obvious that the international monetary game is rigged tighter than a new tennis racquet with Rothschild-controlled central banks, bullion dealers, and mining interests in England, Germany, France, South Africa and the U.S. (Kuhn, Loeb & Company, whose partner, Lewis Strauss, was Nixon's chief money raiser, is a Rothschild operation.) The financial ministers of these countries do not represent their sovereign nations, but instead cooperate with the *Insiders* in rigging the world monetary situation. But the super-inflation planned by Nixon will

---

*There is a possibility that Galbraith may deliberately play a part in ensuring the re-election of RMN in 1972 — far-fetched as that would seem to those who are not aware that he and Nixon are part of the same conspiracy — by dividing the Democratic Party. Columnist John Chamberlain stated in the October 31, 1970 issue of *Human Events*: ". . . the so-called New Democrats, taking their cue from the new Galbraith book, *Who Needs The Democrats?*, are already busy sowing the dragons' teeth that will, as sure as sin, disrupt the Democratic convention of 1972 if the radicals in the party do not succeed in getting their way.

"An extremely significant symposium, engineered by the editors of the journal called *The New Democrat* (they happen to be Stephen Schlesinger, the son of Arthur Schlesinger Jr., and Grier Raggio, a Mayor John Lindsay functionary in New York City), shows what the Democratic party faces.

"Addressing a letter to 30 prominent intellectuals, the Schlesinger-Raggio team posed this question: 'Do you believe the Democratic party is still capable of aggressively reforming itself by the 1972 convention, or do you believe that a fourth party is the only conceivable means of effecting change in 1972?'

"To this, 18 intellectuals gave their answers, and even those who do not favor going out into the wilderness to start a fourth party look with complaisance on the idea of using such a party as a prod to force a radical platform and candidates on the existing Democratic organization."

This strategy may be the reason Galbraith wrote his article. It appears in a magazine whose circulation is limited almost exclusively to New York City, and may be the "transmission belt" informing camp followers that Nixon is really the *Insiders'* boy.

augment some forty billions of dollars already in the hands of Europeans, who can exchange them for gold, and the situation could get out of control. Europeans are planning to create a European-bloc gold-backed currency, which could be instituted if and when the U.S. cuts the dollar loose from gold for foreigners as it has done for its own citizens.

This threat may be used to force acceptance of the plan to turn the International Monetary Fund (IMF) into a world central bank, controlling all money of all nations. William McChesney Martin, despite the fact that he had already retired as chairman of the Federal Reserve Board, gave a speech in Basel, Switzerland, on September 14, 1970, at a symposium sponsored by the Per Jacobson Foundation, entitled "World Central Bank: Essential Evolution," in which he advocated just that. [32] What area of control could be more decisive than control of world money? World money control means world people control.

Meanwhile, reports persist, albeit unconfirmed, that the U.S. is preparing a new money. *Myers Financial Review* of November 6, 1970 stated:

> The rumors keep coming in. They are past the point where I can ignore them. Still I can't confirm them. The reports are these:
> The U.S. Treasury has already printed up an enormous supply of new currency differing markedly from the present denominations. The report is that the new currency will be used internally in the U.S., and that all the old currency within the U.S.A. will be called in. The old currency, as long as it continues to exist, will be used outside the U.S.A.
> I have no inside way of knowing whether this is true. But for many months I have been receiving reports that the Treasury has been stocked with huge new color presses. I am inclined to lean toward the truth of the report, since in Canada we are already getting a fancy new currency. The $20 bill looks like Disneyland. It is swiftly replacing all old $20 bills. It gives one the impression of a kind of scrip. There has been no explanation of why we have replaced our old $20 bills with these curiosities.
> It seems to me that this internal U.S. currency would be no

good outside the country. Not redeemable, it could not be converted into Euro-dollars. It would in itself be a most effective foreign exchange control. In order to get your money out of your banks to make foreign purchases, you would probably have to get special licence from the government.

We may be heading not just for devaluation but for a collapse of all money, and a new U.S. paper dollar in exchange for several old ones. The November 1970 report of international currency expert Franz Pick maintains: "The only open door will be to change the official gold value of the MINI-dollar or to exchange 3 or 4 present dollar bills for 1 new one."[33]

What does the Nixon Game Plan mean? Many economists are predicting a superboom (based on inflation, not increased productivity), with a Dow Jones rising to possibly 1500, beginning in the latter part of 1971 and extending through the 1972 election. Then, in 1973 or '74, these economists are predicting that the false boom will lead to economic collapse and a depression that will make 1929 seem like prosperity by comparison. If this happens the cry will be that "capitalism has totally failed."

Gigantic unemployment, particularly among Negroes, would lead to nationwide riots, giving the appearance at least of a full-scale revolution. The general population would demand a socialist dictatorship to end the economic and social chaos. And the Nixon administration would be only too happy to comply — "the familiar yielding to pressure," as Galbraith says. Nixon is merely following the Game Plan established for him by his fellow *Insiders*, who plucked him out of political oblivion following his loss of the governorship of California in 1962, brought him to New York, and financed and promoted his ascent to the Presidency. A Democratic administration could not get away with it, because the Congressional Republicans would expose the Game Plan and possibly prevent it. Now most of them remain silent, or silenced, all in the name of "party unity."

In 1934, FDR prohibited Americans from owning gold to protect themselves from government money manipulation. Since that time the government has destroyed about 80 per cent of the purchasing power of the dollar through increases in the money supply. Economist Henry Hazlitt has written:

> No sound monetary system is possible so long as governments operate on the premises of the new economics.
>
> The real reforms that are needed are all in the opposite direction. Strict limits must be put on the further issue of paper money. Ultimately the world must work back to a real gold standard.
>
> But no nation can achieve sound monetary reform so long as its government embarks on huge spending programs, so long as it runs unending budget deficits, so long as it keeps printing more money and so long as its unions are encouraged to force up wage rates to levels that need more inflation to sustain them. In brief, sound money is impossible in the welfare state.

Major nations forbidding their citizens to own gold in modern times include: Communist Russia, National Socialist Germany, Socialist England, Communist China, and the U.S.A. All dictators fear the private ownership of gold. Since FDR's prohibition of gold ownership was not passed by Congress but was imposed by inserting an "Executive Order" in the Federal Register, Mr. Nixon could abolish this dictatorial edict with the stroke of a pen, issuing an "Executive Order" voiding FDR's. This would go a long way toward restoring liberty and fiscal sanity in America. But there is no more chance that Richard Nixon will restore this liberty than there is that Mao Tse-tung will convert to Christianity. Why? Why can't Americans own gold? Isn't that an interesting question?

Barron's Financial Weekly reports that well over a decade ago Malcolm Bryan, president of the Federal Reserve Bank of

Atlanta, bluntly told an audience: "We should have the decency to say to the money saver, 'Hold still, Little Fish! All we intend is to gut you.'" In the end we shall all be gutted if the Whittier Machiavelli's Socialist Game Plan is not exposed and reversed.

References
1. *Human Events*, November 14, 1970.
2. *Los Angeles Times*, March 26, 1969.
3. *U.S. News & World Report*, July 6, 1970.
4. *Washington Sunday Star*, January 26, 1969.
5. *Tax Fax* No. 100, July 1, 1969.
6. *Watch Washington*, June 27, 1969.
7. *Los Angeles Times*, August 12, 1969.
8. *Human Events*, September 28, 1968.
9. *Los Angeles Times*, October 27, 1968.
10. *U.S. News & World Report*, July 15, 1968.
11. *Christian Crusade Weekly*, May 17, 1970.
12. *Ibid.*
13. *Wall Street Journal*, January 16, 1969.
14. Henry Hazlitt, *Battle Line*, February 1970.
15. United Press International, February 3, 1970.
16. *Battle Line*, April 1970.
17. *Indianapolis Star*, January 8, 1969.
18. *Congressional Record*, August 14, 1970.
19. *Indianapolis Star*, April 21, 1970.
20. *U.S. News & World Report*, May 11, 1970.
21. *Wall Street Journal*, April 14, 1969.
22. *Human Events*, June 27, 1970.
23. *Ibid.*
24. *Wall Street Journal*, September 7, 1969.
25. *Los Angeles Times*, January 31, 1970.
26. *International Harry Schultz Letter*, October 27, 1970.
27. *Los Angeles Times*, September 13, 1968.
28. New York Times News Service, March 22, 1970.
29. *New York Times*, December 4, 1965.
30. *Indianapolis Star*, editorial, May 26, 1970.
31. *Time*, January 12, 1970.
32. *Wall Street Journal*, September 15, 1970.
33. *Myers Financial Review*, January 16, 1970.

CHAPTER XV

The End Is Power

It was early in the Nixon administration that Senator Hugh Scott bragged that while the Conservatives were getting the words, the Liberals got the action. Two years later, in December 1970, the American Conservative Union's newsletter, Republican *Battle Line*, lamented: "Well, at mid-point, we think we can say conservatives are no longer even getting the words. Only the knife."

Those who have followed Nixon's career closely were not surprised. Nixon courts the Conservatives when he needs help and the rest of the time treats them like lepers. Yet Nixon still manages to retain his overall image as a Conservative and comes under hard attack from the Left. Stewart Alsop, in a column titled "Nixon to the Left of Himself," discusses this phenomenon:

> In his farewell address at the White House, President Nixon's favorite liberal Democrat, Daniel P. Moynihan, credited the Nixon Administration with "much genuine achievement." "And yet," he added, more in sorrow than in anger, "how little the Administration is credited with what it has achieved . . . Depressing, even frightening things are being said [by Liberals] about the Administration. They are not true."[1]

Alsop claims that if Nixon were judged by his deeds instead of his ancient image, the Liberals' attitude toward him would be different. If only the Liberals' Pavlovian response to the Nixon name could be eliminated, says Alsop, they would realize how far Left he is. Therefore Alsop substitutes a hypothetical "President Liberal" for President Nixon:

> ... If President Liberal were actually in the White House, it is not at all hard to imagine the reaction to his program. The right would be assailing President Liberal for bugging out of Vietnam, undermining American defenses, fiscal irresponsibility, and galloping socialism. The four basic Presidential policy positions listed above would be greeted with hosannas by the liberals . . . .
>
> Instead, the liberals have showered the President with dead cats, while most conservatives have maintained a glum silence, and thus the Administration has been "little credited" for "much genuine achievement." But there are certain special reasons, which Pat Moynihan omitted to mention, why this is so.

Alsop goes on to explain how it helps Nixon in passing the Liberal Democrats' program to have the reputation of being an enemy of Liberal Democrats:

> For one thing, there is a sort of unconscious conspiracy between the President and his natural enemies, the liberal Democrats, to conceal the extent to which his basic program, leaving aside frills and rhetoric, is really the liberal Democratic program. Richard Nixon is the first professional politician and "real Republican" to be elected President in 40 years – and it is not in the self-interest of the liberals to give credit to such a President for liberal initiatives. By the same token, it is not in the self-interest of the President to risk his conservative constituency by encouraging the notion that he is not a "real Republican" after all, but a liberal Democrat at cut rates . . . .
>
> There are plenty of examples of the mutual obfuscation which results from this mutual interest. The withdrawal of half a million men from Vietnam is quite obviously the greatest retreat in American history. But the President talks as though it were somehow a glorious advance, certain to guarantee a "just and lasting peace." When the President – like any commander of a retreat – resorts to spoiling actions to protect his dwindling rear guard, the liberals howl that he is "chasing the will-o'-the-wisp of military victory."

... When the President cuts back real military strength more sharply than in a quarter of a century, the liberals attack him for failing to "reorder priorities." The President, in his rhetoric about a "strong defense," plays the same game. The result, as John Kenneth Galbraith accurately noted recently, is that "most people and maybe most congressmen think the Administration is indulging the Pentagon even more than the Democrats," which is the precise opposite of the truth ....

Alsop continued what is probably the most damnifying column ever written about Richard Nixon by noting the role that the mass media have played in portraying to the public an image that is the reverse of the truth:

... There is also a human element in this exercise in mutual obfuscation. To the liberals, especially the liberal commentators who dominate the media, Richard Nixon is Dr. Fell ("The reason why I cannot tell, but this I know and know full well, I do not like thee, Dr. Fell"). This is not surprising. Not too many years ago, Richard M. Nixon was one of the most effective — and least lovable — of the conservative Republican professionals of the McCarthy era.

The columnist, himself a member of the ADA, speculated on what the "old Nixon" would have had to say about the "new Nixon":

... on his past record, it is not at all hard to imagine R.M. Nixon leading the assault on the President for his "bug-out," "fiscal irresponsibility," "galloping socialism," and all the rest of it. So how can one expect Mr. Nixon to defend President Liberal's program with the passionate conviction that a President Robert Kennedy, say, would have brought to the defense of such a program?

Alsop has revealed the *real* Nixon. He could not be more pleased. Those who voted for Nixon aren't quite so happy — or shouldn't be. If you liked the Richard Nixon who ran for the Presidency, then you cannot, if you are consistent, like the Richard Nixon who is President. Nixon and his fellow "moderates" have turned the Republican elephant into a donkey in elephant's clothing. On June 19, 1959, Vice President Nixon gloated: "In summary, the Republican administration produced the things that the Democrats promised." It looks as if it's happening again!

A year and a half earlier Nixon had been warbling a different tune:

> If we have nothing to offer other than a pale carbon copy of the New Deal, if our only purpose is to gain and retain power, the Republican Party no longer has any reason to exist, and it ought to go out of business.[2]

Alsop is right. According to the "old Nixon," the Republican Party should disband. Norman Thomas said, in effect, that the American people would not knowingly vote for socialism, but under the guise of "Liberalism" they would adopt socialist measures until one day they would be living under a socialist state without knowing how it all came about.[3]

U.S. News & World Report noted:

> The late Norman Thomas, who ran unsuccessfully for President six times on the Socialist Party ticket, observed in 1964 that the Democrats "have through the years taken over measures once regarded as Socialist, but then so have the Republicans but to a slightly less degree."[4]

If Thomas were alive today, he would applaud the Nixon administration with great glee. The Republicans have been conquered by Fabian-Socialist patient gradualism. First we oppose, next we endure, then we embrace. That is the tragic story of the Republican party. Republican support of Nixon merely lends respectability to his implementation of the Marxist programs described by Alsop. Democrats have long accused Nixon of being tricky. Republicans tended to react to the accusation in a Pavlovian manner, accusing the Democrats of partisan political slander. Actually, though the Democrats have badly misinterpreted Nixon's true ideology, they have understood his character very well. And many Republicans who have worked closely with Nixon in past campaigns know that he is tricky. He is also cunning and clever. He has been an actor and debater since his youth and he knows all the tricks of the trade. Nixon tries to cover his reputation for deviousness by seeming to go overboard in his speeches to be fair. He also prefaces statements with phrases like "let me make it perfectly clear," "putting it bluntly," "speaking quite frankly," or "to be perfectly candid." What follows is usually anything but clear, blunt, frank or candid.

Democrats have accused Nixon with more than a little validity of having been on every side of every issue. Many of them resent his appropriating their pet issues. However, most political analysts dismiss Nixon's incursions into the land of Liberalism as symptomatic of his pragmatism. Now, Nixon claims to be a pragmatist; but in his book, *Six Crises*, he claimed:

> . . . My philosophy has always been: don't lean with the wind. Don't do what is politically expedient. Do what your instinct tells you is right. Public opinion polls are useful if a politician uses them only to learn approximately what the people are thinking, so that he can talk to them more intelligently. The politician who sways with the polls is not worth his pay. And I believe the people will eventually catch up with the man who merely tells them what he thinks they want to hear.[5]

Washington Post political reporter David Broder wrote in a column on April 8, 1969:

> Pragmatism is the operating philosophy of this Administration. The Nixon White House, as one insider remarked, is not "an intensely ideological environment." Lacking ideology or even a

strong set of goals and values, the Administration has a tendency to drift.[6]

Baloney! The alleged "pragmatism" is merely a cover-up for the "genuine achievement" of Liberal aims (socialism) of which Alsop spoke.

Most people look at the Nixon administration and see only the confusion produced by the President's alleged pragmatism. Kevin Phillips wrote: " . . . the Nixon administration's mixture of hard rhetoric with contradictory programming and overall lack of vision wins no plaudits."

Nixon is not bungling or stupid, he is brilliant and cunning. And what he is doing is not stupid but brilliant — from the standpoint of the *Insiders.* Author G. Edward Griffin has said:

> It's always a source of amazement to me when I hear someone criticize our leaders for being confused in the area of foreign policy, or reversing their position, of bungling the job and not having any long-range goals. These men are *not* bungling the job. They're acting in accordance with a definite, well thought out plan, and they've been executing that plan with brilliant precision. We may or may not like the plan, but let's not kid ourselves into thinking that there isn't any . . . .
>
> The Grand Design has absolutely nothing to do with partisan politics. These men aren't nearly as much Republicans or Democrats as they are *world* politicians. They've got bigger things to occupy their minds than mere party labels. To them, partisan politics is only a game to amuse the masses who crave the showmanship of big national conventions, the excitement of partisan campaigns, and the satisfaction of casting a vote in the illusion that, somehow, they're really helping to decide the important issues of the day. But, with precious few exceptions, for the past two decades the American voter has had to make his choice between Grand Designer A and Grand Designer B . . . .[7]

And Thomas Jefferson once observed:

> Single acts of tyranny may be ascribed to the accidental
> opinion of a day; but a series of oppressions, begun at a
> distinguished period, and pursued unalterably through every
> change of ministers, too plainly prove a deliberate, systematical
> plan of reducing us to slavery.[8]

Benjamin Disraeli, the British statesman much admired by
Nixon, wrote a novel called *Coningsby* whose chief characters
were thinly disguised take-offs on the Rothschilds. Disraeli
was a close friend of the Rothschilds and a Rothschild agent.
In his book he has a "Rothschild" say: "So, you see, my dear
Coningsby, the world is governed by very different person-
ages from what is imagined by those who are not behind the
scenes."[9]

Nixon is now a man who works for the men behind the
scenes — the Rothschild-Rockefeller world empire which
helped to establish and now controls Communism. David
Broder writes in his book on the Republican Party: "For
Richard Nixon, the end is power — specifically the incom-
parable power of the presidency . . . . "[10] Nixon now has
power — fantastic power — over the lives of 200 million
Americans. He has more power than a good man would want
or an evil man should have. Richard Nixon, the man of
unbounded and, unfortunately, unprincipled ambition has
reached the top of the political heap. And at the same time
he has acquired considerable wealth — something else he has
always wanted. He has been rewarded well for his services.
The only thing left for him now would be to head a world
government.

The fact that Nixon is a Republican is all the better for the
Insiders. Unfortunately, many Republicans take it as a
personal attack on themselves when it is suggested that there
is a conspiracy working within their own party. They should
not be offended. It is no reflection on the rank and file —
unless they continue to tolerate it once the conspiracy has

been exposed. It is only natural for a conspiracy to try to control both (or all) political parties. It would not do to have a pro-conspiracy party and an anti-conspiracy party or a pro-socialist party and an anti-socialist party. The "antis" would ruin the game by exposing it. And exposure is the one thing a conspiracy cannot stand. The voters would have "a choice, not an echo." When both parties are infiltrated, pleas for party unity can be made that take the spotlight off the conspirators. As the two parties become more alike, elections center around personalities and means, not goals. The *Insiders* believe that Conservatives are trapped within the party. As the late Thomas E. Dewey, a top *Insider* and possibly the most important man to Richard Nixon's presidential aspirations, once arrogantly expressed it: "Let them [Conservatives] write letters, let them petition, let them pass resolutions; just as long as they have no place else to go, forget them."[11]

Without a pipeline to the councils of the *Insiders*, it is impossible to predict just what their exact plans and timing are for the coming years. But one needs no pipeline to tell that they are moving very swiftly toward their final goal — a one-world socialist government that they will control. In order to accomplish this, Nixon is doing everything possible to centralize power in the federal government, so that control of the federal government will mean automatic control over all state and local governments. Then from the federal government sovereignty can be transferred to a world government. When Franklin D. Roosevelt was Governor of New York, he said: "Now, to bring about government by oligarchy masquerading as democracy, it is fundamentally essential that practically all authority and control be central- ized in our National Government."* Later, as President,

---

*Interestingly, Nixon's favorite President is Woodrow Wilson, the man who started us on the road to rule by the *Insider* oligarchy by establishing the progressive income tax, direct election of Senators, and the Federal Reserve System.

Roosevelt was to go a long way toward bringing about the government by oligarchy which he predicted. What we are going to see is a dictatorship of the elite disguised as a dictatorship of the proletariat.

Much, if not all, of the solidification of power will come between 1972 and 1976. In all probability the *Insiders* want Nixon to have a second term because they believe there will be far less resistance if the *coup de grâce* is administered to the American Republic by a Republican rather than a Democrat. Because the socialism enacted by previous administrations is really catching up with the American economy, it may be necessary for the *Insiders* to institute a fourth party on the far left, possibly headed by John Lindsay, in order to divide the Democrat vote and re-elect Richard Nixon. Although Richard Nixon's popularity is down as this is written, he has many weapons with which to create a false euphoria to facilitate his re-election in 1972. A seeming end to the Vietnam war, combined with the semblance of a return to prosperity at home, would be a tough combination to beat.

After re-election in 1972 Nixon would have no political brake on his final drive to socialism, unless enough Constitutional Conservatives who understand the conspiracy can be elected in 1972 to head the *Insiders* off at the pass. It is apparent that Nixon would like to celebrate the 200th anniversary of the founding of the United States by instituting a United States of the World — a step that would be ballyhooed as the most significant event in world history since the Declaration of Independence. It would be PR'd as bringing permanent peace and prosperity, but in reality, it would be a world dictatorship, bringing with it a *1984*-style slavery. As the *Insiders'* mouthpiece James Reston noted:

> ...He [Nixon] will zig zag [left and right] to avoid the torpedoes and take advantage of the wind, but his destination is to preside over the great festival of freedom in 1976, and to get there from here he must eventually go to the left.

References

1. *Newsweek*, January 11, 1971.
2. *Almanack of Poor Richard Nixon*, Cleveland, World Publishing Co., 1959, New York, January 20, 1958.
3. Harold P. Poeschel, *It Is High Time*, Independent Publishers, Inc., 1963, p. 20.
4. *U.S. News & World Report*, July 14, 1969.
5. Richard Nixon, *Six Crises*, Garden City, N.Y., Doubleday & Co., p. 143.
6. *Battle Line*, April 1969.
7. G. Edward Griffin, *The Grand Design*, Thousand Oaks, Calif., American Media, Inc., 1968.
8. *The Works of Thomas Jefferson*, Vol. 1, p. 130.
9. Benjamin Disraeli, *Conningsby*, Century Edition, 1903, p. 233.
10. Stephen Hess and David Broder, *The Republican Establishment*, New York, Harper & Row, 1967, p. 143.
11. Poeschel, *op. cit.*, December 1964 supplement.
12. *Indianapolis News*, January 24, 1970.

CHAPTER XVI

Turn The *Insiders* Out

Communism will not come to the United States under that name. It will be called the New Freedom, the New Politics, Participatory Democracy, the Greater Society, the New Federalism, or some other such vacuous slogan. Almost all Americans are against Communism, but they don't know what it is. America can stop the Communists when the *Insiders* are exposed and the public realizes that the primary threat against the Republic comes from within, not from without. In the coming years the government will assume more and more emergency powers to meet various "temporary crises." Of course, the crises will not be temporary, and neither will the assumption of power. If the last steps down the long road to dictatorship are taken by a Republican President, the job of the conspirators will be easier. The *Insiders* realize this and will have one of their own, Richard Nixon, doing an acting job as a "Conservative Republican." In the name of "party unity" good Republicans will swallow docilely gigantic increases in dictatorial government power which, if instituted by Democrats, they would resist tenaciously. Many Republicans will actually defend such depredations (if a bit sheepishly), just as Republicans defended Dwight Eisenhower as he broke his campaign promises, one after another.

Fourteen signposts on the road to totalitarianism were compiled some years ago by historian Dr. Warren Carroll and a refugee from Yugoslavian Communism, Mike Djordjevich.

The original list was not in any particular order, nor is the order in which the points are listed here of any particular significance. The imposition of any one of these new restrictions on liberty (none of which are now in effect) would be a clear warning that the total state is very near; and once a significant number of them — say five — have been imposed, we will be justified in concluding that the remainder, or most of the remainder, will not be far behind, and that the fight for freedom and the preservation of the Republic has been lost in this country. The fourteen signposts are:

1.   Restrictions on taking money out of the country and on the establishment or retention of a foreign bank account by an American citizen.

2.   Abolition of private ownership of hand guns.

3.   Detention of individuals without judicial process.

4.   The requirement that private financial transactions be keyed to social security numbers or other government identification, so that government may conveniently record these transactions and feed the record into a computer.

5.   Use of compulsory education laws to forbid attendance at presently existing private schools.

6.   Compulsory non-military service.

7.   Compulsory psychological treatment for non-government workers or public school children.

8.   The official declaration that anti-Communist organizations are subversive, and subsequent legal action to suppress them.

9.   Laws limiting the number of people allowed to meet in a private home.

10. Any significant change in passport regulations that makes passports more difficult to obtain or use.

11. Wage and price controls, especially in a non-wartime situation.

12. Any kind of compulsory registration with the

government of the individual's place of employment.

13. Any attempt to restrict freedom of movement within the United States.

14. Any example of a new major law made by executive decree (that is, actually put into effect, not merely authorized, as by existing executive orders).

Steps 1,2,5,6,7,8,11,12 and 13 have already been proposed and some are being actively campaigned for by organized groups. For example, Step 1 — The Travel tax urged by President Johnson would have required the declaration of the amount of money being taken out of the country, and in the discussion of this proposal it was seriously suggested that a flat dollar limit be placed on the amount that could be removed. Step 5 — Increased government control over private schools of many kinds is proposed annually in many state legislatures. Step 6 — Compulsory non-military service — a universal draft of all young men and women, with only a minority going into the armed services — has been discussed by the Nixon administration as an alternative to the draft. Step 7 — Sensitivity training is already required for an increasing number of government workers, teachers, and school children. Step 8 — As long ago as 1961, Victor Reuther proposed that Right-wing anti-Communist groups and organizations be investigated and placed on the Attorney General's subversive list. Step 11 — Prospects for wage and price controls were discussed in Chapter 14. Step 2 — The propaganda war in process to force registration or confiscation of firearms is the number one priority of all the collectivists — an armed citizenry being the major roadblock to a totalitarian takeover of the United States.

How can a dictatorship in America be headed off? Truth is a powerful weapon — but only when it is used properly. Not everyone has the courage to face the facts, but facts must be faced, even when they are discouraging. Any action taken on the basis of truth is better than action taken on the basis of falsehood, misconception, and self-deceit. The facts contained in this book are so powerful that some may choose to run and hide — others to ignore them — while still others will throw up their hands in discouragement. This is exactly what the *Insiders* want you to do. City Hall wants you to believe you can't fight City Hall. The salvation of America requires an army of educators, armed with truth and facts and tenaciously dedicated to principle. Many have tried to bypass the education step in the process and go directly to political action, and this has resulted only in the wasting of precious time. Action that is not based upon knowledge and understanding is really worse than no action at all. It is not too late to save America if a sufficient number of Americans will stand up, face reality, and go to work.

The fact is that the Republican party is now little more than a name. America's two-party system has quietly been replaced by the virtual dictatorship of an "invisible government." Today, the Council on Foreign Relations and the *Insiders* behind it control our federal government at practically every level and in every branch. But it need not control Congress. The Senate must ratify all treaties and confirm all appointments. The Senate, therefore, can stop the Council on Foreign Relations and save America, if the people will demand that their Senators live up to their oath to uphold the Constitution of the United States. By the Constitution, all spending bills must originate in the House of Representatives. No matter who is in the White House, our Congressional representatives can cut spending drastically and force the executive branch to return America to a sound currency and sane fiscal policy.

This is the answer to the question: If not Nixon, who? Americanists are going to have to face up to the reality that almost short of a miracle they are not going to elect an anti-conspiracy Conservative to the Presidency in

1972. To back one of the conspiracy's candidates because he appears to be slightly less Leftist than the other makes no sense at all.

There is no denying that the *Insiders* start with many advantages — big money, big power, big press, and a big bag of campaign tricks perfected since 1936. The one thing the *Insiders* and their pawns, the moderates, do not have is a grass-roots following of political activists within the party. This is their Achilles' heel. They attempt to overcome it by constantly preaching unity to the Conservatives. Unity with one's enemies is always a trap. A known enemy in the open is better than a false friend in ambush. And Liberal Republicans are as much the enemies of Conservative Republicans as Liberal Democrats are — maybe more so. Every Conservative must stand up and proclaim to the world that he will not be part of a unified socialist Republican party.

One of the conspiracy's chief weapons is the desire of most people for respectability or social prestige. To question "party unity" is to become unrespectable. Unfortunately, some people are more interested in saving their social respectability than they are in saving their lives and their country. For many of these people, nominal Republicans, the primary difference between a Democrat and a Republican administration in Washington is that when the Republicans are in they get invited to gala social functions, and when the Democrats are in they don't. (But there won't be any cocktail parties in the concentration camps.) Conservative Republicans must face the fact that most GOP Liberals at the local level, while certainly not conspirators, are social climbers who are more interested in being invited to the "right" parties by the "right" people than in what is happening to the country. These people are Republicans for social or business purposes, not for ideological reasons. And since the knowledgeable Left within the Republican Party will always use the media to paint Conservatives as "extremists," the so-called moderates will always be the ones carrying the aura of respectability. Americanists have to forget these shallow phonies and recruit honest concerned Americans from the Democratic party.

In 1936, Al Smith, who had been the Democrat party's presidential candidate eight years earlier, had the courage to speak out about what he saw happening in his party, just as many Republicans today are being forced to speak out about what is happening to theirs. Smith said:

> Make a test for yourselves. Just get the platform of the Democratic party and get the platform of the Socialist party and lay them down on your dining room table side by side and get a heavy lead pencil and scratch out the word Democrat and scratch out the word Socialist and let those two platforms lay there . . . .

Ninety percent of what was in the Socialist Party platform of the '30's has now been adopted as the law of the land under the leadership of the Democrats. Take a look at the 1968 Republican party platform. Does it promise to repeal socialism? Or only to run it more efficiently? If the Democrat party takes us into socialism and the Republican party perpetuates it, then freedom is doomed. Expediency leads to slavery. The middle of the road is the path to ever-increasing doses of Marxian socialism.

Al Smith said:

> I suggest to the members of my party on Capitol Hill here in Washington that they take their minds off the Tuesday that follows the first Monday in November. Just take their minds off it to the end that you may do the right thing and not the expedient thing.

And he stated further:

> You can't mix socialism or Communism with [the Constitution]. They are like oil and water . . . . They refuse to mix. It is

all right with me if they want to disguise themselves as Norman Thomas or Karl Marx or Lenin or any of the rest of that bunch, but what I won't stand for is to let them march under the banner of Jefferson, Jackson or Cleveland.

Today, a Republican Al Smith must speak up and say that Republican socialists won't be allowed to march under the banner of Lincoln and Taft.

Smith concluded by saying:

> Let me give this solemn warning. There can be only one capitol, Washington or Moscow. There can only be one atmosphere of government, the clear, pure, fresh air of free America or the foul breath of Communist Russia. There can be only one flag, the stars and stripes, or the red flag of the Godless Union of the Soviet. There can be only one national anthem, the Star Spangled Banner or the Internationale.

The Republican party needs its own Al Smith.

Earl Browder, then general secretary of the Communist Party, in an address before the National Press Club in Washington in August 1936 told the assembled reporters:

> The program of the Socialist Party and the program of the Communist Party have a common origin in the document known as the Communist Manifesto. There is no difference, so far as the program is concerned and final aim.

The socialists follow the lead of the Communists, the Democrats follow the lead of the socialists, and the Republicans follow the lead of the Democrats. *Before we can go Communist, we must first go socialist.* Who cares whether the collectivist dictator is theoretically a Republican or a Democrat? Most Republican nominees for high offices have completely ceased even to use the word "socialism" in their attacks on the Democrats. They bleat only of wasteful spending, not of big spending, and promise efficiency and leadership in running the programs the Democrats have already legislated. But either you believe in the principles of Karl Marx or you believe in the principles of the Declaration of Independence and the Constitution: there can be no middle ground. If the grass-roots Republican activists will not force their party to stand for principle, then it will continue to be a cheap imitation of Socialist Party A.

We have indeed witnessed bipartisan treason in Washington. The vast majority of Republicans have supported Nixon's continuation of Lyndon Johnson's no-win policy in Vietnam. Most have said nothing of the fact that the United States is financing both sides of the war through aid and trade with the Communist bloc. They have also said little or nothing of the organized and subversive elements that are running the street revolution in America. If the public had known the truth about these events, the course of American history would have been changed for the better. The Republican party has enough money and power at its command to make sure that the truth does get to the public. Yes, the party could do it if it really wanted to. The mass media may be in the hands of Liberal Democrats, but the advertisers are, for the most part, theoretical Republicans. Since the media would collapse without the advertising dollar, the advertisers could bring pressure to bear on the media to stop propagandizing the American public and tell them the available facts. If purged of Liberals and *Insiders*, the Republican National Committee could publish its own newspaper and see that it got wide distribution. The Republican party could serve as a vehicle for getting the truth to the American people — but only if the enemies of the truth are purged, in the way that Conservatives have been systematically purged from high places in the party since Republican Advance was formed in 1950.

The Republican party can again be the great party it was. But to do so it must stand for principle and refuse to compromise between right and wrong. It must shun the temptation to pander to assorted voting blocs. It must show that Communism can be defeated short of warfare by simply stopping the practice of propping it up every time it falls on its face. The main issues must be American sovereignty and independence, the return to a sound dollar, and an end to something-for-nothing promising contests. The Republican Party platform must avow that those who advocate bloody revolution and criminals will be subjected to swift and just punishment. The lives and property of law-abiding citizens must once again become the primary concern of our courts. Above all, the target must be the real enemy, Communism, and the *Insiders* behind it.

Weaklings will whine, "Conservatives can't win." There is much evidence to the contrary, but even if it were true, men and women of morality and principle have no other choice than to stick by their guns in defense of what is right. For if the Republican party must become socialist in order to win elections, then the elections are not worth winning. By copying the enemy instead of fighting him, all chance of defeating him will be lost.

Conservatives need to develop articulate spokesmen who can use the techniques of the modern mass media to get their message to the public. The Conservative message of individual liberty is the "politics of hope," the real and only genuine solution for the problems that beset us. Most important, we must go on the offensive, calling the enemy by his right name. The weakness of the Conservative is supposed to lie in his failure to be all things to all people. He can turn these lemons into lemonade. The public will respond favorably to a public figure who takes a stand for principle, even if they do not altogether agree with the principle. Principles transcend personalities. When the tide begins to turn, the "pragmatists" will jump on the Americanist bandwagon. As *Battle Line* noted in December 1969:

It is for this very reason that conservatives should and must fight for their beliefs within the Republican Party. Pragmatists are notoriously susceptible to pressure, and in the absence of commitment to principle, this is understandable. This means that conservatives must speak out and be heard or lose their case.

Conservatives must find candidates whose convictions run deeper than merely the ability to select ghostwriters, as was the case with Goldwater. In 1964, Conservatives put all their emotional eggs into a very shallow basket. Goldwater was more interested in playing with his ham radio than in doing his homework by reading von Mises, Bastiat, or Evans. Conservatives must learn to put their faith in principles, not in personalities.

Conservatives must find candidates who will be Americans first and Republicans second; who will dare to be mavericks within their own party and not sell out principles every time the moderates wail about party unity. Most Republicans have a simple platform — get elected. Any unified GOP can only become the same thing that the unified Democrat Party has become: an unprincipled prostitute. Men of principle are against "unity" and blind loyalties. There is no person or secular institution in the world to which we owe or should feel blind loyalty. We should be for what we know is right, regardless of race, color, kin, or previous condition of misinformation.

Americans must readjust their political thinking; they must learn to think in terms of Council-on-Foreign-Relations versus anti-Council-on-Foreign-Relations politicians. Now is the time for all good men to *forget* the Party. The Republican Party is nothing more than a tool, an instrument. Intrinsically, it deserves no loyalty.

Once a Conservative has been elected, we must pay attention to what he does after the election. Many people are elected as Conservatives, only to turn Liberal. When all the effort to elect a man has been successful, the job has only begun. Grass-roots Conservatives must keep track of what their man is doing. These candidates must be tied down with a commitment to remain independent — loyal to principle, not to party. The best way, of course, is to start with an honorable man and make sure he knows the kinds of pressure he must expect once he gets into office. Candidates must understand the conspiracy, its goals, and how it operates.

The candidate must be willing to face and accept the fact that if he does an honest and honorable job he may have only one term in office. One of the major sicknesses in any legislature is that as soon as a man is elected, being re-elected becomes his prime concern. The rationalization used by many who begin their careers as Conservatives is that "losers don't legislate." Their whole object then becomes merely to win elections and stay in office, and this is accomplished by compromising until victory becomes meaningless. Typical is this statement made to Congressman John G. Schmitz when he was in the California State Senate, by a fellow State Senator:

> I'm just as conservative as you are. It's just that I realize that you've got to win. You have to go along to get along. You have to play the game. Look at me. I'm a committee chairman of the [blank] committee.

Senator Schmitz's answer was, "Yes, as long as you keep putting out liberal votes, they are going to keep you chairman of that committee."

In order to make sure that your local representatives stay on the track and don't succumb to the temptation to "play the game," every local area should have a watchdog committee to keep track of its elected representatives. No politician is going to like this, and the ones most apt to compromise are the ones who will like it the least. The watchdog committee must have the courage (and it takes courage) to tell the representative that if he doesn't stand 100 per cent for principle, he will be opposed in the next primary. This may result in the temporary election of a Democrat, but the next Republican elected to office from that district will stand 100 per cent for principle because he *knows* what is going to happen to him if he doesn't. This is the only practical way to deal with politicians; it is the way all politicians understand.

The real Republicans must declare war on ersatz Republicans and kick the conspirators and their social-climbing flunkies out of the party. Conservatives who attempt to do this will, of course, be vilified by the press and news media. They will be accused of everything the Liberals have actually done, particularly of following a rule-or-ruin policy. But New York and its *Insiders* can no longer dominate the Republican party as they once did. New York is no longer the sole financial center for the nation, and the growth of the South and West has shifted political power away from the Eastern seaboard. Therefore, the *Insiders* cannot control the body of the Republican party; but they still control the apex. It is their control that can be and must be severed. Conservatives must use their grass-roots control over party organizations to re-establish the Republican party as a Conservative party. Funds must be channeled to selected local Conservative candidates rather than sent to the Republican National Committee, which is always controlled by the Eastern Liberal Establishment — although almost every GOP mailing from House, Senate, and other national campaign groups emphasizes the fact that there is a difference between the Democrats and the GOP, that one party is Leftist, while the other holds to traditional Conservative principles of fiscal prudence, anti-communism, and limited government.

The fallacy in total acceptance of this Republican argument has never been better illustrated than in a recent interview with Senator John Tower of Texas, chairman of the Senate Republican Campaign Committee. Tower, a Conservative in his own right, sees his campaign post solely as a funnel through which to dispense funds to Republican candidates, regardless of their personal political views or party loyalty. Senator Tower told the *New York Times Magazine* in April 1970:

> I don't care whether a Republican candidate is liberal or conservative. The only thing I am interested in is whether or not they are electable — I'm in a numbers game right now, not a philosophical game.

By turning the *Insiders* out, real Republicans will only be doing what the *Insiders* have been doing to them since the birth of Republican Advance in July 1950. Even the outer wheels of this wheels-within-wheels conspiracy have gotten into the act of emasculating the party's Conservatives.

Dorothy Ray Healey, official chairman of the Southern California Communist Party, writing in the December 1964 issue of *Political Affairs* (the official Communist theoretical journal, in which the "party line" is laid down for the comrades), calls for the expulsion of anti-Communists from the Republican party. She states that it is perfectly legitimate for Republicans to complain of "high taxes and rising crime" as long as there is no discussion of Communism. Although no cause and effect relationship can be proven, within months of the Communist Party's call for the expulsion of anti-Communists from the Republican party, Liberal and Moderate leaders within the party began calling for the purge of all John Birch Society members from party ranks. There may have been no connection between the Communist Party directive and the actions of Republican leaders, but at the very least, they were doing exactly what the Communists wanted.

Any worthwhile movement takes courage. The easiest thing to do is to continue to drift with the tide, even when the tide is running Leftward. If you are tempted to stand for principle you will be told, "You are throwing your vote away" by refusing to support all Republican candidates. Actually, you are throwing your freedom away if you do support them all indiscriminately. The dilemma most often faced by Conservative political activists is that of being dissatisfied or disillusioned with the Republican candidate, yet knowing that the Democrat will be even worse. If Conservatives are willing to be satisfied with the lesser of two evils, they will never have anything but evils to choose between. This is the primary way in which Liberals and opportunists have effectively disenfranchised Conservatives who stand for principle. By withholding your vote, or voting for a protest candidate, you are not throwing your vote away. You are, in fact, making it felt in the strongest possible way. You throw your vote away only when you are willing to compromise. It is time to vote for an outsider.

You will be told that you are destroying the two-party system if you stand for principle, but in fact we no longer have a two-party system, and by voting for principle you will be taking the only measure that can reestablish it. It is those who will accept a Richard Nixon because he is not quite so socialistic as a Hubert Humphrey who are in reality throwing their votes and their birthright away. If one candidate wants to go toward socialism at one hundred miles an hour and another candidate wants to go toward that same goal at only fifty miles an hour, they are both headed toward the same goal and both will eventually get there. The choice between going toward slavery faster and going more slowly is no choice at all. These are false alternatives. The real choice is between true freedom and slavery.

Political activists always make up a small percentage of the population. If Conservatives are willing to settle for a candidate who is slightly less socialistic than the Democratic candidate, then the broad masses of the American public will never be presented with the real issue of freedom versus slavery. Americans will be led to believe that the choice is merely between aspirin and some other pain killer, as they were in 1960. Many political activists are unknowingly playing games with the *Insiders*, using their rules. You can't win with a stacked deck. It takes courage to stand against the tide and to oppose what is morally wrong. But in your heart you know you have no other choice.

George E. Sokolsky, writing in the *New York Herald Tribune* of March 29, 1937, described what it was like when a tiny minority of Communists took over in Russia:

Long before the Communist revolution transferred political power from Kerensky to Lenin, the workers had destroyed all rights and private property . . . . Private property disappeared before the rights of human beings disappeared.

What were intelligent, educated people doing? What were businessmen and bankers doing? At that moment each man was looking after himself. Some were seeking to get in under the tape. They would assist the Bolsheviks; then the Bolsheviks would let them live. Some were attempting to save a few effects . . . . Others were trying one compromise after another . . . . Even their newspapers ceased to print articles favorable to them, because their reporters and writers were organized in unions and they would permit only such news and views to be printed as the union ordered.

. . . The businessmen applauded with merriment. They would make money, they felt, no matter what kind of politician was in power. In the end they had nothing. Their property, their human rights and their lives were taken from them.

. . .The organized minority had focused its will on the seizure of property and government. The majority was engaged in every occupation but the defense of the rights of property and rights of man. The minority smashed the majority because only the minority knew what it wanted. The majority was destroyed because it could not believe that it had to organize to fight and live. Yes, they woke up later, but it was too late . . . . Their tactical advantage was to resist every suggestion of compromise while they still possessed power, but they lost themselves in painful disputations concerning humane considerations until humanity itself was crushed. Compromise destroyed their one weapon for resistance — the army . . . .

I saw all this from July in 1917 until March 1918. I saw this process .... I have witnessed too many poisons mixed in the melting pot of compromise; I have seen too many Pandora's boxes opened by the intriguing fingers of compromise.

There are not two sides to some questions .... As I write of those days in Russia I think of the seizures of property in this country ....

Revolutions are successful when an organized minority discovers that the majority is split, is confused, is without vigilance. Then it uses revolutionary tactics to confound and confuse the majority by side issues, by speeches on humane subjects, by beating the drums of progress and liberalism.

... The revolutionists and the compromisers repeat the slogans and the adages of all the centuries and of all countries. They play upon distress; they create emergencies; they ridicule fundamentals. And all sorts of people are taken in by these tricks and they bow to the golden calf of humane proposals. Only too late do they learn that this emphatic humanity is only a veneer, only a sham in the rise to power.

The minority stand upon the shoulders of those whom they fool only as long as they need protection. When they want to come to earth they destroy the props that supported them ....

The American people do not yet realize that they are in the first stage of a revolution. Yet all experience with revolution shows that the seizure of private property by lawless bands before whom government stands impotent is the first major battle in the destruction of any government.

The battle lines have been drawn. The Republican party must accept as its first political premise that you never gain anything when you give up principle. (Oh, how the Liberals and Moderates hate that word "principle!") To know what is right and not to do it is the worst sort of cowardice. And if it's morally wrong it can't be politically right. Republicans must listen to St. Paul's admonition: "Follow not a multitude to do evil."

Numerous well-meaning individuals have tried to stop me from publishing this book. Some said the timing was bad. Others said that I would be smeared and that no one would believe the truth. Others wanted to know what it would accomplish and said I should not attack the Republican party. They felt we should take the best candidate we can get and try to work with him. This book is not an attack on rank-and-file Republicans, but an attempt to let them know that it is the *Insiders* who have been stampeding the Elephant. Any individual who is willing to compromise with the conspirators is not the best we can get because he is not ours.

A man's judgment is no better than his information. If this book makes enough people aware that we are in a life-and-death struggle with a conspiracy, it will have accomplished more than enough to make the *Insiders* wish it had never been written. Until grass-roots Republicans realize that they are up against a conspiracy which is seeking to control both major political parties, their efforts are doomed to frustration and failure. For many years the author believed it was merely the "Liberal mentality" that was the enemy. The "Liberal mentality" is an enemy, but there is more behind America's problems and the takeover of the Republican party by the Left than just the "Liberal mentality." For it is a conspiracy, not an ideology, that is taking over our country. The American people have not swallowed and did not vote for the concepts that are now being thrust down their throats by Richard Nixon as President — or as an *Insider* of the conspiracy. They voted, in fact, for almost exactly the opposite concepts, proclaimed by Richard Nixon the candidate. And Nixon was elected President largely because of the rising revulsion against the very pro-Communist policies that he is now carrying out with regard to both our foreign affairs and our domestic system. So let me repeat: It is the conspiracy that is our enemy and our danger.

The American people must make sure, next time they go through the quadrennial ritual of turning the rascals out, that it is the real rascals they turn out. We will stay on the same merry-go-round, merely switching brightly colored horses, unless a sufficient number of people wake up to the con game that has been perpetrated by an exceedingly cunning gang of international monopolists for the past six decades. It makes no difference whether the man who throws out the CFR gang and their philosophy comes from within the Democrat, the Republican, or the Amalgamated Intergalactic Party; but the candidate must be irreversibly committed to carrying out that act before he is elected.

Yes, there is a conspiracy, and the only way to defeat it is to turn the bright light of unequivocal and unwavering truth on it. What the conspirators count on most in this whole struggle for the world is the short memory, colossal ignorance, good-natured gullibility, and incredible apathy of the American people. We are all being "played for suckers" in a gigantic confidence game in which the stakes are both our freedom and our lives. And all it will take, even now, to escape the net that is being pulled tight around us is to wake up enough people to the fact that there is a net.

If five per cent of American citizens wake up and go to work, the *Insiders* will see the rewards of their decades of careful planning disintegrate like a pane of glass hit with a sledgehammer.

Epilogue

When one is attacked it is only natural to attempt to defend oneself and reassure one's friends. This author wrote an article for the October 1968 issue of *American Opinion* magazine which, while striving to be objective, nevertheless presented much condemnatory evidence concerning Richard Nixon. Nixon campaigners screamed like so many banshees. Doubtless, the same attempts at obfuscation and rationalization will be made in the effort to dull the impact of this book, and these ploys are therefore worth examining.

The Nixon-Agnew Campaign Committee sent out this reply to Republicans who were disturbed about the 1968 article:

> The article that you referred to is a slickly-written hatchet job that consists of a great many half-truths. It is instructive to note that the primary authority for the author of the article was William Costello. Mr. Costello was hired by the Democratic National Committee to write a book on Mr. Nixon for the 1960 campaign. I think you'll agree that any book inspired by the Democratic National Committee on a probable Republican presidential candidate, can hardly be described as dispassionate or objective.

We accept as a compliment the statement that the article was "slickly written," but the charge that it was a "hatchet job that consists of a great many half-truths" is one that Nixon-Agnew apparently felt no need to document, nor could they have documented it. And of course William

Costello was not "the primary authority for the author." The aim of Costello (and of the Democratic National Committee, if they did indeed instigate his book) was anything else than to show that RMN was a Fabian Socialist, internationalist, welfare-state Liberal. The book presented Mr. Nixon basically as a "reactionary," an "anti-Communist," and an "economic Neanderthal." Costello's admissions of Liberal stands by Nixon were clearly admissions against interest that had to be made to keep the book honest.

Human Events, a generally excellent and Conservative newsweekly whose Achilles' heel is its refusal to deal with the Council on Foreign Relations web of conspiracy, defended its pro-Nixon stand by claiming that this author's article was "riddled with factual errors, exaggerations and misinterpretations." It too felt no necessity to cite chapter and verse concerning the author's alleged journalistic sins. He was to be sentenced to life as a galley-proof slave, to be burned alive at the literary stake, or at least to have his literary license revoked, without being afforded any opportunity to refute the evidence (if any) on which he was charged.

In retrospect, the *American Opinion* article projected a much more accurate picture of Nixon than did features in other Conservative publications. Readers of *American Opinion* knew what to expect from the Nixon administration. Readers of other Conservative publications are in a state of shock today, and today these publications still criticize Nixon's policies but never come to grips with the character of the man and his integrity, or lack of it.

One can hardly expect those who have a strong vested interest in any particular politician to throw in the towel when their boy is exposed. Mr. Nixon himself is unlikely to go on national television and announce: "O.K. The jig is up. I confess!" Instead, phrases such as "half-truths," "distortions," "factual errors," "exaggerations," and "quotes out of context" will be used in an effort to cover up.

Doubtless there are errors in this book despite all the pains taken by the author and his editors to eliminate them. The author has tried to do his homework faithfully and document his case thoroughly, but sources can be erroneous and he is not omniscient. There has never been a historical-political-biographical book written that did not contain errors. Probably no book of any sort has ever been published that did not contain at least one typographical error. And all quotations are "out of context" unless the entire speech, statement, book or article is reproduced. The cry, "I was quoted out of context," is often a red herring. Quoting out of context is reprehensible only if the author has done it deliberately to give a distorted or dishonest connotation different from the intended meaning. Nit-pickers will try to get the reader to focus on trivia and minutiae rather than on the mountains of evidence that prove the case against Nixon.

Other critics have complained that the author in his 1968 magazine article relied heavily on Liberal commentators to prove that Nixon was a Liberal. Since we Conservatives don't believe these Leftist sources on other things, these critics ask, why should we believe them when they tell us that Nixon is a Liberal? Isn't this a trick to discredit Nixon in the eyes of Conservatives? These are good questions. However, we don't remember that the Establishment columnists, in their efforts to discredit such authentic Conservatives as Robert Taft, Joseph McCarthy, William Knowland, and Barry Goldwater, ever told us that these men were Liberals. We think it much more likely that these *Insider* pundits were being used as a transmission belt to carry the word to the Liberals that RMN really is O.K. after all.

Another complaint regarding the article was that it did not quote Nixon himself sufficiently. After all, we were told, Nixon himself had covered many of the situations described, in his book, *Six Crises*. The author was asked why he didn't give Nixon's version of the story instead of someone else's. In

his memoirs Nixon naturally indulged in a great deal of
self-justification and succumbed to the very human temptation to leave out of his narrative some of the key facts,
especially those that reflected no credit on him. This author's
aim was merely to fill in the omissions. Conservatives would
not blindly accept all the facts in an opus titled *The True
Story Of My Administration*, by "Honest Lyndon" Johnson,
and they should be just as critical of any other politician's
recreation of his public life while he is still running for
political office. The present book has quoted Mr. Nixon
himself extensively many times, but we doubt if his
defenders will like these quotations much better.

We hope the reader will apply the same standards to the
attackers of this book as to the book itself. Make them
document their assertions against it. Make them document
their conviction that there is no Council on Foreign
Relations, and no interlocking web of elitist organizations
forming a supra-government. Make them document their
belief that the continual movement to the Left over nearly
forty years has been mere coincidence. Make them document
their denial that we have propped up the Communist world
time after time, and their insistence that it is just an accident
that our foreign policy toward the Communists doesn't
change from administration to administration. Make them
document, too, their contention that Nixon has not really
staffed his administration with more than one hundred CFR
members. Don't let the obfuscators con you with nebulous
dismissals of this book. Americans are destined for slavery
unless the CFR *Insiders* and those who are controlled by
them can be purged from the government.

Five years ago, anyone who thought there was anything
seriously wrong with America was ridiculed as an alarmist.
Today, those who can't see that something is drastically
amiss are targets for ridicule. Let's go on the offensive!

Index

Abt, John J., 137, 231
Acheson, Dean, 80, 143, 161, 162, 170, 171, 174, 175
Ackley, Gardner, 351
Adair, E. Ross, 338
Adams, Sherman, 104, 108, 119, 166, 168, 201
Agnew, Spiro T., 5, 24, 31, 39, 49, 50, 160, 187
Aldrich, Winthrop, 89, 116
Alexander, Holmes, 309, 310
Alsop, Joseph, 247, 260, 341
Alsop, Stewart, 4, 5, 36, 39, 127, 128, 134, 155, 202, 209, 247, 265, 266, 393, 394, 396
Anderson, John, 245
Anderson, Robert B., 81, 169, 280
Andrews, Phillip, 126
Annenberg, Walter, 255
Arvey, Jake, 110
Ashbrook, John, 25, 234
Attila, 253
Aydelotte, Frank, 68, 69

Bachelder, Joseph, 260, 261
Balfour, Arthur, 69
Ball, George, 80, 85, 277
Barmine, Gen Alexander, 111
Barnes, Harry Elmer, 65
Barnes, Joseph Fels, 97, 111

Barnett, Doak, 276
Bartlett, Charles, 367
Bartley, Robert, 63
Baruch, Bernard, 112, 167, 201
Bastiat, Frederic, 412
Beam, Jacob, 85, 287
Behr, Edward, 49
Benson, Ezra Taft, 169
Bentley, Elizabeth, 182
Benton, William, 80, 303
Berle, Adolph, 109
Biddle, Francis, 102, 103
Biossat, Bruce, 316
Bliss, Ray, 237
Bloomfield, Dr. Lincoln P., 312
Bohlen, Charles E., 276
Bowles, Chester, 80, 109
Bozell, Brent, 213
Braden, Spruille, 108
Brandeis, Louis, 126
Brett, Reginald Baliol (Lord Esher), 69
Brewster, Kingman, 280
Bricker, John, 182, 183, 194, 304, 309
Broder, David, 15, 28, 238, 397
Brooke, Edward W., 246
Browder, Earl, 409
Brown, Edmund W. (Pat), 36, 51, 218-222
Brown, Rap, 339

Brownell, Herbert, 104, 157, 168, 175, 218
Bryan, Malcolm, 390
Buchanan, Sir George, 71
Buckley, William F. Jr., 171, 193, 194, 285
Budenz, Louis, 111, 171,
Buffett, Howard, 169
Bulganin, Marshal, 194
Bunker, Ellsworth, 80, 85
Bundy, McGeorge, 80, 81
Burch, Dean, 237
Burdick, Usher, 94
Burns, Arthur, 22, 85, 287, 334, 360, 361, 362n, 383
Buttenwieser, Benjamin J., 143n
Buttenwieser, Helen Lehman, 143n
Byrnes, James, 58
Byrnes, John, 334

Cardozo, Benjamin N., 126
Carmichael, Stokely, 339
Carnegie, Andrew, 299
Carroll, Dr. Warren, 403
Carswell, G. Harrold, 39
Case, Clifford, 80, 104, 192, 221
Castro, Fidel, 185, 195
Chamberlain, John, 386n
Chambers, Whittaker, 65, 111, 137-144
Chiang Kai-shek, 149, 184
Childs, Marquis, 184
Chodorov, Frank, 115
Clark, Evans, 360n
Clark, Grenville, 293
Clark, Ramsey, 261
Clausen, Don, 27
Clay, Lucius, 168
Cleveland, Grover, 409
Cleveland, Harlan, 85

Clubb, Oliver, 161
Coleman, Dr. Arthur P., 113
Conant, Prof. Michael, 355
Connolly Reservation, 296, 297
Cooley, Prof. Oscar, 356
Costello, William, 131, 132, 135, 183, 184, 203, 421, 422
Cowles, John, 117
Cox, Edward, 135
Cronkite, Walter, 162
Crocker, George N., 97
Currie, Lauchlin, 77, 161
Curtis, Lionel, 74

Davenport, Marcia, 91, 92, 95, 96
Davenport, Russell, 90, 91, 96, 102
De Goulevitch, Arsène, 70
De Sola, Ralph, 107
De Toledano, Ralph, 20, 237, 278, 284
Dewey, Thomas E., 80, 97-101, 108, 114, 136, 151, 151n, 154-156, 159, 199, 201, 209, 212, 218, 247, 400
Dewey, Thomas E. Jr., 151n
Dies, Martin, 141, 142, 144
Dillon, C. Douglas, 81, 116, 170, 264, 278
Dirksen, Everett McKinley, 280
Disraeli, Benjamin, 51, 328, 399
Djordjevich, Mike, 403
Dobbs, Zygmund, 350n
Dodd, Dr. Bella, 72
Dodd, Norman, 76
Dole, Robert, 281
Donovan, Robert J., 3, 232, 271
Douglas, Helen Gahagan, 111-112, 144-148, 220
Douglas, Melvyn, 144
Douglas, Paul, 109

Douglas, William O., 111
Downey, Sheridan, 144
Drummond, Roscoe, 6, 7, 8, 327
Dubinsky, David, 80, 109
Duffee, Warren, 240
Dulles, Allen W., 169
Dulles, John Foster, 104, 134, 137, 140, 167, 169-174, 177, 183, 184, 201, 303, 304
Dunlop, John, 352
Dworshak, Henry, 191

Edson, Peter, 158
Eisenhower, Dwight D., 6, 7, 12, 22, 23, 48, 50, 77, 78, 83, 97, 105, 108-121, 144, 150-157, 159, 160, 162, 165-171, 174-194, 199, 200, 200n, 204, 207, 209, 210, 215, 217, 218, 240, 247, 254, 264, 269, 273, 281, 286, 287, 295, 297, 303, 307, 368, 372, 403
Eisenhower, Dr. Milton, 111, 166, 195, 201, 303
Emerson, Thomas I., 127
Engels, Friedrich, 359
Evans, M. Stanton, 32, 37, 41, 186, 232, 412
Evans and Novak, 42, 43, 246, 279, 282, 285

Filene, Edward A., 360n
Finch, Robert H., 22, 23, 49, 287, 317, 325, 328
Finder, Leonard, 109-111
Findley, Paul, 298, 304
Finletter, Thomas, 303
Flanders, Ralph, 104, 178
Flanigan, Peter, 277, 278
Flemming, Arthur, 281
Flemming, Harry, 281

Folger, Clifford, 218
Ford family, 63
Ford, Henry II, 303
Forrestal, James, 67
Foster, William C., 303
Fowler, Henry, 80
Frank, Dr. Glenn, 89
Frankel, Max, 49
Frankfurter, Felix, 143
Freeman, Dr. Roger, 319, 374
Frelinghuysen, Peter, 28
Friedman, Dr. Milton, 361
Fritchey, Clayton, 369
Fulbright, J. William, 303

Galbraith, John Kenneth, 80, 127, 346-350, 353-355, 357-362, 365, 366, 382, 384-386, 386n, 387n, 389, 395
Gallup, George, 40, 97, 261, 316
Gardner, John W., 325
Garment, Leonard, 254, 279
Gates, Thomas S., 169
Gavin, Gen. James M., 18
Gibbons, Sam, 371
Goldberg, Arthur, 80, 277
Goldwater, Barry, 6, 32, 38, 41, 81, 96, 191, 207, 208, 227-240, 249, 250, 253, 263, 304, 412, 423
Goodpaster, Gen. Andrew J., 85, 170
Graham, Billy, 251
Graham, Phillip, 117
Gray, Gordon, 170
Green, Edith, 340
Grey, Albert (Lord), 69
Griffin, G. Edward, 398
Gross, H.R., 28, 29, 234, 362, 370, 378, 385
Gubser, Charles S., 27

Gunther, John, 111
Guthrie, Randolph, 355

Haberler, Gottfried, 352
Hagerty, James, 200n
Halleck, Charles, 98, 189
Hanighen, Frank, 156
Hannegan, Robert, 101
Harris, Fred, 28
Harris, Louis, 40, 41
Harris, Richard, 261
Harris, Seymour, 351-352
Harris, Sidney, 3
Hatfield, Mark, 304
Haynsworth, Clement F., 39, 280
Hazlitt, Henry, 364, 365
Healey, Dorothy Ray, 415
Heller, Walter W., 327, 351
Henderson, Leon, 127
Herter, Christian, 104, 134, 135, 136, 169, 201, 304
Hess and Broder, 238, 239
Hiestand, Edgar, 221
Hillman, Sidney, 106, 112, 113
Hiss, Alger, 65, 77, 99, 137-144, 161, 163, 175, 182, 275, 276, 301, 310
Hiss, Mrs. Priscilla, 143
Hitler, Adolf, 90, 275, 350
Ho chi Minh, 184
Hoffman, Paul, 80, 105, 106, 108, 109, 154, 156, 167, 168, 178, 179, 187, 189, 190, 201
Hoover, J. Edgar, 59, 139n, 165, 186
Hoover, Herbert, 77, 83, 95
Hopkins, Harry, 96, 166, 280
Hosmer, Craig, 28
House, Col. Edward M., 87, 102, 166, 170, 278
Houthakker, Hendrik, 352

Hughes, Charles Evans, 126
Hughes, Emmett John, 200n
Hull, Cordell, 58
Humphrey, Hubert H., 3, 5, 19, 27, 33, 51, 80, 82, 201, 253, 254, 256, 259, 261-263, 265, 270, 295, 296, 303, 325, 366, 412
Humphreys, Robert, 150
Hunter, Edward, 276

Ickes, Harold, 101
Innis, Roy, 246

Jackson, Andrew, 409
Janin, General, 70
Janssen, Richard, 351, 369
Javits, Jacob, 3, 80, 104, 190, 221, 233, 295, 303
Jefferson, Thomas, 228, 398-399, 409
Jenner, William, 171, 190
Johnson, Joseph E., 275, 276
Johnson, Lyndon B., 6, 18, 19, 21, 23, 24, 26, 32, 41, 50, 78, 81, 144, 200, 212, 214, 229, 231, 232, 237, 243, 246, 263, 264, 272, 277, 283, 286, 287, 307, 325, 326, 342, 350, 351, 362, 366, 367, 368, 370, 372, 377, 378, 382, 383, 384, 410, 424
Johnston, (Sir) Harry, 69
Jones, Eugene, 260
Jones, Richard, 219

Kahn, Herman, 276
Karenga, Ron, 341
Katzenbach, Nicholas, 80, 276
Keating, Kenneth, 104
Kefauver, Estes, 301-302, 303

Kennedy family, 63
Kennedy, David, 361, 380
Kennedy, Edward M., 33
Kennedy, John F., 18, 21, 23, 24, 26, 31, 50, 77, 78, 80, 144, 176, 212, 214, 215, 216, 221, 222, 231, 232, 235, 246, 252, 254, 264, 265, 270, 271, 283, 286, 307, 327, 350, 351, 352, 367, 372
Kennedy, Robert F., 5, 80, 248, 328, 395
Kerensky, Alexander, 70, 71, 360, 383, 417
Kerr, Clark, 303
Keyes, Paul, 255
Keynes, John Maynard, 350, 352
Khrushchev, Nikita, 185, 204, 205
Killian, James R. Jr., 170
Kilpatrick, James Jackson, 20, 272, 273, 284, 307, 308, 333
King, Martin Luther Jr., 244, 245, 251
Kirk, Russell, 272, 273
Kissinger, Henry A., 50, 58, 85, 162, 287, 303
Knowland, William F., 126, 220, 423
Konoye, Prince, 97
Kraft, Joseph, 10, 57, 83, 113, 269

Lamont, Corliss, 89
Lamont, Flora, 89, 93
Lamont, Thomas W., 74, 89, 92, 93, 94
Landon, Alfred M., 89, 90
Larson, Arthur, 269, 270, 276
Lattimore, Owen, 77, 161
Lavine, Harold, 150, 192

Lehman, Herbert, 303
Lenin, Nicolai, 106, 291, 409, 417
Lerner, Max, 50
Lewis, Fulton Jr., 178
Lewis, Ted, 324
Lincoln, Abraham, 67, 257, 354
Lindsay, John V., 228, 303, 387n, 401
Lippmann, Walter, 10, 264, 326
Lisagor, Peter, 379
Lodge, Henry Cabot, 85, 104, 109, 114, 119, 170, 178, 229
Lodge, John Davis, 104
Loeb, William, 21, 308
Loory, Stuart, 277, 278
Lorwin, Lewis, 135
Lothian, Lord, 93, 94
Lubell, Samuel, 100, 121, 186
Luce, Henry, 90, 92, 104, 108
Luciano, Lucky, 66
Lyons, Leonard, 223

MacArthur, Gen. Douglas, 116, 117, 136, 148, 149
McCarthy, Eugene, 8, 80, 253, 256, 303, 328
McCarthy, Joseph 176-181, 190, 194, 208, 287, 423
McCloy, John, 81
McCone, John A. 81, 170
McCracken, Paul, 85, 352, 359, 380
McGill, Ralph, 2
McGinniss, Joe, 255-258
MacGregor, Clark, 245
McGrory, Mary, 8, 9
McKinney, Jack, 257-259
McKissick, Floyd, 245, 246
McManus, Charles A., 27
McNamara, Robert, 81, 276, 277

Machiavelli, Niccolo, 332
Maddox, Lester, 324
Maillard, William S., 27
Mahon, George, 377
Malone, George, 190
Mao Tse-tung, 253, 345, 390
Marcantonio, Vito, 145-147
Marshall, George C., 97, 98, 105, 108, 135, 166, 303
Martin, William McChesney, 388
Marx, Karl, 102, 133, 289, 291, 315, 347, 352, 357, 359, 408, 410
Massing, Hede, 111
Mathias, Robert, 28
Matthews, J.B., 177
Mazo, Earl, 126, 174, 214, 215, 247
Mazo and Hess, 137, 145-147, 151, 311
Merchant, Livingston T., 170
Mesta, Perle, 372
Meyer, Eugene, 89
Meyer, Frank S., 173, 328
Mezek, Frank W. Jr., 35, 36, 37, 41
Miller, J. Irwin, 280
Millin, Sara, 68
Milner, Alfred (Lord), 69-71
Mills, Ogden, 89
Mills, Wilbur, 333, 377
Mitchell, James P., 169
Mitchell, John N., 22, 42, 43, 50, 223, 273, 287, 309
Mollenhoff, Clark, 162
Morgenstern, George, 117
Morgan, J.P., 74, 78, 79, 94
Morse, Wayne, 109
Morton, Thruston, 104
Moscow, Warren, 114
Moynihan, Daniel P., 9, 22, 50,

280, 287, 325, 328, 330, 339, 393, 394
Mundt, Karl, 139
Murphy, Robert, 85, 170
Muskie, Edmund, 33
Mussolini, Benito, 350

Newton, Huey, 339
Nicholas II, 70
Niles, David K., 280
Nix, Robert, 50
Nixon, Donald, 219
Nixon, Mrs. Hannah, 219
Nixon, Mrs. Pat, 127, 159, 223
Nixon, Richard M., *passim*
Novak, Robert, 272
O'Brien, Lawrence F., 33, 36, 286
O'Brien, Pat, 251
Okun, Arthur, 351
Olds, Dr. Glenn, 276, 277
Olson, Arnold, 372
Oppenheimer, J. Robert, 360n
Orwell, George, 59, 333
Otten, Alan, 44, 48, 50, 51

Passman, Otto, 337
Patman, Wright, 320, 355
Pepper, Claude, 109, 145
Percy, Charles, 34, 206, 228
Perdue, Bill, 127
Perlo, Victor, 182
Perry, Herman, 129
Peurifoy, Jack, 139
Phillips, Kevin, 32, 33, 34, 35, 37, 38, 41, 42, 43, 398
Pick, Franz, 389
Pillsbury, John, 93
Polowasky, Joseph, 156
Pomeroy, Col. Eugene, 294
Powers, Harold ("Butch"), 218
Pressman, Lee, 137

Price, John, 330
Price, Raymond, 255
Pulliam, Eugene, 296

Quigley, Carroll, 59-64, 68-72, 74-76, 79, 89

Rafferty, Max, 221
Raggio, Grier, 387n
Rankin, John, 138
Rarick, John, 363
Reagan, Ronald, 36, 253
Rebozo, Charles ("Bebe"), 215
Redding, Jack, 101
Reed, Douglas, 294
Reid, Ogden, 80, 93
Reid, Mrs. Ogden, 93
Reston, James, 10, 11, 12, 13, 14, 233, 253, 264, 266, 280, 326, 401
Reuther, Walter, 80, 111, 235
Rhodes, Cecil, 68, 69, 298
Rhyne, Charles S., 303
Richardson, Elliot, 298
Riesel, Victor, 112, 280
Rinfret, Pierre, 365, 369
Roberts, Owen J., 301
Rockefeller, David, 80, 208
Rockefeller, John, 80
Rockefeller, Nelson A., 52, 66, 80, 102, 106, 134, 136, 139, 139n, 170, 179, 205-210, 216, 217, 223, 228, 237, 238, 246-249, 253, 273, 278, 281, 285, 287, 304, 305, 324n, 330
Rogers, William P., 58, 178, 218, 287, 298, 311
Romney, George, 34, 244, 304, 317
Roosevelt, Eleanor, 111
Roosevelt, James, 109

Roosevelt, Franklin D., 7, 39, 44, 47, 48, 50, 56, 67, 78, 88, 90, 97, 98, 103, 144, 162, 166, 167, 187, 192, 204, 211, 283, 284, 327, 350, 390, 400
Roper, Elmo, 302
Rosebery, Archibald Philip, 69
Rosenberg, Anna, 105-108, 179
Rostow, Walt W., 80
Roth, William, 320
Rothschild family, 71, 387
Rothschild, Meyer Amschel, 61, 62
Rothschild, Nathan Meyer (Lord), 68, 69
Roudebush, Richard, 234
Rousselot, John, 221
Rovere, Richard, 59, 346
Rowan, Carl T., 9, 246
Royster, Vermont, 248
Rubottom, R. Richard, 276
Rumsfeld, Donald, 340, 341
Rusk, Dean, 80
Ryskind, Morrie, 168

Satterthwaite, Joseph C., 170
Scammon, Richard, 41
Schary, Dore, 109
Schiff, Dorothy, 117
Schiff, Jacob, 71, 117
Schiff, John, 71
Schlafly, Mrs. Phyllis, 238, 282-283
Schlesinger, Arthur Jr., 80, 303, 360n, 387n
Schlesinger, Arthur Sr., 12
Schmitz, John G., 384, 385, 413
Schoeppel, Andrew, 191
Scott, Hugh, 1, 104, 393
Scott, Paul, 319, 363, 364
Scott, William L., 364

Scranton, William, 229, 230, 238, 304
Seaborg, Dr. Glenn T., 85
Seale, Bobby, 281
Seeger, Murray, 374
Semple, Robert, 48
Sennholz, Prof. Hans, 362n
Service, John Stewart, 161
Shakespeare, Frank, 255
Shannon, Don, 184
Shaw, George Bernard, 93
Shell, Joe, 216-218, 223
Sherwood, Robert, 114
Shultz, George P., 359
Silvermaster, Nathan, 182
Sisco, Joseph J., 85
Skousen, W. Cleon, 59, 60, 61, 72, 77
Smathers, George, 145
Smith, Al, 408, 409
Smith, Dana, 157
Smith, Gerald, 85
Smoot, Dan, 77, 78, 83, 165, 166
Sokolsky, George, 92, 117, 417
Sorenson, Theodore, 36
Sparks, C. Nelson, 93
Spengler, Oswald, 68
Stalin, Joseph, 106, 133, 162, 291
Stassen, Harold, 80, 201
Stead, William T., 69
Stein, Herbert, 351
Stevenson, Adlai, 110, 111, 112, 121, 143, 157, 160, 161, 165, 168, 175, 254, 303
Strauss, Lewis L., 169, 201, 358, 387
Streit, Clarence, 299-301 304-306
Stripling, Robert, 141-143
Sukarno, Achmed, 185
Sulzberger, Arthur Hays, 118

Sutton, Antony, 72
Symington, Stuart, 80
Synon, John 309

Taft, Robert A., 93, 94, 97, 98, 99, 101, 103, 108, 110, 114-121, 136, 152-157, 168, 169, 179, 194, 208, 209, 229, 236, 247, 266, 423
Taft, Mrs. Robert A., 93
Taft, Robert (Jr.), 370
Talbott, Harold, 116
Talcott, Burt, 28
Teague, Charles, 28
Ter Horst, J.F., 352
Thant, U, 298
Thompson, Dorothy, 118
Thomas, Norman, 48, 187, 396, 409
Thurmond, Strom, 6, 9, 271
Tower, John, 6, 414, 415
Treleaven, Harry, 254-255, 255n, 256, 260
Trohan, Walter, 19, 20, 325, 375
Trotsky, Leon, 135, 151n, 358
Truman, Harry S., 50, 78, 99-103, 111, 114, 138, 140, 144, 148, 160, 161, 166, 169, 174, 175, 181, 187, 192, 193, 283, 284, 303, 307
Tugwell, Rexford Guy, 90

Udall, James, 128
Udall, Morris K., 28
Upton, Dr. Arthur, 126
Utt, James, 27

Valachi, Joseph, 66
Vance, Cyrus, 80
Vandenberg, Arthur H., 108
Vincent, Mrs. Clifford, 126

Vincent, John Carter, 161, 171
Vinson, Fred, 157
Volpe, John, 357
Von Mises, Ludwig, 47, 412
Voorhis, Jerry, 129-133

Wade, Richard C., 35
Wadsworth, James J., 170
Wallace, George C., 31, 34, 38, 39, 45, 250, 251, 252, 263, 264, 270, 325
Wallace, Henry A., 99, 127, 147
Wallas, Graham, 370
Wallich, Henry, 352
Walter, Francis, 176
Wanniski, Jude, 17
Warburg, Felix, 62, 87
Warburg, James, 289
Warren, Earl, 99, 108, 119, 152, 153, 156, 157, 188, 297
Washington, George, 290
Watson, Thomas, 303
Wayne, John, 251
Weber, John, 358
Weinberg, Sidney J., 102, 115, 136, 166, 167, 168, 201
Welker, Herman, 190
White, Cliff, 227

White, Harry Dexter, 99, 137, 175
White, Theodore Jr., 192, 206, 208, 224, 227, 229, 231
Whitney, George, 116
Whitney, John Hay, 116
Wicker, Tom, 214, 285, 339
Wilcox, Francis O., 170
Wiley, Alexander, 190
Williams, John J., 365
Willkie, Wendell, 90-97, 111, 114, 115, 168, 212
Wills, Garry, 200n
Wilkinson, Bud, 257-259
Wilson, Charles, 28
Wilson, Richard, 4, 202, 214, 350
Wilson, Woodrow, 166, 278, 400n
Witcover, Jules, 217
Witt, Nathan, 137
Wittfogel, Dr. Carl, 111
Woodring, Harry H., 97
Wroble, Lester, 128

Yarmolinsky, Adam, 80, 276, 277
Yost, Charles, 85
Young, Philip, 181

Zhukov, Marshal, 194
Zwick, Charles, 368